P143 COM

The
Comparative
Method
Reviewed

The Comparative Method Reviewed

Regularity and Irregularity in Language Change

Edited by
Mark Durie
Malcolm Ross

New York   Oxford
OXFORD UNIVERSITY PRESS
1996

OXFORD UNIVERSITY PRESS

Oxford   New York
Athens   Auckland   Bangkok
Calcutta   Cape Town   Dar es Salaam   Delhi
Florence   Hong Kong   Istanbul   Karachi
Kuala Lumpur   Madras   Madrid   Melbourne
Mexico City   Nairobi   Paris   Singapore
Taipei   Tokyo   Toronto

and associated companies in

Berlin   Ibadan

Published by Oxford University Press, Inc.
198 Madison Avenue, New York, New York 10016

Library of Congress Cataloging-in-Publication Data
The comparative method reviewed : regularity and irregularity
in language change
edited by Mark Durie, Malcolm Ross.
       p.   cm.
    Includes bibliographical references.
    ISBN 0-19-506607-3
    1. Comparative linguistics.
    2. Linguistic change.
I. Durie, Mark, 1958–   .   II. Ross, Malcolm.
P143.C66   1996   94-40954
410—dc20

Printing (last digit): 9 8 7 6 5 4 3 2 1

Printed in the United States of America

on acid-free paper

Preface

Comparative linguistics tends to be a conservative field; within the context of the latter, this book contains much that will be controversial. Historical reconstruction relies upon the comparative method, which itself crucially depends upon the assumption of the regularity of change. This regularity includes the famous "Neogrammarian Hypothesis" of the regularity of sound change: "sound change takes place according to laws that admit no exception." However, the comparative method is not restricted to the consideration of sound change, nor is the assumption of regularity thus limited: syntactic, morphological, and semantic change all are amenable, in varying degrees, to comparative reconstruction, and each type of change is constrained in ways that enable the researcher to distinguish between what are, in some sense, regular changes and irregular or exceptional changes.

The notions of "regularity" and "irregularity" are controversial ones, and so this volume takes as its focus regularity, irregularity, and the comparative method. It brings together a set of empirical studies that provide a forum for theoretical and practical discussion of the limitations and potentials of the comparative method. These studies also include applications of the comparative method under challenging conditions.

The emphases of this volume distinguish it from many standard treatments of the comparative method. An introductory chapter provides a critical commentary on these differences, the most important of which include the following: there is a preponderance of non-Indo-European comparative data; some challenging implications of more "exotic" kinds of language contact situations are explored; detailed treatments are offered of issues involved in semantic and morphological change and reconstruction; and a central group of chapters explores different kinds of irregularity in sound change and the diverse motivations for such changes, all in the context of comparative reconstruction.

Special care has been taken to provide worked examples of comparative data, with an eye to both theoretical and methodological implications. Chapters are intended to be accessible to various types of readers; they have been written in a way which assumed no knowledge of any specific language family. At the same time, a very general understanding of the comparative method is assumed, since this volume is not intended as an introduction to the method itself. It should be suitable as a source of readings in a comparative-historical linguistics course. The at times controversial formulations of its contributors should prove thought-provoking and challenging.

The original idea for this volume was conceived by Mark Durie in 1987. Toward the end of 1988 he invited a group of prospective contributors to participate. An early plan for a conference on the subject, to be held in Australia, proved impractical for both financial and logistical reasons. Instead, the project was rethought and a collection of essays was the result. In 1992 Malcolm Ross agreed to become coeditor of the book, and the final selection and editing of essays was undertaken jointly by Durie and Ross.

Many thanks go to all the contributors, some of whom waited years to see their work appear in print. The encouragement of Cynthia Read, our acquiring editor at Oxford University Press, has been much appreciated. Robert Blust provided valuable initial encouragement and helpful suggestions about how to proceed.

Parkville, Australia   M.D.
Canberra, Australia   M.R.
April 1995

Contents

1 Introduction   3
MALCOLM ROSS and MARK DURIE

2 The Comparative Method as Heuristic   39
JOHANNA NICHOLS

3 On Sound Change and Challenges to Regularity   72
LYLE CAMPBELL

4 Footnotes to a History of Cantonese:
Accounting for the Phonological Irregularities   90
JOHN NEWMAN

5 Early Germanic Umlaut and Variable Rules   112
MARK DURIE

6 The Neogrammarian Hypothesis and
Pandemic Irregularity   135
ROBERT BLUST

7 Regularity of Change in What?   157
GEORGE GRACE

8 Contact-Induced Change and the Comparative Method:
Cases from Papua New Guinea   180
MALCOLM ROSS

9 Reconstruction in Morphology   218
HAROLD KOCH

10 Natural Tendencies of Semantic Change and
the Search for Cognates   264
DAVID WILKINS

Subject Index   307
Language Index   313
Name Index   318

The
Comparative
Method
Reviewed

1 Introduction

MALCOLM ROSS AND MARK DURIE

1 PRELIMINARIES

This book is about the classical comparative method of historical linguistics.[1] When historical linguists talk about the 'comparative method', what they usually have in mind is not just a method but also an associated theory, and the contributors to this volume are no exception to this generalisation. For over a century a mainstay of the associated theory has been the 'Neogrammarian hypothesis', set out by Osthoff and Brugmann (1878) in the manifesto which sought to bring scholarly rigour to historical linguistics: '[E]very sound change, inasmuch as it occurs mechanically, takes place according to laws that admit no exception.' (translated in Lehmann 1967: 204).

This association between method and theory is captured in the title and subtitle of this volume: *The comparative method reviewed: Regularity and irregularity in linguistic change*. We find it convenient at various points in this introduction to distinguish between the comparative method in this 'wide' sense (the method with its associated theory) and the comparative method in a 'strict' sense (the method itself).

Each of the contributors has had long experience of working with the comparative method (in the wide sense) in one or more language families. In order to keep the connection between method and theory as strong as possible, contributors were asked to choose topics associated with the method which their work had brought to the fore, focusing on regularity and irregularity in linguistic change. The result is a collection of empirical studies which provide examples of applying the comparative method in its strict sense, together with discussions of the results of these applications and their bearing on the comparative method in its wide sense.

In the introduction we have drawn together a number of threads from our contributors' discussions in a way which is intended to be provocative, believing as we

3

do that this is a time of theoretical change and the right time for a review of the comparative method in its wide sense. Thus, we hope that the contributions to this volume, including the introduction, will provide material for the ongoing debate about the Neogrammarian hypothesis and other theories associated with the comparative method.

The range of language families from which the contributors draw their primary data is wide. It includes two subfamilies of Indo-European, Slavic (Nichols) and Germanic (Durie); the Mayan family of Native American languages (Campbell); Chinese (Newman); several geographical regions within Austronesian, namely, its western region (Blust), Papua New Guinea (Ross), and New Caledonia (Grace); Papuan (Ross); and the Pama-Nyungan family of Australia (Koch, Wilkins).[2] The contributions here are all concerned, in one way or another, with issues of method. Chapter 2 examines what the comparative method *is* and, importantly, what it is not. Chapters 3 through 7 are all concerned with cases in which the data appear to challenge the Neogrammarian hypothesis. Chapter 8 looks at certain data (outcomes of language contact) which the comparative method traditionally ignores, and chapters 9 and 10 examine the application of the comparative method to morphology and to semantics, areas which have received only limited attention in previous discussions of the method.

The body of this introduction falls into two parts. In the first we examine the steps of the comparative method in its narrow sense and indicate how the contributions to this volume tie in with those methodological steps. In the second we take the suggestions and implications contained in all the contributions to this volume—that the comparative method in its wide sense is undergoing a paradigm change—and seek to discern the outlines of the coming paradigm.

2 THE COMPARATIVE METHOD (NARROW SENSE): WHAT IT ISN'T AND WHAT IT IS

The contributions to this volume are all concerned with the linguistic comparative method. Unfortunately, there are several extant misunderstandings about what the comparative method in its wide sense is, and we will refer to five of these before we proceed.

The first misunderstanding equates the comparative method with its application to Indo-European languages. Today, perhaps, this misunderstanding prevails only in some European universities, where the 'Department of Comparative Linguistics' is in fact a department of comparative Indo-European linguistics. The equation is also reflected in the title of Szemerényi (1990), *Einführung in die vergleichende Sprachwissenschaft* ('Introduction to Comparative Linguistics'), which is not about comparative linguistics or comparative methodology, but is an introductory survey of work in Indo-European comparative linguistics. Hopefully the range of language families to which the comparative method has been applied by the contributors to this volume will give the lie to this equation.

The second misunderstanding confuses the comparative method with the techniques of lexicostatistics and glottochronology. Lexicostatistics is the use of the percentages of assumed cognates (that is, items in related languages which are directly inherited from a common ancestor) shared by pairs of languages on a standard word list to arrive at a 'family tree' of those languages. Although its outcome—a family tree—looks like one of the outcomes of the comparative method, the lexicostatistical method is different in both practice and principle from the comparative method (despite occasional claims by lexicostatisticians that they are practising the comparative method; e.g. Dyen et al. 1992) and there is sometimes a radical difference between the family trees attained by the two methods.[3] Glottochronology is a technique for dating the nodes in the family tree and has no equivalent in the comparative method.

The third misunderstanding is a more dangerous one. It confuses the comparative method with the technique of 'multilateral comparison', sometimes known as 'mass comparison', used, for example, by Greenberg (1987) in his work on the linguistic prehistory of the Americas. We will return to this later. Suffice it for now to say that multilateral comparison is not a variant of the classical comparative method of historical linguistics.

The fourth misunderstanding confuses the comparative method with the typological comparison of the phonological, morphological, and syntactic systems of different languages. This kind of comparison has assumed an increasingly important role in linguistics in the three decades since Greenberg (1963b) was published, but it is different in method and objectives from the comparative method. Practitioners of the comparative method compare languages and use the results of this comparison to reconstruct their prehistory, whereas the goal of typological comparison is to determine the universal parameters along which languages vary (see, for example, Comrie 1989 or Croft 1990). Typological comparison also has a diachronic dimension: the study of how typological change occurs in linguistic systems. Work in this area has tended to focus on morphosyntax (see, for example, Hopper & Traugott 1993). Obviously universals of synchronic systems and of system change are vitally important to historical linguists because they provide criteria for assessing the plausibility of a reconstructed protolanguage (Comrie 1993). But typological comparison itself is not a part of the comparative method, and attempts to use typological comparison to establish genetic relationships simply do not work (see below [sec. 2.1] and Ross, this volume).

The fifth misunderstanding has to do with typological comparison of another kind and with the fact that the term 'comparative method' is used in different ways in different disciplines. For practitioners of disciplines other than linguistics, especially archaeologists and ethnologists, the significance of the linguistic comparative method is that it provides independent evidence about human prehistory and culture history. Its independence resides in the fact the linguistic comparative method (in its wide sense) is radically different from the comparative method of ethnological reconstruction. The latter is based on typological similarities, whereas the linguistic comparative method operates with arbitrary historical particulars. These particulars are linguistic signs: morphemes and their lexical collocations which a group of related languages has inherited from a common ancestor. It is a characteristic of linguistic signs that their signifiers are made up of phones which have no intrinsic meaning. As a result, the morphemes of a language (other than onomatopoeic and certain other marginal types of morpheme) show arbitrariness in regard to what phoneme sequence is used to represent what meaning. Since each language has at least a dozen, and more usually several dozen phonemes, and the rules for building phoneme sequences in any given language allow for a huge inventory of possible morphemic forms, two different languages are unlikely to have by chance any more than a miniscule percentage of (nonmarginal) morphemes which match each other in form and meaning (see Nichols, this volume).

A feature of language which is especially important for the linguistic comparative method is that, if the sounds of a language change over time, they do so in a largely regular manner (the word 'largely' here is perhaps controversial, and we will return to it later), such that sound x becomes sound y under statable conditions not just in some morphemes but in all morphemes that meet these conditions.[4] The result is that the sounds of reasonably closely related languages will correspond to each other in a regular manner, and this regularity allows the linguist to identify cognate items and to distinguish these from borrowings and accidental similarities. There is effectively no chance that a correspondence like the one exemplified in the initial consonants of Ancient Greek *pod-*, Sanskrit *pad-*, Gothic *fōt-*, Modern German *Fuss*, all meaning 'foot', Ancient Greek *pénte*, Sanskrit *pañca*, Gothic *fimf*, Modern German *fünf* 'five', and Ancient Greek *polús*, Sanskrit *pulu-*, Gothic *filu*, Modern German *viel* 'much, many', has arisen by accident. The same is true of the correspondence of the root-final consonant of the 'foot' set and of 'eat': Ancient Greek *ed-*, Sanskrit *ad-*, Gothic *it-* and Modern German *ess-*.

Once the sound correspondences among earlier written languages (in the case of Indo-European mentioned earlier) and/or among contemporary languages (in the cases of language groups with no written records) have been charted, the sound systems of earlier stages (protolanguages) can be inferred by established procedures. From data of which we have given a very small sample, historical linguists reconstruct the Proto-Indo-European morphemes **pod-/ped-* 'foot', **penkʷe* 'five', **pļu-/pelu-* 'much, many', and **ed-* 'eat'.[5] These reconstructions provide the baseline for working out which languages share which innovations relative to their reconstructed ancestor. For example, Gothic and German (and English, Friesian, Dutch, Afrikaans, Danish, Swedish, Norwegian, and Icelandic) share an innovation whereby Proto-Indo-European **p-* became *f-*. They also share several other innovations, indicating that they are descended from a more recent common ancestor, Proto-Germanic, in which these innovations occurred. As such, they constitute a genetic subgroup of the Indo-European language family.

Innovations diagnostic of a subgroup are not always regular sound changes. Other kinds of significant innovation include an idiosyncratic change in the form of a particular morpheme, the replacement of one form by another, or any type of change in which the chances of independent parallel innovation are tiny. The technique of subgrouping by shared innovations is used recursively to identify subgroups within subgroups, that is, to construct what is conventionally called the 'family tree' of a group of related languages.

The comparative method (in its strict sense) can be summarised as a set of instructions:

1. Determine on the strength of diagnostic evidence that a set of languages are genetically related, that is, that they constitute a 'family';

2. Collect putative cognate sets for the family (both morphological paradigms and lexical items).

3. Work out the sound correspondences from the cognate sets, putting 'irregular' cognate sets on one side;

4. Reconstruct the protolanguage of the family as follows:

    a. Reconstruct the protophonology from the sound correspondences worked out in (3), using conventional wisdom regarding the directions of sound changes.

    b. Reconstruct protomorphemes (both morphological paradigms and lexical items) from the cognate sets collected in (2), using the protophonology reconstructed in (4a).

5. Establish innovations (phonological, lexical, semantic, morphological, morphosyntactic) shared by groups of languages within the family relative to the reconstructed protolanguage.

6. Tabulate the innovations established in (5) to arrive at an internal classification of the family, a 'family tree'.

7. Construct an etymological dictionary, tracing borrowings, semantic change, and so forth, for the lexicon of the family (or of one language of the family).

Fellow comparativists would doubtless come up with other breakdowns. Some might want to include the reconstruction of syntax. The steps given by Nichols, Grace, and Koch in their contributions to this volume are rather different from these, but the difference is one of focus, not of substance. Nichols, for example, is concerned with how linguistic relatedness is demonstrated and proven, whereas our breakdown attempts to codify those steps in applying the method which are assumed or referred to in the contributions to this volume (not that the contributors would necessarily agree with our codification!). These steps, listed above as sequential, are in practice often recursive. For example, as the steps beyond step 1 are executed, more diagnostic evidence for the family may well be found. As the protolanguage is reconstructed and the internal classification of the family is worked out, languages previously thought to be unrelated may also be recognised as members of the family.

We will discuss each of these six steps, looking at potential problems and matters of controversy associated with each, and especially relating them to the contributions in this volume.

2.1 Diagnostic Evidence

Step 1 may appear rather surprising, as it is often assumed that the whole application of the comparative method has something to do with demonstrating relatedness. However, Nichols (this volume) examines the conventional theory and practice of Indo-Europeanists—and especially of Antoine Meillet, whose work epitomises Indo-European comparative linguistics before 1960—and shows that their determination of relatedness is logically quite separate from the succeeding steps of the method. It is based on evidence of the kind that Nichols terms 'individual-identifying', that is, 'evidence that firmly identifies a unique individual protolanguage' because 'its probability of multiple independent occurrence among the world's languages is so low that for practical purposes it can be regarded as unique and individual'. In the Indo-European tradition the main (although not the only) source of such evidence is whole paradigms of morphological forms, preferably with multiple paradigmaticity, as in the case of the inflections which mark the intersecting categories of the Indo-European nominal system with its three genders, its phonologically defined declension classes, and its case-marking paradigm.

Nichols shows that the nature of evidence used to diagnose relatedness was clearly recognised by Meillet, both explicitly (1958: 91) and implicitly (in his practice). However, as well as naming and defining this kind of evidence, she operationalises the concept of individual-identifying evidence statistically. She defines a statistical threshold for 'individual-identifying' by combining a single language's probability of occurrence among the several thousand on earth with a conventional level of statistical significance, then calculates the probability of occurrence of various samples of individual-identifying evidence in Indo-European, including the nominal system. These samples include the various kinds of evidence which Meillet treated as individual-identifying: morphological paradigms, lexical sets (e.g. the lexemes of the counting system), and individual words with complex or lengthy forms. But, as Nichols notes, to say that something is individual-identifying is only to say that all the languages which have it have acquired it from a single source. In the case of morphological paradigms, comparativists assume that acquisition is by inheritance, discounting borrowing as improbable. In the case of individual words, however, borrowing is quite possible, and this is why Nichols argues that the evidence of individual lexical items is at best supportive of diagnosed relatedness, rather than itself diagnostic. Comrie (1988) provides an example where both lexical borrowing and syntactic restructuring have occurred, so that only morphological paradigms remain as evidence of genetic relatedness.

We referred earlier to the technique of 'multilateral comparison' applied by Greenberg (1987) to divide the languages of the Americas into families and to determine the internal structure of the largest of these, Amerind. The proponents of multilateral comparison claim to be working within the framework of the comparative method (see, for example, Greenberg & Ruhlen 1992), and publications by nonlinguists sometimes fail to distinguish between language families determined by the classical comparative method and those based on multilateral comparison or other nonclassical approaches (see Nichols, this volume, for references). By showing that the diagnosis of relatedness is logically separate from the other steps of the comparative method, however, Nichols also shows that multilateral comparison and other techniques (like lexicostatistics) which omit our step 1 are in a fundamental way not applications of the comparative method. Instead multilateral comparison takes as its evidence simultaneous sound/meaning similarities across a number of languages. And, Nichols shows, these fall short of the statistical threshold for 'individual-identifying' and are therefore not evidence of relatedness at all (for another statistical argument against multilateral comparison, see Ringe 1992).[6]

The attraction of multilateral comparison and other techniques of 'long-range comparison' is that they claim to reach much further back into time than the comparative method has been able to do. However, if they do not provide evidence of relatedness which could not have arisen by chance, the 'families' they establish must be treated with skepticism.[7] It can of course be argued that at great time-depths the morphological paradigms which form the backbone of diagnostic evidence under the comparative method must have decayed or shifted function to such a degree that their reflexes will be nonexistent or unrecognisable, and that to demand them as a prerequisite of the comparative method is ridiculous. But whether the presuppositions of decay and functional shift are correct or not (and the degree of survival of morphological paradigms in the Indo-European and Austronesian families suggests they are not), any technique which purports to delineate language families must produce individual-identifying evidence of that family's protolanguage. One way of doing this might be to treat a potential 'macrofamily' in the same way as one would have to treat a family of isolating languages (which would have no morphological paradigms), namely to seek individual-identifying evidence in the form of lexemes organised into paradigmatic sets. But in such cases, as Nichols emphasises for isolating languages, each set would have to be reflected in its (near) entirety in all language families claimed as members of the macrofamily. Such reflexes would also presuppose regular sound correspondences.

Quite distinct from multilateral comparison are the long-range comparison techniques used to reconstruct etyma in Proto-Nostratic (the putative protolanguage superordinate to Proto-Indo-European, Proto-Uralic, and various other language families) and the protolanguages of certain other putative macrofamilies (e.g. Sino-Caucasian; Starostin 1982, 1984). Multilateral comparison compares morphemes with similar sounds and similar meanings, but makes no attempt to generate sound correspondences. It thereby bears only the most superfical resemblance to the comparative method and cannot meet any of the criteria mentioned in the previous paragraph. On the other hand Nostratic long-range comparison seeks to follow the comparative method from step 2 onward and presents rudimentary morphological paradigms and cognate sets which may take it towards the eventual fulfilment of step 1 and meeting the individual-identifying criterion.[8] It is therefore regretable that some writers do not distinguish clearly between the two approaches (for example, Shevoroshkin & Manaster Ramer 1991).

If the comparative method simply does not provide results which stretch back beyond, say, Proto-Indo-European or Proto-Austronesian, then it may well be that linguists will have to resort to quite different methods in order to research earlier periods, as Nichols (1992) suggests, but the results will not be in terms of genetic relationships. It is worth asking, however, *why* the time-depths accessible to the comparative method are limited. The received answer is that beyond a certain time-depth lexical replacement erases cognate sets to such a degree that there is insufficient material to work out sound correspondences, let alone to recognise morphological paradigms. But if this were uniformly true, then we would expect in a large language family like Austronesian, within which a diachronic series of interstage protolanguages is reconstructable, to find progressive degradation of the evidence throughout the family as we reconstruct successively earlier interstages. But we do not find this: Instead we find great variation in the rate of lexical retention in different parts of the Austronesian family (Blust 1981), correlating with factors which have to do with language contact (Pawley & Ross 1993).

The data require a more sophisticated hypothesis about the time-depth limitations of the comparative method. Bellwood (1984,1991) and Renfrew (1987) propose that the world's major language families achieved their status because of the demographic muscle which their speakers gained through the acquisition of agriculture. As these speakers expanded, slowly but inexorably, in search of new meadows or paddy-fields, they outnumbered and often absorbed hunter-gatherer populations, eliminating their societies and their languages. It is implicit in this model that speakers of early Indo-European, early Afro-Asiatic, early Austronesian, and their peers eliminated their own neighbour-relatives, quite possibly without trace. If this is so, the fact that practitioners of the classical comparative method cannot find the immediate relatives of Proto-Indo-European, Proto-Afro-Asiatic, and Proto-Austronesian is not surprising: It is because these relatives have disappeared without trace. There are, however, areas of the world where the agricultural expansion model does not apply. These include Australia (without agriculture) and New Guinea (with agriculture but little expansion). In New Guinea there appears to have been continuous and relatively undisturbed human habitation from much greater time-depths than in the cases of the world's major language families. The comparative method has yet to be systematically applied across the entirety of such an area,[9] but it would not be surprising to find that it can penetrate to a time-depth considerably greater than received wisdom allows. The difficulties we would expect the comparative method to encounter here are not so much those of simple degradation as those caused by ongoing language contact, discussed later in section 3.6.[10]

2.2   Cognate Sets and Sound Correspondences

In practice, step 2—collecting putative cognate sets for the family—overlaps with step 3 because the researcher inevitably develops hypotheses about sound correspondences in the course of searching for cognates and uses these hypotheses to further that search. Indeed, comparativists have tended to be rather cavalier about the semantics of potential cognates, assuming 'that any vocabulary set displaying the regular sound correspondences is in fact cognate, however far-fetched the semantic correspondences' (Nichols, this volume). The presupposition which underlies this assumption is that semantic change is not characterised by any crosslinguistic commonalities and is therefore unlike phonological change, where the comparativist recognises that some kinds of change are far more likely to occur than others. The contributions to this volume suggest, however, that this presupposition is false, and that there are at least two aspects of semantic change which can be codified and used by the linguist in judgments of cognation. The first of these aspects has to do with natural semantic shifts, the second with contact-induced change.

Wilkins, in his contribution to this volume, argues that the meanings of lexical items are subject crosslinguistically to natural shifts about which we can make generalisations parallel to those which comparativists make about phonological and morphological changes. These natural semantic shifts can be used, as Wilkins demonstrates from Australian data, to justify the inclusion in a single cognate set of items with different meanings. Conversely, they may sometimes imply the implausibility of such an inclusion. He thus demonstrates the role of a science of comparative etymology in the comparative method.

In Ross' contribution it is suggested that one aspect of certain kinds of contact-induced change resulting from bilingualism is that the semantic structures of one language may become the model for another. When this happens, the ranges of meaning of the lexical items of one language are expanded, contracted, or otherwise altered to bring them into line with their perceived equivalents in the model language.

Probably every experienced comparativist has learned not to take step 3—working out sound correspondences from cognate sets—for granted. Chapters 3 to 7 are all concerned with cases where sound change appears to have been 'irregular', resulting in cases where words clearly form cognate sets but produce irregular sound correspondences.

In his contribution Campbell argues that, although irregularities in sound change undoubtedly occur, we should not give up the basic concept of the regularity of sound change since many irregularities can be explained by linguistic and sociocultural factors which may 'interfere' with regularity but do not undermine the principle of regularity itself. Linguistic factors include morphological conditioning (discussed from a different perspective in Koch's contribution) and the avoidance of homophony. Sociocultural factors mentioned by Campbell are (i) onomatopoaeia and affective/expressive sound symbolism, including institutionalised forms where the relationship between two or three sounds expresses a semantic relationship in a number of word pairs or triplets; (ii) entry into the phoneme system of new phonemes as a result of extensive lexical borrowing, followed by the replacement of inherited phonemes by the new phonemes in some inherited words; and (iii) language death, where imperfect learning of the language can result in considerable irregularity. Campbell also takes issue with those who have suggested that the regularity of sound change is somehow suspended in 'exotic' languages on the mistaken assumption that 'primitive' or unwritten languages behave differently from 'civilised' or written languages.

In his chapter Newman describes the traditional Chinese philological tradition, arguing that, where the forms it attributes to Middle Chinese differ from those that would be reconstructed by a comparativist from modern Chinese dialect data, the Middle Chinese forms need to be taken seriously as preserving information which has been lost in all modern dialects. With this in mind, he examines a number of irregularities in modern Cantonese forms. Some of these are true irregularities, in the sense that they are due to factors which have interfered with regular development: The factors he exemplifies are the influence of Chinese writing on a few forms and the avoidance of taboo forms. Others are only irregularities at first sight: If comparativists are careful about the way they order the sound changes they reconstruct, then some 'irregularities' become regular by the ordered application of natural changes.

Blust discusses two cases of lexically sporadic sound change in Austronesian languages which he calls 'pandemic', that is, they occur independently in a large number of different languages. He shows that one of these, the crossover of initial /k/ and initial /g/, is probably the result of a natural perceptual difficulty due to the acoustic similarity of the two segments. The other—the widespread but sporadic tendency for

a homorganic nasal to be inserted before a word-medial stop in a range of languages—
has occupied a number of scholars, but Blust finds none of their explanations satisfactory, leaving this phenomenon to tantalise future students of Austronesian.

Durie presents a case of a rather different kind, taken from one of the longest-
studied language families. He suggests that there are genuine sound changes which
are not categorically regular, yet it is inappropriate to speak of 'exceptions' because
the phonetic conditioning of the change is probabilistic in its effect. Durie thus seeks
to blur the traditional distinction between regular and exceptional change. Grace presents us with a case where, when he put the 'irregular' cognate sets on one side, he
discovered that he had nothing left: There were plenty of cognate sets, but none that
he could label as 'regular'. We will consider Durie's and Grace's contributions below, when we turn to the comparative method in its wider sense.

2.3   Reconstruction

Step 4 is the reconstruction of the protolanguage of the family. Describing approaches to the reconstruction of prehistoric languages, Anttila (1989: 341) suggests that
there are two schools of thought among linguistic prehistorians. 'Formulaists'[11] assume that the symbols used in reconstruction are simply cover-symbols for sound correspondences. 'Realists' assume that the symbols used in reconstruction not only represent the phonemes of the protolanguage but also tell us something about the
articulation of these phonemes. Indeed, realists assume in general that they are reconstructing something approximating a 'real' language. The formulaist/realist debate receives little attention today, but the interest which comparativists take in check-
ing the plausibility of reconstructed protolanguages against the findings of language
typologists betrays an almost universal acceptance of some version of the realist position. A recent and thoughtful discussion of this issue is provided by Lass (1993).
Our statement of step 4a—reconstruct the protophonology from the sound correspondences worked out in step 3, using conventional wisdom *regarding the directions
of sound changes*—betrays a realist bias, since one cannot discuss the directions of
sound changes unless one believes that one's reconstructions consist of potentially
'real' phonemes affected by 'real' sound changes.

At step 4b the comparativist uses the newly reconstructed protophonology to reconstruct the morphemes of the protolanguage from the cognate sets of step 2. These
morphemes include both lexical items and paradigms of grammatical morphemes. If
steps 2, 3, and 4a have been successfully executed, then the reconstruction of lexical
items usually follows almost automatically from them. The reconstruction of morphology, however, is a different matter. In his contribution to this volume, Koch distinguishes between sound change in morphemes and morphological change. Where
different diachronic stages in the development of a morpheme are shown to be related by regular sound changes, then Koch speaks only of 'sound change', reserving the
term 'morphological change' for cases which, viewed phonologically or semantically, are 'irregular'. However, what is phonologically irregular is not necessarily morphologically irregular. Just as the comparative phonologist uses a typology of sound
change as a check on the plausibility of the phonological history he reconstructs, so
the comparative morphologist may use a typology of morphological change to decide

among reconstructive hypotheses, that is, to determine which encapsulates greater diachronic regularity. Koch provides us with just such a typology.

Ross, in his contribution, touches on morphological changes induced by language contact. These are changes in grammatical function rather than changes in form, and they arise in the context of the more general morphosyntactic change ('metatypy') which occurs when one language is restructured by bilingual speakers on the model of another. Ross makes the point that when, in the course of step 4b and step 4c (the reconstruction of syntax), the comparativist finds sudden restructurings of morphosyntax, he should not put them aside as unexplained residues but, if his data allow, investigate the possibility that metatypy has occurred. The other side of this coin is that syntactic change can occur with great ease, is far from meeting the individual-identifying criterion, and should never be used to establish genetic relationships (controversy over the putative Altaic and Trans New Guinea genetic groupings illustrates this; see respectively Unger 1990 and Foley 1986).

Because the focus of this volume is on regularity and irregularity in linguistic change, the contributors have mostly focussed their attention on steps 2, 3, and 4 of the comparative method, and so discussion of steps 5 and 6 lies outside the scope of this introduction.

3 THE COMPARATIVE METHOD (WIDE SENSE): A PARADIGM SHIFT IN PROGRESS?

We remarked at the beginning of this introduction that the term 'comparative method' is often used in linguistics to refer not only to the method itself but also in a 'wide' sense to its associated theory. For most of the method's lifetime, the central pillar of the theory has been the Neogrammarian hypothesis of the regularity of sound change. In recent years, however, the hypothesis has been subsumed by a growing body of sociohistorically based theory. The regularity hypothesis has been questioned ever since it was proposed, but historical linguists have continued to work with it because regularity *is* a major feature of language change and because there has been no systematic substitute for the hypothesis. Comparativists have constantly encountered data which seemed to challenge the hypothesis, and eight of the contributions to this volume (chapters 3 to 10) deal with such data.

The causes of irregularity advanced by the contributors are many and complementary. Apart perhaps from the effects of analogy and morphological conditioning (Koch), none of the causes has its locus in the language system itself. Instead, most refer in one way or another to the *speaker* of the language. This reference may be to the speech organs and speech processing (Blust), to cognition (Campbell on onomatopoaeia and affective/expressive sound symbolism; Wilkins on universal semantic change), to communicative exigency (Campbell on avoidance of homophony), to politeness (Newman on taboo), or to bilingualism and to contact between speakers of different languages (Campbell on borrowed phonemes; Ross; Grace). Comparativists find themselves moving from the quasi-Darwinian Neogrammarian paradigm which underlies the regularity hypothesis to a speaker-oriented paradigm which has a place for both regularity and irregularity.

The basic assertion of the Neogrammarian hypothesis is that a sound change occurs without exceptions, apart from the outworkings of analogy and borrowing. Whilst the regularity hypothesis certainly reflected its authors' desire for rigorous scholarship, its conceptual roots go deeper. The Neogrammarians adopted it from the work of August Schleicher, who—in the heyday of Darwinism—argued that languages are natural organisms following natural (and therefore exceptionless) laws, and that linguistics is therefore a natural science (1863: 6). Hermann Paul, whose *Prinzipien der Sprachgeschichte* is a Neogrammarian manual of the comparative method and of historical linguistics, regarded language as a *psychischer Organismus* ('psychic organism'), subject to a selection process analogous to Darwin's natural selection. The functionality of a linguistic pattern, defined by how well it was suited to the organs of speech, determined its extinction or survival (Paul [1880] 1920: 25, 32, 56).[12]

The view of language as an organism had its continuation (at least metaphorically) in the Saussurean concept of language as a system and in the idea that paradigms have their own internal dynamic (Lass 1980: 120). This 'Neogrammarian heritage' is recognised by Weinreich et al. (1968: 119), and our use of the term 'Neogrammarian' from this point also subsumes Structuralist historical linguistics (as described, for example, by Bynon 1977: chap. 2).

The metaphorical power of this idea has remained strong, and historical linguists have often been loath to look outside language systems to explain changes within those systems.[13] As numerous commentators have pointed out, there has long been an unease with the organism metaphor. There has also been a recognition that language is spoken by speakers and language change is subject to socio-historical factors. Paul and Meillet both knew this (Weinreich et al. 1968: 104–8, 176–77), but historical linguistics waited until the publication of Weinreich, Labov, and Herzog's 'Empirical foundations for a theory of language change' in 1968 for the first outline of a speaker-oriented, socially embedded paradigm.

Why did the shift to a speaker-oriented approach take so long? In retrospect we see that the shift was the outcome of changes over which linguists had no control, especially the reorientation of anthropological and sociological theory away from social Darwinism, a reorientation associated with the names of Franz Boas and Emile Durkheim. A practical result of the new paradigm in cultural anthropology was a growth in fieldwork in unwritten languages and consequently in knowledge and experience of spoken languages in a range of community contexts. The new sociology provided a framework for interrelating language, speakers, and the community; concomitant developments in social statistics allowed the analysis of linguistic data collected in that framework. But it is increasing access to computing technology which has made it possible for historical linguists to start processing the immense amounts of data which must be analysed if a speaker-oriented historical linguistics is to have an empirical foundation, as we see from the publications of Labov and his associates, Le Page & Tabouret-Keller, Lesley and James Milroy, and Durie (this volume).

Keller's (1990) study of the conceptualisation of language change depicts historical linguists as trapped between two unviable alternatives. On the one hand, a language is clearly not an organism. On the other hand, it is not an artefact like art, science, or philosophy, since these have a history directly attributable to human intention (Keller 1990: 73). Instead, Keller argues, language change is usually an 'invisible hand process' (the term comes from the eighteenth-century philosopher-economist Adam Smith), the kind of process which takes place when members of a population act in a similar way with similar intentions, yet their collective acts have a result beyond their intentions. A simple invisible hand process occurs when many people take the same short cut over a grassed area, with the unintended result that they trample a track across it. A language change takes place because, for example, a sufficient number of speakers perform the same 'act of identity' (Le Page & Tabouret-Keller 1985), that is, adopt a feature from the speech of some other group of speakers in order to identify more closely with that group, with the unintended result that the sum of their adoptions becomes a change in the language system.[14]

When people perform similar actions with similar intentions in what turns out to be an invisible hand process, their behaviour can be influenced by an awareness of others' behaviour in the circumstances: A sees B taking a short cut and follows him, or A sees the beginnings of the trampled track, recognises its use, and follows it. Similarly in a language change, one speaker hears an innovatory feature in the speech of another and adopts it. As Milroy and Milroy (1985: 345–48) argue, it is necessary to distinguish between speaker 'innovation' and language 'change'. A speaker innovation may or may not be copied by other speakers. If it is copied, it may be adopted only by people in the speaker's immediate community, or it may be copied into other communities via other innovators. The linguist who observes the result of this invisible hand process labels it 'language change'.

3.1 Explaining Language Change

This brings us to what Weinreich et al. (1968: 102) call the 'actuation problem': 'Why do changes in a structural feature take place in a particular language at a given time, but not in other languages with the same feature, or in the same language at other times?' As one can infer from the foregoing discussion, the explanation of an invisible hand process is always complex.[15] If the *explanandum* is the change in the language system, then the immediate efficient cause of that change is the cumulative adoption of the relevant innovation by a large number of speakers. But the adoption itself is explicable in terms of a final cause, namely the speakers' motive(s) for adopting the innovation. Also to be explained are the identity of the innovator and the eligibility of the innovator(s) to be copied by whom (what are these speakers' positions in the speech community? why them and not others?) and how the innovation comes to be in the innovator's speech in the first place (what classes of innovation can occur? how do they get there?).

When we question these elements in relation to a particular language change, then we are asking historical questions, and these require historical answers. A historical answer applies generalisations to events after they have happened in order to help explain them: it does not predict specific future events.[16] For ease of presentation, we will discuss these elements and the kinds of generalisations relevant to them in the following order:

1. the identity of the innovator and the copiers and their relationships within the speech community;

2. the entry of innovations into the innovator's speech and human constraints on possible or preferred innovations;

3. speakers' motives for adopting innovations.

When explanations of particular language changes are given within the Neogrammarian framework, they are largely given in terms of a 'speakerless' version of (2) alone, that is, in terms of the language system to the exclusion of human (physiological and cognitive) constraints. The Neogrammarian framework has no explicit theoretical place for the speaker, as required by our formulation, nor for the speech community as required by (1). On the other hand, when explanations are given within the speaker-oriented paradigm, they often consist only of answers to (1) and (3), to the neglect of (2). That is, emphasis falls on sociohistorical factors, to the neglect of physiology and cognition. However, as Wilkins (this volume) argues with regard to semantic change, both human (in the case of semantics, cognitive) and sociocultural factors play a role in explaining language changes.

3.2 Speech Communities and Innovators

Our earlier formulation of (1) presupposes a definition of the speech community, but a rigorous definition is difficult to formulate. Grace (this volume) writes of the definition of 'speech community': 'In its modified form it might read, "A speech community consists of those people who communicate with one another or are connected to one another by chains of speakers who communicate with one another." But to be entirely satisfactory it would also need to recognize that community is a matter of degree. . . .'

As Grace says, the speech community has commonly been defined by its speakers' language, but this definition fails for the case he describes because the speech community uses a *pool* of languages and there is no one language coterminous with the community. The last sentence of the quotation refers to the fact that a speech community can be viewed schematically as a series of roughly concentric circles (e.g. hamlet, village, village group, region, and so on) to which there is no specified upper limit—a view which will work just as well in a traditional village situation as in a metropolitan urban setting.

A current speaker-oriented view of the speech community which meshes with the previous paragraph (and on which Grace draws) is one which has been developed through research in Belfast and views the speech community in terms of a social network of links between speakers (Milroy 1992, Milroy 1993, Milroy & Milroy 1985, Milroy 1980, Milroy 1987, Milroy & Milroy 1992). A network is characterised by the density of its links (the number of people who relate to each other) and by the intensity (in terms of time spent and intimacy) and the multiplicity of those links (the number of purposes for which two people relate to each other) (Milroy 1980: 20, 49–52, 139–44). A virtue of this model, unlike the social-class model of urban sociolinguistics, is that it can be applied to speech communities everywhere (see, for example, Schooling 1990).

Milroy and Milroy (1985) suggest that innovators are people who are marginal to the local community which will adopt the innovation, but who have a large number of weak and uniplex ties outside it to people who in general do not know each other. Their outside ties make them candidates for adopting innovations from people outside the community; their marginal position means that they are less susceptible to norm-enforcement within the local community and that innovations have less significance for them as social markers. If a speaker innovation diffuses into the community, it does so because it is copied from the innovators by people whom Milroy and Milroy call 'early adopters'. These are people who are central to the network: They have strong ties with a relatively large number of people who also have ties to each other, they conform to community norms, and they provide a model for conservative members of the community. Once an innovation is adopted by them, the middle of the S-curve of innovation diffusion has been reached, and the innovation diffuses with increasing speed into the rest of the community (Milroy 1992: 172–85).[17] This account presupposes, of course, that innovations are always introduced to the community from without, but this is not necessarily the case.

Neogrammarian explanations of (2) look at the entry of the innovation into the language system as a whole, rather than into the *innovator's* speech. They appeal to either borrowing, system-internal change, or analogy (which is also a form of system-internal change). But the speaker-oriented model of language change renders the well-worn Neogrammarian distinction between borrowing and system-internal change less clear-cut, as every change begins (from a community perspective) in the speech of innovators, diffusing into the community via early adopters. As Wang (1979: 362) remarks, it doesn't matter how a sound change is actuated ('internally' or 'externally')—its method of implementation (spread) will be the same. This is vividly clear in the situation described by Grace (this volume).

3.3   The Innovator's Language System and Constraints on Innovation

The question of how an innovation comes to be in an innovator's speech in the first place presupposes a theory of the individual's speech in relation to the language system of the community. It is by now a truism of sociolinguistics that the language system of a community entails orderly variation. But it is also true that each speaker's speech is characterised by orderly variation, even though individual speakers may not have access to all the variants of the system (Weinreich et al. 1968: 100–1, 159; Milroy & Milroy 1985: 346–47). Apart from the introduction of new lexical items, which may be *additions* to an open system, innovations arise as *variants* in the innovating speaker's language system. These variants may be lexical, phonological, or morphological, but our discussion here will be largely limited to phonological innovations, as scholars operating with a speaker-oriented model have paid more attention to these. Whether an innovator acquires a new variant from outside the community or whether it arises spontaneously within his speech makes little difference to its diffusion within the community or to the constraints to which it is subject within the innovator's linguistic system.

Weinreich et al. (1968: 183–84) labelled the question of what language changes are likely and why they are likely 'the constraints problem'. This is an area of historical linguistics which has received little attention since the Neogrammarian heyday, and so it is gratifying that this volume contains several contributions which refer to it. Blust touches on articulatory and acoustic constraints, Durie on systemic constraints, Wilkins on constraints on semantic change, and Koch on constraints on morphological change.

Experienced comparativists know that certain sounds (e.g., nasals; cf. Baldi 1990a 1990: 6–8) are less prone to change than other sounds and that certain sound changes are far more likely to occur than others, and they use this knowledge in doing reconstructions. What the comparativist knows, informally, is what sound changes are 'natural', that is, normal within the constraints of human physiology and cognition (or sometimes just common within the language family the linguist works with). It was evidently this insight which inspired attempts during the Neogrammarian era to catalogue and classify sound changes which, it was assumed, were universal,[18] but these endeavours declined with the growth of Structuralism, and there has been little interest in the phonological aspect of the constraints problem in recent literature, with the exception of Ferguson (1978, 1990) and the work of Stampe, Donegan, and Ohala referred to later.

Structuralist historical phonology has emphasised the relationships between changes within a language's phonological system, either because one change seems to trigger the next (as in the chains of changes recognised by Martinet [1952, 1955]). Or because several changes entail an alteration of the same componential feature. Foley (1977) also shows that a feature change affects a set of phonemes in a predictable diachronic sequence. But further progress with the problem of phonological constraints is only possible if the innovating speaker is allowed to emerge from the wings, complete with organs of speech and hearing and with a mind which perceives, processes, and produces. Mainstream phonology has tended to take the physiology of speech for granted (or, like Foley, to declare it irrelevant) and to take account of naturalness only by incorporating markedness conventions into phonological representations. But markedness conventions only capture the outcomes of naturalness; they cannot characterise naturalness itself. What the comparativist needs is a characterisation of naturalness in terms of the physiology and cognition of speech and an account of the relationship between naturalness and sound change. For this we have to look beyond mainstream phonology to research directions which offer speaker-oriented insights into the constraints problem. Two such directions are Stampe's 'natural phonology' (see, for example, Donegan 1993, Donegan & Stampe 1979, Stampe 1979) and Ohala's laboratory phonology (see, for example, Ohala 1993, 1974, 1989), both of which take the interactions between the organs of speech, hearing, and cognition as basic elements of theory.[19]

We are aware that objections of various kinds have been raised against natural phonology (for a sympathetic statement of these, see Anderson 1985: 342–47), but for the comparativist it provides a sensible research framework in a way that its competitors cannot. Firstly, it reserves a special place for naturalness, rather than treating it as merely a formal convention. Fundamental to natural phonology is a distinction between phonological processes, which have their basis in natural constraints imposed by the organs of speech and hearing, and morpho-phonological rules, which are purely conventional.[20] Secondly, two kinds of phonological processes are recognised, fortitions, and lenitions, which, as we will note, are relevant in the description of certain sound changes.

Fortitions (or paradigmatic processes) are processes which work to limit the inventory of 'possible' (intentionally pronounceable/perceivable) segments in a language. For example, the vowel [ɒ] requires both opening the mouth wide (the feature 'low') and narrowing the lips by rounding (the feature 'round'). These gestures are obviously in conflict, and there are several fortitive processes which can be used to remedy this difficulty: after a period of variation, one of the features is abandoned, giving [ɑ] or [o], or they are sequenced in a diphthong, giving [ɑŏ] or [oɑ̆]. Fortitive processes are not learned, but follow naturally from the physical features of the organs of speech. Instead, what *is* learned is the ability to overcome the difficulty of producing and perceiving, for example, the vowel [ɒ]. The fortitive process applies when this ability is not acquired or is lost. Fortitive processes 'are part of the speaker's native *incapacity*' (Donegan 1993: 109). Fortitive processes allow us to account for the fact that there are 'default' phoneme inventories which are particularly well distributed among the world's languages (e.g., the system of five cardinal vowels).

Lenitions (or syntagmatic processes) in natural phonology are processes which overcome difficulties associated with producing and perceiving segment sequences. Lenitive processes are, for example, vowel nasalisation before nasals or stop fricativisation between vowels. Hearers unconsciously 'undo' lenitive (allophonic) processes in order to recognise a phoneme sequence.

The means by which natural processes become speaker innovations has been described by Ohala (1993, 1989).[21] Phonological processes result in innovations when hearers misinterpret what they hear. Modern instrumental phonetic analysis shows that rule-governed phonetic variation, resulting from the competing demands of fortition and lenition, is a ubiquitous trait of speech. Hearers constantly make perceptual corrections for this variation. Sporadically, however, they 'hypocorrect', that is, they fail to correct what they hear. One kind of hypocorrection occurs when speakers fail to detect the difference between two acoustically similar sounds and treat one as the other.

Hypocorrection may apply to both fortitive and lenitive processes and may lead to the creation of new phonemes. If a hearer fails to recognise [ɑ] or [oɑ̆] as an allophone of /ɒ/, a natural fortitive process is allowed to operate, and some or all instances of /ɒ/ are reinterpreted (variably in the first instance) as /ɑ/ or /oɑ/.[22] If a hearer fails to interpret nasalisation on a vowel as a feature of the adjacent nasal consonant (i.e., fails to 'undo' a lenition) and instead interprets it as a feature of the vowel, then the hearer's phonological system may acquire a new set of nasal vowel phonemes (especially if nasal consonants in this context are underarticulated). It is worth recalling in all this, as Donegan, Ohala, and Blust (this volume) all do, that although phonetic events occur in the organs of speech and hearing, the acts of perception, interpretation, and instructions to produce sounds are essentially mental.

Sometimes hypocorrection leads to the confusion or merger of two phonemes. Blust (this volume) points out that the acoustic difference between voiced and voiceless velar stops is smaller than at other points of articulation, with the result that the hearer fails to recognise a lightly voiced [g] as /g/ and instead interprets it as /k/. This results in the merger of Proto-Austronesian *k* and *g* in many daughter languages (allowing a fortitive process to operate), or, in languages which retain the distinction, in their confusion word-initially in a number of etyma.

We are now in a position to understand the actuation of the chains of changes described by Martinet (1952, 1955) and Foley (1977). We have no means of predicting when the first shift in a chain will arise in the orderly variation of an innovator's speech, but we know that once it has occurred, the probability of the next shift occurring is much greater than if the first shift had not occurred. Once the 'hardest-to-articulate' sound in a sub-system has undergone fortition or lenition, the next hardest is likely to follow, for reasons which evidently have to do with economy in the interaction of the speech organs and cognition. It is sometimes argued that chains of changes are provoked by the need to fill a 'gap' in a subsystem. In the speaker-oriented paradigm, however, a gap is nothing exceptional: complete effacement is simply the most extreme form of lenition.

The kind of chain which most readily springs to mind is a vowel fortition chain like the Great Vowel Shift in English. But another kind of chain is exemplified by the intervocalic lenition of stops, where it seems that the probability of the lenition of /t/ or /d/ to [r] or [ð] is close to zero if the corresponding velar /k/ or /g/ has not already been lenited (usually to [ɣ]), but quite high if it has. Of course, this does not tell us how quickly or slowly the next shift in the chain will occur. Eckert's (1980) careful study of a chain of vowel shifts in southwestern France shows that a chain shift can continue over generations, each sound change eventually triggering the next.

Our intent in the preceding paragraphs has been to indicate the shape of theories which may offer answers to the phonological constraints problem, and we have touched only in the briefest way on research in both natural and laboratory phonology.[23] The claims implicit in these paragraphs are (i) that there is a growing body of theory, albeit away from the mainstream, from which we can predict which sound changes (and which chains of changes; see Labov 1981: 299) will be more common; and (ii) that innovations do not have to be 'borrowed' to enter the innovator's language system.

3.4   Motives for Innovation

The third element in the explanation of language change consists of speakers' motives for adopting an innovation. When the innovation is the adoption of a new lexical item, a fairly straightforward sociohistorical-cum-linguistic explanation seemingly suffices. For example, as Keller (1990: 109–27) shows in eloquent detail, the word *englisch* 'angelic' was replaced in mid-nineteenth-century German by *engelhaft* not simply because it was homophonous with *englisch* 'English' (speakers do not invariably avoid homophony; cf. Malkiel 1979) but because at this time *englisch* 'English' and *englisch* 'angelic' both increased in usage, one because of the rise of English/German industrial competition, the other because it had become an aspect of the female ideal and had a more readily available morphological alternative. Such an elegant answer presupposes generalisations (as Keller says). One is that speakers seek to avoid homophony when homophonous words rise in frequency of usage (see Campbell, this volume). Another is that a regular way of avoiding homophony is the adoption of a morphological alternative. Whether these particular generalisations

whose stem belongs to the /æ:/ class *have* been redistributed: *manning*, like *man*, has /æ:/ (285).

Now, all these exceptions could be explained by appeal to analogy, but other cases cannot. Labov and his coworkers found lexical diffusion in progress in Philadephia. They found that there was variation between /æ/ and /æ:/ in certain words with following nontautosyllabic /n/ or /m/ (i.e. where only /æ/ 'ought' to occur). Among these *planet* occurred with /æ:/ with significantly greater frequency than other words of this class, especially in children's speech. *Planet* was followed at a distance by *damage* and *manage*, with *camera* and *family* lagging further behind (293–4). Thus the evidence indicated that these words were undergoing redistribution from the /æ/ to the /æ:/ class. They also found that the same redistribution was affecting words where /æ/ was followed by /l/: *personality* and *pal* were shifting, but *algebra* and *California* were not. At some point in the past, this redistribution has also affected words where /æ/ was followed by tautosyllabic /d/: *bad*, *mad*, and *glad* have moved into the /æ:/ class, whilst *sad* and *dad* retain /æ/ (286, 295). Here, lexical diffusion has been arrested along the way.[27]

Labov is also able to point to plenty of vowel changes in his studies of urban American English where the regularity hypothesis applies. However, there is a significant difference between the Neogrammarian version of the regularity hypothesis and Labov's. The Neogrammarian version looks at a completed sound change and says that every word eligible for the change has been affected, except for cases where analogy and borrowing (and perhaps certain other factors) apply. Labov looks at instrumentally measured sound change in progress, applies variable rule analysis to it, and shows it to be regular when fine-grained phonetic conditioning and socially conditioned variation are taken into account. But under this version of 'regularity' there is predictable variation clustered around a mean, a fact captured in steps (i) and (ii) of our reformulations of the two competing hypotheses above. The question is: Does the regular variation observed by Labov necessarily result in a completed sound change which affects every eligible word, as the Neogrammarian hypothesis claims?

Durie (this volume) shows that the answer is 'no'. Applying variable rule analysis to certain ancient vowel changes in Germanic languages, he shows that fine-grained phonetic conditioning is probabilistic, not exceptionless. The probability factor is evidently the diachronic reflex of synchronic variation. Upon reflection, this is not surprising. Step (iii) of our speaker-oriented version of the regularity hypothesis (p. 23, this volume) asserts that steps (i) and (ii) apply equally and immediately to all items in the lexicon which contain the relevant sound in the relevant environments'—but steps (i) and (ii) consist in variation between the old and the new sound, and, although the variation itself applies to all eligible lexical items, when this particular pattern of variation ceases, it is to be expected that some items will end up with the old sound rather than the new. In the cases described by Durie, the variation of reflexes of Proto Germanic **u* between [u] and [o] ceased with the attrition of the phonetic conditioning enviroments and the resulting phonemic split in which the reflexes were assigned to either **u* or **o*. Thus 'regular' sound change as it is observed in progress by Labov will not necessarily be exceptionless in its outcome. Experience suggests that this might as well be worded 'will rarely be exceptionless in its outcome'—but we will return to this case briefly later.

The redefinition of 'regular sound change' to include probabilistic sound change obviously reduces the distinction between 'regular' change and lexically diffused change. Since both kinds of change have their beginnings in the same natural processes, as we indicated in our reformulations, we may suspect with Labov (1981: 304) that there is a whole array of sound change types ranged between the two poles of exceptionlessness and lexical diffusion. It is nonetheless convenient to focus our discussion on the two polar types.

What determines whether a particular innovation becomes a regular sound change or is diffused lexically? Labov does not give a completely definitive answer, nor can we, but some observations are in order.

Durie (this volume) provides a vivid example of the difference. His analysis specifies phonetic conditions under which the Proto-Germanic high vowels *u and *i were likely to be lowered respectively to [o] and [e]. In Old High German, however, there is a significant difference between the behaviours of the two protovowels, and Durie shows that this is attributable to the asymmetric structure of the Proto-Germanic vowel system. Proto-Germanic had no back mid vowel *o, but it *did* have a front mid vowel *e. As a result, lowering of *i to [e] is partially blocked in order to avoid merger of *i and *e, whereas there is no such blockage to lowering *u to [o].

In many cases of lexical diffusion, the speaker evidently recognises the output sound as 'different' because it is already another phoneme and the application of the innovation will result in a merger. This was also the case with the Middle English /ɛ:/. A shortening innovation applied, giving *bread, head, dead, breath, sweat*, but, because /ɛ/ was also a phoneme, the innovation had limited application, leaving other cases of /ɛ:/ which later rose via /e:/ to /i:/ (*bead, lead, mead, read*) (Jespersen 1949: 242–3; Labov 1981: 297). There is, incidentally, no doubt that some cases of lexical diffusion result from the borrowing of forms from a neighbouring dialect into the innovator's speech, but the effect of these is not essentially different from the scenario we have presented (Wang & Lien 1993).

Thus, some innovations lead in the direction of change in the phonemic make-up of affected words, whereas others do not. Where an innovation does not affect the phonemic make-up of words (i.e. it results only in allophony or in a difference in the realisation of the phoneme) it applies regularly (i.e. without exception or probabilistically). But where an innovation threatens to alter the phonemic make-up of words, speakers are liable to block its regular application, with the result that it spreads by lexical diffusion. (We write 'liable to block' rather than simply 'block' because we believe that this account is in need of much refining. Phonemic mergers do occur, and we often do not know whether these are cases of completed lexical diffusion or of Neogrammarian regularity.)

If the lexically diffused change from /æ/ to /æ:/ described by Labov had applied without exception, it would not have altered the number of vowels in the system, as there was earlier no /æ:/—so why should speakers have applied it lexically? The answer is implicit in Labov's statement that we find 'lexical diffusion in the redistribution of an abstract word class into other abstract word classes'. Labov explains that the lax-to-tense shift is a complex one, in which 'the whole set of phonetic features changes at once' (Labov 1981: 299): the phonological distinction between lax and tense, or short and long, is phonetically complex and not, for example, a simple difference in length, and it is this complexity which he captures with the word 'abstract'. It seems that, cognitively, the speaker recognises the output [æ:] as a 'different' sound from the input [æ], and blocks its exceptionless application. And once it has applied to turn two homophones into a minimal pair (like *can* /kæ:n/, 'tin can', vs. *can* /kæn/, the modal) or to create a subminimal pair (like *mad* /mæ:d/ vs. *sad* /sæd/), then a new phonemic distinction has been created.[28]

It is possible that the probabilistic sound change from Proto-Germanic *u to [o] described by Durie belongs in this category (rather than the category of 'regular' sound change): it behaves more predictably than the phonemically obstructed change from *i to Old High German [e], but is far from exceptionless. One may speculate that speakers perceived the output [o] as 'different' from the input [u] by analogy with the difference between /e/ and /i/ and that this contributed to the probabilistic operation of phonetic conditioning.

Undoubtedly lexical diffusion still needs more research attention from comparativists. Two topics spring to mind, both concerning the typology of lexically diffused changes. Firstly, in an insightful article, Phillips (1984) characterises two types of lexical diffusion. The words which change first are, in one type, those which occur *more* frequently; in the other type, they are those which occur *less* frequently. Interestingly, changes of the first type are (in terms of natural phonology) lenitions, those of the second type fortitions. (This observation is ours, based on Phillips' account, and it is one which also underlines the value of natural phonology.)[29] Secondly, the cases of lexical diffusion we have referred to above all have their genesis in natural articulatory tendencies, but Blust (this volume) describes one whose genesis lies in perceptual difficulty. Where two sounds are acoustically close but phonemically distinct, they are liable to be confused or merged. A number of Austronesian languages merge or show a tendency to confuse word-initial /k/ and /g/. Blust attributes this to a physiological factor which makes the voicing distinction between velar stops harder to hear than that between labial or alveolar stops.

We conclude this discussion of the two kinds of sound change with an example, drawn from the Polynesian language Samoan, which again underlines the need for research into kinds of sound change and the factors that determine them. It is interesting for two reasons. Firstly, Labov (1981: 296) compiles a number of features of regular sound change and lexical diffusion,[30] among which he claims that lexical diffusion is phonetically discrete, whilst regular sound change is not; but the Samoan example shows that regular sound change may also be phonetically discrete. Secondly, Samoan illustrates rather nicely our suggestion that the criterion for deciding between the two kinds of change is whether or not the phonemic make-up of words will be changed.

Samoan has two major lects, which we will term Old and New Samoan. Old Samoan represents the older form of the language, where /t/ remains [t]. It continues to be used for formal purposes. New Samoan is the colloquial form of the language, in which /t/ became [k]. These changes seem to have been in progress around the year 1800 (Hovdhaugen 1986). Although the change [t] to [k] is phonetically discrete, it is regular and apparently exceptionless. In Old Samoan, Proto Polynesian *p, *t, and *k were reflected as /p/, /t/, and /ʔ/ respectively; that is, there was no /k/, so the change [t] to [k] is simply a change in phonetic output which leaves the phonemic make-up of words undisturbed. Its regularity is therefore not surprising, and we can see that Labov's suggestion that regular sound changes are not phonetically discrete is a product of his concern with vowel changes. A regular sound change may or may not be phonetically discrete. What is more, even a phonetically discrete sound change may on occasion be exceptionless.

The motivation for speaker rejection of sound change outlined here, namely, that the speaker recognises the output sound as another phoneme and avoids merger, is exactly parallel to the motivation for a number of the morphological changes described by Koch (this volume). In these cases, if regular sound change applied to a morpheme, a merger would occur. Because affixes and clitics are often subject to phonological reduction, speakers use a variety of innovatory strategies to avoid merger.

3.6   Where the Comparative Method Fails—or Does It?

The comparative method relies on the retention of archaic features in daughter languages. When something is independently lost in all the attested languages of a family, there can be no way of reconstructing it. In this sense it is uncontroversial that the comparative method can 'fail'. Grace (this volume) describes a different kind of failure, a case in New Caledonia where the comparative method failed or 'succeeded only to a quite limited extent'.[31] As he notes, however, this seeming semifailure is worth reporting because of the circumstances which give rise to it. In other words, the semifailure itself is diagnostic of a particular kind of sociolinguistic prehistory and is in this sense not a failure at all.

The distinctive characteristic of the sociolinguistic prehistory described by Grace is that the boundaries of language and speech community have long been noncoterminous. Although each village probably recognised one language as emblematic of its inhabitants' identity, more than one language was evidently used in each village, and most or all villagers probably spoke two or more languages. Some languages were evidently spoken in more than one village, but this did not particularly identify them as a community. Rather, the larger community was a collection of villages with a repertoire of several languages, which, as it happened, were genetically quite closely related to each other.

The linguistic result of this intensive bi- and multilingualism is a *Sprachbund*, in which the languages have similar phonologies and similar morphosyntax but considerable lexical diversity. Because the languages were closely related in the first place, the *Sprachbund* effect—the adoption of common structural features—has been intensified. But unlike a 'normal' group of genetically related languages each of which has been used in a relatively discrete community, these languages pose an enormous problem for the comparativist. Grace was unable to work out a consistent set of sound correspondences; instead he found multiple correspondences with just a few examples of each correspondence—in other words, multiple unconditioned reflexes of each phoneme of the shared protolanguage. One might expect, as Grace originally did, that some reflexes could be attributed to borrowing, but he was unable to isolate borrowings and therefore unable to separate regular from 'irregular' sound correspondences. That is (as we noted earlier), he was unable to complete step 3 in his application of the comparative method.

Grace infers that it is impossible to separate 'regular' (inherited) from 'irregular' (borrowed), not because the irregularities are too complex, but because this dichotomy is not a proper characterisation of what has occurred. Where speakers regularly use two or more lects, they have an intuitive grasp of their sound correspondences and use these to convert the phonological shapes of words from one lect to another. It is easy to see that if the converted word has been the object of a lexically diffused change or if it includes the reflex of a protophoneme which has merged with another protophoneme in the 'donor' language (but not in the 'recipient'), then the phonological shape which results from the conversion will not be the same as it would have been if the word had been directly inherited by the recipient language. If this kind of interplay continues between several languages over centuries, then the result will be of the kind that Grace has uncovered.

The rise of regular sound correspondences requires (as Grace observes) that the corresponding languages each be spoken by a network of people who have stronger ties with each other than with speakers of the other languages. But in the case Grace describes, there was apparently no significant difference in strength between the two sets of ties. And where a language does not coincide with a relatively strong network, norm-enforcement is weak and language change can meet less resistance.

The cases described by Ross (this volume) are also set in Melanesian villages and bear some resemblances to the situation Grace analyses. Both entail bilingualism and consequent semantic and morphosyntactic restructuring. However, in the situations Ross reconstructs, one language is clearly the emblematic language of the village, the other a genetically unrelated intergroup language. The emblematic language thus coincides with a relatively strong network (one or more villages), whilst the intergroup language is used by a larger speech community composed of villages with weaker ties between them (and the intergroup language is also the emblematic language of one or more villages). These strong village networks ensure 'regularity' of change, and the functional inequality of the languages means that the diffusion of innovations has been largely one-way: from intergroup language to emblematic language. In Grace's New Caledonian case it seems to have been bi- or multidirectional. Other differences in outcome are that in New Caledonia Grace found a levelling of phonological differences between languages and the lexical interplay we referred to earlier; neither of these phenomena is significant in Ross' Papua New Guinea cases (although Maisin has borrowed extensively). Ross observes that phonological levelling is due to language shift (rather than to diffusion from an intergroup language), and one can imagine that language shift by individuals must have been ubiquitous in the New Caledonian scenario. Also important in both New Caledonia and Papua New Guinea is the fact that speech communities are small, and this favours language change because norm enforcement depends on only a few speakers in each generation.

Both Ross and Grace argue that the cases they describe are not merely marginal. Ross says that the kind of contact-induced change he describes leaves recognisable and consistent patterns in the data, but that these patterns are of a kind often ignored by the comparative method. Grace describes the outcome of another kind of contact-induced change and concludes that 'we do not know enough about diachronic processes in situations where there is not a close association between linguistically defined units and communities.' The kinds of situation described by both writers occur where small groups speaking different languages rub shoulders with each other. Inevitably, these situations *are* marginal in the spread zones (the term is from Nichols 1992: 13) of Indo-European, Uralic, or Afro-Asiatic, but the increasing application of the comparative method to languages in areas away from the well-known spread zones and accessible only to the fieldworker can be expected to throw up a growing number of cases where the comparative method, to use Grace's word, 'fails'.

Significantly, there is a sprinkling of cases in the recent literature which resemble Grace's not only in their outcomes but in their sociolinguistic histories. Particularly interesting in this regard is the set of Australian patrilects (lects of patriclans) described by Johnson (1990), where, allowing for the fact that the genetic relationship among these lects is closer than between Grace's languages, the linguistic outcomes are rather similar to the New Caledonian case: the patrilects share a common phonological system, but there are considerable irregularities in sound correspondence as well as lexical differences between the lects. These outcomes are attributable to community structure: every person belongs to an exogamous patriclan which has an emblematic patrilect, but people move about in somewhat unstable hunter/gatherer bands with around fifty members drawn from different patriclans and speaking their own and each other's patrilects. The patrilects are maintained because they are emblematic of the patriclan, membership of which gives the right to land use and thereby to a living. What is striking here is that the sociolinguistic situation observed by Johnson in the Cape York Peninsula resembles the one reconstructed by Grace: the patrilect and the local speech community (the band) do not coincide.[32]

Boretzky (1984), in a paper which sets out to show that change in 'exotic' languages may have outcomes different from those in Indo-European languages, examines data from the Arrernte dialects of central Australia and describes a set of linguistic outcomes similar to those in the Cape York Peninsula: identical phonologies, irregular variation in the phonological shapes of cognates, and divergence in lexicon. Unfortunately, his ethnographic information is limited, but he recognises the small size of dialect groups and intermarriage as probable contributing factors to the absence of regular sound correspondences. Heath (1978, 1979, 1981) provides a detailed account of the diffusion of innovations between Australian languages in Arnhem Land. This situation differs from New Caledonia, Cape York, and central Australia in that the languages are genetically only very distantly related and the social structure is somewhat different from that in Cape York—but, like Ross' Papua New Guinea cases, account must also be taken of contact in order to reconstruct their prehistories.[33]

Finally, Leer (1990) reconstructs the prehistory of the Tlingit language of southern Alaska. Tlingit is related to the Athabaskan languages and Eyak, but, as in the New Caledonian case, there are too many sound correspondences. Modern Tlingit shows little dialect variation, but Leer suggests that such variation did exist in the past. However, the networks associated with the various dialects collapsed into a single network, so that people speaking different dialects came to have close ties to each other. There was no social motivation to maintain these dialects, and Leer argues that words containing different reflexes of the protophonemes came to be part of the common language. This prehistory resembles that in New Caledonia in that it posits the use of different lects side by side in the same speech community. It differs from it in that in New Caledonia the lects have retained their emblematic significance, whereas in Tlingit they have lost it and have merged.

We have rehearsed these histories briefly here because they illustrate the fact that the cases described by Grace and Ross, in which the comparative method either 'failed' or neglected significant data, are part of an emerging pattern. It is probably true that all the steps of the comparative method, as we listed them earlier, can never be applied to southern New Caledonia or the Cape York Peninsula, and that if they and they alone are applied to Ross's Papua New Guinea or Heath's Arnhem Land cases, significant patterns will be missed. But Grace's very 'failure' in New Caledonia (i) enables him to reconstruct the *kind* of linguistic prehistory the region experienced and (ii) points to the more general fact that, even if the comparative method cannot be applied in the same way as it has been applied to Indo-European (and numerous other language groups), the patterns which emerge from the analysis nonetheless inform us about the prehistory of the languages we are investigating. What we do not yet understand well is just what linguistic outcomes are diagnostic of just what sociolinguistic prehistories.

4 CONCLUSIONS

Comparativists have tended to argue (at conferences rather than in print, perhaps) that irregularity is so undermining to the comparative method that it cannot be recognised but should be explained away at any cost. The cost, however, as the contributions to this volume show, is not only that one distorts one's data but also that one ignores patterns of irregularity which can reveal a great deal about linguistic prehistory. The burden of part 3 of this introduction has been that, whilst much of language change is regular, there clearly *are* irregularities of change and we can understand these better within a speaker-oriented framework than within a language-oriented framework of the kind which has tended to dominate the comparative method since the Neogrammarian revolution.

What are the implications of this paradigm shift for the comparative method in its narrow sense? On one level, they are very slight: the steps of the method as we set them out in part 2 of this introduction will not change. On another level, namely that of scale, the implications are substantial indeed. If we want to be able to identify probabilistic sound changes, or to track lexical diffusion, or to reconstruct complex sociolinguistic histories, then we will need to work with far larger and more complete quantities of data than has often been the case. The appearance of regularity is often the result of data bases limited to comparative lists of a few hundred words of 'core' vocabulary. At the same time, a false appearance of irregularity can be the result of using small data bases. The larger the database, the larger the reconstructed lexicon and morphology. The larger the reconstructed lexicon and morphology, the more our attention will be drawn to the various kinds of irregularity that we have referred to, the larger will be the empirical foundation for a theory of language change which is more isomorphic with reality, and the greater will be our understanding of the prehistory of the world's languages. And the larger, the more detailed, and the more precise the lexicons we reconstruct, the greater our insight into the cultural history of the speakers whose linguistic prehistory we seek to reconstruct.

Perhaps the greatest difference between comparative work on Indo-European and work on the languages of traditional societies is a difference in *depth* of lexicological research. For example, most dictionaries of Pacific island languages are weakest where there is perhaps the greatest richness—in the domains of terms for plants, animals, fish, reef fauna, and so on. As reconstructions are pursued to greater time-depths, the incompleteness of the lexical data bases becomes increasingly critical. For non-Western societies the cultural distance between the researcher and the language's speakers is a major factor limiting the collection of lexical material.

A commonality of a number of the contributions to this volume is an insistence on the 'regularity of irregularity'. Campbell rightly attacks those who argue that 'exotic' or 'primitive' languages are simply not governed by the same norms of sound change as Indo-European and other written languages. Durie argues that one form of 'irregularity' is in fact regular. Grace and Ross argue that the 'irregularities' they describe are in fact regularities of contact-induced change. As Blust writes, 'Irregularity is not mere chaos. Rather . . . irregularity appears to be an integral part of the natural process of language change'.

NOTES

1. This is not a textbook on the comparative method. We would refer the reader who is seeking a general introduction to works such as Anttila (1989), Bynon (1977), Crowley (1992), or Hock (1986).

2. Although a range of language families are referred to in this volume, these are not its primary focus. The reader seeking a survey of the applications of the comparative method to various language families is referred to Baldi (1990).

3. A good recent account of lexicostatistical and glottochronological approaches is given by Embleton (1991). Bynon (1977: 266–72) provides a brief critique of lexicostatistics from the standpoint for the comparative method. Differences in the outcomes of lexicostatistics and the comparative method are discussed for Australian languages by Dixon (1980: 254, 1990: 399–401) and Johnson (1990: 430–32) and for Austronesian languages by Blust (1990: 146–48).

4. We take this to be a substantive empirical insight about language change, one which the Neogrammarian hypothesis seeks to capture as a law. Thus we do not view the Neogrammarian hypothesis as simply true by definition, that is, a 'sound change' is not merely regular by definition.

5. It is a convention of the comparative method to write reconstructed forms with a preceding asterisk. The alternating forms here reflect a feature of Proto-Indo-European morphology known by the German term *Ablaut*.

6. Heath (1981) refers to two cases where a diagnosis of genetic affiliation which was based on the lexicon (whether by lexicostatistics or by multilateral comparison) would yield results utterly at odds with those obtained from diagnosis by individual-identifying evidence. The cases involve Australian languages, which are sociolinguistically very unlike Indo-European languages. One is Anindhilyagwa (338), whose affiliation is hardly visible lexically, and Ngandi and Ritharngu, which share a substantial portion of their lexica (including items on Swadesh's hundred-word list for lexicostatistics) but are genetically among the most distantly related languages in Australia. Comrie (1988) describes a similar case in Papua New Guinea.

7. It is true that Greenberg's (1963) grouping of African languages, also based on multilateral comparison, is now the received view among Africanists. However, this is because the languages of Africa 'prove to have been underanalyzed raw material for comparative work' (Nichols 1992: 5) whereas those of Greenberg's Amerind grouping lack material which meets the individual-identifying criterion.

8. Reconstructed grammatical morphemes are included in Shevoroshkin and Manaster Ramer (1991). We are uncertain how to assess macrofamilies like Nostratic and Sino-Caucasian, firstly because published materials accessible to us (Bomhard 1990; Lamb and Mitchell 1991; Shevoroshkin and Markey 1986;

Shevoroshkin 1992) give cognate sets whose members are all ancient protolanguages (Proto-Indo-European, Proto-Uralic, etc.) without supporting data from extant or written languages, and secondly because we lack the expertise to make accurate evaluations of data from such a wide range of language families.

9. Much of Australia is occupied by the Pama-Nyungan family, which is well established by the comparative method. The north of Australia, however, is occupied by a diversity of language groups on which systematic comparative work is only now beginning.

10. Austerlitz (1991) says he finds long-range comparisons hard to believe in because of the opportunities for language contact which must have existed among ancient languages spoken by hunter/gatherer and early agricultural populations.

11. Anttila evidently derived the label 'formulaist' from Bloomfield's statement that 'A reconstructed form . . . is a formula that tells us which identities or systematic correspondences of phonemes appear in a set of related languages' ([1933] 1935: 302).

12. For an account of the history of the Neogrammarian hypothesis, see Jankowsky (1990). Keller (1990: 68–77) discusses the Neogrammarian view of language as an organism, whilst Hermann Paul's view of language is discussed by Weinreich et al. (1968: 104–20).

13. See, for example, Marcel Cohen [1947] 1970. In the introduction we read: 'Since linguistics is part of the natural sciences, and more particularly of the life sciences, it offers valuable possibilities for the formulation of evolutionary laws and, in this way, renders service to other branches of biology'.

14. Ironically, Keller seems not to be aware of the relationship between his work on linguistic epistemology and the work of scholars under the speaker-oriented paradigm, and his few linguistic examples are rather poor.

15. We are well aware that there has been copious discussion of the words 'explanation' and 'explain' in historical linguistics circles (Lass 1980; Romaine 1982; Koopman et al. 1987; Keller 1990) and that our use of them will be unacceptable to some. However, in the lay vocabulary of nonphilosophers, these *are* the cover-terms for what we are about, and we make no apology for using them.

16. Whether a historical explanation is qualitatively different in this respect from an explanation in the natural sciences or merely quantitatively different is a matter of debate. On this, see Ohala 1993: 267.

17. These definitions essentially divide the characteristics of Labov's (1980) description of the innovator between the innovator and the early adopter.

18. Attempts of this kind began with the Neogrammarian Sievers ([1876] 1901: 268–304), and continued with Saussure's disciples Roudet (1910) and Grammont (1933) in France, with Sweet (1877) in England and in the Kazan School of Baudouin de Courtenay ([1895] 1972: 114–212) and his student Kruszewski ([1881] 1978: 64–91).

19. As Anderson (1985: 40, 74–5, 346) observes, natural phonology is in a number of respects a continuation of the linguistic tradition of Baudouin and Kruszewski (the natural phonologist's distinction between processes and rules matches Baudouin's between divergences and correlations), Ohala's work a continuation of Grammont's concerns.

20. This distinction corresponds roughly to the distinction in current mainstream phonology between 'post-lexical' and 'lexical' rule applications, but the latter 'is not presented as a difference between rules with and without synchronic phonetic motivation' (Donegan 1993: 126; see also Milroy 1992: 25).

21. It is important not to confuse a natural process with a sound change. Weinreich et al. (1968: 115–16) point out that the Neogrammarian exceptionless hypothesis of Osthoff and Brugmann (1878) has its origins in an unwarranted extrapolation from a natural lenitive process (the assimilation of /n/ to [ŋ] before /k, g/ in Kerenz-German) to sound change.

22. Andersen (1973) introduced the concepts of 'abductive' and 'deductive' change. The cognition of the innovating speaker plays an important role in Andersen's account of these processes, which differs somewhat from our summary account here. From his examples, however, it is clear that in the terminology used here his abductive changes are hypocorrections of fortitions which entail the loss of a feature (e.g., [ɑ] as an allophone of /ɒ/ comes to be reinterpreted as /ɑ/), and his deductive changes are are hypocorrections of fortitions which entail the sequential separation of features (e.g. [oɑ] as an allophone of /ɒ/ comes to be reinterpreted as /oɑ/).

23. For example, the converse of hypocorrection is hypercorrection, which results in dissimilation but never in new phonemes (Ohala 1993: 255–56).

24. Andersen (1988: 71–4) outlines concepts which resemble Thurston's, although the two scholars have evidently developed their concepts independently. Thurston's concepts apply to *languages*, which seems appropriate in this context, whereas Andersen's refer to *communities*. Andersen distinguishes *two*

parameters: a sociodemographic 'open'/'closed' parameter and an attitudinal 'exocentric'/'endocentric' parameter. An open community evidently has a weaker network with more/stronger external ties, a closed community a stronger network with fewer/weaker external ties (Milroy 1993: 228). Endocentricity values community solidarity and eschews outside influence, exocentricity the reverse. Andersen's terms 'open' and 'exocentric' correspond roughly to Thurston's 'exoteric', his 'closed' and 'endocentric' to Thurston's 'esoteric'. Andersen argues for both parameters with the example of the city of Cologne, where, he claims, speakers have maintained their distinct dialect because of community solidarity (endocentrism) despite frequent communication with speakers of other dialects and of Standard German ('open'-ness). It is unclear, however, that the two parameters affect language change independently or differently. We suspect that a finer-grained account of network structures may offer a solution to the Cologne problem. However, we should note that not all lects of open communities are exoteric, that is, have intergroup use, and not all lects of closed communities are esoteric.

25. The term 'lexical diffusion' remains a source of confusion. In the very issue of *Language* containing Labov (1981) on lexical diffusion, for example, the term is also used by Heath (1981) in a completely different sense (of the large-scale borrowing of vocabulary between languages).

26. There are more languages in the chain than Lincoln refers to in his article. Ross has extended the database to more languages and more words, confirming Lincoln's result.

27. Wells (1982: 288–9) mentions that a similar split and redistribution has occurred (or is perhaps still occurring) in some varieties of British Received Pronunciation, but suggests that it is generally limited to cases where /d/ follows (/æ/ in *pad, lad,* but /æ:/ in *bad, glad*) and that it is basically an adjective/noun split. However, in Ross lect, *clad* has /æ/ (*pace* Wells), and *man* and *can* ('tin can') have /æ:/ (but *slam* has /æ/), and *family* (but not *planet,* etc.) has moved into the /æ:/ class.

28. In their account of lexical diffusion within the Lexical Phonology framework, Kiparsky (1988) and Harris (1989) claim that a change like [æ] to [æ:] in Philadephia results in phonologisation as a lexical rule, that is, the distinction between [æ] and [æ:] occurs in the lexical segment inventory (the output of lexical rules), not in the underlying segment inventory, and that only such changes diffuse lexically. This is not at odds with our account, framed in a traditional Structuralist framework. An important reason for their interpreting the [æ] ~ [æ:] contrast as introduced by a lexical rule is that rough conditioning applies. Note, however, that Lexical Phonology is not a speaker-oriented theory and offers no hypothesis as to why this this particular change became phonologised as a lexical rule rather than as a postlexical rule (in Labov's terms, a low-level output rule).

29. Phillips (1984) characterises the two types of lexically diffused change as 'physiologically motivated' and 'other' (337). It lies beyond the scope of this Introduction to justify the matching of these with 'lenition' and 'fortition', as defined by Donegan (1993). Another research area is the lexical diffusion of morphosyntactic change: Ogura (1993) shows that *do*-periphrasis in English affected less frequently used verbs first.

30. He notes, for example, that the phonetic conditioning of exceptionless sound change is precise, that of lexical diffusion rough, and that lexical diffusion is subject to grammatical conditioning, whilst exceptionless sound change is not (as the /æ/ ~ /æ:/ case illustrates).

31. Various aspects of the New Caledonian case have been discussed by Grace in several articles (1981, 1986, 1990, 1992).

32. The social situation of Cape York Peninsula is also described by Sutton and Rigsby (1979), but without an elaboration of its linguistic implications.

33. In the Papua New Guinea case described by Comrie (1988), languages belonging to quite different genetic groups are structurally very similar, apparently as a result of metatypy—but we do not yet have information on the sociolinguistic background to these changes.

REFERENCES

Andersen, H. (1973). Abductive and deductive change. *Language* 49: 765–93.

———. (1988). Centre and periphery: Adoption, diffusion and spread. In J. Fisiak, ed., *Historical dialectology* 39–85. Mouton de Gruyter, Berlin.

Anderson, S. R. (1985). *Phonology in the twentieth century: Theories of rules and theories of representations.* University of Chicago Press, Chicago.

Anttila, R. (1989). *Historical and comparative linguistics.* 2nd rev. ed. John Benjamins, Amsterdam.

Austerlitz, R. (1991). Alternatives in long-range comparison. In S. M. Lamb and E. D. Mitchell eds., *Sprung from some common source: Investigations into the prehistory of languages* 353–64. Stanford University Press, Stanford.

Baldi, P. (1990a). Introduction: The comparative method. In P. Baldi, ed., *Linguistic change and reconstruction methodology* 1–13. Mouton de Gruyter, Berlin.

————, ed. (1990b). *Linguistic change and reconstruction methodology.* Mouton de Gruyter, Berlin.

Baudouin de Courtenay, J. ([1895]1972). *Versuch einer Theorie phonetischer Alternationen.* Strassburg and Cracow. English translation in E. Stankiewicz, ed.), *A Baudouin de Courtenay anthology* 144–212. Indiana University Press, Bloomington.

Bellwood, P. (1984). A hypothesis for Austronesian origins. *Asian Perspectives* 26: 109–17.

————. (1991). The Austronesian dispersal and the origin of languages. *Scientific American* 265 (1): 88–93.

Bloomfield, L. (1935). *Language* Allen and Unwin, London (U.S. ed.: Holt, New York, 1933).

Blust, R. A. (1981). Variation in retention rate among Austronesian languages. Paper presented to the Third International Conference on Austronesian Linguistics, Denpasar.

————. (1990). Summary report: Linguistic change and reconstruction in the Austronesian language family. In P. Baldi, ed., *Linguistic change and reconstruction methodology* 133–53. Mouton de Gruyter, Berlin.

Bomhard, A. R. (1990). A survey of the comparative phonology of the so-called "Nostratic" languages. In P. Baldi, ed., *Linguistic change and reconstruction methodology* 331–58. Mouton de Gruyter, Berlin.

Boretzky, N. (1984). The Indo-Europeanist model of sound change and genetic affinity, and change in exotic languages. *Diachronica* 1: 1–51.

Burling, R. (1966). The addition of final stops in the history of Maru (Tibeto-Burman). *Language* 42: 581–86.

Bynon, T. (1977). *Historical linguistics.* Cambridge University Press, Cambridge.

Chen, M., and W. S.-Y. Wang. (1975). Sound change: Actuation and implementation. *Language* 51: 255–81.

Cheng, C.-C., and W. S.-Y. Wang. (1977). Tone change in Chao-Zhou Chinese: A study in lexical diffusion. In W. S.-Y. Wang, ed., *The lexicon in phonological chang* 86–100. Mouton, The Hague.

Cohen, H. (1970). *Language: Its structure and evolution.* University of Miami Press, Miami. Trans. by Leonard Muller from *Le langage: structure et évolution*, 1947.

Comrie, B. (1989). *Language universals and linguistic typology.* 2nd ed. Blackwell, Oxford.

————. (1993). Typology and reconstruction. In Charles Jones, ed., *Historical linguistics: Problems and perspectives* 74–97. Longman, London.

Croft, W. (1990). *Typology and universals.* Cambridge University Press, Cambridge.

Crowley, T. (1992). *An introduction to historical linguistics.* 2nd ed. Oxford University Press, Auckland.

Dixon, R. M. W. (1980). *The languages of Australia.* Cambridge University Press, Cambridge.

————. (1990). Summary report: Linguistic change and reconstruction in the Australian language family. In P. Baldi, ed., *Linguistic change and reconstruction methodology* 393–401. Mouton de Gruyter, Berlin.

Donegan, P. (1993). On the phonetic basis of phonological change. In C. Jones, ed.), *Historical linguistics: Problems and perspectives* 98–130. Longman, London.

Donegan, P. J., and D. Stampe. (1979). The study of natural phonology. In D. A. Dinnsen, ed., *Current approaches to phonological theory* 126–73. Indiana University Press, Bloomington.

Dyen, I., J. B. Kruskal, and P. Black. (1992). An Indoeuropean classification: A lexicostatistical experiment. *Transactions of the American Philosophical Society*, 82 (5).

Eckert, P. (1980). The structure of a long-term phonological process: The back vowel chain shift in Soulatan Gascon. In W. Labov, ed., *Locating language in space and time* 179–219. Academic Press, New York.

Embleton, S. (1991). Mathematical methods of genetic classification. In S. M. Lamb and E. D. Mitchell, eds., *Sprung from some common source: Investigations into the prehistory of languages* 365–88. Stanford University Press, Stanford.

Ferguson, C. A. (1978). Phonological processes. In J. H. Greenberg, C. A. Ferguson, and E. A. Moravcsik, eds., *Universals of human language.* Vol. 2: *Phonology* 403–42. Stanford University Press, Stanford.

————. (1990). From esses to aitches: Identifying pathways of diachronic change. In W. Croft, K. Denning, and S. Kemmer, eds., *Typology and diachrony* 59–78. John Benjamins, Amsterdam.

Foley, J. (1977). *Foundations of theoretical phonology*. Cambridge University Press, London.

Foley, W. A. (1986). *The Papuan languages of New Guinea*. Cambridge University Press, Cambridge.

Grace, G. W. (1981). Indirect inheritance and the aberrant Melanesian languages. In J. Hollyman and A. Pawley, eds., *Studies in Pacific languages and cultures in honour of Bruce Biggs* 255–68. Linguistic Society of New Zealand, Auckland.

————. (1986). Hypotheses about the phonological history of the language of Canala, New Caledonia. In C. Corne and A. Pawley, eds., *Le coq et le cagou: Essays on French & Pacific languages in honour of Jim Hollyman*. Linguistic Society of New Zealand, Auckland.

————. (1990). The "aberrant" (vs. "exemplary") Melanesian languages. In P. Baldi, ed., *Linguistic change and reconstruction methodology* 155–73. Mouton de Gruyter, Berlin.

————. (1992). How do languages change? (More on "aberrant" languages). *Oceanic Linguistics* 31: 115–30.

Grammont, M. (1933). *Traité de phonétique*. Delagrave, Paris.

Greenberg, J. H. (1963a). *The languages of Africa*. Indiana University Press, Bloomington.

————, ed. (1963b). *Universals of language*. MIT Press, Cambridge, Mass.

————. (1987). *Language in the Americas*. Stanford University Press, Stanford.

Greenberg, J. H., and M. Ruhlen. (1992). Linguistic origins of Native Americans. *Scientific American* November: 60–65.

Harris, J. (1989). Towards a lexical analysis of sound change-in-progress. *Journal of Linguistics* 25:35–56.

Heath, J. (1978). *Linguistic diffusion in Arnhem Land*. Australian Institute of Aboriginal Studies, Canberra.

————. (1979). Diffusional linguistics in Australia: Problems and prospects. In S. A. Wurm, ed., *Australian linguistic studies* 395–418. *Pacific Linguistics,* C-54. Australian National University, Canberra.

————. (1981). A case of intensive lexical diffusion: Arnhem Land, Australia. *Language* 57: 335–67.

Hock, H. H. (1986). *Principles of historical linguistics*. Mouton de Gruyter, Berlin.

Hopper, P. J., and E. C. Traugott. (1993). *Grammaticalization*. Cambridge University Press, Cambridge.

Hovdhaugen, E. (1986). The chronology of three Samoan sound changes. In P. Geraghty, L. Carrington, and S. A. Wurm, eds., *FOCAL II: Papers from the Fourth International Conference on Austronesian Linguistics* 313–31. *Pacific Linguistics,* C-94. Australian National University, Canberra.

Jakobson, R. ([1929]1962). Remarques sur l'évolution phonologique du russe comparée à celle des autres langues slaves. In R. Jakobson, ed., *Selected writings* 1: 7–116. Mouton, The Hague.

Jankowsky, K. R. (1990). The Neogrammarian hypothesis. In E. C. Polomé, ed., *Research guide on language change* 223–39. Mouton de Gruyter, Berlin.

Jespersen, O. (1949). *A modern English grammar on historical principles*. Vol. 1: *Sounds and spellings*. Allen & Unwin, London.

Johnson, S. (1990). Social parameters of linguistic change in an unstratified Aboriginal society. In P. Baldi, ed., *Linguistic change and reconstruction methodology* 419–33. Mouton de Gruyter, Berlin.

Keller, R. (1990). *Sprachwandel*. Francke, Tübingen.

Kiparsky, P. (1988). Phonological change. In F. W. Newmeyer, ed., *Linguistics: The Cambridge Survey.* Vol. 1: *Linguistic theory: Foundations* 363–415. Cambridge University Press, Cambridge.

Koopman, W, F. van der Leek, O. Fischer, and R. Eaton, eds. (1987). *Explanation and linguistic change.* John Benjamins, Amsterdam.

Kruszewski, Nicolai. ([1881]1978). *Über die Lautabwechslung*. Kazan. (English translation in P. Baldi and R. N. Werth, eds.) *Readings in historical phonology: Chapters in the theory of sound change* 64–91. Pennsylvania State University Press, University Park).

Labov, W. (1981). Resolving the Neogrammarian controversy. *Language* 57: 267–308.

Labov, W., and W. Harris. (1986). De facto segregation of black and white vernaculars. In D. Sankoff, ed., *Diversity and diachrony* 1–24. John Benjamins, Amsterdam.

Lamb, S. M., and E. D. Mitchell, eds. (1991). *Sprung from some common source: Investigations into the prehistory of languages*. Stanford University Press, Stanford.

Lass, R. (1980). *On explaining language change*. Cambridge University Press, Cambridge.

————. (1993). How real(ist) are reconstructions? In C. Jones (ed.), *Historical linguistics: Problems and perspectives* 156–89. Longman, London.

Le Page, R. B., and A. Tabouret-Keller. (1985). *Acts of identity: Creole-based approaches to language and ethnicity.* Cambridge University Press, Cambridge.

Leer, J. (1990). Tlingit: A portmanteau language family? In P. Baldi, ed., *Linguistic change and reconstruction methodology* 73–98. Mouton de Gruyter, Berlin.

Lehmann, W. P. ed. (1967). *A reader in nineteenth-century historical Indo-European linguistics.* Indiana University Press, Bloomington.

Lincoln, Peter C. (1973). Some possible implications of POC *t as /l/ in Gedaged. *Oceanic Linguistics* 12: 279–93.

Malkiel, Y. (1979). Problems in the diachronic differentiation of near-homophones. *Language* 55: 1–36.

Martinet, A. (1952). Function, structure and sound change. *Word* 8: 1–32.

———. (1955). *Economie des changements phonétiques.* Francke, Berne.

Meillet, A. (1958). *Linguistique historique et linguistique générale.* Librairie Honoré Champion, Paris.

Milroy, J. (1992). *Linguistic variation and change: On the historical sociolinguistics of English.* Blackwell, Oxford.

———. (1993). On the social origins of language change. In C. Jones, ed., *Historical linguistics: Problems and perspectives* 215–36. Longman, London.

Milroy, J., and L. Milroy. (1985). Linguistic change, social network and speaker innovation. *Journal of Linguistics* 21: 339–84.

Milroy, L. (1980). *Language and social networks.* Basil Blackwell, Oxford.

———. (1987). *Language and social networks.* 2nd ed. Blackwell, Oxford.

Milroy, L., and J. Milroy. (1992). Social network and social class: Toward an integrated sociolinguistic model. *Language in Society* 21: 1–26.

Nichols, J. (1992). *Linguistic diversity in space and time.* University of Chicago Press, Chicago.

Ogura, M. (1993). The development of periphrastic *do* in English: A case of lexical diffusion in syntax. *Diachronica* 10: 51–85.

Ohala, J. J. (1974). Experimental historical phonology. In J. M. Anderson and C. Jones, eds., *Historical linguistics* II: *Theory and description in phonology* 353–89. North Holland, Amsterdam.

———. (1989). Sound change is drawn from a pool of synchronic variation. In L. E. Breivik and E. H. Jahr, eds., *Language change: Contributions to the study of its causes.* Mouton de Gruyter, Berlin.

———. (1993). The phonetics of sound change. In C. Jones, ed., *Historical linguistics: Problems and perspectives* 237–78. Longman, London.

Osthoff, H., and K. Brugmann. (1878). Morphologische Untersuchungen auf dem Gebiete der indogermanischen Sprachen. Vol. 1. S. Hirzel, Leipzig.

Paul, H. ([1880]1920). *Prinzipien der Sprachgeschichte.* 5th ed. Niemeyer, Halle.

Pawley, A. K., and M. D. Ross. (1993). Austronesian historical linguistics and culture history. *Annual Review of Anthropology* 22: 425–59.

Peeters, B. (1986). Téléologie et besoins communicatifs. *Folia linguistica* 20: 539–43.

Phillips, B. S. (1984). Word frequency and the actuation of sound change. *Language*, 60: 320–42.

Renfrew, C. (1987). *The puzzle of Indo-European origins.* Cambridge University Press, Cambridge.

Ringe, D. A. (1992). On calculating the factor of chance in language comparison. *Transactions of the American Philosophical Society* 82 (1): 1–110.

Romaine, S. (1982). *Socio-historical linguistics: Its status and methodology.* Cambridge University Press, Cambridge.

Ross, M. D. (1988). *Proto-Oceanic and the Austronesian languages of western Melanesia.* Pacific Linguistics C-98. Australian National University, Canberra.

Roudet, L. (1910). *Eléments de la phonétique générale.* Welter, Paris.

Schleicher, A. (1863). *Die Darwinsche Theorie und die Sprachwissenschaft.* Weimar.

Schooling, S. (1990). *Language maintenance in Melanesia: Sociolinguistics and social networks in New Caledonia. Publications in Linguistics* 91. Summer Institute of Linguistics at the University of Texas at Arlington, Arlington.

Shevoroshkin, V., ed. (1992). *Reconstructing languages and cultures: Abstracts and materials from the First International Interdisciplinary Symposium on Language and Prehistory.* Brockmeyer, Bochum.

Shevoroshkin, V., and A. Manaster Ramer. (1991). Some recent work on the remote relations of languages. In S. M. Lamb and E. D. Mitchell, eds. *Sprung from some common source: Investigations into the prehistory of languages* 178–99. Stanford University Press, Stanford.

Shevoroshkin, V. V., and T. L. Markey, eds. (1986). *Typology, relationship and time*. Karoma, Ann Arbor.

Sievers, E.. ([1876]1901). *Grundzüge der Phonetik zur Einführung in das Studium der Lautlehre der indogermanischen Sprachen*. 5th ed. Breitkopf und Härtel, Leipzig.

Stampe, D. (1979). *A dissertation on natural phonology*. Indiana University Linguistics Club, Bloomington.

Starostin, S. A. (1982). Proto-Yenisey and the external relations of the Yenisey languages. *Ketskij sbornik*. Nauka, Moscow. [In Russian].

———. (1984). Hypotheses about the genetic relationship of Sino-Tibetan to Yenisey and north Caucasian. *Lingvisticheskaja rekonstrukcija i drevnejshaja istorija vostoka*. Nauka, Moscow. [In Russian].

Sutton, P., and B. Rigsby. (1979). Linguistic communities and social networks on Cape York Peninsula. In S. A. Wurm, ed., *Australian linguistic studies* 713–32. *Pacific Linguistics* C-54. Australian National University, Canberra.

Sweet, H.. (1877). *Handbook of phonetics*. Clarendon, Oxford.

Szemerényi, O. (1990). *Einführung in die vergleichende Sprachwissenschaft*. 4th corr. ed. Wissenschaftliche Buchgesellschaft, Darmstadt.

Thurston, W. R. (1987). *Processes of change in the languages of northwestern New Britain. Pacific Linguistics* B-99. Australian National University, Canberra.

———. (1989). How exoteric languages build a lexicon: Esoterogeny in West New Britain. In R. Harlow and R. Hooper, eds., *VICAL 1, Oceanic languages: Papers from the Fifth International Conference on Austronesian Linguistics* 555–79. Linguistic Society of New Zealand, Auckland.

Unger, J. M. (1990). Summary report of the Altaic panel. In P. Baldi, ed.), *Linguistic change and reconstruction methodology* 479–82. Mouton de Gruyter, Berlin.

Wang, W. S.-Y. (1969). Competing sound changes as a cause of residue. *Language* 45: 9–25.

———, ed. (1977). *The lexicon in phonological change*. Mouton, The Hague.

———. (1979). Language change—a lexical perspective. *Annual Review of Anthropology* 8: 353–71.

Wang, W. S.-Y., and C.-C. Cheng. (1977). Implementation of phonological change: the Shuang-Feng Chinese case. In W. S.-Y. Wang, ed., *The lexicon in phonological change* 148–58. Mouton, The Hague.

Wang, W. S.-Y., and C. Lien. (1993). Bidirectional diffusion in sound change. In C. Jones, ed., *Historical linguistics: Problems and perspectives* 345–400. Longman, London.

Weinreich, U., W. Labov, and M. Herzog. (1968). Empirical foundations for a theory of language change. In W. P. Lehmann and Y. Malkiel, eds., *Directions for historical linguistics* 95–195. University of Texas Press, Austin.

Wells, J. C. (1982). *Accents of English*. Cambridge University Press, Cambridge.

2 The Comparative Method as Heuristic

JOHANNA NICHOLS

1 INTRODUCTION

Nonlinguists are not always able to distinguish easily between genetic groupings established by the comparative method and those proposed on other grounds. A much-publicized recent example is Cavalli-Sforza et al. (1988), where the very deep macrogroupings the authors assume for languages of the Pacific and New World are treated as the same kind of grouping as Indo-European or Uralic. Another example is Renfrew 1991, where, following Illič-Svityč, Nostratic is described as based on the same comparative method as Indo-European (1991: 6). More tangential to linguistic questions, Stoneking and Cann (1989), analyzing mitochondrial DNA divergences in human populations, estimate the rate of evolution by assuming that Papua New Guinea, Australia, and North America each constitutes a single population of a single age. This amounts to an implicit assumption that each of these areas was colonized only once, an assumption compatible with the linguistic macrogroupings of Indo-Pacific, Australian, and Amerind. In these and other works, nonlinguists working on human prehistory assume or implicitly assume that macrogroupings are the same kind of entity as families like Indo-European, that they are established by the same comparative method as Indo-European was, and that the received view in linguistics takes them as established or plausible. Works like these, or the macrogroupings they assume, are cited with approval in popular works such as Turner 1988 and Gould 1991.

Comparative linguists distinguish between genetic groupings established on the basis of the standard comparative method and those not so established, which they generally view as probabilistic or speculative or even fanciful. Much of the work done by comparative linguists, including much of the reconstruction of the unique protolanguage for each established family, involves comparison of lexical items and grammatical elements; but the groupings which comparativists regard as speculative are also based on comparison of lexical items and grammatical elements. What is the difference?

Some linguists would appear to maintain that the difference is only one of degree: that the standard comparative method and the other procedures differ chiefly in the fact that the standard comparative method requires regular sound correspondences, a rigorous account of semantic change (e.g. a theory of the derivational morphology that has produced changes in lexical semantics), at least some protoroots which have more than two consonantal segments amenable to comparison or reconstruction, a fair frequency of ancient roots in most daughter vocabularies, and attestation of at least some roots in most or all daughter languages. This would appear to be the position of most long-range comparativists (e.g. Greenberg 1987, Kaiser & Shevoroshkin 1988, and numerous others), and seems to be implicitly subscribed to in statements of some standard comparativists (e.g. Campbell 1988, Matisoff 1990).

On the other hand, many explicit statements make it clear that comparativists see a difference of kind, not degree. The received view would appear to be that the comparative method is not a heuristic: that when applied to vocabulary it does not demonstrate relatedness, but simply assumes relatedness and proceeds to describe the relationships between the daughter languages. Newman (1970, in press) makes this clear:

> The proof of genetic relationship does not depend on the demonstration of historical sound laws. Rather, the discovery of sound laws and the reconstruction of linguistic history normally emerge from the careful comparison of languages already presumed to be related. (Newman 1970: 39)

> By now, people should know that the Comparative Method is a technique for reconstructing aspects of a protolanguage by the systematic comparison of languages already understood to be related. (Note, for example, Hoenigswald's (1960: 119) definition of the Comparative Method as a "procedure whereby morphs of two or more sister [i.e. genetically related] languages are matched in order to reconstruct the ancestor language".) It has never been an essential tool in the establishment of relationship as such, although it has often been helpful in sorting out problems of subgrouping. (Newman in press)

Thomason & Kaufman (1988: 201–2) describe the comparative method as

> two different tasks, the establishment of genetic relationship for a group of languages and then the reconstruction of features of the protolanguage from which those related languages arose. . . . But when one looks at the criteria that are used to arrive at the initial hypothesis [of relatedness], the distinction between the two tasks breaks down. . . . Properly applied, then, the Comparative Method is a means by which a hypothesis of genetic relationship is demonstrated through the following kinds of evidence: not only (1) the establishment of phonological correspondences in words of same or related meaning, including much basic vocabulary, but also (2) the reconstruction of phonological systems, (3) the establishment of grammatical correspondences, and (4) the reconstruction of grammatical systems, to whatever extent is possible. Where more than two languages are involved, a thorough exploitation of the Comparative Method also in-

cludes (5) construction of a subgrouping model for the languages and (6) the elaboration of a diversification model.

That is, the result of applying the comparative method is both a demonstration of relatedness and a reconstruction.

This chapter will argue that demonstration of relatedness through systematic correspondences in vocabulary is not the operating procedure for the classic application of the comparative method to the Indo-European languages going back to the late eighteenth century; nor—and this is perhaps more important—is it the definition of 'comparative method' assumed in the classic secondary literature on Indo-European and general comparative linguistics. The comparative method involves a heuristic component, but that component is distinct from the work of lexical and grammatical comparison that establishes the correspondences and produces the reconstructions. It is important to codify the standards for proof of relatedness assumed in the comparative method, both in the practice of the classic Indo-European comparativists and in their theoretical and methodological pronouncements, and such a codification will be offered here. The criteria of adequacy demanded of grammatical evidence in the classic Indo-European works, though widely agreed upon, are only implicit, and the first task is to make them explicit. To do this I survey some of the history of the Slavic philological tradition and its background in Indo-European studies.

The procedure employed by the classic comparative method may be summarized as follows. An initial assumption of relatedness is made on the basis of solid evidence that firmly identifies a unique individual protolanguage; that evidence is primarily grammatical and includes morphological material with complex paradigmatic and syntagmatic organization. The initial assumption of relatedness is made for some, though not necessarily all, daughter languages. Once relatedness is assumed, then the labor-intensive process of working out the correspondences and cognate sets begins. Since relatedness is assumed, this lexical work makes the further assumption that any vocabulary set displaying the regular sound correspondences is in fact cognate, however far-fetched the semantic correspondences. This work ultimately yields a detailed picture of the branching structure of the family tree, and it often brings into the family additional languages that did not figure in the initial assumption of relatedness. It also yields additional individual-identifying evidence for the relatedness of the daughter languages.

The next three sections utilize the history of Slavic philology and aspects of Indo-European philology to argue that the assumptions and operating procedure are as just outlined.

2 SLAVIC AND INDO-EUROPEAN PHILOLOGY

How and when was it first established that Slavic is a language family and a branch of Indo-European? The history of this discovery has received little attention among historians of Slavic philology, and it is difficult to find works, even prescientific works, whose authors did not already assume these things at least implicitly.

2.1 Slavic as a Language Family

For the Slavic languages, there was no moment of discovery and no published announcement that they constituted a language family. For the Western philological tradition, awareness of the Slavic language family appears to have come from German philological scholarship, which was aware by the beginning of the seventeenth century of the existence and relatedness of the Slavic languages. Leibniz (1646–1716) studied various aspects of Slavic philology and antiquities, and was interested among other things in the possibility of drawing up a uniform pan-Slavic alphabet (Jagić 1910: 62, quoting Leibniz's letters). He and his contemporaries and followers used the terms *Slav* and *Slavic* (in contemporary Latin, *Slavi, lingua Slavonica*) and used them to refer to any and all Slavs and Slavic languages. (For some of the authors and their works, see Jagić 1910: 59 ff.) They obviously borrowed the term and its meaning from the Slavs themselves.

Native Slavic tradition, going back to Common Slavic times, uses *slověne* 'Slavs' and *slověnĭsk-* 'Slavic' as a generic ethnonym for all Slavs. The native Slavic theory of ethnic identity implicitly distinguishes two levels. The lower level is that of the tribe or local ethnicity. Examples include the Poliane and the Dregovichi, East Slavic tribes which had ceased to have any political or ethnic autonomy by the early Middle Ages, but whose reality was a matter of memory and is recorded in medieval chronicles; the Czechs, a tribe-like group that grew into a feudal entity and then into a protokingdom; and the Ljakhs, roughly the Poles or perhaps all northern West Slavs in medieval references. At some time after the Proto-Slavic breakup and before the first Slavic chronicles, all of these groups evidently had political and ethnic reality, for medieval writings and folklore record origin myths which trace each group to a mythic ancestor. The higher level of ethnic identity is that of the **językŭ*, literally 'language', but in medieval Slavic it also refers to any set of ethnic groupings to whom a common ancestry or origin was imputed on the basis of communality or closeness of language (and hence this word could translate Greek *ethnos*). **językŭ slověnĭskŭ(jĭ)* thus refers, in medieval Slavic, either to the Slavs ('Slavic ethnicity, Slavic nation, Slavic race') or to their common language ('Slavic language'). The name of the ethnicity was primary, and the name of the language was derived from that.

The following are a few representative medieval Slavic passages illustrating the sense of *językŭ*. I use the standard translations, boldfacing the relevant words and adding the Slavic original in brackets (citing it in the nominative singular, regardless of the case and number used in the original). From the *Life of Constantine* I quote a piece of diplomatic correspondence (Kantor 1983: 67):

> God, who will have all men come unto the knowledge of the truth and raise themselves to a greater station, having noted your faith and struggles, arranged now, in our time, to fulfill your request and reveal a script for your **language** *[językŭ]*, which did not exist in the beginning but only in later times, so that you may be counted among the great **nations** *[językŭ]* that praise God in their own **language** *[językŭ]*.

From the Russian Primary Chronicle I quote three passages dealing with the origin and dispersal of the Slavs (Cross 1953: 52–3, 62, and 63); all three make clear the two levels at which ethnicity is identified:

Over a long period the Slavs settled beside the Danube, where the Hungarian and Bulgarian lands now lie. From among these Slavs, parties scattered throughout the country and were known by appropriate names, according to the places where they settled. Thus some came and settled by the river Morava, and were named Moravians. . . . The Slavs also dwelt about Lake Il'men', and were known there by their characteristic name. They built a city which they called Novgorod. Still others had their homes along the Desna, the Sem', and the Sula, and were called Severians. Thus the Slavic **race** *[jazykŭ]* was divided, and its **language** [*gramota*, more properly 'writing, writing system, written text'] was known as Slavic. (52–3)

There was at the time but one Slavic **race** *[jazykŭ]* including the Slavs who settled along the Danube and were subjugated by the Magyars, as well as the Moravians, the Czechs, the Lyakhs, and the Polyanians, the last of whom are now called Russes. It was for these Moravians that Slavic books were first written, and this **writing** *[gramota]* prevails also in Rus' and among the Danubian Bulgarians. (62)

But the Slavs and the Russes are one **people** *[jazykŭ]*, for it is because of the Varangians that the latter became known as Rus', though originally they were Slavs. While some Slavs were termed Polyanians, their **speech** [*reč'*, 'speech, discourse'] was still Slavic, for they were known as Polyanians because they lived in the fields. But they had the same Slavic **language** *[jazykŭ]*. (63)

For some of these examples, the context makes it clear whether 'language' or 'nation, race, ethnicity' is the proper translation of *językŭ*; for others, especially the last one, the choice of translation is fairly arbitrary. Such examples show that the medieval Slavic concept of ethnicity bases ethnic affiliation on language. By the early Middle Ages, dialect differentiation in Slavic was considerable and incipient language separation was underway, so that to regard all of Slavic as a single language required a certain amount of abstraction. Thus *slověnĭskŭ(jĭ) językŭ* 'Slavic language/race', meant to a medieval Slav exactly what 'Slavic' means to a historical linguist or philologist: a language (or dialect) family.

To summarize, no linguist discovered that Slavic was a language family. That knowledge entered the central and western European philological traditions from the Slavic tradition, where it was a matter of oral and written memory and was furthermore self-evident, as the Slavic languages preserve to this day some degree of mutual intelligibility as well as the shared ethnonym 'Slavic'. (The Proto-Slavic concept of ethnicity is further discussed in Nichols 1993.)

2.2   The Slavic Family as a Branch of Indo-European

In the second half of the eighteenth century, both Mikhail Lomonosov (1711–1765), the founder of modern Russian science, and Josef Dobrovský (1753–1829), the founder of Slavic philology, independently, were aware that Slavic was related to Greek, Latin, etc. Lomonosov's unpublished writings demonstrate a clear sense of Indo-European family tree structure whereby Slavic was most closely related to Lithuanian and more distantly related to Latin, Greek, and Germanic (Smirnov et al. 1980: 21–2; Lomonosov 1952: 658–9).

2.3 Balto-Slavic as a Family

Native Slavic tradition as revealed in the medieval sources does not group the Balts with the Slavs, but the pervasive similarities of grammar and vocabulary between the Slavic and Baltic languages have suggested a Balto-Slavic branch of Indo-European since the first attempts at comparative work. Lomonosov's assumption that Slavic and Baltic were closely related was based on comparison of grammar as well as vocabulary (Smirnov et al. 1980: 22). In the first half of this century, the received view, at least among Indo-Europeanists, shifted: The similarities, though pervasive and self-evident, were shared conservatisms, typological resemblances, and/or areal features. To a Slavist or Balticist, the fact that each of the two groups helps explain developments and protoforms in the other was more important than whether the sharings were unique, and Balto-Slavic continued to be regarded as a unit if not a true family among Slavists. By now, the majority view among Slavists, Balticists, and Indo-Europeanists is again in favor of a Balto-Slavic branch, partly on accentological evidence (Baltic and Slavic share accentual paradigms and accent shifts that operate on them, and cognate roots generally have the same accent paradigm) and partly on segmental evidence (Baltic and Slavic share lengthening of root vowels before reflexes of Indo-European plain voiced stops, and subsequently they merge the plain voiced and voiced aspirate series, see Winter 1978). For any scholar who has taken an explicit stance on the issue, the evidence accepted as probative of Balto-Slavic has been not shared lexemes but shared sound changes and/or grammar. The attitude toward the lexical evidence for Balto-Slavic is revealing. There are a number of uniquely shared lexical and affixal roots, uniquely shared senses of Indo-European roots, and uniquely shared derivational treatments, all with regular sound correspondences and well attested in the basic vocabulary of Balto-Slavic. These have always been recognized, but have never been taken as sufficient evidence to establish a Balto-Slavic grouping. This example shows that, in standard procedure, lexical sharings do not suffice to prove family status, even when the lexical sharings are grounded in basic vocabulary, show regular sound correspondences, and include some individual affixal roots with arguably "grammatical" function.[1]

2.4 The Received View

To summarize this section, none of the linguists mentioned here—and, more generally, no scholar whose work had substantial impact on comparative Slavic linguistics—ever used lexical evidence to establish the genetic nature of Slavic or Balto-Slavic, or to establish that (Balto-) Slavic was Indo-European. The status of Slavic as a family is simply self-evident. The probative evidence for Balto-Slavic is not lexical but grammatical, and it involves uniquely shared sound changes and whole sets of morphological paradigms. The secondary literature of Slavic linguistics and philology contains numerous statements to support this view of how the comparative method works. The Slavist and Indo-Europeanist F. F. Fortunatov, in an introductory and theoretical lecture on the comparative method, describes its task as follows ([1901–2]1956: 25): "Thus, the task of comparative linguistics—studying human language in its history—requires, as you see, a definition of the genetic relations among individual languages, and comparative study of those languages that have a common history in the past, i.e. which are related in origin."[2] This passage makes it clear that a determination of genetic relatedness is a prerequisite of comparative work, which can be done only on languages already presumed to be related. That is, relatedness is presupposed or assumed, not established, by comparative linguistics.

Dobrovský had come to his own conclusion about proof for genetic relatedness in the late eighteenth century, as reported by Jagić (1910: 107): "Dobrovský, for example, was already aware by this time [1792] that the degree of relatedness of languages is determined not on the basis of some quantity of resemblant words, but on the basis of identity of the grammatical organism."[3] The wording makes it clear that Jagić (another leading philologist) also subscribes to this view.

The genetic unity of Slavic, then, never required argument. But when the question of diagnostic evidence for relatedness arose—when the external relationship to Baltic was at issue, or when methodological principles needed to be demonstrated—then the critical evidence was never drawn from the lexicon. The next section will argue that this situation—transparency of relatedness and recognition of grammar rather than lexicon as the source of diagnostic evidence of relatedness—was the standard assumed in both operating procedure and secondary pronouncements of the classic Indo-European comparative method. Furthermore, this is the situation that obtains not only for the individual daughter branches of Indo-European (Germanic, Slavic, Celtic, etc.) but also for many other families such as Algonkian, Polynesian, Bantu, and Kartvelian.

3 THE STATUS OF INDO-EUROPEAN AS A FAMILY

Sir William Jones is generally credited with the founding statement about Indo-European as a protolanguage, made in 1786:

> The Sanskrit language, whatever may be its antiquity, is of wonderful structure; more perfect than the Greek, more copious than the Latin, and more exquisitely refined than either; yet **bearing to both of them a stronger affinity, both in the roots of verbs and in the forms of grammar, than could have been produced by accident**; so strong that **no philologer could examine all three without believing** them to have sprung from some common source, which, perhaps, no longer exists. **There is a similar reason, though not quite so forcible, for supposing that both the Gothic and Celtic, though blended with a different idiom, had the same origin with the Sanskrit; and the old Persian might be added to the same family.** (quoted from Mallory 1989: 12; boldface added)

There are three important points to be emphasized in this passage (the relevant parts are boldfaced). First, the evidence Jones refers to is "forms of grammar", which obviously refers to morphological paradigms; and "roots of verbs". The latter may seem at first glance to be simply a reference to basic vocabulary and hence to lexical comparison. However, the notion "root of verb" relies on a theory (based on Greek, Latin, and Sanskrit) of parts of speech, basic versus derived form, root versus theme versus desinence, morphophonemic root canon, and inflectional classes. Hence Jones'

notion of diagnostic affinity consists of grammatical paradigms plus their phonologically specific fillers (the actual verb root forms), which will be shown later to provide the most clearly individual-identifying evidence. In sum, then, the initial assumption of relatedness offered by Jones was made on the basis primarily of
grammatical evidence; lexical evidence figured only to the extent that it fit into the
grammatical structure. The relevant grammatical evidence involves whole paradigms
and sets of paradigms, not individual forms. In the case of Indo-European, the grammatical evidence has what can be called *multidimensional paradigmaticity,* that is, relationships of grammatial patterning among ordered sets of disjunct forms as in the
following segment of adjectival morphology for Latin, Greek, and Sanskrit:

	Masculine	**Feminine**	**Neuter**
Latin:			
Nominative	-us	-a	-um
Accusative	-um	-am	-um
Greek:			
Nominative	-os	(*)-ā	-on
Accusative	-on	(*)-ān	-on

This table shows two dimensions of paradigmaticity: case (nominative, accusative) and gender (masculine, feminine, neuter). Number, not shown here, would
be a third. In both languages, the masculine and neuter adjectival endings are identical to *o*-stem noun endings, the feminine adjectival endings are identical to *a*-stem
noun endings, and these declensional identity relations constitute a fourth dimension.
The two languages have cognate endings with identical distributions along all four
dimensions. In addition to the abstract paradigmaticity, there are phonologically specific fillers and grammatically specific functions for the slots in the paradigms. This
was the kind of evidence Jones regarded as probative: entire shared systems with multiple paradigmaticity and a fair degree of phonological and functional specificity.

Second, the relatedness Jones assumes is self-evident to the philologically trained
("no philologer could examine all three without believing them to have sprung from
some common source"). The "philologer" of Jones' time had been trained not only in
the principles of comparative method and reconstruction, but also in the texts and
grammars of individual languages. The modern analogs are the philologist and the
family specialist.

Third, the initial assumption of relatedness is made only for Greek, Latin, and
Sanskrit. Other languages now known to be Indo-European are mentioned by Jones
as likely candidates for inclusion. And the Baltic and Slavic languages, though their
existence was well known to philologists—at least central European philologists—in
the late eighteenth century, are not mentioned at all.

Neither the notion of linguistic relatedness nor the awareness of descent from a
common source through gradual change over time is new with Jones in this passage;
both ideas had been familiar to philologists for at least a century (and, as we have
seen, the notion of language family and common origin of daughter languages was

part of the native Slavic theory of ethnicity going back to before the Middle Ages). The novelty attributed to Jones by linguists is the recognition that the protolanguage is not identical to any daughter language ("some common source, which, perhaps, no longer exists"). But in this passage, which is now accepted as the intellectual source of the standard notion of language family and linguistic genetic relatedness, we can also see three important assumptions of the comparative method. First, relatedness is established on the basis of grammatical evidence involving paradigmaticity and the full paradigmatic system is attested *in its entirety* (or nearly so) in at least some daughter languages. Second, that the evidence points to relatedness is self-evident to one trained in text philology. Third, the case for an initial assumption of relatedness can rest on a few clearly related languages, though other prospects may also be noted in the initial statement.

These three assumptions continued to be asserted in general and methodological pronouncements of the later Indo-Europeanists. The statements of Antoine Meillet, the leading Indo-Europeanist of his time, provide the best illustration of received view in the late nineteenth and early twentieth centuries. On the first point, the importance of grammatical paradigms in establishing relatedness, Meillet says:

> Grammatical correspondences are proof, and only they are rigorous proof, provided one makes use of the material detail of the forms and that it is established that particular grammatical forms used in the languages under consideration go back to a common source. (1958: 91)[4]

> While one can initially establish vocabulary resemblances between two or several languages as an indication of where to do further research, this cannot furnish a definitive demonstration; vocabulary can only orient the research, and proof comes from elsewhere. (1958: 97)[5]

On the self-evidence of relatedness:

> The resemblances between the languages of each group [Romance, Germanic, Slavic, etc.] are obvious; the classification is consistent with the practical fact that one who knows one of the languages of the group can acquire the others more easily. (1958: 77)[6]

> Wherever the phonological and grammatical systems are in precise agreement, regular correspondences make it possible to recognize the shared origin of the words and the phonological system, and the systems of grammatical forms can be explained on the basis of a shared prototype, genetic relatedness is obvious. (1958: 88)[7]

> Transformed and distant from the ancient Indo-European type though Tokharian (recently discovered in Central Asia) is, it was immediately recognized as Indo-European: the number of Indo-European grammatical particularities conserved in Tokharian is still great. (1958: 97)[8]

On obvious relatedness holding for only some languages of a family:

> If it were not for the ancient Germanic dialects and for Latin, the relatedness of English and French would not be demonstrable. (1958: 90)[9]

Related languages eventually come to differ so greatly that their common origin is impossible to recognize. If, for example, we had only French, Bulgarian, and modern Armenian as representatives of Indo-European, it would not be easy to establish the relatedness of these three languages, and there would be no possibility of setting up a comparative grammar for them. (1958: 93)[10]

4 HOW THE COMPARATIVE METHOD WORKS

The purpose of this section is to codify classical comparative method and to formalize its standard for proof of relatedness and probative value of evidence. The standard method as discussed above can be broken down into four steps: (1) Assume genetic relatedness on the strength of diagnostic evidence; (2) work out sound correspondences and cognate sets, thereby establishing an internal classification for the family; (3) uncover and reconstruct more diagnostic evidence; (4) bring more languages into the family as daughters.

4.1 First Step: Assume Relatedness of a Set of Languages, Based on Diagnostic Linguistic Evidence

As mentioned earlier, the evidence taken as probative of relatedness is not individual items but whole systems or subsystems with a good deal of internal paradigmaticity, ideally multiple paradigmaticity, and involving not only categories but particular shared markers for them. Such evidence may include structural categories together with their (phonologically specific) markers, or lexical categories with some of their (phonologically specific) member lexemes. Examples of both kinds of evidence will be given below.

The kinds of evidence accepted as probative in the standard method vary, but all share a property which I propose to take as definitive of probative evidence: its probability of multiple independent occurrence among the world's languages is so low that for practical purposes it can be regarded as unique and individual. Statements like that of Jones (quoted earlier), and examples of diagnostic sharings discussed by Meillet and set out below, make it clear that the Indo-European tradition has explicitly sought to base its claims of relatedness on the kind of evidence that identifies a unique individual protolanguage rather than on evidence that identifies a set of languages or a type of language. The former can be called *individual-identifying* evidence, or features; the latter is *type-identifying* and is simply low in identificational value. Type-identifying features include (to cite some modern examples) such things as verb-final word order, ergativity, presence of genders, nonconfigurationality, and so on—features found in enough unrelated language families that comparative structural linguistics views them as typological. For an explicit discussion of the difference between descent from a unique protolanguage and shared structural type, we can again turn to Meillet :

Chinese and a language of Sudan or Dahomey such as Ewe, for example, may both use short and generally monosyllabic words, make contrastive use of tone, and base their grammar on word order and the use of accessory words, but it does not follow from this that Chinese and Ewe are related, since the concrete detail of their forms does not coincide; only coincidence of the material means of expression is probative. (1958: 90)[11]

It is easy to define a statistical threshold for individual-identifying. Since there are now a few thousand languages on earth, a probability of occurrence of one in a few thousand (i.e. the order of 0.001) is at the level of the individual language. A scientific notion of individual-identifying needs to combine this level with at least a conventional level of statistical significance, say 0.05 or 0.01. One in a few thousand multiplied by 0.05 or 0.01 yields figures in the vicinity of 0.000 01 to 0.000 005, that is, one in a hundred thousand or less. This level of probability is less, by two orders of magnitude, than that of a random individual language happening to turn up. I will assume that a probability of occurrence of one in a hundred thousand or less is individual-identifying at a statistically significant level, and a probability of one in ten thousand is at least interesting and borderline useful.

Note that the number of individuals against which the probabilities for protolanguages are measured is not the number of (known or probable) protolanguages in the world, but the number of languages. I am assuming that a protolanguage like Proto-Indo-European was, in its own time, just one individual language among the world's languages, and that the number of languages attested in the last two or three centuries is of the same order of magnitude as the number that existed a few millennia ago, at the time of Proto-Indo-European. The amount of linguistic extinction that has accompanied the spread of imperial, colonial, and standard national languages in the last centuries suggests that there may have been a good many more individual languages a few millennia ago than there are now; but surely the total number of languages is of the same order of magnitude. I assume there have been a few thousand individual languages on earth at least since the time—about thirty thousand years ago—when modern humans spread from the tropics to colonize all kinds of climates and all continents. Thus today's individual-identifying level of probability is also valid for Proto-Indo-European times and earlier, probably much earlier.

Note also that this procedure does not ask what the probability is of finding some form (or set of resemblant forms) in two languages, or three, or two out of three, or five out of ten, etc. That question is asked whenever lexical sets are used as heuristic, and it has been much discussed. Here, the only point at issue is how good the form (or paradigm) itself is as a piece of diagnostic evidence, and not how many languages must exhibit it. Nor will it be asked here how many pieces of individual-identifying evidence it takes to establish sure relatedness (though it can at least be noted that well-established families have several to many in the realm of grammar and very many in the lexicon). The only thing that matters here is how good the particular piece of evidence is.

Most, and perhaps all, of the grammatical evidence taken by Indo-Europeanists as probative of the genetic relatedness of Indo-European turns out to fall within the individual-identifying probability of occurrence. Four examples of individual-identifying features, drawn from Indo-European studies, follow. Though it was emphasized ealier that the probative evidence is usually grammatical and paradigmatic, I will, for the sake of clarity, begin with a lexical example.

Meillet (1954: 36–7) observes that, while lexical evidence is generally not probative of genetic relatedness, an occasional word is long enough or otherwise sufficiently structured that it can be a good diagnostic. One such word is the Indo-European word for 'widow', *widhewa,* with four consonants: *w, *y, *dh, *w. The chances of a word having these four consonants in this order are computed as follows. Assume that most languages have around twenty consonants (as the Indo-European daughter languages generally do). Then the worldwide average probability of any given consonant appearing in any given position is one in twenty, or 0.05.[12] In this word we are dealing with the chances of getting *w in first position and *y in second position, and so on. The occurrence of each of these consonants is independent of the other (in that there is nothing in the phonetics of [w] that predisposes the next consonant to be [y], and so on). The probability of a string of independent occurrences is computed as the product of the individual conjunct probabilities. Thus the probability of a word with *w-*y-*dh-*w is $0.05 \times 0.05 \times 0.05 \times 0.05 = 0.000\ 006\ 25$, or less than one in a hundred thousand. This word, then, lies securely in the individual-identifying range: substantially less than one of the world's languages can be expected to have this word. On the other hand, the probability of occurrence for a word containing, say, only *w and *dh (or any other two consonants) is $0.05 \times 0.05 = 0.0025$, or two in a thousand; several of the world's languages can be expected to have such a word by chance.

Saying that this word is individual-identifying amounts to saying that all the languages having it have acquired it, ultimately, from a single source. The languages need not all be descended from that source; the word could be a loan in some of the languages. (This is why lexical evidence alone is only weak evidence of relatedness.) But the loans are ultimately traceable to the same unique source.

Now consider a grammatical example, the miniparadigm of *good* and *better* in English and its sisters. This example is mentioned as diagnostic of relatedness by Newman (1980: 21). Again I assume a probability of 0.05 for any consonant, and 0.2 for any vowel (both are actually high for Germanic languages, which have over twenty consonants and well over five vowels). The paradigm of comparison can be analyzed as a three-way opposition of positive, comparative, and superlative, or as a two-way opposition between positive and comparative/superlative. On the three-way analysis, the chances of a particular suppletive root falling into one of the three categories are one in three, or 0.33; on the two-way analysis, 0.5. Here I will assume the two-way analysis in order to favor the null hypothesis. Each of the roots *good* and *bett-* has chances of $0.05 \times 0.2 \times 0.05$. There is a fifty-fifty chance of *good* being the positive member, in which case, assuming that we are dealing with a closed suppletive set, *bett-* must be comparative/superlative. The total probability of occurrence of this miniparadigm is $0.05 \times 0.2 \times 0.05 \times 0.05 \times 0.2 \times 0.05 \times 0.5 = 0.000\ 000\ 125$, or one in a million. Either of the two roots by itself has a probability of 0.0005, or five in ten thousand—a level that is not individual-identifying, as perhaps ten of the world's languages might have either root. It is the integration of these two roots into a suppletive grammatical paradigm that gives them their high individual-identifying value.

Now consider a more typical example from the realm of grammar: the probability of occurrence of an Indo-European gender system. By "Indo-European gender system" I mean a system of noun classification with three genders marked by agreement; their nominative singular endings *-s, *-m, and *-H; a particular kind of intersection with a set of declension classes, defined phonologically as *e/o, *ā (i.e. *-H), and *C (the latter subsumes any consonant, including *i and *u); and the gender "semantics" of masculine, feminine, and neuter. (For ease of exposition, this presentation reduces the system to its core classes and their typical combinations.) The probabilities are shown in Table 2-1. What is computed is the chance of having the three genders and the endings and the declension classes and the semantic categorization, and these probabilities are independent. Since the probability of the co-occurrence of independent multiple events is the product of the individual probabilities, the probabilities shown in the left-hand column are multiplied to give the overall probability for the Indo-European gender system.

The overall probability is less than one in a million, securely individual-identifying. (Furthermore, the probability has been inflated by such measures as reducing the declension classes to three, not computing additional restrictions on the distribution of

TABLE 2-1
Probability of finding an Indo-European gender system in a randomly chosen language.

0.27	Probability of having genders. (*Source:* the database of Nichols 1992).
0.50	Probability that those genders will number more than two.[a] (*Source:* same.)
0.0033	Chances of having the following set of endings as gender markers, calculated as:
	*-s 0.20 Estimate of the probability of having -s in any given ending.[b]
	*-m 0.33 Estimate of the probability of having -m in any given ending.
	*-H 0.05 Probability of any random one of twenty consonants occurring in any given position in any morpheme.
0.0359	Chances of having this set of endings distributed across *e/o and *a declension classes, and a partly different system for *C stems:
	*e/o 0.33
	*a 0.33
	*C 0.33
0.0359	Chances of having the three gender markers code respectively masculine, feminine, and neuter (in the commonest paradigms). These gender categories can be defined cross-linguistically: masculine = assigned to animate nouns referring to males, and arbitrarily to inanimates; feminine = assigned to animate nouns referring to females, and arbitrarily to inanimates; neuter = assigned to no animates, and arbitrarily to inanimates.[c]
	masculine 0.33
	feminine 0.33
	neuter 0.33

Overall probability = 0.000 000 57

[a]The chances of having exactly three genders are much lower: 5 languages out of 174, or 0.03. As computed in the text, the combined probability of having genders at all and of having specifically more than two genders is $0.27 \times 0.5 = 0.135$. I use this higher probability just in order to give the null hypothesis every opportunity to stand.

[b]Nasals are more frequently found in grammatical endings than other consonants are. I have simply estimated the probability of finding s and m in endings, based on my impressions of how common they are. These estimates may be too high; I have deliberately tried to err in the direction that will inflate probabilities and favor the null hypothesis.

[c]The probabilities here refer to the chances of having a particular gender associated with a particular form or paradigm or ending, and not to the chances of finding masculine, feminine, and neuter genders as defined here in a three-gender system. In fact any three-gender system is likely to have genders definable in this same way. It seems to be a universal that gender systems include one gender associated with male animates and some arbitrary set of inanimates, and one associated with female animates and some arbitrary set of inanimates (Nichols 1992: sec. 4.3).

the three endings, computing the chances of having more than two genders rather than the much smaller probability of having exactly three, and so on.) This is why the classic Indo-European gender and declension system can be considered to identify an individual—Proto-Indo-European—and not a batch of languages or a type of language.[13]

These two grammatical examples show why paradigmaticity is of critical importance in the grammatical evidence offered in demonstration of relatedness. Paradigmaticity imposes co-occurrences and an ordering on a set of forms each of which, if taken individually, would be much too short for its consonantal segments to reach the individual-identifying threshold. The co-occurrences and ordering allow a probability level for the whole subsystem to be computed as the product of the probabilities of the individual forms and categories. It is my impression that what is offered as grammatical evidence in long-range comparisons generally lacks paradigmaticity. For instance, the grammatical evidence for Amerind offered by Greenberg (1987: 271ff.) consists almost entirely of single lexemes or morphemic roots, including pronominals, plural markers, negatives, and tense affixes. Very few of these have any systematically traced allomorphy. An example of one-dimensional paradigmaticity, a three-way opposition in person markers in a large South American grouping, is discussed (44–46), but outside of this discussion paradigmaticity is not demanded of the grammatical evidence. Kaiser and Shevoroshkin (1988: 313–15) offer grammatical evidence for Nostratic which again consists of individual endings and lexical roots of fairly abstract semantics, with no requirement of paradigmaticity. Taken as individual root morphemes, such comparative evidence has a high probability of occurrence and is not even close to individual-identifying; that is, it is of no diagnostic value.

Meillet (1954: 2 ff.) also admits whole structured systems of vocabulary as probative evidence, provided the relation of paradigmaticity to phonological form of coding is arbitrary (and not, say, phonosymbolic). His example is the set of Indo-European numerals, and indeed, even if we consider only the first five numerals and only the first two root consonants of each, the probability of occurrence of such a system is infinitesimal. Again I assume a flat 0.05 probability for any individual consonant. The probability of finding this entire segment of the Indo-European numeral system, with the forms in order and the consonants ordered as shown in the individual forms, is the following:

1	*y, n*	$0.05 \times 0.05 = 0.0025$
2	*d, w*	$0.05 \times 0.05 = 0.0025$
3	*t, r*	$0.05 \times 0.05 = 0.0025$
4	*k^w, t*	$0.05 \times 0.05 = 0.0025$
5	*p, n*	$0.05 \times 0.05 = 0.0025$

Total: $(0.0025)^5 = 0.98 \times 10^{-13}$ (i.e. 0.000 000 000 000 098)

Compare, in contrast, the likelihood of finding a single resemblant numeral root in each of two languages, as with IE *septm̥* and Kartvelian *šwid-* '7', both of which contain first a fricative, then a labial, then a dental stop. If we again consider only the first two root consonants in the two languages as was done just above, the chances are 0.0025, as for any one numeral in the table above. This is the probability for two identical consonants. If the requirement is relaxed to mere similarity (as between IE *s and Kartvelian *š, or IE *p and Kartvelian *w), the probability increases. Here is a calculation of the probability of a root shaped like the IE and Kartvelian roots for '7' occurring in the world's languages:

*s or *š $0.05 + 0.05 = 0.10$ (Indo-European had only one sibilant fricative, but since the sole Indo-European fricative can be compared to two Proto-Kartvelian ones the probability is computed for two consonants)

*p or *b or *m or *w (i.e. any labial) $0.05 + 0.05 + 0.05 + 0.05 = 0.20$

*t or *d $0.05 + 0.05 = 0.10$

Total: 0.002

Two languages in a thousand, or six to eight of the world's languages, might have such a form by pure chance. The similarity in this pair of Indo-European and Kartvelian words, though striking, is not individual-identifying.[14]

Now let us calculate the probability of occurrence of the root forms compared in this Nostratic set (Kaiser & Shevoroshkin 1988: 314; the double-asterisked form is Proto-Nostratic):

**wete 'water' > IE *wed-; Uralic *wete; Altaic: Proto-Tungusic *ödV; Dravidian *otV-/*wetV 'wet'

Let us take the reconstruction for granted and ask what the probability is of a root of the shape **wete occurring in the world's languages. We have initial *w, followed by what is not so much a particular vowel as a vowel slot, since the root *e in the IE form is an abstraction used in citation forms of roots when the actual words had ablaut, so no single vowel can be reconstructed. Then follows a dental stop, and after it an *e which again is not a particular vowel but an abstraction covering generic vowels of Tungusic and Dravidian. The probabilities, again assuming one-in-twenty chances for any consonant, are:

*w	0.05	
vowel	1.00	(Estimate of the chances of having a vowel slot in a lexical root)
dental stop	0.10	(Combined probability of *t and *d, assuming 0.05 each)
vowel	0.5	(Estimate of the chances of having a second vowel in a two-consonant root)
Total:	0.0025	

Three languages in a thousand, or perhaps ten to fifteen of the world's languages, might have such a form by accident.

The probability is actually less than this for either of the first two reconstructed family protoforms. The probability of finding the Indo-European form is 0.05×0.05 for the two consonants $*w$ and $*d$, multiplied by some fraction representing the probability of finding a representative of Indo-European vowel ablaut and some very small fraction representing the probability of finding a representative of Indo-European $*r/n$-stem declension. I am not certain how the chances for the ablaut and $*r/n$ representatives are to be computed, but even if we simply estimate the chances of getting regular ablaut in IE roots at 0.8 and the chances of finding the $*r/n$ declension at an unrealistically high one in twenty, we reach 0.0001, or one in ten thousand. For the Proto-Uralic form we have two specific consonants and one specific vowel; assuming a worldwide average of five vowels per language (it is actually closer to eight among the languages of my database) we have a total probability of 0.0005 for Uralic $*wete$—not quite individual-identifying at five in ten thousand, but small enough to be interesting and an order of magnitude less than for the Nostratic form.

Personal pronouns offer a good example of a systematically structured and phonologically filled lexical field that nonetheless does not yield individual-identifying probabilities of occurrence. The problem with personal pronouns is that the forms of first and second persons, and of singular and plural numbers, are not independent; that is, in a personal pronoun system the relation of paradigmaticity to coding phonological form is nonarbitrary. These words tend to use consonant symbolism which shows their paradigmatic relationships and their deictic semantics (Nichols, in press), just as "mama"-"papa" words do (Jakobson 1971), so that the presence of a nasal in at least one of the personal pronoun forms is to be expected and the presence of a labial in one of the forms makes it quite likely that the other person or number form (or both) will contain a dental.

Let us try to compute the identificatory value for the first-person n and second-person m posited for Amerind by Greenberg (1987: 49 ff.). Crosslinguistically, nasals have a high frequency of occurrence in closed sets of paradigmatically organized morphemes (such as case endings, deictic roots, and nuclear-family kin terms). I estimate the chances of finding n in a personal pronoun root as one in five, and likewise for m. For the first person, n may be sought in a number of different forms: the independent singular form, the independent plural (exclusive) form, the singular possessive, the plural possessive, the singular subject marker for verbs, the plural subject marker, etc. Likewise, m may be sought in a number of different second-person forms. Though Greenberg presents the issue as one of first-person n AND second-person n, the citation of evidence (49 ff.) indicates that the de facto design of the search was to find n in one OR another first-person form OR m in one OR another second-person form.[15] The probabilities for success in such a search are shown in Table 2-2. Surveying four forms is exemplified by seeking the n or m in the singular and plural independent roots and in singular and plural bound forms; or in singular and plural nominative roots and singular and plural oblique roots. Probabilities are given for three frequency estimates: the one-in-five chance of finding n in first person assumed here; the one-in-twenty chances assumed above of getting an arbitrarily chosen consonant in an arbitrarily chosen position in an arbitrarily chosen lexical root; and a one-in-ten chance of getting n (a high-frequency phoneme) in any position in an arbitrarily chosen root morpheme.[16]

TABLE 2-2
Probabilities of finding first-person *n* or second-person *m* for the various numbers
of pronominal forms surveyed and various assumptions of the likelihood of finding
n in a lexical morpheme of deictic or abstract meaning belonging to a closed,
paradigmatically structured set.

Assumed probability of *n* in pronoun	No. of forms surveyed	*n* in first person	*n* in first person or *m* in second person
0.20	1	0.20	0.36
	2	0.36	0.59
	3	0.49	0.74
	4	0.59	0.83
0.05	1	0.05	0.10
	2	0.10	0.19
	3	0.14	0.26
	4	0.19	0.34
0.10	1	0.10	0.19
	2	0.19	0.34
	3	0.27	0.47
	4	0.34	0.56

Probabilities for *m* in the second person are the same as those for *n* in the first person. For the computation of probabilities, see Excursus.

The chances of finding one or the other of two high-frequency consonants in one or another of four form categories each are quite good: If each of the consonants by itself has a one-in-five chance of occurring randomly in a pronoun root, then the probability of finding one or the other in one or another form is 0.83. Even if we assume that nasals have no more than their normal lexical frequency in pronominal roots, the probability of finding first-person *n* or second-person *m* is still good: 0.34. In lay terms this means that 34% of the searches for first-person *n* or second-person *m* in individual languages should lead to success if nasals have no special affinity for pronominal roots, and upwards of 80% of the searches can be expected to lead to success if (as is generally accepted) nasals do have a special affinity for pronominal roots. The chances of success increase as the inventory of forms to be surveyed increases. They also increase if the consonants sought are broadened from *n* or *m* to any dental and any labial (Greenberg 1987: 49 ff. lists only forms in *n* for the first person, but his examples of second-person *m* include *p, b,* and *f* as well). On the other hand, the probability of success decreases rapidly if we demand both first-person *n* AND second-person *m* in the most basic or most frequent form in the singular number only. Such a definition specifies two-dimensional paradigmatic organization. Here the probability of success, even assuming one-in-five chances of each nasal in pronominal roots, is only 0.04, or four in a hundred. This is far from the individual-identifying threshold, but it is much less than eighty-three in a hundred, or 83%, which shows again the importance of paradigmaticity in grammatical evidence of genetic relatedness.

The figure of 83% success is a good illustration of the fact that the likelihood of finding random similarities is inflated if one seeks among grammatical morphemes and does not require paradigmaticity of the evidence. The assumptions of all long-range lexical comparison with which I am familiar are that pronominal root consonantism is not phonosymbolic, that the various pronominal roots are phonologically independent of each other, and that grammatical evidence can be taken piece by piece with no requirement of paradigmaticity. It is little wonder that comparison on this basis leads to enormous macrogroupings and often straight to Proto-World. The working assumptions provide a virtual guarantee of success. But such comparisons are of absolutely no diagnostic value.

Received wisdom has long recognized the non-arbitrary form-meaning relation of personal pronoun systems: In the words of Meillet (1958: 89–90):

> It goes without saying that in order to establish genetic relatedness of languages one must disregard everything that can be explained by general conditions common to all languages. For instance, pronouns must be short words, clearly composed of easily pronounced sounds, generally without consonant clusters. The consequence is that pronouns are similar in almost all languages, though this does not imply a common origin. On the other hand, pronouns often show little resemblance in languages that are otherwise quite similar; compare, for example, the pronouns of Armenian with those of Gothic or Irish. Even forms that descend from the same protoform, like French *nous* and English *us*, may no longer have a single element in common (the French *s* is purely graphic). Therefore, pronouns must be used with caution in establishing relatedness of languages. (1958: 89–90)[17]

To complete the discussion of the first step in comparison, it should be noted that individual-identifying evidence may at first emerge clearly from only a core set of languages. The important announcement of Sir William Jones was made on the basis of Latin, Greek, and Sanskrit, and it was only these three that he regarded as definitively having "sprung from some common source." He listed some other good candidates, all of which have subsequently been brought firmly into the Indo-European family, but only as a result of later scholarship.

4.2   Second Step: Work Out Sound Correspondences and Cognate Sets, Thereby Establishing an Internal Classification for the Family

That these sound correspondences must be regular and systematic is so well known that this point need not be illustrated. What may require some discussion, however, is that in the standard method the sound correspondences need not be exceptionless. For instance, Russian *drozd* 'thrush, blackbird' and its cognates have always been assumed to be cognate to Engl. *thrush*, Lat. *turdus*, and so on, although the Slavic word inexplicably shows a voiced initial. (For the full set of cognates and references to the literature on this word, see Vasmer 1964: s.v.) We now know that a few dozen Slavic words of unquestioned Indo-European origin show comparable voicing irregularities (see Shevelov 1964: chap. 24). No uniform explanation (such as a conditioned sound change) can be given, nor can a separate correspondence be set up; all that can be said is that Slavic shows a sporadic tendency to voice Indo-European voiceless consonants, and that this happens most often in initial position and where the word contains another voiced consonant. That is, this sporadic change is not reduced to a phonological irregularity, but is rather seen as a probabilistic indication of subgrouping: It occurs specifically in the Slavic branch of Indo-European. It does not weaken the case for Indo-European or for Slavic; it simply shows how Slavic fits into Indo-European. This is because relatedness had already been assumed for Slavic and for Indo-European before the sound correspondences in question began to be worked out. The point about regular correspondences may be worth insisting on in view of Greenberg's lengthy discussion (1987: 10 ff.) of whether comparative practice takes irregular correspondences to undermine genetic relatedness. In standard comparative practice, as we have seen, relatedness has already been assumed by the time correspondences are being worked out. Irregular correspondences neither strengthen nor weaken the case for relatedness; they simply assist in the description of the family tree. And, as Matisoff (1990: 109, n. 9) points out, "only the idealized assumption of regularity makes it possible to identify 'irregularities' in the first place."

Even more misunderstood is the comparative method's position on semantic similarity or regularity. The actual working assumption in this second step is that, since the languages are presumed related, all vocabulary is presumed native and cognate until shown otherwise. The burden of proof lies on any claim of noncognacy; for such cases an external source must be found and the borrowing must be explained. If the correspondences are regular, the set of words is cognate, however unlikely the semantics. That is, structural grounds—regular correspondences—are sufficient for establishing cognacy, while semantic grounds are neither necessary nor sufficient.

Examples of reliance on this working assumption can be found in Meillet 1961, a good representative of the kind of lexical work done by Indo-Europeanists. Its second part deals with nominal morphology, and in it Meillet goes through the nouns of canonical Old Church Slavic, grouped by root or stem type, and traces both their etymological connections and any changes in their stem types. The result is a picture of the Slavic evidence for (and adjustments to) the reconstructed Indo-European nominal paradigms. Three illustrative examples follow.

> *slava* 'glory', cf. Lith. *slově* with a different suffix. The Lithuanian word is often regarded as a Slavic borrowing, but this is mistaken (see Leskien, Bild., 281): the circumflex accentuation of the *o* (acc. *slõvė*) is not definitive because -*je* derivatives, though less prone to circumflex metatony than certain other -*j*- suffixes, are not immune to it (F. de Saussure, M.S.L., VIII, 441, n). In formation and accent type, *slově* is precisely comparable to *srově* 'current', *zolė* 'herb, grass', whose native standing is not in doubt. [Lithuanian forms respelled in modern orthography] (1961: 208)[18]

The accentological issue is that Slavic **sláva* has acute accent while Lithuanian *slově* has circumflex accent, so there is some question as to whether they can be cognate. Meillet argues that they are cognate. This passage makes it clear that a word is considered native even when no cognates can be found, that the burden of proof is on one who claims non-native status, and that grammatical patterning is sufficient evidence for assuming native status. (A Lithuanian dialect form with acute accent is now generally taken as the direct cognate, confirming cognacy; see Vasmer 1964: s.v. *slava*.)

In the next example, the semantic connection is not self-evident, and the derivational category is unique in the corpus. "**ostĭ* 'point, tip' (Russ. *ost'*, S. *ostĭ*, Pol. *ość*): the root **ak₁-* is indicated by Lith. *asakà* 'fishbone', Gk. *akís*, Gk. *aké*, Lat. *acies*,

Skt. *acánih*, OE *egl* 'thorn, sting', Arm. *ase\n* 'needle', etc." (Meillet 1961: 209)[19] Only because cognacy is assumed unless there is explicit evidence to the contrary, and because the formal correspondences are correct, can this semantic connection be proposed. (Vasmer 1964: s.v. *ost'* now cites a Lithuanian word with the same derivational morphology as *ost'*, which overrides Meillet's etymology.)

In the following example Meillet deals with a type of compound whose supposed second element is otherwise unknown in Indo-European and whose derivational form is also unknown in Indo-European.

> Agentive nouns in *-čĭja-* are separate; they are either ancient compounds (per M. Jagić, Archiv, XX, 522) or derivatives in *-ĭja-* of words in *-ĭcĭ*, e.g. *lovĭčĭjĭ* 'fisherman' from *lovĭcĭ* (?). The Old Church Slavic texts have only a small number of examples, e.g. *krŭmĭčĭjĭ* 'steersman' (Supr. 360, 27), from *krŭma* 'stern', *kŭnjigŭčĭjĭ* 'scribe'. . . . (1961: 362)[20]

Here the assumption of cognacy overrides the lack of Indo-European attestation. Slavists would now regard the second element as a borrowing of Turkic *ci* as a suffix-forming agent and sometimes instrument nouns in Slavic, especially Russian. Other examples include Russian *zodčij* 'architect', *sobačej* 'dog seller'. Non-Indo-European oriental vocabulary in Slavic is something Meillet was not particularly familiar with, so, in the absence of positive evidence for borrowing and an identifiable source, he relied on the default assumption that Slavic vocabulary is Indo-European.

In summary, comparative work on an assumed or established family proceeds almost entirely along formal lines. Semantics can be almost entirely disregarded. For this reason, cognate sets can and do involve considerable semantic latitude in root morphemes, most of it accounted for by attested derivational morphology. There has been some discussion of constraints on semantic distances in the search for deeper genetic connections; most statistically-based heuristic procedures require virtual identity of semantics for root word sets (e.g. Bender 1969, Dogopol'skij 1964, Oswalt 1992; Rankin 1992 discusses the consequences of permitting semantic latitude). In practice, though, lists of putative cognates offered in support of deeper relationships tend to show just as much root semantic variation as the cognate sets in etymological dictionaries of Indo-European languages do, but without reconstructed derivational morphology to account for it. If the method used to compile Indo-European etymological works like those just cited (Vasmer 1964, Meillet 1961) and the method used to compile lexical support for long-range groupings (e.g. Illič-Svityč 1971ff., Greenberg 1987: chap. 4) were of the same sort, one would naturally expect that, say, Indo-European root dictionaries and Amerind or Eurasiatic root lists would be comparable in such features as the semantic latitude of entries. But the methods are not of the same sort and the etymological dictionaries have different purposes: Dictionaries of groupings like Indo-European are compiled only after relatedness is assumed or proven, and they serve to reconstruct and subgroup, while dictionaries of the long-range groupings are offered as evidence of relatedness. Semantic constraint or latitude within word sets is crucial to heuristics in that it can make or break a grouping, but irrelevant to the status of groupings like Slavic or Indo-European. That is because relatedness is *established* by lexical comparisons in the heuristic measures, but *assumed* in the lexical comparison stage of the standard comparative method.

4.3 Third Step: Uncover and Reconstruct More Diagnostic Evidence

The sound correspondences and cognate sets that result from step 2 point to more grammar of the individual-identifying type. A good example is Indo-European ablaut, which was worked out only after the relatedness of Indo-European was assumed and in connection with research on etymology and sound correspondences. A basic understanding of ablaut made it possible to unify more inflectional and derivational paradigms in the daughter languages. This in turn added more phonological and grammatical precision to bodies of evidence like the Indo-European gender system, increasing their individual-identifying value. Another example is the Indo-European laryngeals, discovered only as a consequence of research on ablaut. An understanding of laryngeals increased the generality of ablaut and hence the conformity of daughter paradigms to Proto-Indo-European models, thereby expanding the inventory of individual-identifying grammar.

4.4 Fourth Step: Bring More Languages into the Family as Daughters

The sound correspondences and additional individual-identifying grammar revealed in the course of the second step also serve to make clearer the relatedness of more languages to the core set. In Indo-European philology, for instance, it was only Greek, Latin, and Sanskrit that offered the naked-eye evidence supporting the initial assumption of relatedness. The result of the second step was to bring Gothic, Celtic, and Old Persian, mentioned by Sir William Jones as possible additional contenders, firmly into the Indo-European fold; and also others such as Balto-Slavic, Armenian, Albanian, and the later-discovered Tocharian and Hittite. But the scholars who did this work were asking and answering very different questions from those of the time of Jones. At his time, in the late eighteenth century, the questions in the air were whether and, if so, how the languages we now know as Indo-European are related, and Jones' much-quoted statement answered both questions definitively and neatly and established the modern notion of language family. The work of subsequent centuries no longer asked whether Indo-European was a family; thenceforth, the question shifted to whether and how a given language or family was related to Indo-European. The philologists who established the Indo-European affiliation of Balto-Slavic, Germanic, Celtic, etc. were performing a kind of bilateral comparison, comparing their stock on the one hand with Proto-Indo-European on the other. This bilateral comparison continues to be a standard form of knowledge in the fields dealing with the branches of Indo-European: for instance, graduate programs in Slavic linguistics generally include coverage of what is known as "Slavic and Indo-European," including early Proto-Slavic developments not evident in the daughter languages but revealed by comparison to Proto-Indo-European, and including mastery of basic sound correspondences between Proto-Slavic and major Indo-European languages. Drawing such bilateral comparisons simultaneously for two languages, Latin and Greek, is the purpose of Buck 1933. And, of course, the same kind of bilateral comparison has been

used more recently to establish the Indo-European affiliation of Hittite. The importance of bilateral comparison in expanding already-established families is worth em-
phasizing in view of Greenberg's emphasis on multilateral rather than bilateral comparison (1987: 25 ff.). Bilateral comparison may or may not be heuristically useful
(Greenberg maintains it is not), but it is standard procedure in describing and expanding established families.

It is important to emphasize again that in the first step, when the initial claim of
relatedness is made, the individual-identifying evidence is attested *as a system* and
more or less entire in each of the core daughter languages, as the Indo-European declension system is attested in Latin, Greek, and Sanskrit. But in the fourth step, when
additional daughter languages are brought into an already established family, the entire system is not required of the additional languages. Armenian and Albanian do not
attest the full Indo-European system of nominal or verbal inflection and derivation,
but once Indo-European was established they could be shown to attest fragments of
the original system.

5 SOME PROBLEMS OF APPLICATION

The previous sections have laid out the abstract essentials of comparative evidence
and comparative method, based on both attested procedure and theoretical pronouncements in Indo-European comparative linguistics. For Indo-European, it was
possible to ascribe individual-identifying levels of probability to protoforms and
reconstructed grammatical subsystems. Matters may be less precise and less straightforward for less precisely reconstructed protolanguages. Application of the individual-identifying criterion as heuristic in the search for new genetic groupings or as an
evaluatory metric in assessing proposed groupings will require consideration of several additional issues in probability, noted here briefly.

5.1   Density of Attestation

Suppose a grammatical subsystem of individual-identifying value has been discovered and a set of languages has been identified as possibly related. In how many
daughter languages or branches must the system be attested in order for it to confirm
genetic relatedness? If it is the sole individual-identifying evidence of relatedness,
then obviously it must be firmly attested in EVERY daughter branch (at the highest level at which daughter branches can be identified and reconstructed). By "firmly attested" I mean that it must be demanded (and not simply tolerated) as a reconstruction for the protolanguage of the branch. If it is not the sole evidence but simply one
of several pieces, then its distribution among the daughter branches can be evaluated
as a binomial distribution: ten out of twelve or nine out of ten is significant, six out
of ten or three out of four is not, etc. (Binomial distributions and levels of significance
for them are discussed in most basic statistics textbooks. A classic example is tossing
a coin: chances are that half the tosses will be heads, and ten heads out of twelve tosses or nine out of ten would be quite unusual.) Since most deep protolanguages will
have only a few first- and second-order surviving daughter branches (Nichols 1990),

in practice this means that unanimous firm attestation among the daughter branches must be required of each piece of individual-identifying evidence.

5.2   Closed Sets Versus Samples

Recall the example of Indo-European 'widow' discussed in section 4.1. It has individual-identifying value because it contains four consonants in a particular order. But this value obtains only if this word is regarded as a unique entity and sought crosslinguistically as a unique entity and a closed class. That is, it cannot be viewed as a representative of a larger lexical class (such as words for female and/or bereaved kin) or as part of a sample (such as the recorded nouns of a language). Proper use of it as evidence would require a search for a word of its form in exactly the sense 'widow', and this search would be a self-standing, complete test and not one of many lexical searches. Such a test would identify languages as having or not having the Indo-European word for 'widow'. Similarly, the example of the first five numerals of Indo-European must be sought as exactly those five numerals, and not as any five sequential numerals or any five numerals.

A clearer example of the consequences of treating a set of elements as part of a sample rather than as a closed set comes from Newman 1980:19 ff., where it is suggested that the assignment of genders to lexemes in Afro-Asiatic is diagnostic of genetic relatedness. For instance, 'blood' is regularly masculine, 'eye' feminine, and 'water' plural, whether or not the nouns are cognate. Newman cites fourteen words with reconstructable protogender. If we assume the chance of a given lexeme being masculine or feminine to be 0.5, and if for simplicity we also extend this probability to the likelihood of 'water' being a plural, the overall probability of the fourteen-word system is 0.000 061, or six in ten thousand.[21] Seventeen words would be sufficient to reach a securely individual-identifying probability of less than one in a hundred thousand. This example assumes that the genders of all the words are independent of each other (as they probably are not in reality: they contain 'sun' and 'moon', which tend crosslinguistically to form a miniparadigm linked by gender symbolism: One is masculine and the other feminine).

Most importantly, this presentation assumes that the fourteen (or seventeen) words form a closed set and are sought as a set, that is, that exactly those fourteen (or seventeen), and no more, are sought. Only the set has individual-identifying value. It is a very different matter if we ask what the likelihood is of finding fourteen nouns with identical gender among the six branches of Afro-Asiatic. Again assuming the chances of either gender to be fifty-fifty, the chances of identical genders in each of six branches are $0.5^6 = \frac{1}{64} = 0.016$ or sixteen out of a thousand. Assuming that for any language the root nouns plus the derived nouns whose derivational morphology does not determine their gender total about a thousand, Newman's fourteen nouns are about what we would expect to find in sampling the basic nominal vocabulary. For samples, we can use standard statistical procedures to determine the likelihood that a result was achieved by chance. Again we are dealing with a binomial distribution. If the fourteen nouns with identical gender represent a surveyed corpus of about one thousand nouns, their frequency is identical to random chance; but if they represent a surveyed corpus of one hundred nouns, then fourteen is a tenfold increase over the expected frequency, and it is highly significant. In fact, a mere seven consistencies out of fifty words in all six branches, provided the gender of each word was independent of that of all others in the sample, would be highly significant and might well indicate genetic relatedness (if it was not due to unsuspected universals of gender classification).

These examples all show the importance of using closed sets and self-contained (or at least coherent, clearly definable) systems when assessing the identificatory value of linguistic sharings. A set of elements has much greater individual-identifying value when taken as a closed set than when taken as a group of trials in a larger sample.

5.3 Spurious Individual-Identifying Evidence

Suppose we find resemblant words in putative daughter languages where one language has *s* and another has *t*. We might choose to symbolize the correspondence by positing an additional stop series, say *t′*, or by positing a sequence *st*. Either way we have increased the apparent individual-identifying value of the reconstructed form: in the first case we increase the consonant inventory, giving each consonant a smaller probability of occurrence, and in the second we put an additional segment in the root. The method of computing identificatory value proposed here uses a flat 0.05 probability for any consonant, no matter how many consonants are posited for the protoinventory, thereby assuring that unduly complex protoinventories do not artificially increase the individual-identifying value of reconstructed morphemes. Spurious sequences can be precluded by requiring (as comparative practice generally does) that sequences be attested as sequences in some daughter languages and that protoforms not depart unduly from the phonotactics and root structure of the attested daughter languages. For Indo-European 'widow', discussed above, all four consonants are attested in most daughter languages.

Here are examples of the application of these principles in practice. Matisoff (1990: 116–17) discusses examples from Benedict 1975 where different daughter reflexes descend from different syllables of the putative protoform, that is, Proto-Austro-Tai *[wa]kləwm[a] 'dog' > Proto-Tai *hma and Proto-Hmong-Mien *klu. With five consonants, this protoform easily reaches the individual-identifying level, but its validity depends on whether all five consonants are attested in some daughter form. This is an extreme example of a technique that is standard. For instance, Haas (1968: 40 ff.), working within the standard comparative method, presents examples where not all proto-syllables are continued in all daughter languages:

Proto-Algonkian		*e	š	k	o	t	eː	w	i		'fire'
	or	*e	š	k	we	t	eː	w	i		
Miami				k	o	t	ä	w	i		
Fox		a	š	k	o	t	eː	w	i		
Kickapoo		o	s	k	o	t	eː	w	i		
Cree		i	s	k	o	t	eː	w			
Menomini		e	s	k	o	t	ɛː	w			
Ojibwa		i	s	k	o	t	eː				
Cheyenne		h	o	ʔ	e	t	a				

Arapaho	(hi)	s	í	t	ee	
Penobscot		s	k	wə̀	t	e
Passamaquoddy		s	k	wə	t		(1968: 43)

Proto-Muskogean	*	i	xʷ	a	N	i/u	'squirrel'
Choctaw			f	a	n	i	
Koasati		i	p	ł	u		
Hitchiti	h	i		ł	-		
Creek		í		ł	u		(1968: 41)

In both sets all correspondences are regular; there is ample and well-described evidence of relatedness in the inflectional and derivational paradigms of both Muskogean and Algonkian; and in both sets some daughter languages preserve all consonants or all syllables of the protoform and some daughter languages preserve both the initial and final portions. These three observations can be proposed as three conditions on appeal to syncope in reconstructions or linearization of partial resemblances: (1) All correspondences must be regular; (2) Such protoforms are not offered as crucial evidence for relatedness; (3) The entire skeleton of the protoform must be attested in some daughter languages, with each posited consonant sequence attested as a sequence. Thus treated, syncopated protoforms are part of the description of language families, not part of the evidence for relatedness; they are worked out in the second step of the comparative method or later. Otherwise, one could create very long pseudo-protoforms for any random set of linguistic data, masking the absence of real and recurrent correspondences by positing a great number of highly specific sequentializations. This possibility is one reason why the standard comparative method does not base genetic relatedness on lexical resemblance alone but requires independent evidence of relatedness.

5.4 Individual-Identifying Evidence in Languages Without Inflectional Morphology

Languages of the isolating type, and to a lesser extent languages with agglutinative morphology, lack the intersecting arbitrary classifications and grammatical accidence that make subsystems like the Indo-European gender system diagnostic of genetic relatedness. Nonetheless, there are various circumstances under which groupings and reconstructions of isolating languages may be said to be consistent with the comparative method. One such situation is where the family is sufficiently shallow that relatedness is self-evident (e.g. Tai, Chinese) or has a written history that makes its relatedness evident (Chinese). Sometimes an isolating group fits into a deeper family that has more morphology and whose relatedness has been established in part on the evidence of that morphology, as Chinese fits into Sino-Tibetan or Vietnamese into Austro-Asiatic or Kwa into Niger-Congo. In principle, genetic relatedness could even be established on purely lexical evidence. If lexemes can be organized into paradigmatic sets and the entire set reconstructed (as was done with the Indo-European numerals in section 4.1 above), then it may be possible to regard the sets as internally structured pieces of individual-identifying evidence. The whole structured set would have to be attested as a set and entire (or nearly so) in each language or language family for which relatedness was claimed. Tone systems are common in isolating languages, and where tone correspondences are regular the tones may be regarded as an arbitrary lexical classificatory device (rather like the gender or declensional and conjugational classes of Indo-European) that incorporates some paradigmatic grammatical organization into the lexicon. But any claim of genetic relatedness among isolating languages that relies simply on lexical comparison—without (tonal or other) arbitrary lexical classification and without paradigmatic lexical sets attested as whole sets in each language—probably cannot be regarded as individual-identifying and thus as consistent with the comparative method, no matter how numerous the compared lexemes.

6 CONCLUSION

This chapter has answered the question of whether the standard comparative method includes a heuristic component by examining the operating procedure and the theoretical pronouncements of classic practitioners and showing that both can be reduced to a clear and generally applicable statistical criterion: the individual-identifying level.

The classic comparative method does recognize certain evidence as diagnostic of relatedness. But this heuristic component does not rely on vocabulary; even the extensive Proto-Indo-European or Proto-Slavic vocabulary now reconstructed, complete with multiple regular sound correspondences, serves only as secondary confirmation of the genetic relatedness of Indo-European or Slavic. The diagnostic evidence is grammatical, and it combines structural paradigmaticity (usually multiple paradigmaticity) and syntagmaticity with concrete morphological forms. The Indo-Europeanists' intuitive feel for what was diagnostic evidence of relatedness corresponds to a computable threshold of probability of occurrence, and the main purpose of this chapter has been to give a simple rule of thumb for judging evidence of relatedness. A grouping can be regarded as established by the comparative method if and only if it rests on individual-identifying evidence.

Classic lexical comparison and reconstruction are then quite limited in their possible achievements: They can only describe and extend relatedness but cannot establish it. Their practical applicability is therefore limited to the time frame within which the individual-identifying grammar, which makes relatedness obvious to the trained philologist, remains intact—perhaps up to eight thousand years (the conventional age of Afro-Asiatic, the oldest family established by the comparative method). Classic lexical comparison is not a heuristic, except in the limited sense of offering the means to bring additional languages into an established family as daughters.

After Sir William Jones' pioneering statement came two centuries of lexical comparison, still ongoing, that have resulted in a precise branching structure for the Indo-European family tree, innumerable etymologies, and etymological dictionaries and similar reference works. This is the work that has received most of the scholarly and lay attention and that made nineteenth-century comparative linguistics the "queen of sciences" in the view of its contemporaries. It is no surprise that this conspicuous phase of the work has been identified with the comparative method of a whole: Measured in pages, years, or fame, it represents most of the work and most of the achievements. But, as has been argued here, equating the comparative method with its second phase is mistaken. This mistake is what has allowed linguists doing lexical comparison in the absence of a prior assumption of relatedness, or in the absence of individual-identifying evidence, to describe their work as based on the comparative method.

What linguistics needs now are heuristic measures that will be valid in situations where comparativists cannot expect to have reliable intuitions, measures that will detect relatedness at time depths at which face-value individual-identifying evidence has disappeared and the standard comparative method cannot apply. And since any such heuristic is likely to be improved if it can take into account the evidence offered by archeology, human biology, and other fields, it is important that communication be improved between historical linguists and other human prehistorians.

The first step toward improving communication will be drawing a clear and easily formulated line between groupings that are established by the comparative method and those that are not. This knowledge is part of received wisdom in mainstream linguistics and readily available in the oral tradition, but evidently difficult of access for nonlinguists. A second necessary step will be for linguists to compile an authoritative reference manual of language classification, one that will draw a clear line between established groupings and likely further relationships, and not venture beyond the latter. Perhaps the greatest single need in this area is for nonlinguists to be made aware of just how much genetic diversity exists among the world's languages. Genetic diversity of languages is a fact of nature, and to explain it away or ignore it is to deny reality.

EXCURSUS ON COMPUTING MULTIPLE DISJUNCT PROBABILITY

What are the chances of finding an *n* in a first-person pronominal root? What are the chances of finding a dental as second consonant in a word for 'water'? These two situations both involve multiple probability. In the case of the pronouns, we need to compute the probability of finding the *n* in the first person singular independent form, or the plural, or one or another bound form, singular or plural. In the case of 'water', we need to compute the probability of finding *t* or *d* or *n* as second consonant in the root. These two situations are quite different: the first involves sequential probability, the second simultaneous probability. The mathematical computations are accordingly different. Since the coverage of probability in elementary statistics textbooks is rarely such as to enable the linguist to discriminate between the two kinds of multiple probability, the reasoning is worth laying out in detail.

For the first example, the case of sequential probability (the chances of finding *n* in any of several first-person pronouns), the design of the survey is a sequence of searches for *n*. We seek an *n* in some cardinal form, say the independent form of the first person singular (the basic word for 'I') in our language. If we find *n* there, the search is successful. We may stop there, or we may examine other forms, but finding additional examples of *n* in other forms does not make the outcome any more successful than finding it in the first form, so for all practical purposes we can describe this search as an experiment which stops after the first success. If we do not find *n* in the first form examined, we proceed to another form, say the independent first-person plural form. If we find *n* there, the search is successful after two steps. If not, we proceed to another form, say the first-person singular possessive form. If we find *n* there, the search is successful after three steps; if not, we continue. And so on.

Multiple probability is often represented as a branching tree. A tree for the probability of finding *n* in a first-person pronoun is shown in Figure 2-1, for an assumed general likelihood of one in five for finding *n* in a pronominal root and for three attempts. Each tier of the tree represents one attempt, and the chances of success at any node are one in five. The chances of nonsuccess are then four in five, and the chance of success at either node in the second tier is computed as one-fifth of the chances of nonsuccess at the first tier: one-fifth of four-fifths = $0.2 \times 0.8 = 0.16$. The chance of success at the second tier after failure at the first tier is $0.2 + 0.16 = 0.36$, and this is the figure entered for two forms in the first part of Table 2-2. That is, the probability of success with the first form OR the second form is computed as the sum of those two probabilities. A mathematical formula that computes this probability is:

$$1 - (1 - P)^n$$

where P = the assumed likelihood of finding an *n* in a pronominal root and n = the number of attempts. For two attempts, $1 - (1 - 0.2)^2 = 0.36$

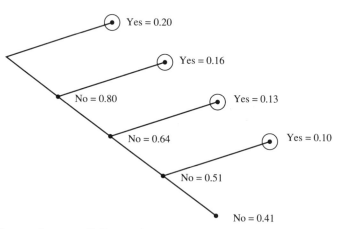

Figure 2-1. Chances of success at finding an *n* in a first-person pronominal form, where up to four forms can be searched and the search is judged a success the first time *n* is found. Circled nodes represent findings of *n*. The universal probability of finding *n* in a pronominal root is assumed to be one in five, or 0.20. The change of finding *n* in any one of the forms searched is computed as the sum of circled nodes at that tier and all previous tiers (i.e. all tiers to the left). This sum is equal to 1 minus the value of 'no' at that tier. For example, at tier three it is: $0.20 + 0.16 + 0.13 = (1 - 0.51)$.

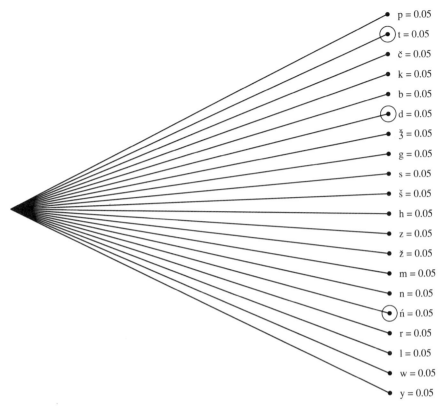

$p = 0.05$
$t = 0.05$
$č = 0.05$
$k = 0.05$
$b = 0.05$
$d = 0.05$
$ʒ = 0.05$
$g = 0.05$
$s = 0.05$
$š = 0.05$
$h = 0.05$
$z = 0.05$
$ž = 0.05$
$m = 0.05$
$n = 0.05$
$ń = 0.05$
$r = 0.05$
$l = 0.05$
$w = 0.05$
$y = 0.05$

Figure 2-2. Chances of finding a dental as second consonant in the word for 'water', was an assumed twenty-consonant inventory and all consonants equally likely to appear. Nodes representing dentals are circled. The probability of finding a dental is the sum of the probabilities of the individual dental consonants.

The total probability for the entire tree, regardless of how many tiers it has, is always 1.00, reflecting the fact that the chances of success and nonsuccess add up to exactly 100% of the attempts.

A probability tree for simultaneous probability, in this case the chances of finding a dental as second consonant in the word for 'water', is shown in Figure 2-2. Here we have one single attempt because there is only one word for 'water' to be examined. The chance of finding any randomly chosen consonant in a given position in any randomly chosen lexeme is assumed to be one in twenty (since the worldwide average number of consonants in inventories is twenty). We seek a dental, and there are three dentals in the basic inventory: *t, d,* and *n*. The chance of finding a dental in the position at issue is the sum of the individual probabilities for *t, d,* and *n*, that is, three out of twenty, or 0.15. Here the individual probabilities are summed directly: because there is a single attempt, any one of the three consonants might come up on that one attempt, and the total probability for all twenty consonants is 1.00.

NOTES

1. The history of the Balto-Slavic question is surveyed briefly, and the evidence summarized, in Bräuer 1961:14–20. Dybo 1979 is a typical representative of recent accentological works in that it refers to Balto-Slavic in its title but is concerned with tracing the Balto-Slavic system back to Indo-European.

2.. "Itak, zadača jazykovedenija—issledovat' čelovečeskij jazyk v ego istorii—trebuet, kak vy vidite, opredelenija rodstvennyx otnošenij meždu otdel'nymi jazykami i šravnitel'nogo izučenija tex jazykov, kotorye imejut v prošlom obščuju istoriju, t.e. rodstvenny po proisxoždeniju." The translation of *jazykove-denie* as 'comparative linguistics' rather than simply 'linguistics' is justified by the pages preceding this quote. (Here and elsewhere translations are my own unless otherwise indicated.)

3. "Dobrovskij, naprimer, znal uže togda [1792], čto stepen' rodstva jazykov opredeljaetsja ne izvest-nym količestvom sxodnyx slov, a tožestvom grammatičeskogo organizma."

4.. "Les concordances grammaticales prouvent, et elles seules prouvent rigoureusement, mais à la condition qu'on se serve du détail matériel des formes et qu'on établisse que certaines formes grammaticales particulières employées dans les langues considérées remontent à une origine commune." (1958: 91)

5. "Si donc on peut d'abord constater des ressemblances de vocabulaire entre deux ou plusieurs langues pour indiquer de quel côté il faut chercher, ce n'est pas de là que peut venir une démonstration définitive; le vocabulaire ne peut servir qu'à orienter la recherche; la preuve se trouve ailleurs." (1958: 97)

6. "Les ressemblances entre les langues qui constituent chacun de ces groupes [Romance, Germanic, Slavic, etc.] sont évidentes; la valeur de ce classement se traduit pratiquement par le fait que si l'on possède l'une des langues du groupe, on acquiert plus facilement les autres." (1958: 77)

7. "Partout où le système phonétique et le système grammatical présentent des concordances précis-es, où des correspondances régulières permettent de reconnaître l'unité d'origine des mots et du système phonétique et où le système des formes grammaticales s'explique en partant d'un original commun, la par-enté est évidente." (1958: 88)

8. "Si transformé, si éloigné de l'ancien type indo-européen que soit le "tokharien" récemment dé-couvert en Asie centrale, on l'a du premier coup reconnu pour indo-européen; le nombre des particularités grammaticales indo-européennes conservées y est encore grand." (1958: 97)

9. "Si l'on n'avait pas les anciens dialectes germaniques d'une côté, et le latin de l'autre, la parenté du français et de l'anglais ne serait pas démontrable." (1958: 90)

10. "A la longue cependant des langues parentes finissent par différer tant que leur communauté d'origine devient impossible à reconnaître. Si par exemple on n'avait que le français, le bulgare et l'ar-ménien modernes pour représenter le groupe indo-européen, il ne serait pas aisé d'établir la parenté de ces trois langues, et l'on ne pourrait songer à en poser la grammaire comparée." (1958: 93)

11. "Le chinois et telle langue du Soudan, celle du Dahomey ou ewe, par exemple, peuvent se servir également de mots courts, en général monosyllabiques, faire varier la signification des mots en changeant l'intonation, fonder leur grammaire sur l'ordre des mots et sur l'emploi de mots accessoires; il n'en résulte pas que le chinois et l'ewe soient des langues parentes; car le détail concret des formes ne concorde pas; or, seule la concordance des procédés matériels d'expression est probante." (1958: 90)

12. In fact, for the languages of the Old World the average is about twenty-five consonants, and the probability of any given consonant appearing in any given position is 0.04. This figure, and the world av-erage of twenty, are drawn from the database in Nichols 1992.

13. The identificatory value of the segments of the Indo-European adjectival concord system discussed earlier in section 3.1 can be computed as follows, using the same probabilities for consonants and genders as were used in table 2-1.

	M = 0.33	F = 0.33	N = 0.33
Nom.	*-s = 0.20	*-H = 0.05	*-m = 0.33
Acc.	*-m = 0.33	*-m = 0.33	*-m = 0.33

The six endings have a specific paradigmatic ordering. In addition, each dimension has a paradigmatic structure as a set of categories: there are several cases (with particular primary functions: subject, direct object, possessor, indirect object, etc.) and three genders (with particular primary functions: masculine, feminine, neuter). I assume that the two dimensions of gender and case are to be regarded as *n* degrees of freedom, and only *n*–1 of them used in computing systemic probability. I use gender rather than case in this computation, since case involves more forms (if the entire case paradigm, and not just the segment shown here, is taken into account) and hence lower probability: a six-case inventory for Proto-Indo-European would give 0.17 for each nominative and accusative. Again, I use the category yielding the higher overall probability just in order to give the null hypothesis every chance to stand. The probability of occurrence of this subsystem is the product of the individual probabilities: 0.000 003 6, or about four in a million. (But it is only 0.000 03, or three in one hundred thousand, if each of the two cases is counted as 0.5 probability and gender is not counted. This would be the appropriate count if the two cases constituted the entire paradigm.) The probability becomes even less if the other two dimensions mentioned in section 3.1, number and declension class, are figured in.

14. This pair is not the only similarity between the Indo-European and Kartvelian numerals; there is a striking resemblance in '6' as well, and less striking similarity in '5', '10', and perhaps '4'. The total probability for all these resemblances would probably be within the individual-identifying range.

15. For first-person *n*, Greenberg (1987: 49 ff.) cites forms in fourteen different categories, that is, first singular possessive, first singular subject of stative verb, first plural possessive, inclusive, first singular transitive subject, of which nine are the sole categories cited for the first person from the given language and five are the sole forms cited for either person. For second-person *m*, he cites nine categories, of which six are the sole forms cited in the second person and four are the sole forms cited from the language. To be sure, many of his citations involve both first-person *n* forms and second-person *m* forms, and for a number of them more than one form category in the person class is cited. But many of them involve a single form from a given language.

16. Gimson 1965: 214 gives a frequency of 7.58% (among consonants) for *n* in English. Delattre 1965: 95 gives 11.46% for *n* in English, 5.22% in French, 16.76% in German, and 12.27% in Spanish. All are text frequencies. I found 13.7% lexical frequency for *n* in Ingush (Northeast Caucasian) stems. Though far from adequate as a sample, these frequencies suggest that an estimate of 10% (one-in-ten chances) for *n* is not too high.

17. "Il va de soi que, pour établir une parenté de langues, il faut faire abstraction de tout ce qui s'explique par des conditions générales, communes à l'ensemble des langues. Ainsi les pronoms doivent être des mots courts, nettement constitués avec des éléments phonétiques aisés à prononcer, et en général sans groupes de consonnes. Il en résulte que les pronoms se ressemblent plus ou moins partout, sans que ceci implique une communauté d'origine. Et, d'autre part, les pronoms se ressemblent souvent assez peu dans des langues d'ailleurs très semblables; qu'on compare par exemple les pronoms de l'arménien avec ceux du gotique ou de l'irlandais. Même des formes qui, en fait, se ramènent à un même prototype, comme nous du français et us de l'anglais, peuvent ne plus offrir un seul élément commun (l's de français nous n'étant que graphique). On ne peut donc tirer parti des pronoms dans la détermination des parentés de langues qu'avec précaution." (1958: 89–90)

18. "*slava* 'gloire', cf., avec un autre suffixe, lit. *slověˊ* ; on tient souvent le mot lituanien pour emprunté au slave, mais sans raison (v. Leskien, Bild., 281); l'intonation douce de o (acc. *szlōvė*) n'est pas probante ici; car, bien que moins sujet à la métatonie douce que certains autres suffixes à -j- initial, le type en -(j)e n'en est pas exempt (F. de Saussure, M.S.L., VIII, 441, n); soit par la formation, soit par l'intonation, *szlovė* est exactement comparable aux mots *srovė* 'courant', *zolė* 'herbe' qui ne sont nullement suspects d'être empruntés." (1961: 208)

19. "**ostī* 'pointe' (r. *ost'*, s. *ostī̆*, pol. *ość*); le thème **ak*ₗ- est supposé par lit. *aszakà* 'arête de poisson'; gr. *akís*; gr. *aké*; lat. *acies*; skr. *acánih*; ags. *egl* 'aiguillon', arm. *aseƚn* 'aiguille', etc. (Meillet 1961: 209)

20. Il convient de mettre à part les noms d'agents in -*čĭja*— qui sont, ou d'anciens composés (d'après M. Jagic, Archiv, XX, 522), ou des dérivés en -*ĭja*- de mots en -*īcī̆*, ainsi *lovĭčĭjĭ* 'pêcheur', de *lovīcī* (?). Les textes vieux slaves n'en présentent d'ailleurs qu'un nombre restreint d'exemples, comme: *krŭmičĭjĭ* 'kubernétes', Supr. 360, 27, de *krŭma* 'poupe'; *kŭnjigŭčĭjĭ* 'grammateús'. . . . (Meillet 1961: 352)

21. The chances are slightly less if, as suggested by Newman, the probabilities of the individual genders are weighted in accordance with their attested frequencies.

REFERENCES

Bender, M. L. (1969). Chance CVC correspondences in unrelated languages. *Language* 45: 519–31.

Benedict, P. K. (1975). *Austro-Thai language and culture*. HRAF Press, New Haven.

Bräuer, H. (1961). *Slavische Sprachwissenschaft.* Vol 1. *Einleitung, Lautlehre.* Sammlung Göschen, vol. 1191/1191a. De Gruyter, Berlin.

Buck, C. D. ([1933]1966). *Comparative grammar of Greek and Latin.* University of Chicago Press, Chicago and London.

Campbell, L. (1988). Review of Greenberg 1987. *Language* 64: 591–615.

Cavalli-Sforza, L. L., A. Piazza, P. Menozzi, and J. Mountain. (1988). Reconstruction of human evolution: Bringing together genetic, archeological, and linguistic data. *Proceedings of the National Academy of Sciences of the United States of America* 85 (16): 6002–6.

Cross, S. H., and O. P. Sherbowitz-Wetzor. (1953). *The Russian Primary Chronicle: Laurentian text.* The Mediaeval Academy of America, Cambridge.

Delattre, P. (1965). *Comparing the phonetic features of English, German, Spanish, and French.* Julius Groos, Heidelberg.

Dolgopol'skij, A. B. (1964). Gipoteza drevnejšego rodstva jazykovyx semej severnoj Evrazii s verojatnostnoj tocki zrenija. *Voprosy Jazykoznanija* 1964 (2): 53–63.

Dybo, V. A. (1979). Baltoslavjanskaja sistema s tipologičeskoj tocki zrenija i problema rekonstrukcii indoevropejskogo akcenta. In T. V. Civ'jan, ed., *Balcanica: Lingvisticeskie issledovanija* 85–101. Nauka, Moscow.

Fortunatov, F. F. ([1901–2]1956). Sravnitel'noe jazykovedenie: Obščij kurs. *Izbrannye trudy.* Vol. 1: 23–197. Gosudarstvennoe ucebno-pedagogičeskoe izdatel'stvo, Moscow.

Gimson, A. C. (1965). *An introduction to the pronunciation of English.* Edward Arnold, London.

Gould, S. J. (1991). Grimm's greatest tale. In *Bully for brontosaurus* 32–42. Norton, New York.

Greenberg, J. H. (1987). *Language in the Americas.* Stanford University Press, Stanford.

Haas, M. R. (1968). *The prehistory of languages.* Mouton, The Hague.

Hoenigswald, H. M. (1960). *Language change and linguistic reconstruction.* University of Chicago Press, Chicago.

Illič-Svityč, V. M. (1971, 1976, 1984). *Opyt sravnenija nostratičeskix jazykov (semitoxamitskij, kartvel'skij, indoevropejskij, ural'skij, dravidskij, altajskij).* 3 vols. Nauka, Moscow.

Jagić, I. V. (1910). *Istorija slavjanskoj filologii.* Enciklopedija slavjanskoj filologii, vol. 1. Academy of Sciences, St. Petersburg.

Jakobson, R. ([1960]1971). Why "mama" and "papa"? In *Selected writings of Roman Jakobson.* Vol. 1, 538–45. Mouton, the Hague.

Kaiser, M., and V. Shevoroshkin. (1988). Nostratic. *Annual Review of Anthropology* 17: 309–29.

Kantor, M. (1983). *Medieval slavic lives of saints and princes.* Michigan Slavic Translations, no. 5. Department of Slavic Languages and Literatures at the University of Michigan, Ann Arbor.

Lomonosov, M. V. (1952). *Polnoe sobranie sočinenij.* Vol. 7. Akademija Nauk, Moscow and Leningrad.

Mallory, J. P. (1989). *In search of the Indo-Europeans: Language, archaeology, and myth.* Thames and Hudson, London.

Matisoff, J. A. (1990). On megalocomparison. *Language* 66: 106–20.

Meillet, A. ([1925]1954). *La Méthode comparative en linguistique historique.* Champion, Paris.

———. (1958). *Linguistique historique et linguistique générale.* Société Linguistique de Paris, Collection Linguistique, 8. Librairie Honoré Champion, Paris.

———. (1961). *Etudes sur l'étymologie et le vocabulaire du vieux slave.* 2nd ed. Institut d'Etudes Slaves, Paris.

Newman, P. (1970). Historical sound laws in Hausa and in Dera (Kanakuru). *Journal of West African Languages* 7 (1): 39-51.

———. (1980). *The classification of Chadic within Afro-Asiatic.* Universitaire Pers, Leiden.

———. (In press).On being right: Greenberg's African linguistic classification and the methodological principles which underlie it. In Taylor, ed.

Nichols, J. (1990). Linguistic diversity and the first settlement of the New World. *Language* 66: 475–521.

———. (1992). *Linguistic diversity in space and time.* University of Chicago Press, Chicago.

———. (1993). The linguistic geography of the Slavic expansion. In R. A. Maguire and A. Timberlake, eds., *American contributions to the Eleventh International Congress of Slavists* 377–391. Slavica, Columbus.

———. (In press). Linguistic diversity and the provenience of New World languages. In Taylor, ed.

Oswalt, R. L. (1992). A method for assessing distant linguistic relationships. In S. M. Lamb and E. D.

Mitchell, eds., *Sprung from some common source: Investigations into the prehistory of languages* 389–404. Stanford University Press, Stanford.

Rankin, R. L. (1992). Review of Greenberg *Language in the Americas*. *International Journal of American Linguistics* 58 (3): 324–51.

Renfrew, C. (1991). Before Babel: Speculations on the origins of linguistic diversity. *Cambridge Archeological Journal* 1 (1): 3–23.

Smirnov, V. S., G. I. Safronov, and P. A. Dmitriev. (1980). *Russkoe i slavjanskoe jazykoznanie v Rossii serediny XVIII-XIX vv.* Leningrad University, Leningrad.

Stoneking, M., and R. L. Cann. (1989). African origin of human mitochondrial DNA. In P. Mellars and C. Stringer, eds., *The human revolution: Behavioural and biological perspectives in the origins of modern humans* 17–30. Edinburgh University Press, Edinburgh and Princeton University Press, Princeton.

Shevelov, G. Y. (1964). *A prehistory of Slavic: The historical phonology of Common Slavic*. Columbia University Press, New York.

Taylor, A. R., ed. (In press). *Language and prehistory in the Americas: Proceedings of the Conference on the Greenberg Classification*. Stanford University Press, Stanford.

Thomason, S. G., and T. Kaufman. (1988). *Language contact, creolization and genetic linguistics*. University of California Press, Berkeley and Los Angeles.

Turner, C. G., II. (1988). Ancient peoples of the North Pacific rim. In W. W. Fitzhugh and A. Crowell, eds., *Crossroads of continents: Cultures of Siberia and Alaska* 111–16. Smithsonian Institution Press, Washington, D.C.

Vasmer, M. (1964). *Ètimologičeskij slovar' russkogo jazyka*. Progress, Moscow.

Winter, W. (1978). The distribution of short and long vowels in stems of the type Lith. *ésti : vèsti : mèsti* and OCS *jasti : vesti : mesti* in Baltic and Slavic languages. In J. Fisiak, ed., *Recent developments in historical phonology* 431–46. Mouton, The Hague.

3 On Sound Change and Challenges to Regularity

LYLE CAMPBELL

1 INTRODUCTION

Broadly speaking, this chapter is about reconstruction by the comparative method. More precisely, it concerns the regularity of sound change, that cornerstone which underlies our ability to recover linguistic history by the comparative method. Specifically, I examine the question "Is sound change regular?," addressing in particular some of the more sociocultural aspects of the issue. I discuss seven topics which have at times been presented as challenges to the hypothesis that sound change is regular: sound symbolism, onomatopoeia and affective/expressive symbolism, avoidance of homophony, morphologically conditioned phonological changes, areal linguistic borrowing, language death, and questions concerning the nature of change in so-called exotic speech communities. To anticipate the conclusion, I argue that these do not, in fact, present true exceptions to the regularity of sound change, but that it is important to take these issues into account in order to attain a full understanding of sound change in particular and of linguistic change in general.

2 SOUND SYMBOLISM

While sound change on the whole obeys standard Neogrammarian regularity, in some languages forms involving sound symbolism (ideophones) may exhibit irregular sound correspondences, which have occasionally been treated as putative exceptions to sound change. By "sound symbolism" I mean just those cases which involve symbolic variation in a language's sounds which depends on "size" and/or "shape." It is not uncommon for otherwise regular sound changes to appear to have exceptions in cases where sound symbolism is not recognized. For example, Mandan *s* corresponds (regularly) to the š of Dakota (and other Mississippi Valley Siouan languages, Chiwere-Winnebago, and Dhegiha [Osage]), and Mandan š corresponds to Dakota *s*. There are exceptions to these, however, which are explained by sound symbolism. In many forms in these languages, sound symbolic variants of the same root exist, where, for example, /s/ represents a smaller or less intense version of the basic meaning, /š/ a medium-sized or medium-intensity version, and /x/ a large or more intense version, as in the Mandan example:

sí 'yellow'   ší 'tawny'   xí 'brown'

Compare now the following cognate sets with sound-symbolic variants, where 'rattle' is a more intense version of the same root as 'tinkle':

Mandan: sró 'tinkle'   xró 'rattle'
Dakota: sná 'tinkle'   xná 'rattle'

The *s* of Mandan 'tinkle' should not normally correspond to the *s* of Dakota, but rather to Dakota's š. If the effects of sound symbolism were not recognized, the irregular correspondence would be unexplained and would be taken as an exception to the regular sound changes. (Cf. Campbell 1975, Ultan 1970, Nichols 1971.)

3 ONOMATOPOEIA AND AFFECTIVE/EXPRESSIVE SYMBOLISM

In some languages, forms involving onomatopoeia or affective symbolism may exhibit irregular sound correspondences. By affective or expressive symbolism, I mean the deployment of certain phonetic aspects of a language to reflect or symbolize affectations, heightened expressive value, or the speaker's attitude. The most basic sort of examples are the expressive use of laryngealization in Latin American Spanish and in Finnish to represent masculinity, nasality in English to indicate something disagreeable, and the stereotypic breathy voice (murmur) to symbolize sexiness. While these instances tend to be employed globally by speakers in order to achieve their expressive or affective ends, in other cases such features may be employed for such purposes only in certain appropriate words. In this view, any use of a phonetic feature for special symbolic, expressive, affective, or connotative purposes fits the notion. For example, for speakers of many dialects of American English, the intervocalic flapping of /t/ and /d/ (in the appropriate environment, that is, basically after a stressed vowel) is automatic, or nearly so (as in my dialect), yet some of these speakers suspend the flapping in *Plato* and *Latin* ([pleyt^{h}ow], [læt^{h}ɪn]) in order to give a more prestigious affect to these words. This affective suspension of the flapping rule makes these two forms seem to be exceptions to the essentially regular change of flapping.

Size-shape sound symbolism (section 2) is certainly related to this, and may even be a subtype thereof, though it tends to be more institutionalized as part of the structural resources of many languages. For example, excessively over-long vowel length may be used expressively to symbolize something big or intense, as for example it sometimes is in English; but the opposition between short and long vowels has no regular status as a marker of bigger versus smaller things in English, as it may have in languages with a more institutionalized sound-symbolism.

An illustrative example where onomatopoeic or affective symbolic forms may exhibit irregular sound correspondences is seen in the non-etymological *r* in Chol and Tzotzil (two Mayan languages).

Before contact with Spanish, the Cholan-Tzotzilan languages had no *r*; rather, *r* was introduced to these languages through Spanish loanwords which contained this sound, for instance in Chol: *arus* 'rice' (< Spanish *arroz*), *rus* 'cross' (< Spanish *cruz*), *araweno* 'mint' (< Spanish *hierbabuena*); in Tzotzil: *martoma* 'custodian' (< Spanish *mayordomo*), *kurus* 'cross' (< Spanish *cruz*), *yaraveno* 'mint' (< Spanish *hierbabuena*).[1] This *r* was later extended to native words (that is, to non-etymological contexts) through onomatopoeia and affective or expressive sound symbolism. That is, after the *r* was introduced via Spanish loans (although *r* is still today quite rare and seemingly not fully integrated into the sound system of the two languages), this new sound—which was apparently exotic from the point of view of the native speakers—came to be employed in certain native words, but for expressive purposes. Nearly all of these involve onomatopoeia or affective/expressive forms. In Chol, such examples are limited mostly to a few adjectives: *buruk-ña* 'buzzing, humming', *burbur-ña* 'noisily', *kirik-ña* 'grunting', *porok-ña* 'breathing when there is an obstruction', *sorok-ña* 'bubbling', *borol* 'truncated, headless, handless'. No etymological source for any of these can be identified in Proto-Cholan or Proto-Mayan (henceforth PM). Apparently the new *r* was utilized in the creation of these new words for heightened expressive value.

The story of the Tzotzil *r* is similar, except that some of the Tzotzil words which now have *r* come from etymological sources which formerly had *l* (replaced by *r*). For example, Tzotzil *ner-iš* 'cross-eyed' (*nel-iš* also still exists) in Colonial Tzotzil had only *l,* that is, *nel-* 'crooked, twisted, slanted' (Laughlin 1988: 271). Similarly, the Proto-Cholan-Tzotzilan single etymon **kelem* 'strong, young man, male' has split into two in modern Tzotzil: *kerem* 'boy (affective)', *kelem* 'rooster'. Colonial Tzotzil had only *kelem* 'boy, bachelor, servant' (Laughlin 1988: 220). As in Chol, however, most of the nonborrowed Tzotzil words with *r* are onomatopoeic or affective symbolic forms. For example, several of these are found in bird names (which are often onomatopoeic in languages of this region): *k'oročoč* 'woodpecker', *puruvok* 'dove', *purkuvič* 'roadrunner', *tararan* 'vulture', and *tsurukuk* 'screech owl'. Other such onomatopoeic or expressive forms include: *pirič'tik* 'unkempt, disheveled', *turič* 'dragonfly', *ts'urupik* 'earwig', and several words for 'throat': *čuruhub, k'orok', koroʔ*, and *turub*.

This increased employment for onomatopoeic and expressive purposes of what started out as a foreign sound in nonborrowed forms illustrates the question about regularity: What is the effect on our interpretation of the hypothesis of the regularity of sound change, given the possibility that new sounds can be utilized in environments other than their etymologically expected ones? Or, to put it more directly, Why is the change of *l* to *r* in forms such as those cited here sporadic and not regular?

The issue is seen more clearly in the following cognate sets from Mayan languages, which exhibit some exceptional forms. (In the case of exceptions, the expected reflexes are given in parentheses.)

(1) 'to drip, drop'

PM	*ts'uh-
Quiche	ts'ux-
Cakchiquel	ts'ux-
Mam	ts'uːx
Teco	ts'ux-
Kanjobal	t'uh- (*ts'uh* is expected)
Tojolabal	t'uh- (*ts'uh* is expected)
Jacaltec	ts'uh
Tzeltal	ts'uh- (some dialects have -*t'uh*-, but *ts'uh*- is the expected reflex)
Tzotzil	-ts'uh-
Chol	t'uh- (*ts'uh* is expected)

In this case, the regular (expected) reflex of PM *ts'* in Kanjobal, Tojolabal, Tzeltal, dialects, and Chol is *ts'*, not the exceptional *t'* seen here.

(2) 'to spit, saliva'

PM	*tʸu(h)b'-
Huastec	tub-
Quiche	ub'-
Pokomchi	ub'-
Kekchí	uːb
Mam	tsub'
Teco	tsuːb'-
Jacaltec	tsub'- (expected *tub'*)
Tojolabal	tsuhb'- (expected *tub'*)
Tzeltal	tuhb'-
Tzotzil	tub'
Cholan	*tuhb'
Yucatecan	túːb'
Itza	tub'

The normal reflex of PM *tʸ* in Jacaltec and Tojolabal is *t*, not the *ts* seen here (compare, for example, Jacaltec *tuh* 'stink', Tojolabal *tuʔuh* 'stink', from PM *tʸuʔh) 'stink').[2]

The exceptional forms cited here involve onomatopoeia, for example, 'drip/drop' and 'to spit/spittle'. That is, the otherwise regular sound changes fail to match expected reflexes only in the cases where imitation of the sound associated with the referent in the real world has complicated the picture, either leading to sporadic change after the sound change or deflecting the sound so that it does not undergo the expected change. In either case, it would not be possible to recognize these as exceptions without knowledge of the regularity generally obeyed elsewhere in these languages. Thus, regularity of sound change remains the principal explanation, while recognition of the involvement of onomatopoeia supplements overall understanding of how languages may change.

Another kind of irregularity (as some have seen it) in sound change involves not deflection or prevention due to onomatopoeia, but rather the deployment of new sounds created by regular sound change in unexpected phonetic environments for onomatopoeic or symbolic reasons (akin to the case of Chol and Tzotzil *r* mentioned previously, but here not limited just to new sounds introduced through borrowing). An example of this is the change of PM *b'* (imploded glottalic) to *p'* (ejective, glottalized) in certain environments in the Yucatecan, Cholan-Tzotzilan, and Pokom subgroups (Campbell 1973, 1977). This change has resisted explanation. For example, as Kaufman and Norman point out for Proto-Cholan, "With the exception of *p'ah*, all the roots [reconstructed for Proto-Cholan] in which /p'/ occurs contain one of the apical [i.e. 'coronal'] consonants /t s n [s]/. However, /b'/ also occurs in roots that contain apicals. . . ." (1984: 85).

This is clearly not the typical statement of a completely regular sound change. Their statement can be refined to reveal more regularity than they found. For example, *b'* before *a* or *ə* does not change to *p'*, regardless of whether it is followed by a coronal consonant or not (e.g. Cholan *b'ət* 'hail', *b'əl* 'contents', *b'ats'* 'howler monkey'.[3] However, this still does not account for all exceptions. After the regular creation of /p'/ in the context of vowel + coronal consonants when not followed by *a* or *ə* (e.g. *b'is* > *p'is* 'measure'), this new ejective *p'* was utilized further for onomatopoeic and affective purposes. For example, PM *b'ax* 'to pound, nail' has apparently split into Cholan *b'ax* 'to nail' (the regular, expected outcome, given that the *b'* is followed by *ə*, and the *x* is not a coronal consonant) and Cholan *p'əx* 'to curse, condemn', where *p'* is deployed outside its original phonetically determined environment for added expressive/symbolic affect. This explanation is particularly evident in cases where Cholan *p'* comes not as it normally does from reflexes of PM *b'*, but in the unexpected instances where the Cholan *p'* is the reflex of PM *p*, for example, *sip'* 'to swell up' (PM *sip*), The employment of *p'* in 'to swell up' (rather than the etymologically expected *p*) seems clearly due to expressive sound symbolism (cf. also *nup'* 'to marry'; in other Greater Lowland Mayan languages *nup*).

This explanation provides the clue to further refinement of the sound change. An additional problem for seeing the change of PM *b'* to Proto-Cholan *p'* as regular stems from the Cholan doublets *b'us* 'piled' and *p'us-pat* 'hunchback' [from *b'us* 'piled' + *pat* 'back']. However, this complication is resolved. The change apparently did not normally take place before *u* either (just as it is lacking in cases before *a* and *ə*); the *p'* was employed for symbolic affect in 'hunchback', in the otherwise phonetically unexpected environment before an *u*. The only other form with *p'* before *u* is Cholan *p'ul* 'with indigestion, smallpox, piled up'; the *p'* in this form appears to be explained as in the case of 'hunchback' as due to affective symbolic factors.

Finally, both *b'* and *p'* can occur word-finally, although *p'* is rare there—only six instances (Kaufman and Norman 1984: 85), not counting *sip'* 'to swell' and *nup'* 'to marry' from final *-p* (see preceding discussion). These six also appear to be due to onomatopoeia or affective symbolism: *top'* 'to break, burst, jump, fly'; *sep'* 'to pinch'; *sop'* 'light and frothy'; *nap'* 'to stick to (to glue)'; *nexep'* 'half-ripe, aged'; and *tep'* 'to wrap a child'. The only remaining exceptions to the sound change are three forms which retain *b'* with coronal consonants, although some of these do not actually fit the environment. For example, Cholan **b'iš* (with alternate *iš*) 'to go' is derived from *b'ih-iš*, cf. **b'ih* 'road', although at the time of the sound change there was no appropriate coronal consonant in the conditioning environment (only *h*). The case of **b'es* 'stammerer' may in fact involve onomatopoeia/affective symbolism in the other direction, with the deployment of *b'* in a coronal-consonant environment where *p'* would be expected; forms in other Mayan and other Mesoamerican languages involve *m* onomatopoeically in words for 'stammerer' and 'deaf-mute' (e.g. *mem, uma?*, etc.; cf. Quiche *moːš* 'dumb, stupid').

The affective (symbolic) and onomatopoeic use of a sound in phonetic environments beyond those associated with its origins from regular sound changes can complicate the investigation of sound change. Nevertheless, it is the basic principle of regularity which leads to understanding, and it is the supplementary information that sounds can on occasion function for onomatopoeic and affective/expressive (and sound-symbolic) purposes which helps to complete the picture. The unraveling here of the complications in the change of **b'* to *p'* in Cholan is a particularly complex illustration of this.

It is generally known in historical linguistics that onomatopoeia may create exceptions to sound changes (cf. Anttila 1972: 87, Campbell and Ringen 1981). However, it is important to point out that without the assumption of the basic regularity of sound change, investigators would not be able to recognize such forms as exceptions. That is, the existence of deflected or irregular reflexes due to onomatopoeia and affective/expressive symbolism, such as those discussed here, do not invalidate the principle of regularity, but rather require the additional explanatory principle, according to which in cases of onomatopoeia occasionally (usually sporadically) sound change in certain forms may not conform to the regular pattern. The outcome may instead reflect the association of the form's meaning with sounds of nature, or it may involve the symbolic-affective uses of speech sounds for heightened expressiveness.[4]

4 AVOIDANCE OF HOMOPHONY

While scholars opposed to teleological explanations in linguistics have never been friends of the explanation of certain changes as due to the avoidance of pernicious homophony, such avoidance is nevertheless solidly documented; that is, it is an undeniable empirical reality (cf. Campbell and Ringen 1981: 59–60). Avoidance of homophony, however, can take several forms. The best known cases involve lexical replacement or loss, as in Gilliéron's French examples, where in Gascony reflexes of Latin *gallus* 'rooster' (commonly *gal* in southern France) were replaced by words meaning 'pheasant' and 'vicar' in exactly those dialects which correspond to the area of the sound change of *ll* to *t*, where *gal* > *gat* would make 'rooster' homophonous with *gat* 'cat' (Gilliéron and Roques 1912). German dialects present several similar examples (cf. Bach 1969:168; Öhmann 1934). Avoidance of homophony can also sometimes block otherwise regular sound changes from taking place in certain forms or trigger irregular or spontaneous changes in forms in order to avoid homophonic clashes. For example, as Menner (1936: 222–3) demonstrates in English, *quean* 'low woman' disappeared because of homophonic conflict with *queen* after Middle English [ɛː] and [eː] fell together, especially in the East Midlands and the Southeast. However, in some regions of the North, initial *wh-* was substituted for the *qu* of *quean*, and the two words survive, avoiding homophonic conflict through this special, sporadic change.[5] Similarly, German dialects where regular sound change (for example, loss of intervocalic *g* and unrounding of *ü*) would have produced homophony for *liegen* 'to lie (down)' and *lügen* 'to lie (tell falsehoods)' illustrate both instances where the changes are blocked (the original sounds preserved only in these words) and cases of deflected changes where sporadic changes take place to preserve the phonetic difference between these two words (Öhmann 1934).

In these cases, we again see that fundamentally the sound changes are regular, and that the seeming irregularity (produced either by preventing the change in instances where pernicious homophony would result or by inducing minor but irregular, or sporadic, changes to deflect the sounds to prevent the homophony) is rendered explicable only against the backdrop of the assumption that sound change is fundamentally regular and by calling upon the avoidance of homophony as a secondary principle also involved in language change.

5 MORPHOLOGICALLY CONDITIONED SOUND CHANGES

In earlier, more formative generative treatments of linguistic change, sound changes exhibiting morphological conditioning occasioned much excitement. They acquired an important role in the overall theoretical outlook with regard to historical linguistics associated with then current theoretical issues in general linguistics, such as the separation of levels, where transformational-generative views contrasted sharply with those of the more traditional American structuralists. At the same time, morphological conditioning of sound change was also proclaimed as a routine historical linguistic matter, expected by the general theory, and thus in no need of additional explanation. According to King, "Once we have determined that *x* becomes *y* in the morphological environment *z*, the story is over, and there is little to do but move on to more interesting things" (1969: 124).

From today's perspective, we have almost the inverse of this view. Such changes no longer generate much excitement, but far from "the story being over," morphological conditioning of sound change itself has become subject to explanation as part of a broader picture of language and language change. It is probably safe to say that most (historical) linguists see language as a more or less integrated whole, with grammatical subcomponents interacting in interdependent ways so that change in one part of the language system may have consequences for other areas of the grammar. This is what lies behind most cases of morphologically conditioned sound change. It is commonly argued that the grammatical/semantic side of language can exert influence on the phonological side (which formally signals the morphosyntactic and lexical categories) either to prevent or deflect otherwise regular sound changes in order to prevent the disruption of the phonological material which signals important morphosyntactic categories. This is seen as another complication for the regularity principle.

Morphological conditioning of a sound change seems to take place only where an otherwise regular sound change would have adverse effects on speakers' ability to process important morphosyntactic functions. Morphological conditioning produces blockage or deflects the sound change in certain grammatical environments (Campbell 1974, Campbell and Ringen 1981). A frequently cited example is the well-known Estonian case. In Northern Estonian, final *n* was lost in regular sound change everywhere except in first person singular verb forms (that is, this is a morphologically conditioned change): compare **kanna-n* 'heel' (gen. sg.) > *kanna*, but **kanna-n* 'I carry', which remained *kannan*. The retention of *-n* in first person singular verb forms prevents the homophony that would occur with second person singular imperatives, as in *kanna* 'carry it!'. In Southern Estonian, however, the final *-n* was freely lost everywhere, including in first person singular verb forms, for instance, **kanna-n* > *kanna* 'I carry'. The change in Southern Estonian was not morphologically conditioned because no homophony with second person imperative forms would have occurred. That is, historically second person imperatives were marked by a glottal stop, for example, *kanna-ʔ* 'carry it'. Since the glottal stop was maintained in the south, the two competing forms remained distinct (*kanna* 'I carry', *kannaʔ* 'carry it!'). However, the final glottal stop was lost in the north, which would have resulted in difficulty in distinguishing the competing forms; therefore, the sound change deleting final *-n* was blocked in this instance, and *-n* was retained in first person singular forms to maintain the distinction (*kanna-n* 'I carry', *kanna* 'carry it!'. (For more discussion of this case and other similar cases, see Kiparsky 1965: 28, Anttila 1972: 79, King 1969: 125, Campbell 1974, Campbell and Ringen 1981.)

A Kekchi (Mayan) case (for details see Campbell 1971: 149–50) may be helpful in understanding the relationship between regularity and morphological conditioning of sound changes. Historically, in Kekchi short vowels of the final syllable in polysyllabic forms were deleted:

**išoq	>	išq 'woman'
**winaq	>	kwinq 'man'
**warik	>	wark 'sleep'
**šulub'	>	šulb' 'flute'

Certain final consonant clusters produced by this rule were further simplified, wherein the final consonant could be lost, for example, *ts'ik* (< *ts'ikn* < **ts'ikin*) 'bird'.

The loss of short vowels from final syllables applied in all cases that fit its structural description, except when it was the vowel of a verb root, in which case the vowel was retained:

t-at-in-k'am
ASPECT-you-I-carry
'I will carry you' (cf. **-k'am* 'carry, take')

t-at-w-il
ASPECT-you-I-see
'I will care for you' (cf. **-il* 'see')

t-at-in-muq
ASPECT-you-I-bury
'I will bury you' (cf. *-*muq* 'bury')

The otherwise regular sound change was blocked in this case because if it had deleted the vowel of the verb root, it would be very difficult to recognize the verb. In particular, if the resulting consonant cluster had subsequently been subject to loss of the final consonant as well, then the CVC pattern typical of Mayan roots would have been reduced to a mere C, making recognition of the root extremely difficult, if possible at all (e.g. *t-at-in-k'am* > *tatin-k'm* > *tatin-k'* [and conceivably on to *tatin*]). Thus, the morphological conditioning in this example appears to have blocked an otherwise regular sound change in this environment so that it would not have deleterious results on speakers' ability to identify the verb root.

I conclude again that sound change is essentially regular, although in the case of morphologically conditioned sound changes a secondary principle can also come into play. That is, languages (or rather speakers of languages) may block otherwise regular sound changes when the result would impede perception of important morphosyntactic functions. (For more discussion, see Campbell and Ringen 1981.)

6 AREAL LINGUISTIC BORROWING

It has been argued that the regularity of sound change can be suspended in cases where sounds are borrowed from other languages in a linguistic area and come to be employed in native words, the borrowed sounds in effect aping sound changes, but often irregular ones (compare, for example, Campbell 1976: 183). For example, the Indo-Aryan retroflexed consonants involve borrowing within the Indian linguistic area from the Dravidian languages; in this region many native Indo-European etyma came to have retroflexed consonants, but their occurrence in native forms is not the result of regular sound change. According to Burrow, "the cerebralization [retroflexion] is not only spontaneous but also sporadic and unpredictable" (1971: 36).[6]

This claim warrants far more study than it has to date been given. In broad outline, however, it is still safe to say that exceptions due to foreign sounds being borrowed and employed in native morphemes could not be identified or dealt with properly without recognition of the basic regularity of internally motivated sound changes that take place within a language. That is, such cases do not constitute true exceptions to the regularity of sound change because we define them as "external" changes, that is, as borrowings, which are outside what we normally understand under the rubric of sound change. Nevertheless, a full explanation of linguistic change is possible only by taking the combined effects of sound change and borrowed sounds into account.

7 LANGUAGE DEATH AND SOUND CHANGE

It has also been claimed that some phonological changes which go on in dying languages may not exhibit the regularity typical of sound changes in fully viable languages (Campbell 1976, Campbell and Muntzel 1989, Cook 1989: 252, Dressler 1972). For example, there is nothing regular about the almost random glottalization of originally plain consonants by Jumaytepeque Xinca semispeakers. (For other examples, compare Campbell 1976, 1994; Cook 1989.) In this case, the irregularity is best attributed to the imperfect learning on the part of not fully competent speakers of the obsolescing languages, rather than to a flaw in the basic notion of how sounds change in fully viable languages. Nevertheless, the existence of such skewed transmittal in the case of a dying language needs to be borne in mind in assessing all the ways languages can change and vary.

8 CHANGE IN EXOTIC LANGUAGES AS A PUTATIVE CHALLENGE TO THE REGULARITY HYPOTHESIS

In this section I address issues raised (inappropriately, I argue) with respect to so-called primitive or exotic languages. Such questions as the following have been asked: Is change in unwritten/primitive/exotic languages fundamentally different from change in nonexotic (and written) languages?, and Is sound change regular in unwritten/exotic languages? Regular sound change is a cornerstone of the comparative method, and the comparative method has been applied successfully to cases of unwritten/exotic languages so often and so consistently that one would expect any doubt to have been abandoned long ago. Unfortunately, the question continues to recur. For example Baldi asks: "The comparative method relies on sound correspondences; what, then, can it do in language families where sound correspondences are irregular and inconsistent? Boretzky (1984), for example, has argued that change in the Arandic languages of central Australia seems to proceed more by abrupt lexical replacement through borrowing than by gradual phonological change" (1990: 11).

This being the case, it may still be necessary to show (yet again) (1) that sound change is not fundamentally different in so-called exotic languages; (2) that the question of written versus unwritten language is irrelevant for sound change; and (3) that the myth that linguistic primitivism affects the nature of sound change should be abandoned.

8.1   The Regularity of Sound Change in So-Called Primitive Languages

There should no longer be any doubt about the regularity of sound change in exotic languages, though in the past this regularity was frequently questioned due to misconceptions concerning the nature of so-called primitive languages. Alluding to these misconceptions, Sapir ([1931]1949: 74) summarized the now almost universal attitude:

> Is there any reason to believe that the process of regular phonetic change is any less applicable to the languages of primitive peoples than to the languages of the more civilized nations? This question must be answered in the negative. . . . If these laws are more difficult to discover in primitive languages, this is not due to any special characteristic which these languages possess but merely to the inadequate technique of some who have tried to study them.

As is now well-known, Bloomfield (1925, 1928) demonstrated the validity of the regularity assumption for sound change in primitive/exotic languages, responding to doubts about the applicability of the comparative method to exotic languages. For example, Meillet and Cohen (1924: 9) in *Les Langues du monde* expressed their misgivings as follows:

> One may well ask whether the languages of America (which are still for the most part poorly known and insufficiently studied from a comparative point of view) will ever lend themselves to exact, exhaustive comparative treatment; the samples offered so far hold scant promise. . . . it is not even clear that the principle of genealogical classification applies. (See also Meillet 1925: vi–vii.)

Rivet (1925) recognized that the lack of regular phonetic correspondences in some exotic languages might lie in the fault of the transcription, but he nevertheless considered it possible that these languages might not conform to "rules as strict as those found in the Indo-European language" (Rivet 1925: 26; cf. Andersen 1990: 189). It was against these sentiments that Bloomfield, in his famous article, (1925: 130) directed the following arguments:

> I hope, also, to help dispose of the notion that the usual processes of linguistic change are suspended on the American continent. (Meillet and Cohen, *Les langues du monde*, Paris, 1924, p.9). If there exists anywhere a language in which these processes do not occur (sound-change independent of meaning, analogic change, etc.), then they will not explain the history of Indo-European or any other language. A principle such as the regularity of phonetic change is not part of the specific tradition handed on to each new speaker of a given language, but is either a universal trait of human speech or nothing at all, an error.

Sapir ([1929]1949: 160–1), who had already engaged in the historical linguistic study of a number of Native American language families, seconded Bloomfield:

> The methods developed by the Indo-Europeanists have been applied with marked success to other groups of languages. It is abundantly clear that they apply just as rigorously to the unwritten primitive languages of Africa and America as to the better known forms of speech of the more sophisticated peoples. . . . The more we devote ourselves to the comparative study of the languages of a primitive linguistic stock, the more clearly we realize that phonetic law and analogical leveling are the only satisfactory key to the unraveling of the development of dialects and languages from a common base. Professor Leonard Bloomfield's experiences with Central Algonkian and my own with Athabaskan leave nothing to be desired in this respect and are a complete answer to those who find it difficult to accept the large-scale regularity of the operation of all those unconscious linguistic forces which in their totality give us regular phonetic change and morphological readjustment on the basis of such change. It is not merely theoretically possible to predict the correctness of specific forms among unlettered peoples on the basis of such phonetic laws as have been worked out for them—such predictions are already on record in considerable number. There can be no doubt that the methods first developed in the field of Indo-European linguistics are destined to play a consistently important rôle in the study of all other groups of languages. (Cf. also Sapir ([1931]1949: 78.)

Since Sapir's and Bloomfield's work, the assumption that sound change is regular has proved itself useful and valid in case after case in work on exotic and unwritten languages.

Some doubts about regularity and about the applicability of the comparative method to exotic languages seem to stem from an often imprecisely articulated belief that change in exotic languages may somehow be fundamentally different from that typical of nonexotic (written) languages. Frequently, Australian languages have been implicated in these doubts (cf. Sommerfelt 1938: 187–8). More recently, Boretzky (1982, 1984) has made similar claims, which have been cited approvingly by Mühlhäusler (1989) and Baldi (1990: 11). Boretzky contrasts Aranta (in Australia) and Kâte (in New Guinea) with Slavic and Romance—that is, "exotic" with "European" languages. Boretzky objects that in exotic languages semantic slots are likely to be filled either by difficult-to-relate morphs, or, conversely, that the phonological differences are so small (in Arandic) that there is no scope for reconstruction; he thinks that change in the Arandic languages proceeds more by abrupt lexical replacement through borrowing than by gradual phonological change (cf. Hoenigswald 1990: 377). This, however, does not invalidate the comparative method for these languages. Dixon (1990: 398) shows that "it is quite clear that Australian languages change in a regular fashion, in the same way as Indo-European and other families." In fact, it was through a demonstration of regular changes that Hale (1964, 1976) was able to show that the languages of northeastern Queensland—with many short monosyllabic words, formerly thought to be quite aberrant—in fact developed regularly from a normal Pama-Nyungan type. Vocabulary may present difficulties in Australia, but lexical borrowings are a fact of linguistic life that the comparative method has to contend with everywhere, not just in Australia or New Guinea (cf. Dixon 1990: 254, Johnson 1990: 430).

8.2 The Overrated and Misperceived Role of Writing

The question about sound change in unwritten languages is really not about writing per se, but rather about the kind of written evidence employed, that is, about whether or not there is an older tradition of written texts. Languages lacking such a tradition have often been considered "exotic" or "primitive", and it is essentially with regard to these that the question of the regularity of sound change, and hence of the applicability of the comparative method, has been raised. While to many the following discussion may seem pretty self-evident (or perhaps like dead-horse beating), it is still worthwhile to rehearse some of the misconceptions regarding "unwritten" languages, both for the lessons offered by the history of linguistics and for the relevance with respect to recent challenges to regularity of sound change.

Haas points out that "[s]ince the existence of written languages . . . was of great strategic importance in the development of our knowledge of Indo-European, some scholars came to believe that the historical and comparative study of languages was impossible without written records of earlier stages of the same or related languages (1969: 20)." This belief persisted in spite of the fact that the comparative study of unwritten/exotic languages has had a long and successful history. Bloomfield's (1925, 1928) famous Algonquian proof shows—though this was not his primary intention—

how writing can not only be overrated but can sometimes actually be an obstacle to reconstruction. For some languages Bloomfield used older written sources; for others he employed his own field data. Frequently the written materials were inadequate for accurate reconstruction. He relied in part on his own field records for Menomini and Cree; his Fox and Ojibwa material was written down by William Jones, a native speaker of Fox, and this provides an important lesson about the value of written sources. Bloomfield's proof of regularity of sound change and of the applicability of the comparative method in unwritten languages was based on the following correspondence sets and reconstructions for Central Algonquian.

	Fox	Ojibwa	Plains Cree	Menomini	PCA
(1)	hk	šk	sk	čk	*čk
(2)	šk	šk	sk	sk	*šk
(3)	hk	hk	sk	hk	*xk
(4)	hk	hk	hk	hk	*hk
(5)	šk	šk	hk	hk	*çk

Bloomfield postulated the reconstruction of *çk for set (5) as distinct from the other sets on the bases of scant evidence, but under the assumption that sound change is regular and the difference in this correspondence set (though exhibiting only sounds that occur in different combinations in the other sets) could not plausibly be explained in any other way. Later, his decision to reconstruct something different for this set was confirmed when Swampy Cree was discovered to contain the correspondence *htk* for set (5), distinct in Swampy Cree from the reflexes of the other four reconstructions. Based on this, Bloomfield (1928: 100) concluded, "As an assumption, however, the postulate [of sound-change without exception] yields, as a matter of mere routine, predictions which otherwise would be impossible. In other words, the statement that *phonemes change* (sound-changes have no exceptions) is a tested hypothesis: in so far as one may speak of such a thing, it is a proved truth."

Moreover, since Fox does not contrast *sk* and *šk*, Jones (as a native speaker of Fox) failed to recognize and record this contrast in Ojibwa. Had the written material available to Bloomfield not failed to represent this contrast, Swampy Cree would not have been the only extant witness to the distinctness of set (5). (Cf. Hockett [1948] 1970: 500–1.) As Bloomfield (1946: 88) reported it,

> "The fuss and trouble behind my note in *Language* [Bloomfield 1928] would have been avoided if I had listened to O[jibwa], which plainly distinguishes sk (< PA çk) from šk (< PA šk); instead, I depended on printed records which failed to show the distinction." (Cf. also Hockett [1948]1970: 506.)

The truth of the matter in the case of Central Algonquian is that the older written materials were rather an obstacle to reliable reconstruction by the comparative method, and it was the accurately recorded field data, the usual currency of unwritten languages, which led to the correct solution.

In part the prejudice in favor of writing reflects a holdover from an earlier stage of comparative linguistics where language change was thought to take place in discrete stages of progress and decay. The languages of "savage" people were thought to be "primitive" relics which had not yet evolved (progressed, through processes of compounding and agglutination) to the state of greater perfection which, it was believed, the older written Indo-European languages, in particular Sanskrit, had attained; modern languages were typically viewed as just decayed reflections (due to analogy and sound changes, which were assumed to be operative only in this later phase) of their more perfect ancestors. Thus, the old written languages, thought to be more perfect, were allotted a special status. By the time of the Neogrammarian movement (cf. Osthoff and Brugmann 1878), comparative linguistics had adopted a uniformitarian position according to which language change was no longer held to take place in discrete stages of either progress or decay, but languages were instead seen to undergo the same kinds of changes at all times throughout their histories. With this reorientation, written language was accorded less a special status, attention turned more towards spoken language, in particular to dialects (cf. Osthoff 1883), and attention to dialectology promoted the development of phonetics and techniques for recording forms of spoken language (cf. Sievers 1876). Thus, speaking of the principle that sound laws are without exception, Delbrück ([1882]1880) affirmed in his influential Neogrammarian introduction to linguistics:

> [T]his natural constitution of language is not manifested in the cultivated tongues, but in the dialects of the people. The guiding principles for linguistic research should accordingly be deduced not from obsolete written languages of antiquity, but chiefly from the living popular dialects of the present day (61). It is of far greater importance to collect further facts from living languages, in order to draw conclusions from them with regard to the ancient languages (126).

Thus, the uniformitarian reorientation led linguists to view spoken language, not written, as the more valuable for linguistic research (cf. Christy 1983: 35–6, 55, 58). By 1900, Henry Sweet (1900: 79) was able to report:

> It is now an axiom of scientific philology that the real life of language is in many respects more clearly seen and better studied in dialects and colloquial forms of speech than in highly developed literary languages.

And Hoenigswald (1990: 379) provides a worthwhile summary of the real value of writing for reconstruction:

> That written records add to the fullness of our basic knowledge and give us a "free ride" into the past is of course true, but it does not change the uncertainty which hangs over our inferences. That written records allow us direct observation of changes along something that can come rather close to a direct line of descent is also true, but it still does not solve the problem of how to describe, classify, and "explain" the changes. The most interesting use of written records lies in their availability for the task of confirming or disallowing inferences, as in the case of Latin and Proto-Romance. It should, however, be understood that neither the comparative method nor internal reconstruction depend[s] on written records.

9 CONCLUSION

I conclude from this survey of purported challenges (mostly of a sociocultural nature) to the regularity of sound change that the basic regularity of sound change is still a viable, essential assumption and a well-founded principle of historical linguistics. Nevertheless, for a full understanding of language change, the story does not end with exceptionless sound changes. In a narrowly circumscribed set of circumstances—that is, those involving onomatopoeia and affective/expressive forms, sound symbolism, morphological conditioning, avoidance of homophony, areal borrowing, and language death—supplementary principles are required for explicating the full picture of linguistic change and for explaining seeming exceptions to the regularity of sound change. In each of these cases, the general assumption of regularity for sound change is necessary in order to recognize the potentially exceptional forms which these supplementary principles explain.

NOTES

1. Chol forms are cited from Aulie and Aulie 1978, Tzotzil examples from Delgaty and Sánchez 1978.

2. Several other Mayan examples also exhibit deflected reflexes due to euphemistic or symbolic tendencies, for example:

PM	*tsa:ʔ 'excrement'
Huastec	taʔ
Pokomchi	sa:ʔ (expected tsaʔ)
Teco	čaːʔ (expected tsa:ʔ)
Mam	ča (expected tsa:ʔ)
Tzeltal	tsaʔ
Tzotzil	tsoʔ
Cholan	*taʔ (expected *tsaʔ)
Yucatecan	*taʔ (expected *tsaʔ)

The *ts* is the expected reflex in all these languages.

For another example, Kaufman (1994) presented cases of seemingly exceptional sound changes in Huastec which are due to onomatopoeia (and sound symbolism)—I quote his conclusion for one of these: "*c* and *c'* [*ts'*] were very common, and in Potosino [one of the two major dialects of Huastec] resisted shifting to [ts, ts'] in [onomatopoeic roots], though they shifted virtually without exception in the general lexicon" (72).

3. Proto-Cholan forms cited here are from Kaufman and Norman 1984.

4. It is, of course, to be borne in mind that there is a potential danger in recognizing the workings of onomatopoeia and affective symbolism as occasionally complicating otherwise regular sound changes. It creates the potential for indiscriminate scholars to abuse this by asserting (but not substantiating) that onomatopoeia and affective/expressive symbolism explain exceptions that they have otherwise failed to account for. It is important to caution against a laissez-faire wielding of these. Appeal to these factors should be a matter of last resort and should require strong prima facie evidence for making such assumptions, for instance when the forms involved clearly suggest the possibility of onomatopoeia or affective/expressive symbolism from their meanings and from the fact that the exception is not isolated to a single form, but involves others of similar character.

5. Interestingly, in the southwestern area, the two vowel sounds remain distinct and the word *quean* still survives there.

6. This example is not altogether uncontroversial. Sanskrit has indigenous rules which also result in retroflexed consonants, for instance the famous ruki rule; it might be argued that such native rules first introduced retroflexed variants of native sounds into the language, which then made sounds in other environments susceptible to the sporadic retroflexion due to language contact. While this could be the case, it is not necessary to view the ruki rule as being strictly about retroflexion, since both Iranian and Slavic have

their own version of the ruki rule which show that *s* is backed in this environment (ultimately becoming *x* in Slavic), but not necessarily retroflexed. The retroflexion in the Indo-Aryan ruki rule may well itself have something to do with Dravidian contact. (Cf. Andersen 1968, Campbell 1976: 190, Kuipers 1967: 98.) If this example proves too controversial for some, plenty of other cases exist of such borrowed sounds (cf. Campbell 1976).

REFERENCES

Andersen, H. (1968). IE **s* after *i, u, r, k* in Baltic and Slavic. *Acta Linguistica Hafniensis* 11: 171–90.

Andersen, J. T. (1990). *Linguistics in America 1769 – 1924*. Routledge, London.

Anttila, R. (1972). *An introduction to historical and comparative linguistics*. MacMillan, London.

Aulie, H. W. and E. W. de Aulie. (1978). *Diccionario Ch'ol-Español, Español-Ch'ol*. Serie de Vocabularios y Diccionarios Indígenas, Mariano Silva y Aceves, no. 21. Instituto Lingüístico de Verano, Mexico.

Bach, A. (1969). *Deutsche Mundartsforschung*, 3rd ed. Carl Winter, Heidelberg.

Baldi, P. (1990). Introduction: the comparative method. In P. Baldi, ed., *Linguistic change and reconstruction methodology* 1–13. Mouton de Gruyter, Berlin.

Bloomfield, L. (1925). On the sound system of Central Algonquian. *Language* 1: 130–56.

———. (1928). A note on sound-change. *Language* 4: 99–100.

———. ([1931]1946). Algonquian. In H. Hoijer, ed., *Linguistic structures of Native America* 85–129. Viking Fund Publications in Anthropology, no. 6. The Viking Fund, New York.

Boretzky, N. (1982). Das indogermanische Sprachwandelmodell und Wandel in exotischen Sprachen. *Zeitschrift für vergleichende Sprachforschung* 95: 49-80.

———. (1984). The Indo-Europeanist model of sound change and genetic affinity and its application to exotic languages. *Diachronica* 1: 1–51.

Burrow, T. (1971). Spontaneous cerebrals in Sanskrit. *Bulletin of the School of Oriental and African Studies* 34: 133–4.

Campbell, L. (1971). Historical linguistics and Quichean linguistic prehistory. PhD diss., Univ. of California, Los Angeles.

———. (1973). On glottalic consonants. *International Journal of American Linguistics* 39: 44–6.

———. (1974). On conditions on sound change. In J. Anderson and C. Jones, eds., *Historical linguistics: Proceedings of the First International Conference on Historical Linguistics*. Vol. 2, *Theory and description in phonology* 88–96. North Holland, Amsterdam.

———. (1975). Constraints on sound change. In K.-H. Dahlstedt, ed., *The Nordic languages and modern linguistics: Proceedings of the Second International Conference of Nordic and General Linguistics* 388–406. Almqvist and Wiksell, Stockholm.

———. (1976). Language contact and sound change. In W. M. Christie Jr., ed., *Current progress in historical linguistics: Proceedings of the Second International Conference on Historical Linguistics* 111–94. North Holland, Amsterdam.

———. (1977). *Quichean linguistic prehistory*. University of California Publications in Linguistics, no. 81. University of California Press, Berkeley and Los Angeles.

———. (1994). Language death. In R. E. Asher and J. M. Y. Simpson, eds., *The encyclopedia of language and linguistics*. Vol. 4: 1960–68. Pergamon Press, Oxford.

Campbell, L. and M. Muntzel. (1989). The structural consequences of language death. In N. Dorian, ed., *Investigating obsolescence: Studies in language death* 181–96. Studies in the social and cultural foundations of language, no. 7. Cambridge University Press, Cambridge.

Campbell, L. and J. Ringen. (1981). Teleology and the explanation of sound change. In W. U. Dressler, O. E. Pfeiffer, and J. R. Rennison, eds., *Phonologica* 57–68. Innsbrücker Beiträge zur Sprachwissenschaft, Innsbruck.

Christy, C. (1983). *Uniformitarianism in linguistics*. John Benjamins, Amsterdam.

Cook, E.-D. (1989). Is phonology going haywire in dying languages? Phonological variations in Chipewyan and Sarcee. *Language in Society* 18: 235–55.

Delbrück, B. ([1880]1882). *Introduction to the study of language: A critical survey of the history and meth-

ods of comparative philology of the Indo-European languages. English Translation of (1880). *Einleitung in das Sprachstudium: Ein Beitrag zur Methodik der vergleichenden Sprachforschung.* Breitkopf and Härtel, Leipzig.

Delgaty, A. H. V. de and A. R. Sánchez. (1978). *Diccionario Tzotzil de San Andrés con Variaciones Dialectales, Tzotzil-Español, Español-Tzotzil.* Serie de Vocabularios y Diccionarios Indígenas, Mariano Silva y Aceves, no. 22. Instituto Lingüístico de Verano, Mexico.

Dixon, R. M. W. (1990). Summary report: Linguistic change and reconstruction in the Australian language family. In P. Baldi, ed., *Linguistic change and reconstruction methodology* 393–401. Mouton de Gruyter, Berlin.

Dressler, W. (1972). On the phonology of language death. *Papers from the 12th Regional Meeting, Chicago Linguistic Society* 448–57.

Gilliéron, J. and M. Roques. (1912). *Étude de géographie linguistique.* Champion, Paris.

Haas, M. (1969). *The prehistory of languages.* Mouton, The Hague.

Hale, K. (1964). Classification of the Northern Paman languages, Cape York Peninsula, Australia: A research report. *Oceanic Linguistics* 3: 248–65.

———. (1976). Phonological developments in particular Northern Paman languages, and phonological developments in a Northern Paman language: Uradhi. In P. Sutton, ed., *Languages of Cape York* 7–49. Australian Institute of Aboriginal Studies, Canberra.

Hockett, C. (1948). Implications of Bloomfield's Algonquian studies. *Language* 24: 17–31. Reprinted in (1970) *A Leonard Bloomfield anthology.* Indiana University Press, Bloomington.

Hoenigswald, H. (1990). Is the "comparative" method general or family-specific? In P. Baldi, ed., *Linguistic change and reconstruction methodology* 375–83. Mouton de Gruyter, Berlin.

Johnson, S. (1990). Social parameters of linguistic change in an unstratified Aboriginal society. In P. Baldi, ed., *Linguistic change and reconstruction methodology* 419–33. Mouton de Gruyter, Berlin.

Kaufman, T. (1994). Symbolism and change in the sound system of Huastec. In L. Hinton, J. Nichols and J. J. Ohala, eds., *Sound Symbolism*, 63–75. Cambridge University Press, Cambridge.

Kaufman, T. and W. M. Norman. (1984). An outline of Proto-Cholan phonology, morphology, and vocabulary. In J. S. Justeson and L. Campbell, eds., *Phoneticism in Mayan hieroglyphic writing* 77–166. Institute for Mesoamerican Studies, Publication no. 9. State University of New York, Albany.

King, R. (1969). *Generative grammar and historical linguistics.* Prentice Hall, Englewood Cliffs, N.J.

Kiparsky, P. (1965). Phonological change. PhD diss., Massachusetts Institute of Technology.

Kuipers, F. B. J. (1967). The genesis of a linguistic area. *Indo-Iranian Journal* 10: 81–102.

Laughlin, R. M. (1988). *The great Tzotzil dictionary of Santo Domingo Zinacantán.* Vol. 1: *Tzotzil-English.* Smithsonian Contributions to Anthropology, no. 31. Smithsonian Institution Press, Washington, D.C.

Meillet, A. (1925). *La méthode comparative en linguistique historique.* H. Aschehoug, Oslo.

Meillet, A. and M. Cohen. (1924). *Les langues du monde.* E. Champion, Paris.

Menner, R. (1936). The conflict of homonyms in English. *Language* 12: 229–44.

Mühlhäusler, P. (1989). On the causes of accelerated linguistic change in the Pacific area. In L. Breivik and E. Jahr, eds., *Language change: Contributions to the study of its causes* 137–72. Mouton de Gruyter, Berlin.

Nichols, J. (1971). Diminutive consonant symbolism in western North America. *Language* 47: 826–48.

Öhmann, E. (1934). Über Homonymie und Homonyme im Deutschen. *Suomalaisen Tiedeakatemian Toimituksia, series B*, 32: 1–143.

Osthoff, H. (1883). *Schriftsprache und Mundart.* Richter, Hamburg.

Osthoff, H., and K. Brugmann. (1878). *Morphologische Untersuchungen auf dem Gebiete der indogermanischen Sprachen.* S. Hirzel, Leipzig.

Rivet, P. (1925). Les Australiens en Amérique. *Bulletin de la Société Linguistique de Paris* 26: 23–63.

Sapir, E. (1913, 1915–1919) Southern Paiute and Nahuatl: A study in Uto-Aztecan. Parts 1 and 2. *Journal de la Société des Américanists de Paris*, 10: 379–425, 11: 433–88. Part 2 is also printed (1915) *American Anthropologist* 17: 98–120.

———. (1929). The status of linguistics as a science. *Language* 5: 207–14. Reprinted (1949), in D. Mandelbaum, ed., *Selected writings of Edward Sapir in language, culture, and personality* 160–6. University of California Press, Berkeley and Los Angeles.

———. (1931). The concept of phonetic law as tested in primitive languages by Leonard Bloomfield. In

S. Rice, ed., *Methods in social science: A case book*, 297–306. University of Chicago Press, Chicago. Reprinted (1949) in D. Mandelbaum, ed., *Selected writings of Edward Sapir in language, culture, and personality*, 73–82. University of California Press, Berkeley and Los Angeles.

Sievers, E. (1876). *Grundzüge der Lautphysiologie zur Einführung in das Studium der Lautlehre der indogermanischen Sprachen*. Breikopf and Härtel, Leipzig.

Sommerfelt, A. (1938). *La langue et la société*. H. Aschoug, Oslo.

Sweet, H. (1900). *The history of language*. J. M. Dent & Co., London.

Ultan, Russell. (1970). Size-sound symbolism. *Working papers on language universals* 3: 1–28. Stanford University.

4 Footnotes to a History of Cantonese: Accounting for the Phonological Irregularities

JOHN NEWMAN

1 INTRODUCTION

It is only natural that one's first priority in writing a phonological history of a language, or a language family, should be an account of the major developments which have taken place. Rules which affect hundreds of words in a language are attended to before minor rules affecting small numbers of words; changes which can be described as rule-governed are given more attention than those which appear to be idiosyncratic. I think this is only natural. One likes to have the larger picture in focus before one tries to understand the detail. This is true of the way in which history in general is approached. A person coming to learn about the history of, say, England typically learns, first of all, a few key dates, the names of the kings and queens, the dates of wars, and so on. But one can learn much (possibly more) about human nature from studying local history as well, where the players are not necessarily grand figures with power over thousands of lives and where events are of a far more mundane nature. In the same way, I believe one can learn much from the study of the minor rules and the occasional exceptions to rules in studying the phonological history of language.

Often, in fact, it is only when one comes to study the irregularities of sound changes that one can appreciate the interplay of forces often associated with sound change. As an example, consider the treatment of a major statement in the phonological history of German: Proto-Germanic *a remains a in Old High German, unless it occurs in an umlauting environment (which need not concern us here). In typical accounts of German historical phonology, such as Penzl (1969: 39), this development is briefly stated and exemplified with a few examples, and a reader could be forgiven for thinking that the rule is perfectly straightforward and exceptionless. It is only in the standard handbook of Braune & Mitzka (1967: 24–5) that one finds, in a footnote, references to exceptions to this rule.[1] The footnote includes references to nineteenth century research, in particular Singer (1886), which reveals a far more complicated (and interesting!) account of Proto-Germanic *a than is normally passed on to students of German historical linguistics. Singer (287–8) draws attention to two classes of exceptions to the rule, where *a appears as o: (a) before sonorants (l, r, and nasals) and (b) in unstressed syllables. Phonologically, these are interesting environments in so far as they refer to classes of sounds which play a role elsewhere in the evolution of German (and other languages). The Indo-European sonorants, for example, are exactly the sounds which develop an epenthetic u before them in Germanic; the vowels of unstressed syllables weaken in Middle High German. The minor developments which Singer focusses on give an insight, then, into natural classes of sounds in the same way that the better known and widely attested rules do. More importantly, studying such minor developments reveals something of the dynamic interplay between opposing trends, as pointed out by Singer himself:

> Wenn wir auf diese weise den neigungen der sprache nachgehn, so stossen wir auf die auffallende tatsache, dass dieselbe zu gleicher zeit conträren neigungen folgt. (1886: 291)
>
> [If we trace the tendencies of language in this way, we discover the remarkable fact that one and the same language is following contradictory tendencies at the same time.—My translation.]

When only the major historical rules are presented, one loses sight of the actual dynamics surrounding the implementation of the rule, and one could easily form the mistaken impression that phonological history is typically exceptionless (and exceedingly dull).

It is not only in introductory works meant for beginners in historical linguistics that one finds an emphasis on the regularities. The same emphasis is found in a large proportion of serious scholarly work. The prominence of the comparative method in historical linguistics, focussing as it does on the regular correspondences between languages, has presumably played its part in determining what avenues of research are rewarding. The more regularity one can discover in correspondences, the more successful one is in applying the comparative method. More and more, however, the irregularities swept under the carpet by the comparative method are being re-examined, especially in the light of Labov's work in sociolinguistics and the theory of lexical diffusion.

As for Cantonese, an account of the major historical phonological developments from Middle Chinese (to be described in the next section) can be found in Chen and Newman (1984–85). Irregularities in rules were noted in that account, but the discussion of them was necessarily brief and usually relegated to footnotes. It seems appropriate, now, to return to these irregularities and to discuss ways of dealing with them (without any presumption of the reader's familiarity with already published work on Cantonese). I will focus on irregularities which cannot be explained away— or rather which I will not explain away—by appealing to the commonly recognized causes of exception, namely analogical change influenced by morphology and dialect mixture. The former is irrelevant to the historical period which I am dealing with since there is no significant morphology in the language. Some interdialectal borrowing into Cantonese can be safely assumed, particularly the borrowing of 'literary' styles of pronunciation from prestigous dialects, but I will not be discussing irregularities due to such borrowing here. Instead I will focus on more unusual types of irregularity resulting from taboo associations, the influence of the written language, and certain types of rule interaction. I begin by discussing some important background to carrying out research on Chinese dialects.

2 PHILOLOGICAL VERSUS LINGUISTIC APPROACHES

It is interesting to reflect on the application of Western linguistic traditions, in particular the comparative method, to Chinese dialects. There is no shortage of examples of the comparative method being applied to non-Indo-European language families, and one has every reason to expect, therefore, that the comparative method would have been applied to the Chinese dialects by now. It may come as a surprise to the reader, then, to learn that there is no complete, published reconstruction of a parent language of all the Chinese dialects, arrived at entirely by application of the comparative method, as it is normally practised. We have reconstructions of earlier stages of the dialects in which comparative evidence does play some part, but to the best of my knowledge, there is no reconstruction based solely on the evidence of the modern dialects—at least there is no such reconstruction which is ever appealed to in historical work on Chinese. Nor do I see such a reconstruction being carried out in the future.

The main reason for this state of affairs is the dominance of a long and venerable philological tradition within Chinese culture. (See Chen 1980; Pulleyblank 1984: 129–45, and Norman 1988: 24–42 for more details.) This tradition, extending back for well over a thousand years, involved the compilation of dictionaries from which important information about the readings of characters can be obtained, relating to the tone, initial, and final of a character. The dictionaries did not communicate the information about the phonetic qualities of characters by resorting to any descriptive phonetic jargon, but relied instead upon a much more modest approach. Characters were grouped together in linguistically significant ways: All the words in the same tone appeared in together in one volume (or two, in the case of the numerically large *píng* tone class); within each tone, characters were grouped into rhyme classes; within each rhyme class, characters were grouped into homophone classes. An arrangement of characters in this way, simple as it is, clearly provides extremely useful information about the historical phonology of Chinese dialects.

Some of these dictionaries even went further. The *Qièyùn* is a dictionary of the utmost importance compiled in A.D. 601, and others after it (and possibly before it) made use of a particular kind of 'spelling' system. Key characters—those heading a subgroup of homophonous characters—were associated with a pair of characters, the first of which was alliterative with the key character (that is, started with the same consonant), the second of which rhymed with it. This can be exemplified with the key character 东, which is associated with the pair of characters 德 and 红 (the transcriptions are added here to show the phonological relationships):

东	is associated with	德	and	红
*$tuŋ^1$		*$tək^4$		*$yuŋ^1$
'east'		'virtue'		'red'
		the alliterating character	+	the rhyming character

A spelling system of this sort thus makes further systematic connections between characters, again without explicitly saying just what the pronunciation of the character in question is. It is the most practicable approach to indicating pronunciation when the intended audience is familiar with the language but not linguistically trained. It is similar to the approach adopted, for example, in Burchfield (1982), a guide to preferred pronunciations of English words, where one finds entries such as: *vitamin* : first syllable as in *wit*; *dour* : to rhyme with *poor* not *power*; *hegemony* : g as in *gun*.

There is a further important fact about the *Qièyùn* which makes it especially interesting for historical linguists. It is now agreed that the distinctions made in the dictionary were not based on any one dialect, but represented instead a kind of norm of pronunciation which incorporated all the possible distinctions of a number of dialects, that is, a diasystem. Earlier phonological distinctions which might have been eliminated in one dialect but preserved in another dialect would therefore have been represented in the dictionary. It set up distinctions which could be construed as historical reconstructions, even if it was compiled as a synchronic overview. The *Qièyùn* is valuable therefore not just because it is an ancient systematization of some Chinese language, but additionally it represents, in effect, a kind of reconstruction of Chinese dialects. The system implied by the *Qièyùn* is referred to as Middle Chinese (MC), corresponding to the Chinese term *zhōng-gǔ-yīn* 'the pronunciation of the Middle Antiquities'.

One can see, then, that there exists an indigenous philological tradition which demands respect because of its antiquity, thoroughness, and sophistication. When one comes to study the history of Chinese dialects, therefore, one is bound to defer to this tradition as the starting point.[2] The weight of the tradition is such that it would take an extremely brave (or arrogant) researcher to dismiss the philological evidence. Where one works with actual phonetic reconstructions of a parent language of the Chinese dialects, one is dealing with the *Qièyùn* system aided by the comparative method, not a system arrived at only by application of the comparative method. The first to make such a phonetic reconstruction, Bernhard Karlgren, proceeded in this way—'He [Karlgren] took the "algebraic" system laid down by the ancient Chinese linguists as given, and proceeded to compare those phonetically undecoded symbols with modern reflexes.' (Chen 1980: 314–5)—and others since him have proceeded in the same way.[3] Fortunately, this approach is not normally a source of frustration to the linguist trained in the comparative method, since the linguist's reconstructions of a parent language of the Chinese dialects will coincide for the most part with the systematization underlying the *Qièyùn*. This is not surprising in the light of the cross-dialectal basis of the *Qièyùn* alluded to above.

TABLE 4-1

	话 'word; talk'	花 'flower'	快 'quick'
Peking	xua³	xua¹ᴬ	k'uai³
Sūzhōu	ɦo³ᴮ	huɒ¹ᴬ (L)	k'uE³ᴬ (L)
		ho¹ᴬ (C)	k'uɒ³ᴬ (C)
Wēnzhōu	ɦo³ᴮ	xo¹ᴬ	k'a³ᴬ
Chángshā	fa³ᴮ	fa¹ᴬ	k'uai³ᴬ
Shuāngfēng	o³ᴮ	xo¹ᴬ	k'ua³ᴬ
Nánchāng	ɸua³ᴮ (L)	ɸua¹ᴬ	ɸuai³ᴬ
	ua³ᴮ (C)		
Méixiàn	fa³ᴬ	fa¹ᴬ	k'uai³ᴬ
Cantonese	wa³ᴮ	fa¹ᴬ	faːi³ᴬ
Xiàmén	hua³ᴮ (L)	hua¹ᴬ (L)	k'uai³ᴬ
	ue³ᴮ (C)	hue¹ᴬ (C)	
Cháozhōu	ue³ᴮ	hue¹ᴬ	k'uai³ᴬ
Fúzhōu	ua³ᴮ	xua¹ᴬ	k'uai³ᴬ

There *are*, however, instances where a reconstruction arrived at by the comparative method does differ from the *Qièyùn* categorizations, giving rise to a conflict between what I will call philological and linguistic approaches in reconstructing protoforms. By 'philological' I mean here an approach which preserves the integrity of the rhyme classes implicit in traditional rhyme dictionaries, as opposed to a 'linguistic' approach involving a comparative method relying on a comparison of forms in contemporary dialects. There is no suggestion here that the *Qièyùn* was mistaken in its treatment of such forms. What it means, presumably, is that some changes have occurred, or some distinctions have become lost, in all the modern dialects available to us, in which case the comparative method fails to throw light on the earlier history.

As a case in point, consider the finals (what comes after the initial consonants) in the forms for 'word', 'flower', and 'quick' in the modern dialects given in Table 4-1.[4] On the basis of such comparative data, a linguist would be inclined to see two classes of finals represented in the data: one final which could be reconstructed as *-ua evident in the words for 'word' and 'flower' and a second final, possibly *-uai, evident in the word for 'quick'. The exact phonetic value of the reconstructions can hardly be established on the basis of such limited data. All that is important, for the present purposes, is to recognize that the evidence points to the reconstruction of an -i offglide in the word 'quick' and no such offglide in the other two words. Admittedly, the offglide in the word for 'quick' is missing in the case of Sūzhōu and Wēnzhōu, and so we must posit for these two dialects (the two Wú dialects) an historical rule which removes the offglide. This is not in itself problematical. One might in fact see evidence of an earlier palatal offglide in the literary pronunciation -uE in Sūzhōu. In any case, the reflexes of the 'quick' final in the Wú dialects are still clearly distinct from the reflexes of the finals in the other two words. Thus, even when the offglide is deleted in the Wú dialects, the result points to keeping the final in the word for 'quick' distinct from the final in the other two words. It may come as a surprise, then, to learn that the MC reconstructions which one works with in Chinese historical phonology are:

话	花	快
'word; talk'	'flower'	'quick'
*ηuai^2	*xua^1	*$k'uai^3$

The reconstructions for 'flower' and 'quick' present no difficulties to the comparative linguist, but a reconstruction of *ηuai^2 for 'word' does. When one tries to account for the development of the MC *-uai final, one must treat the non-appearance of the offglide in all the 'word' reflexes as exceptional in *every* dialect. Other words which show a similar MC offglide unwarranted by the comparative method are: 罢 'to cease' *bai^2 (Cantonese wa³ᴮ), 挂 'to hang' *$kuai^3$ (Cantonese kwa³ᴬ), 画 'to draw' *ηuai^3 (Cantonese wa²ᴮ).

As another example, consider the fate of MC *-p and *-t (in syllable-final position). These are subject to various types of change in the dialects: In Peking dialect, for example, they disappear altogether; in Fúzhōu, they both become glottal stops; in Nánchāng, the distinction is neutralized in favour of -t. In Cantonese, the final stops are preserved. These regular developments can be seen in the words 'to hunt' and 'to split' shown in Table 4-2. Compare these forms with the reflexes and the MC reconstruction for 捏 'to hold between fingers'. The comparative data points to a *-p for both 'to hold between fingers' and 'to hunt', in contrast to a *-t final for 'to split', without any need for exceptional reflexes in the dialects. The MC reconstruction of 'to hold between fingers', on the other hand, requires us to treat the appearance of a final -p in Cantonese, Xiàmén, etc. as irregular reflexes of MC *-t. But, again, this is an irregularity which only appears as such when one takes the philological evidence as primary.

There are also irregularities which must be recognized as such regardless of which approach one takes as basic (the philological or the comparative linguistic). An example of this is the irregular replacement in Cantonese of MC *-p by -t in the word 'to press', as shown in Table 4-3. In this case, the comparative method agrees with

TABLE 4-2

	捏 'to hold between fingers'	猎 'to hunt'	裂 'to split'
MC	*niat⁴	*liap⁴	*liat⁴
Peking	nie¹ᴬ	lie³	lie³
Sūzhōu	nia?⁴ᴮ	la?⁴ᴮ	liɤ?⁴ᴮ
Wēnzhōu	ɲia⁴ᴮ	liɛ⁴ᴮ, li⁴ᴮ	li⁴ᴮ
Chángshā	ɲie⁴	nie⁴	nie⁴
Shuāngfēng	ɲi¹ᴮ	nie¹ᴮ	nie¹ᴮ
Nánchāng	ɲiɛt⁴	liɛt⁴	liɛt⁴
Méixiàn	ɲiap⁴	liap⁴ᴮ	liɛt⁴ᴮ
Cantonese	nip⁴ᴮ	lip⁴ᴮ	lit⁴ᴮ
Xiàmén	liap⁴ᴬ	liap⁴ᴮ (L)	liat⁴ᴮ (L)
		la?⁴ᴮ (C)	le?⁴ᴮ (C)
			li?⁴ᴮ (C)
Cháozhōu	niəp⁴ᴮ	la?⁴ᴮ	li?⁴ᴮ
Fúzhōu	nie?⁴ᴮ	la?⁴ᴮ	lie?⁴ᴮ

TABLE 4-3

	压 'to press'	鸭 'duck'
MC	$*ʔap^4$	$*ʔap^4$
Peking	ia^{1A}	ia^{1A}
Sūzhōu	$ɒʔ^{4A}$	$iaʔ^{4A}$ (L), $aʔ^{4A}$ (C)
Wēnzhōu	a^{4A}	a^{4A}
Chángshā	ia^4 (L), $ŋa^4$ (C)	ia^4 (L), $ŋa^4$ (C)
Shuāngfēng	$ŋa^{3A}$	$ŋa^{1B}$
Nánchāng	$ŋat^4$	a^4
Méixiàn	ap^4	ap^4
Cantonese	$ŋa{:}t^{4A}$	$ŋa{:}p^{4A}$
Xiàmén	ap^{4A} (L), $teʔ^{4A}$ (C)	ap^{4A} (L), $aʔ^{4A}$ (C)
Cháozhōu	$iəp^{4A}$	$aʔ^{4A}$
Fúzhōu	$aʔ^{4A}$ (L), $taʔ^{4A}$ (C)	$aʔ^{4A}$

the philological evidence in treating the final of 'to press' as identical with the final of 'duck', with the Cantonese reflex representing an irregularity.

As a final and striking example of conflict between the philological and comparative linguistic approaches, consider the MC reconstruction of *lap for 拉 'to pull' shown in Table 4–4. Here we see no trace at all of a final *-p in the comparative data. The offglide -i in Cantonese is exceptional, but one would still not posit a final *-p in attempting to account for it. In all the other dialects, there is no hint of any final stop or offglide. This should be compared with 腊 'sacrifice; salted meats' where we see p as the the regular reflex of MC *-p in various dialects, including Cantonese. When one works with a MC reconstruction of *lap^4 for 'pull', therefore, one must recognize the reflexes as exceptional in *every* dialect.

There is undeniably a great advantage to being able to utilize the *Qièyùn* material, and this has been recognized by all who have studied Chinese historical phonolo-

TABLE 4-4

	拉 'to pull'	腊 'sacrifice; salted meats'
MC	$*lap^4$	$*lap^4$
Peking	la^{1A}	la^3
Sūzhōu	$lɒ^{1A}$	$laʔ^{4B}$
Wēnzhōu	la^{1A}	la^{4B}
Chángshā	na^{1A}	na^{4A}
Shuāngfēng	na^{1B}	na^{1B}
Nánchāng	la^{1A}	lat^{4A}
Méixiàn	la^{1A}	lap^{4B}
Cantonese	$la{:}i^{1A}$	$la{:}p^{4B}$
Xiàmén	la^{1A}	$liap^{4B}$
Cháozhōu	la^{1A}	$laʔ^{4B}$
Fúzhōu	la^{1A}	$laʔ^{4B}$

gy. It allows us to project back to an early stage of Chinese which, in some cases, cannot be retrieved simply by the comparative method. At the same time, there are certain complexities which arise just because one is relying primarily on the *Qièyùn* categorizations rather than the comparative method. In particular, there are forms whose reflexes appear as irregular in all the dialects which would be perfectly regular, or at least less irregular, had one relied solely on the comparative method for one's reconstruction.[5] Interestingly, the special nature of these 'philologically induced' irregularities shows up when one looks at statistics of correspondences between MC and Cantonese, and it is thus appropriate to consider the relevance of these statistics in researching the history of Cantonese.

3 SOME STATISTICS

It is possible, when researching the phonological history of Chinese dialects, to obtain quick statistics on ancient-modern correspondences by using the Chinese Dictionary on Computer (DOC), the computerized database incorporating the information contained in *Zìhuì*, compiled at Berkeley. By using DOC, one can obtain immediate figures for correspondences for all the categories (tones, initials, finals). The statistics for correspondences between MC initials and their dialectal reflexes, obtained in this way, have in fact been published separately as part of Cheng and Wang (1971). In studying the development of initials in the Chinese dialects, then, we already have available to us a quantified summary of changes in each of the dialects. To illustrate the usefulness of these statistics in identifying exceptional changes, I will consider the MC stops/affricates and their Cantonese reflexes.

Figure 4-1 summarizes these correspondences. The reconstructed MC initials appear on the left in the order bilabial stops, dental stops, dental affricates, retroflex affricates, palatal stops, palatal affricates, and velar stops. The Cantonese reflexes of these initials include the zero sign Ø, meaning a consonant has been deleted. From Figure 4-1 one can immediately see the major correspondences by observing where the clustering of numbers occurs; these major correspondences can be summarized as shown in Figure 4-2. Forms which depart from this pattern stand out in a most striking way in Figure 4-1 as isolated numbers in what is otherwise an empty space. In this way, our attention is drawn immediately to certain unusual developments. There are, for example, twelve MC *k'* initials which have *f* reflexes, all occurring in words such as 寬 'roomy' MC *$k'uan^1$* > fun^{1A}, where *k'* is followed by a labial glide. Presumably, the path of development here involves spirantization of *k'* to *x*, followed by a coalescence of the velar fricative and labial onlglide, *xw* > *f*. Each of these rules is in fact independently supported in Cantonese, although the spirantization process is sensitive to literary versus colloquial distinctions. There is no reason, therefore, to think of these twelve forms as in any way exceptional. The single MC *k* which is deleted occurs as the initial in 鍋 'pot' MC *kua^1* > $wɔ^{1A}$. While this is exceptional behaviour for a MC *k*, it is reminiscent of the regular deletion of MC *y* when followed by a labial onglide, as in 混 'to mix' MC *$yuən^2$* > wan^{3B}. The disappearance of the initial in the word for 'pot', though exceptional, is not entirely unusual because of the similarity of the change to what happens with the velar fricative.

MC	p	p'	f	t	t'	n	l	ts	ts'	s	k	k'	h	∅
p	82	(5)	33											
p'	(1)	39	14											
b	29	42	35											
t				68	(2)	(1)								
t'				(2)	58									
d				51	47									
ts								83	(2)					
ts'								(1)	53					
dz								29	29					
ṭṣ								26						
ṭṣ'									26					
ḍẓ								9	6	(5)				
t̂				(1)				37						
t̂'								(1)	11					
d̂				(1)				24	28	(2)				
tś								70						
tś'								(3)	25					
dz								(1)		15				
k							(1)				215	(12)		(1)
k'			12								(3)	28	47	
g											21	30		

◯ 'exceptional' exceptions   ◯ 'unremarkable' exceptions

Figure 4-1

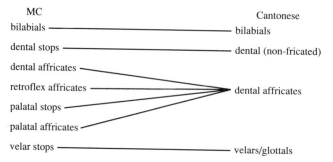

Figure 4-2

Putting aside these changes, we are left with just three cases where there has been a switch across the major categories of Cantonese initials. These three cases are shown with a dark circle in Figure 4-1. The words are:

爹	'father'	MC $*tia^1$	Cantonese $t\varepsilon^{1A}$
瞪	'to stare'	MC $*di\partial\eta^3$	Cantonese $ta\eta^{3B}$
脸	'face; honour'	MC $*kiam^2$	Cantonese lim^{2B}

It turns out, in fact, that the development of the initials in these words is exceptional in *all* the dialects, not just Cantonese. As such, they fall into the same class of irregularities discussed in the preceding section, namely those which arise out of assuming the philological tradition rather than just applying the comparative method.

Within the boxes in Figure 4-1 where there are clusters of numbers, one can identify other exceptional developments—these are shown with a lighter circle. A number without any circle around it indicates that there is a well-motivated phonological rule to account for the development of these forms. So, for example, the MC voiced stops and affricates have both aspirated and unaspirated reflexes, conditioned by the tonal categories. There is, however, no regular historical process which brings about aspiration or de-aspiration of the voiceless stops or affricates. Thus, a change in aspiration of these initials must be considered exceptional. One can easily see that the MC voiceless initials in Figure 4-1 have a relatively small number of exceptions with respect to aspiration.

The advantage of a table like that given in Figure 4-1 is that it enables the linguist to immediately make at least a tentative distinction between 'extraordinary' and 'ordinary' exceptions by distinguishing the 1s which stand by themselves and do not form part of a recurring pattern, and those 1s and 2s which cluster with the major correspondences. Admittedly this can only be an initial and tentative distinction pending a closer examination of these isolated 1s. Nevertheless, by making such a distinction within the set of exceptions, one can set oneself more realistic goals in explaining away the exceptions. By restricting one's attention to the 'ordinary' exceptions of a particular dialect, one can more realistically hope to give some phonological account of the developments.

4 THE INFLUENCE OF CHARACTERS

A number of exceptions can be attributed to the influence of related characters. The reading of a relatively rare character, often limited to the literary layer, changes to become identical to the reading of a more common character which is graphically very similar. Hashimoto (1972) details suspicious cases of such 'analogical readings', looking at such changes case by case, and I am indebted to her for the groundwork which she has done in this area. As a typical example, consider the following two characters:

揣 'to estimate (L)' MC $*t\!\!\!\!/s'ui^2$ should have become $ts'\alpha y^{2A}$, but instead becomes $ts'yn^{2A}$, presumably by analogy with:

喘 'to pant' MC $*t\!\!\!\!/s'yan^2 > ts'yn^{2A}$ (which is regular).

Since there is no semantic association between the two words, one naturally looks to the written forms of the words to find an association. The characters, as can be seen, are very similar. They differ only in their radicals (on the left side of each character), with the phonetic element (on the right side of each character) the same in each case. Becaue of the striking similarity in the written form of the two characters, it seems reasonable to infer that the graphic similarity has influenced the reading of the first character. It may seem far-fetched to suppose that the written form should be so crucial in a language in which most of the speakers would have been illiterate in the past. But one must remember that we are dealing here with the reading of a character from the literary layer rather than colloquial spoken language, and to the extent that speakers would know the pronunciation of the morpheme, they would tend also to know the written character.

The exceptional reading in the previous example involved a change in the pronunciation of the final part of the syllable. It can also involve a change in the expected manner of articulation of the initial, especially in the feature *aspiration*:

柏 'cypress' MC $*pac^4$ should have become $pa:k^{4A}$, but instead becomes $p'a:k^{4A}$, presumably by analogy with:
拍 'to clap' MC $*p'ac^4 > p'a:k^{4A}$ (which is regular)

汀 'land along a river (L)' MC $*t'e\acute{n}^1$ should have become $t'i\eta^{1A}$, but instead becomes $ti\eta^{1A}$, presumably by analogy with:
丁 'man' MC $*te\acute{n}^1 > ti\eta^{1A}$ (which is regular)

It can involve a change in the place of articulation of the initial:

晌 'part of the day' MC $*\acute{s}ia\eta^2$ should have become $s\oe\eta^{2A}$, but instead becomes $h\oe\eta^{2A}$, presumably by analogy with:
响 'sound' MC $*xia\eta^2 > h\oe\eta^{2A}$, or 向 'direction' MC $*xia\eta^3 > h\oe\eta^{3A}$

It can involve a change of tone:

抓 'to grab, scratch' MC $*\mathrm{t}\d{s}au^1$ should have become $\mathrm{t}\d{s}a:u^{1A}$, but becomes instead $\mathrm{t}\d{s}a:u^{2A}$, presumably by analogy with:
爪 'claw' MC $*\mathrm{t}\d{s}au^2 > \mathrm{t}\d{s}au^{2A}$

妨 'to hinder' MC $*f'ya\eta^1$ should have become $f\mathrm{\mathit{ɔ}}\eta^{1A}$, but instead becomes $f\mathrm{\mathit{ɔ}}\eta^{1B}$, presumably by analogy with:
防 'to guard against' MC $*vya\eta^1 > f\mathrm{\mathit{ɔ}}\eta^{1B}$ (which is regular)

It may appear as if there are two exceptional features (tone and intial) in the readings of some characters:

唤 'to call out' MC $*xuan^3$ should have become fun^{3A}, but instead becomes wun^{3B}, presumably by analogy with:
换 'to exchange' MC $*yuan^3 > wun^{3B}$

堤 'dyke' MC $*tei^1$ should have become tai^{1A}, but instead becomes $t'ai^{1B}$, presumably by analogy with:

提 'to carry' MC $*dei^1 > t'ai^{1B}$ (which is regular)

In such cases, however, the low (B) tones would follow if one assumes the initials first changed their voicing (x to y, t to d).

In all the previous cases, there is no semantic basis for relating the two characters. There are some other cases, however, where a semantic connection is arguably present, in addition to the shared phonetic element:

佃 'to rent land (L)' MC $*den^3$ should have become tin^{3B}, but instead becomes $t'in^{3B}$, presumably by analogy with:

田 'field' MC $*den^1 > t'in^{1B}$ (which is regular)

悄 'quiet (L)' MC $*ts'iau^2$ should have become $ts'iu^{2A}$, but instead becomes siu^{1A}, presumably by analogy with:

宵 'night' MC $*siau^1 > siu^{1A}$ (which is regular)

肚 'animal's stomach' MC $*to^2$ should have become tou^{2A}, but instead becomes $t'ou^{2B}$, presumably by analogy with another reading and meaning of the same character:

肚 'human stomach' MC $*do^2 > t'ou^{2B}$

It is very rare to be able to establish the influence of some other semantically related but graphically unrelated (in both simplified and traditional), character. Hashimoto (1972: 655) suggests the following:

什 'miscellaneous' MC $*\acute{z}ep^4$ should have become sap^{4B}, but instead becomes $tsa:p^{4B}$, presumably due to the influence of:

杂 'miscellaneous' MC $*ȡap^4 > tsa:p^{4B}$

5 WORD ASSOCIATIONS

The importance of taboo associations of morphemes in the history of Peking has been well demonstrated by Stimson (1966). In the history of Cantonese, too, one can see the effects of taboo in certain phonological irregularities.

Consider *kau* type syllables. MC *-u* and *-iu* both regularly give rise to Cant. *au*, including those cases where the final follows velar initials. Some examples of these changes are shown in Table 4-5. In the light of these regular developments, we would expect to find kau^{1A} as the reflex of MC $*k(i)u^1$. It is of some interest, therefore, that MC $*k(i)u^1$ syllables do not, in Hashimoto's (1972) data, develop in this way, as Table 4-6 shows. *Zihui* in fact does show kau^{1A} as the reflex for words in this category without any commentary on a taboolike quality. I will follow here Hashimoto's description, which differs from *Zihui* in its description of these two forms, but

TABLE 4-5

		MC	Cantonese
狗	'dog'	$*ku^2$	kau^{2A}
苟	'careless'	$*ku^2$	kau^{2A}
构	'to construct'	$*ku^3$	kau^{3A}
九	'nine'	$*kiu^2$	kau^{2A}
救	'to rescue'	$*kiu^3$	ka^{3A}

which accords better with information I have obtained from native speakers. The ŋau^{1A} form is unremarkable as an alternative to au^{1A}, since [ŋ] occurs as a variant of the zero initial in a number of forms, but the disappearance of the MC $*k$ in 'hook' and 'to cancel' is quite exceptional. In *Zìhuì*, there is only one such instance: 锅 MC $*kwak^1$ 'pot, boiler' > Cant. wɔ^{1A}. In this case, however, a MC reconstruction of $*\gamma wak$ can also be posited, as in the *Zìbiǎo* (1981) and Hashimoto (1972), in which case the elision of the velar fricative before the velar glide is perfectly regular. The aspiration of MC $*k$ evident in 'ditch' and 'turtledove' might appear less exceptional, since there are some other forms which show the same change (in the *Zìhuì* data, 12 forms have kʻ out of a total of 228 from MC $*k$). In a number of cases, the aspiration can be attributed to analogical readings of more common characters, but this does not appear to be the case with the characters for 'ditch' and 'turtledove'. We are left therefore with a pair of phonologically irregular changes to the initial, with the consequence that there are no reflexes of the kau^{1A} type in modern Cantonese.

In fact it is not difficult to find an explanation for these odd developments. There exists in Cantonese an extremely vulgar word kau^{1A} 'penis' (which is however used as an obscenity and for which my informants were not able to provide a character). The existence of this word makes the kau^{1A} syllable taboo, and it is the avoidance of this taboo syllable which motivates the irregular phonological developments. (This connection between the taboo syllable and the historical irregularities can be found, incidentally, in Hashimoto 1972: 641.) There are other Cantonese words which are similarly obscene, namely lan^{2A} 'penis' and hai^{1A} 'vagina', although these are not the expected reflexes of any MC forms and do not appear to motivate any exceptional changes. Hashimoto (1972: 658) does speculate on a possible connection between the taboo lan^{2A} and a pronunciation of lœn^{1B} for 崑 'the second character in the name of the Kunlun Mountains' and 论 lœn^{3A} 'to discuss', instead of lan. In these cases, however, there is no need to resort to avoidance of the taboo syllable, since both lœn and lan are almost equally likely as reflexes of MC $*luən$. Furthermore, the taboo

TABLE 4-6

		MC	Cantonese
钩	'hook'	$*ku^1$	au^{1A}, ŋau^{1A}
勾	'to cancel'	$*ku^1$	au^{1A}
沟	'ditch'	$*ku^1$	kʻau^{1A}
鸠	'turtledove'	$*kiu^1$	kʻau^{1A}

syllable occurs in Tone 2A, so that even a reflex of *lan* for these words would not be identical to the taboo syllable with its specific tone.

Apart from the *Zìhuì*, some older dictionaries do include *kau*[1A] pronunciations for some characters: Ball (1908) has the compound *pa:n*[1A] *kau*[1A] 'turtledove'; Cowles (1965), a dictionary compiled in the early part of this century, has a total of twelve characters to be read as *kau*[1A], none of which is pronounced in this way by my Hong Kong informant. Perhaps, then, *kau*[1A] has only established itself as a taboo syllable in the course of this century? The only occasions when my other informants allowed *kau*[1A] were in those cases where the *kau*[1A] morpheme occurred in their speech as part of a larger compound. So, for example, one informant only used it in the compound *pa:n*[1A] *kau*[1A] 'turtledove' referred to above; another informant only used it for the 'ditch' morpheme as part of a larger compound.

Another instance where word association appears to play a role concerns the MC rhyme *i*. This rhyme has three reflexes in Cantonese: *ai* after the labiovelars *k'w* and *kw*; *i* after after a sibilant or the zero initial; *ei* elsewhere. These developments are illustrated in Table 4-7.

There are two interesting exceptions to the preservation of -*i* after sibilants: the colloquial pronunciations of 死 'to die' MC *si²* > Cant. *sei*[2A] and 四 'four' MC *si³* > Cant. *sei*[3A]. (The literary pronunciations have a regular *i* final.) Some speakers distinguish the two forms differently, using *ši* for the regular cases and *si* just for the two words in question. Various hypotheses can be made about how such a state of affairs could have arisen—*sei* might be a vestige of an older pronunciation, or possibly it represents a later development; perhaps the word for 'to die' was the first to have the *sei* pronunciation, or perhaps it was the word for 'four', or perhaps both words began to be pronounced with the colloquial pronunciation more or less at the same time. Rather than speculate on the prehistory of these developments, I will just comment on the result which presents itself to us in modern Cantonese.

As the only two common forms which exhibit the syllable type *sei* in the contemporary language, the two words are distinguished as a special pair. The phonological oddity of the pair is matched by the easy association many speakers are able to make between the two wods and between the two concepts. So, for example, 'four' is traditionally held to be an unlucky number amongst Cantonese speakers who readily point out the phonetic similarity of the Cantonese words for 'four' and 'to die'.

TABLE 4-7

		MC	Cantonese
貴	'expensive'	*kui³*	kwai³A
亏	'to lose'	*k'ui¹*	k'wai¹A
丝	'silk'	*si¹*	si¹A
知	'to know'	*ti¹*	tsi¹A
以	'because of'	*i²*	ji²B
悲	'sad'	*pi¹*	pei¹A
梨	'pear'	*li¹*	lei¹B
基	'basis'	*ki¹*	kei¹A

Where the number 4 is a salient part of some price or label of some object, there is even an expression available in Cantonese which highlights the unfavourable connotations of 'four': sei^{2A} sei^{2A} $sɛŋ^{2A}$ 'die-die-sound', that is, 'sounds like death'. (Certain combinations of numbers can, however, allow 'four' to be used in a favourable manner: the number '148' jat^{4A} sei^{3A} pat^{4C}, for example, was regarded by one speaker as a lucky number because it sounds in Cantonese like 一世发 jat^{4A} sai^{3A} $fa:t^{4C}$ 'one (whole) lifetime rich'.)

A close association between the words for 'four' and 'to die' can be found in other Chinese dialects and Japanese. Zhang (185: 230), for example, notes the phonetic similarity between $siɹ^{2A}$ (one) pronunciation of 'to die' and $siɹ^{3A}$ 'four' in the Chongming (Wú) dialect and also observes that the word for 'four' is avoided. As an example, Zhang notes that the fourth younger brother is referred to as 'fifth younger brother' and the fourth uncle is referred to as 'fifth uncle' as a way of avoiding using the word for 'four'. In Japanese, the Kanji characters for 'four' and 'to die' are both read as *ši* and here, too, there is a traditional association of the two concepts. The number 42 *ši-ni*, for example, attracts a strong and unfavourable connotation on account of its homophony with the first two morphemes in the inflected verb form of 'to die' *šinimasu*. (Typically, there will be no room number 42 in Japanese hotels.)

Regardless of what the actual stages of evolution were, it seems reasonable to see the special association which exists between 'four' and 'to die' in the Chinese-Japanese cultural sphere as an important factor in the phonological development of the two words in Cantonese. Both words have undergone an exceptional development, with the result that their contemporary colloquial pronunciation makes them a very distinctive pair. This special phonological property of the two words reflects the special semantic bond which exists between them.

6 RULE INTERACTION

There is a tendency to view the history of Chinese dialects in terms of correspondences between MC and reflexes in the dialects and to see a set of such correspondences as the goal of writing a phonological history of a dialect. While it is helpful to identify such correspondences, an historical account based only on correspondences is tantamount to assuming only mutually non-interacting and unordered rules. The view of historical phonology implied in such accounts is extremely impoverished and unrealistic. A more realistic view of the time dimension in historical processes must make provision for a time span during which a rule takes effect, an order in which rules apply, and interaction between rules (cf. Wang 1978: 237–8). Some of the irregularities in the history of Cantonese are best understood, I believe, by positing particular types of rule interaction. I will examine three types of irregularity to illustrate this.

Consider, first of all, the fate of MC *a.[6] In general, MC *a's do not remain (short) a in Cantonese. Instead, they undergo one of three changes:

1. In cases where there is a preceding palatal onglide and no following segment, the vowel changes its quality to a front mid vowel. So, for example, 写 'to write' MC *sia^2 > $sɛ^{2A}$, 夜 'night' MC *ia^3 > $jɛ^{3B}$. (The combination of this

vowel with the velar onglide is generally only found after velar initials, in which case the velar onglide is treated as part of a complex initial kw, or $k'w$).

2. When MC $*a$ is flanked by segments in the final (onglide as well as off-glide/coda), it disappears: 建 'to build' MC $*kian^3 > kin^{3A}$, 儉 'thrifty, frugal' MC $*giam^2 > kim^{3B}$, 苗 'young plant' MC $*miau^1 > miu^{1B}$, 票 'ticket' MC $*p'iau^3 > p'iu^{3A}$. (Forms containing a MC $*u$ onglide before a MC $*a$ do not undergo this change, as the onglide undergoes separate developments.) The exact mechanism by which the a disappears is not entirely clear. Possibly, the deletion does not take place in one step, but rather passes through an umlauted -$i\varepsilon X$ stage, before disappearing altogether (as argued for in Newman 1985). We need only note here the result, which amounts to an elision of the a, with the original i onglide taking over the role of the syllable nucleus. We will simply refer to the relevant rule as NUCLEUS DELETION.

3. Where there is no preceding onglide, MC $*a$ lengthens: 奶 'milk' MC $*nai^2 > na:i^{2B}$, 閙 'to disturb' $*nau^3 > na:u^{3B}$, 慢 'slow' $*man^3 > ma:n^{3B}$. We will label this process LENGTH.

In short, MC $*a$ does not generally remain a in Cantonese. There is one distinct class of exceptions and that involves the MC final $*-iai$, which becomes -ai: 泥 'mud' MC $*niai^1 > nai^{1B}$; 閉 'closed' MC $*piai^3 > pai^{3A}$. To prevent NUCLEUS DELETION from applying just to the -iai final, that is, -$iai >$ (possibly -$i\varepsilon i$) $> -ii > i$, one would have to attach special conditions to an otherwise very general rule (a deletes between segments within the syllable), blocking the rule just in case the final segment is i. If possible, of course, one would like to dispense with special conditions on rules, allowing rules to be expressed in their most general and most natural way.

A low a vowel would be preserved if there were no palatal onglide. This could be achieved by assuming a rule of palatal dissimilation (PALATAL DISM), whereby the palatal offglide triggers dissimilation in the palatal onglide, that is, -$iai > -ai$. This is not an artifical device for removing the onglide, as dissimilation between onglides and codas of syllables is well attested in other Chinese dialects (cf. the rule of palatal dissimilation in the history of Peking dialect in Chen 1976: 191). In Cantonese, too, there is an historical process of dissimilation by means of which final labial consonants become dental/alveolar when there is a labial intial or onglide in the same syllable. This new -ai, which comes about by PALATAL DISM, may only come into existence after LENGTH has run its course. Otherwise, one would expect -ai to become -$a:i$ by LENGTH. Furthermore, PALATAL DISM must take place before NUCLEUS DELETION, otherwise we would be left with the development described above where the a disappears. The order we must postulate is therefore LENGTH, followed by PALATAL DISM, followed by NUCLEUS DELETION. The application of these rules is illustrated in Table 4-8.

It is possible, then, to account for 泥 'mud' MC $*niai^1 > nai^{1B}$ as resulting from the application of PALATAL DISM, without resorting to special conditions on other rules. This can be done in a straightforward way by assuming an ordering of rules with PALATAL DISM sandwiched between the other rules affecting the a nucleus. The preservation of the a nucleus just in the -iai final is therefore not exceptional—it follows from three general und uncomplicated rules taking effect in a particular order.

TABLE 4-8

	奶 'milk'	泥 'mud'	建 'to build'
MC	*nai^2	*niai^1	*kian^3
LENGTH	naːi^{2B}	—	—
PALATALDISM	—	nai^{1B}	—
NUCLEUS			
DELETION	—	—	kin^{3A}

TABLE 4-9

	笨 'stupid'	翻 'to turn'	揀 'to choose'
MC	*buən^2	*pyan^1	*kan^2
Labiodentalization	—	fuan^1	—
LAB-DISM	bən^2	fan^1	—
LENGTH	—	faːn^1	kaːn^2
Other rules	ban^{3B}	faːn^{1A}	kaːn^{2A}

Secondly, some irregularities can be understood as the result of a reversal of the usual rule order. A case in point concerns the rules of Labial Dissimilation (LAB-DISM) and LENGTH. The former removes an -u onglide after an initial labial; the latter lengthens -a when not preceded by an onglide, and LENGTH has already been referred to. By removing an onglide, LAB-DISM can create an environment in which LENGTH may apply. The normal order which one must assume for these two rules is in fact the feeding order in which both rules do indeed apply: LAB-DISM first, then LENGTH. These rules are illustrated in Table 4-9, with 翻 'to turn' MC *pyan^1 > faːn illustrating the application of both rules. If LENGTH were to apply before LAB-DISM in the history of faːn^{1A} 'to turn', then the nucleus a would not be lengthened. Thus, LAB-DISM before LENGTH is necessary in such cases.

However, there are a few forms where the reverse order must be assumed. These involve the MC final *-yai after labials, which shows up as Cantonese -ai, not -aːi as one would expect. The relevant forms are 肺 'lung' MC *p'yai^3 > fai^{3A}, 吠 'to bark' MC *byai^3 > fai^{3B}, 廢 'to cancel' MC *pyai^3 > fai^{3A} (these being all the instances of *-yai after labials).[7] The feeding order of LAB-DISM before LENGTH in (a) leads to wrong results; instead, one must assume the counterfeeding order of LENGTH before LAB-DISM in (b).

(a)

	肺 'lung'
MC	*p'yai^3
Labiodentalization	fuai^3
LAB-DISM	fai^3

LENGTH	fa:i^3
Other rules	fa:i^{3A} (wrong!)

(b)

	肺
	'lung'
MC	*$p'yai^3$
Labiodentalization	fuai^3
LENGTH	—
LAB-DISM	fai^3
Other rules	fai^{3A}

One might wish to avoid the necessity of a rule reversal by appealing to inter-dialectal borrowing for these three forms. It would be difficult to find motivation for borrowing, however, when the words for 'lung' and 'bark' are not literary words. In any case, there is no source for a fai pronunciation in the other dialects included in *Zìhuì*, as can be seen from the list below, which is representative of the three words under discussion:

	肺
	'lung'
Peking	fei^{3A}
Sūzhōu	fi^{3A}
Wēnzhōu	fei^{3A}
Chángshā	fei^{3A}
Shuāngfēng	xui^{3A}
Nánchāng	ɸui^{3A}
Méixiàn	fi^{3A}
Xiàmén	hui^{3A} (L), hi^{3A} (C)
Cháozhōu	hui^{3A}
Fúzhōu	xie^{3A}

One might argue that it is the feature of vowel *shortness* which is borrowed from, say Mandarin, rather than an actual vowel quality, but as such it would be a rather un-orthodox type of borrowing. Positing a reversal in rule order, therefore, seems to be the most straightforward way of handling these cases. One would also like to have an explanation for why there should have been a reversal of rules. Unfortunately, I am not in a position to provide such an explanation, though the theory of lexical diffu-sion does suggest itself.

As a third example, consider the fate of MC *-*iən* and *-*iət*. Generally, ə in these finals undergoes lowering to a in Cantonese, and the palatal onglide is removed by a late rule which completes the phonotactic restructuring of syllables. This is exempli-fied in Table 4-10. After MC dentals, however, these finals behave erratically: Some-times they end up with the a vowel and sometimes they end up with a æ vowel, as il-lustrated in Table 4-11. The total number of each type of reflex in Hashimoto's (1972) data is as in Table 4-12.

TABLE 4-10

		MC	Cantonese
宾	'guest'	$*pi\partial n^1$	pan^{1A}
贫	'poor'	$*bi\partial n^1$	$p'an^{1B}$
七	'seven'	$*ts'i\partial t^4$	$ts'at^{4A}$
失	'to lose'	$*\acute{s}i\partial t^4$	sat^{4A}
银	'silver'	$*\eta i\partial n^1$	ηan^{1B}
殷	'abundant'	$*\Uparrow i\partial n^1$	jan^{1A}

TABLE 4-11

		MC	Cantonese
信	'to believe'	$*si\partial n^3$	$sœn^{3A}$
新	'new'	$*si\partial n^1$	san^{1A}
秦	a surname	$*\dot{}\!\dot{z}i\partial n^1$	$ts'œn^{1B}$
亲	'relatives'	$*ts'i\partial n^1$	$ts'an^{1A}$
邻	'neighbour'	$*li\partial n^1$	$lœn^{1B}$

TABLE 4-12

	MC $*i\partial n$		MC $*i\partial t$	
Cantonese reflexes	œn	an	œt	at
After: *t, t', d, n, l	5	—	1	—
*ts, ts', dz, s, z	8	4	—	5

The rounding which takes place in the development of $*i\partial n/t$ to $œn/t$ is quite unexpected. None of the segments flanking the vocalic nucleus is normally associated with rounding. Rather than posit a totally exceptional type of rounding in such cases, Chen and Newman (1984–5: 365–70) assumed instead a partial merger of these finals in the direction of $*y\partial n/t$ which consistently have $œn/t$ as their modern reflexes in Cantonese in this environment. Instead of the (a) account, of Figure 4-3, we proposed (b).

The development of $*-i\partial n/t$ to $œn/t$ is thereby broken down into two more readily understandable changes: First, the palatal onglide is rounded to y, and then the rounded onglide coalesces with the following mid vowel to form a mid round vowel $œ$. An approach appealing to a partial merger with the $*-y\partial n/t$ finals also has some motivation in terms of the system of phonological contrasts in MC. The distribution of the $*\partial n/t$ type of finals after dental initials in MC is represented in Table 4-13, based on Hashimoto's (1972) data.

It can be seen that the distinction between no onglide and an u onglide (the 'open' versus 'close' distinction of traditional Chinese philology) is virtually non-existent after dental initials. The distinction, which is otherwise pervasive in MC, is neutral-

Figure 4-3

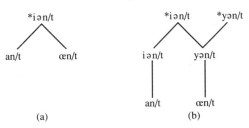

(a)   (b)

ized in favour of *uən/t. The distinction between an *i* onglide and a *y* onglide also amounts to absence versus presence of rounding in the onglide and is naturally construed as the same phonological distinction as that between no onglide and an *u* onglide. (In traditional Chinese philology, *uən/t is the 'close' counterpart of the 'open' *ən/t, in the same way as *yən/t is the 'close' counterpart of the 'open' *iən/t.) The view of events proposed here treats the partial merger of *iən/t and *yən/t as a continuation of the neutralization process evident in MC.

Once again, we can throw some light on the irregularities by appealing to an interaction between rules, in this case positing a preliminary rule splitting *iən/t into two separate finals which then undergo further rules characteristic of those two finals. In this way, one can establish some motivation for the exceptional rounding we observe in the development of *iən/t.

7 CONCLUDING REMARKS

I hope to have shown here that the study of the phonological irregularities in the history of Cantonese can be fruitful and rewarding. The phonological regularities demanded by the comparative method and favoured in introductory textbooks will probably always occupy centre-stage in historical linguistics. The achievements of the comparative method are, after all, undeniable. In a more general way, the regularities allow the linguist and the teacher of undergraduate linguistics courses to routinize procedures, and there are clearly intellectual and organizational benefits derived from approaching historical phonology in this way. It helps to make linguistics a 'science'. But there comes a time when one must confront the irregularities, and here we find ourselves having to talk about such things as perceived similarities between the shapes of Chinese characters and taboo associations of sounds. It is this which helps to make linguistics a 'human science'.

TABLE 4-13

	Finals			
	*ən/t	*uən/t	*iən/t	*yən/t
Dental spirant initials	—	11	17	5
Other dental initials	1	15	6	15

NOTES

1. The neglect of exceptions in Penzl's book must not be interpreted as a lack of awareness of them on the part of the author. As one of the foremost scholars in the field of German linguistics, Professor Penzl will be aware of these exceptions. My comments relate only to the style of presentation in the book.

2. The existence of a long philological tradition has also given rise to a very literary bias in Chinese historical linguistics. Typically, the raw data one works with are the dialect readings of characters, which may not reflect very well the spoken dialect. I welcome the suggestion in Norman (1988: 42) that one might pursue an alternative approach, whereby the modern spoken dialects are the basis of the reconstruction.

3. One should also note that Karlgren's reconstructions took into account Vietnamese, Japanese, and Korean readings of characters.

4. Dialect forms, unless stated otherwise, are taken from *Zìhuì* (1962). This is a comparative dialectological dictionary recording, in modified IPA, the pronunciation of 2,444 characters in seventeen Chinese dialects, covering all the major dialect groups in mainland China. The transcription is broad. *Zìhuì* also includes the traditional philological categorization of each character, in terms of its initial, rhyme, and tone class. The Middle Chinese reconstructions follow the phonological interpretations of Chen (1976). The superscript numbers refer to the historical tone classes: ^{1} refers to the *píng* 'even' category, ^{2} to the *shǎng* 'ascending' category, ^{3} to the *qù* 'departing' category, and ^{4} to the *rù* 'entering' category. Some of these categories have split into two or more sub-categories, indicated by 1A, 1B etc., in certain dialects. The actual phonetic realization of each tone class varies across dialects. L or C in parenthesis after a form indicates a literary or colloquial reading, respectively.

5. As Hashimoto (1978: 5) says, 'In general, there are many distinctions of sound classes in Ancient Chinese [i.e. Middle Chinese] for which there are no known modern correspondents. No phonological distinction in a modern dialect has been found [*sic*] which there is no Ancient correspondent.'

6. Some approaches to Chinese dialectology would never raise the question of how MC *a develops in dialects. It is not untypical to find historical accounts of dialects couched in terms of the traditional rhyme categories, rather than individual phonemic segments. Since MC *a occurs in different rhyme categories, it would not be an object of investigation in these approaches.

7. Huang (1976: 151) records a long nucleus for Cantonese *faːi*^{3A} 'lung'. All other dictionaries I have consulted, however, agree with Hashimoto (1972) in listing this word with a short nucleus.

REFERENCES

Ball, J. D. (1908). *The Cantonese made easy vocabulary*. Kelly and Walsh, Hong Kong.

Braune W., and W. Mitzka. (1967). *Althochdeutsche Grammatik*. 12th ed. revised by W. Mitzka. Max Niemeyer, Tübingen.

Burchfield, R. (1982). *The spoken word*. A BBC guide. Oxford University Press, New York.

Chen, M. Y. (1976). From Middle Chinese to modern Peking. *Journal of Chinese Linguistics* 4.2/3: 113–277.

———. (1980). How Proto-Chinese was reconstructed. In K. Koerner, ed., *Progress in linguistic historiography*. Studies in the History of Linguistics, vol. 20: 311–22. John Benjamins, Amsterdam.

Chen, M. Y., and J. Newman. (1984–5). From Middle Chinese to Modern Cantonese. Parts 1–3. *Journal of Chinese Linguistics* 12.1: 148–94; 12.2: 334–88; 13.1: 122–70.

Cheng, C.-C. and W. S.-Y. Wang. (1971). Phonological change of Middle Chinese initials. *The Tsing Hua Journal of Chinese Studies*, n. s. 9, (1–2) 216–69.

Cowles, R. T. (1965). *The Cantonese speaker's dictionary*. Hong Kong University Press, Hong Kong.

Hashimoto, O.-K. (1972). *Phonology of Cantonese*. Cambridge University Press, Cambridge.

Hashimoto, M. J. (1978). *Phonology of Ancient Chinese*. Vol. 1. Study of Languages and Cultures of Asia and Africa, 10. Institute for the Study of Languages and Cultures of Asia and Africa, Tokyo.

Huang, P. P.-F. (1976). *Cantonese dictionary*. Yale University Press, New Haven.

Newman, J. (1985). Spurious flip-flops in Cantonese and Wenzhou. *Computational Analyses of Asian and African Languages* 24: 169–80.

Norman, J. (1988). *Chinese*. Cambridge University Press, Cambridge.

Penzl, H. (1969). *Geschichtliche deutsche Lautlehre*. Max Hueber, Munich.

Pulleyblank, E. G. (1984). *Middle Chinese: A study in historical phonology*. University of British Columbia Press, Vancouver.

Singer, S. (1886). Zum althochdeutschen Vocalismus. *Beiträge zur Geschichte der deutschen Sprache und Literatur* 11: 287–309.

Stimson, H. M. (1966). A tabu word in the Peking dialect. *Language* 42: 285–94.

Wang, W. S-Y. ([1969]1978). Competing changes as a cause of residue. In P. Baldi and R. N. Werth, eds., *Readings in historical phonology: Chapters in the theory of sound change*, 236–57. Pennsylvania State University Press, University Park. First published in *Language* 45: 9–25.

Zhang, H. (1985). Irregular sound change and taboo in Chinese. *Computational Analyses of Asian and African Languages* 24: 227–31.

Zìbiǎo. (1981). *Fāngyán Diàochá Zìbiǎo*. (Word-list for dialect survey). Shāngwù Yìnshūguǎn, Běijíng.

Zìhuì. (1962). *Hànyǔ Fāngyín Zìhuì*. (A Pronouncing Dictionary of Han Dialects). Wénzì Gǎigé Chúbǎnshè, Běijíng.

5 Early Germanic Umlaut and Variable Rules

MARK DURIE

1 INTRODUCTION

The comparative method assumes that sound change is a regular process, in the sense that it affects all instances of a given allophone or phoneme in a particular context, rather than proceeding on a word by word or random basis. As a consequence, in describing phonological change, the classical procedure involves writing rules which take the form: In such-and-such an phonological context, such-and-such a change takes place. In the sense that such statements are categorical, that is intended to apply to all cases which satisfy the structural description, they model *regular* changes. In practice, it is the experience of every comparative linguist that even the best rule system will be come up against a corpus of 'exceptions': cases that do not fit the rule.[1] The historical linguist will seek to explain or motivate these exceptions in a number of ways: There may be borrowings involved; there may be specific morphological (e.g. analogical) processes at work; particular kinds of expressive effects may have applied; certain types of change such as haplology or metathesis are widely recognized to be inherently irregular; and the exceptions may be items of small grammatical categories that often manifest exceptional changes (e.g. pronouns). A discussion of explanations for some such 'irregularities' is provided by Lyle Campbell in this volume.

If the comparativist is forced at times to stipulate that a rule only applies sometimes or sporadically—that is, that it is not a regular rule—the conservative approach is to regard this as a case of an unsolved problem, for which the best rule system and/or explanations of exceptions have not yet been discovered. In practice this is of course quite a common occurrence. Comparativists are aware of many cases, some quite striking, where what had been claimed to be an intractable problem of this kind has later found a solution, or where a fairly speculative solution has found confirmation through, for example, the discovery of new data. So often it takes many decades of comparative work before a long-standing problem can be solved, whether involving a single etymology or a whole class of 'exceptions'. Because of this, linguistics who specialize in historical work are characteristically most unwilling to conclude that any particular instance of a seemingly irregular change cannot be solved, and no one expects that all exceptions can be explained. This mind-set, which is at once optimistic and sceptical, has made many comparativists immune to a considerable body of evidence that certain types of sound change can be lexical in nature, proceeding on a word-by-word basis, and thus phonologically irregular (see Labov 1981 for a discussion of the problem and references to case studies).

   In this chapter I wish to examine some problematic changes from Germanic historical linguistics which involve a rather large class of 'exceptional' data. The problem is one that has attracted repeated investigation over the course of more than century. I will apply a statistical technique—variable rule analysis—to help account for the exceptions. At first sight the analysis I propose is an example of the time-honoured approach of accounting for exceptional data by improving the analysis, thus demonstrating regularity where there had seemed to be irregularity. However, as I will argue in the conclusion, the success of this technique depends upon a revised notion of 'regularity' that may be viewed as a challenge to the classical method.

2 THE GERMANIC SHORT VOWELS

Proto-Germanic (PG) had a short vowel system of just four phonemes, as shown in Figure 5-1.[2] We know that PG had reduced the Indo-European (IE) five-vowel system by merging *o with *a to give PG *a, for example, IE *agros > Gothic *akrs* 'field', IE *oktō > Gothic *ahtau* 'eight'. The system of short vowel correspondences from IE was as follows.

PIE	PG
*i	*i
*e	*e
*u	*u
*o *a }	*a

   In each of the Germanic daughter languages, with the exception of Gothic, the PG four-vowel system had early on been transformed into a five-vowel system by an umlaut[3] process, lowering *u to o. At the same time there was a tendency to lower *i to e, and raise *e to i. This is represented in Figure 5-2.

Figure 5-1. Proto-Germanic short vowels   *i   *u

                                             *e

                                                   *a

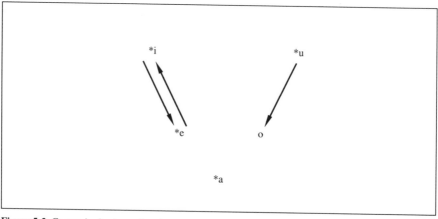

Figure 5-2. Germanic short vowel umlaut

The structural asymmetry in the Proto-Germanic short vowel system, and perhaps also the merger *i and *e in Gothic, has tempted some Germanic philologists to treat *i and *e as having fully merged at the PG level. Meillet puts it as follows:

> . . . in reality the *i*'s and the *e*'s of the different dialects correspond to ancient *i or *e almost indifferently [this is far from true, as we shall see—MD], and the distribution of *i* and *e* is defined by rules peculiar to each of the Germanic dialects. Everything has happened then almost as if there had been in common Germanic a single vowel, which became *i* or *e* according to the cases. Moreover, in the conditions where *e* appears in each dialect, we observe that ancient *u is ordinarily represented by short *o*, which does not correspond to an ancient Indo-European *ŏ but is a Germanic creation. (1970: 32)

Twaddell (1948), Marchand (1957), and Antonsen (1961) came down more emphatically than Meillet on the side of the full merger analysis—going further than Meillet's hedging 'almost'—and attempted to develop an account of the rather numerous exceptions that the merger has to deal with. Objections have been raised against the full merger analysis by a number of scholars (see Lehmann 1961: 70-1; Antonsen 1963: 197, 1964, 1965: 27; Beeler 1966; Benediktsson 1967: 187–91; Lloyd 1966). Hock (1973) summarized these objections, agreeing that PG *i and *e did not merge, but arguing that the umlaut phenomena—the phonemicization of *o* and the rephonemicizations of instances of *e* and *i*—are to be located in the pre-Northwest Germanic period. It remained for Cercignani (1979, 1980) to show that "since even the results of the 'earlier umlaut' phenomena affecting */i e u/ in the various dialects point to the rise of allophonic variations in partly different environments, all the pre-literary vowel modifications produced by both vocalic and consonantal influences should be ascribed to the prehistory of the individual Germanic languages . . ." (Cercignani 1980: 126).

Part of the peculiar difficulty of the Germanic data lies in the considerable number of exceptions to any hypothesis. These exceptions provide the material for the following two sections, which will examine the treatment of Germanic *i, *e, and *u in three languages: Old Icelandic (OI), Old High German (OHG) and Old English (OE).

2.1   Germanic *u

In early Germanic dialects except for Gothic it seems clear that at some stage the PG *u phoneme had allophones, basically according to the following environments:

$$[u] \Bigg/ \underline{\quad} \left\{ \begin{array}{l} NC \\ C^n \left\{ \begin{array}{l} i \\ j \\ u \end{array} \right\} \end{array} \right\}$$

[o]   elsewhere (with a following [−high] vowel in the next syllable).

In due course the Germanic dialects lost or greatly reduced the vowels of the inflectional endings, and of final, unstressed syllables in general, thus turning these allophones into two contrasting phonemes. For example, Proto-Germanic nom. sg. *$xurna$[4] 'horn' became OHG, OI, and OE *horn*, whilst PG nom. sg. *$lustiz$ 'desire' became OHG *lust*, OE and OI *lyst*. Indeed the conditioning environment of the following vowel was significantly eroded by the time most Germanic languages were preserved in writing.[5] Other umlaut processes had sometimes also applied, for example the fronting of *u to y in OE and OI before i or j of the following syllable.

For nominals (including adjectives, whose inflections form one family with those of nouns), inflectional class membership had an important bearing upon the outcome of the phonemicization. In the Germanic philological tradition each inflectional class is characterized by a vowel or consonant which originally concluded the stem throughout the inflectional paradigm: Further back in IE this segment had been part of the stem itself. For example, Proto-Germanic *$luftiz$ 'air' was an i-stem. The -z reflects the IE nominative singular -s inflection, with *lufti*- reflecting the original stem. Given this morphological structure, the inflectional class can be regarded as the conditioning context for the $u : o$ allophony, and the diachronic treatment of PG *u can be predicted in terms of the inflectional class of a nominal stem. In accordance with the above phonological rule, the i-stem, u-stem, ja-stem, $jō$-stem and (weak[6]) jan-stem, $jōn$-stem, and $īn$-stem inflectional classes were raising environments, resulting in u, whilst the a-stem, $ō$-stem, and (weak) an-stem and $ōn$-stem classes were lowering environments, resulting in o. Consonantal stems, which originally ended in a consonant, not a vowel, characteristically had a [−high] vocalism throughout most of their paradigm (see Prokosch 1939:249ff), so they too constituted a lowering environment. Although a number of inflectional classes had one or two inflectional endings which were 'aberrant'—raising instead or lowering or vice versa—the effect of these variants on the stem vowels have been almost invariably levelled.[7]

By the time we have materials attested for OE, OI, and OHG, there had already been considerably attrition and reanalysis of the inflections and levelling of stems, so that the conditioning thematic vowel or semivowel had often been deleted or replaced by paradigmatic reanalysis. For example OI *bogi* 'bow' was an old Germanic an-stem, PG *$buga(n)$, and regularly had o in the stem, reflecting *$u > o$, since Proto-Germanic an-stems had [−high] vocalism throughout their inflectional endings, including the nominative singular. The OI ending -i of the nom. sg. *bogi* reflects a late restructuring of the an-stem paradigm peculiar to Old Icelandic—most of the other inflectional endings of *bogi* still showed a [−high] vocalism (see the paradigm below)—and as such it did not affect the vocalism of the stem:

Old Icelandic Inflectional Paradigm for *bogi* 'bow'

Singular	Nominative	bogi
	Accusative	boga
	Genitive	boga
	Dative	boga
Plural	Nominative	bogar
	Accusative	boga
	Genitive	boga
	Dative	bogum

For weak verbs a parallel distinction can be made between stems taking an infinitive in *-jan*, which were raising, and those in *-ōn* or *-ēn* or *-nan*, which were lowering (these are known as classes I–IV respectively). Thus we have OI *fylla*, OE *fullan*, OE *fyllan* < PG *fulljan* 'to fill', and OI *þola*, OHG *tholēn* and OE *þolian* < PG *þulēn*[8] 'endure, suffer'. In the strong verbs, whose stem vowels varied according to old IE ablaut series, PG *u* appeared only in the preterite plural and past participle stems of some verb classes (classes II, III, and IV). The Germanic preterite plural inflectional endings, with a *-u-* vocalism in the indicative and *-ī-* in the subjunctive (Meillet 1970: 76), constituted a raising environment for the preterite plural stem. The past participle ending *-ana* (Meillet 1970: 79) constituted a lowering environment for the past participle stem (except for those stems ending in -NC). Thus OHG *liogan* 'to lie' has preterite plural *lugum* 'we lied' and past participle *gilogan* 'lied' (cf. OI *ljúgan, lugu, loginn*; OE *lêogan, lugon, logen*).[9]

I will give here two pieces of evidence that the phonemic split of *u* into *u* and *o* occurred after the division of Proto-Germanic into its daughter dialects.[10] Firstly, there are quite a number of cases where a cognate set displays different inflectional class membership in different Germanic languages, implying a change in inflectional class in one or more languages.[11] Such class shifts are often accompanied by divergent effects for the *u/o* vocalism. Examples are given below in their nom. sg. forms:

OI	OHG	OE	
lopt	luft	lyft	'air'
(*a*-stem)	(*i*-stem)	(*i*-stem)	
kør	kuri	cyre	'choice'
(*a*-stem)	(*i*-stem)	(*i*-stem)	
ormr	wurm	wyrm	'worm'
(*a*-stem)	(*i*-stem)	(*i*-stem)	
rugr	rocko	ryge	'rye'
(*i*-stem)	(*an*-stem)	(*i*-stem)	

Consider the case of PG *luftiz* 'air', the first item in the above list. In OHG and OE *i*-stem inflectional class membership correlates regularly here with high *u* in the stem

(> *y* in OE), whilst in OI *a*-stem class membership correlates regularly with lowered *o* in the stem. If **u* had lowered to *o* before the breakup of the dialects, and thus before the shift of **luftiz* to an *a*-stem in OI, we would have expected OI to have ***lupt*. That we do not indicates that lowering of **u* to *o* followed the division of PG into daughter dialects.

Another important piece of evidence for the relatively late phonemic split of **u* into *u* and *o* is the main point of this chapter: In around 20% of cases where *o* would be expected in a lowering environment we get *u* instead, and this 'failed' lowering affects *different* words in different Germanic languages. A typical cognate set is the following, derived from the Germanic *an*-stem **guman* 'man':

OI	**OHG**	**OE**	
gumi	gomo	guma	'man'
(*an*-stem)	(*an*-stem)	(*an*-stem)	

Note the inconsistent treatment of the *an*-stems *bogi* 'bow' and *gumi* 'man' in Old Icelandic: By the rule both should have been lowered. Similar irregularity is observed where the conditioning environment is a [−high] vowel in the second syllable of the stem, as for example in the following cognate set for the disyllabic stem 'honey', where in OI and OE a lowering environment exceptionally does not result in *o*.

OI	**OHG**	**OE**	
hunang	hona(n)g	huneg	'honey'

Apart from perhaps a very few cases, the failed lowering at a rate of approximately 20% cannot be explained away by appeal to morphological analogy or reanalysis, as Hock (1973) tried to do. First, there are no plausible morphological arguments that will distinguish all the 'exceptions' (see Cercignani 1979, 1980 for discussion), and second, the phenomenon is also noted where the lowering environment is part of the stem, as for 'honey' in OI and OE.

Also we note that the opposite effect, irregular occurrences of expected *u* as *o*, are very rare; much less frequent than the approximately 20% exceptions to lowering of **u*. Of Germanic **u* cognates in a raising environment I found only three putative cases of exceptional *o*, and it is significant that in each case a convincing explanation exists for the anomaly.

1. In OHG the *i*-stem *holī* 'hole' (cf. OI *a*-stem *hola*, OE *i*-stem *hylu*) can be explained as a late derivation or re-derivation from the adjective *hol* 'hollow', which has *o* quite regularly, since it is an adjectival *a*-stem. The derivation of de-adjectival *i*-stem nominals is a quite productive process in Old High German, so it would seem that *holī* was a more recent formation.

2. The OI *u*-stem *sonr* 'son' (cf. OE, OHG *sunu*) presents a more complex picture. For this word Old Norse forms existed with both [+high] and [−high] vocalism with the same ending.[12] Thus in the nominative singular there was OI *sonr* alongside East Norse *sunr*: other doublets were dat. sg. *syni/søni*, nom. pl. *synir/sønir* (Zoëga 1910).[13] In the genitive singular no doublet was attested, with only *sonar*.[14] This form

is significant because the characteristic inflectional stem vowel *u* did not ever immediately follow the stem in the original *u*-stem genitive singular, as attested by the genitive singular ending *-aus* of Gothic *u*-stems, which reflects the IE *-ous* (Szemerényi
1970: 161), as well as by the Icelandic genitive singular *u*-stem ending *-ar*. Gen. sg.
forms of *u*-stems were also not subject to *u*-mutation (cf. the nom. sg. *völlr* 'level
ground' alongside gen. sg. *vallar*). This suggests that the genitive singular must have
formed the basis for an exceptional analogical levelling of the paradigm in favour of
the [−high] vocalism. At first sight this would seem implausible. But it is an Old Icelandic idiosyncrasy that the genitive singular form *sonar* had a high frequency, both
in lexical compounds and as a free form in discourse. It was used in many frequent
and culturally significant compounds such as *sonarlát* 'loss of a son', *sonarkván*
daughter in law', *sonardauði* 'death of a son', *sonarbœtr* 'reparation payment for the
death of a son' and *sonarsonr* 'grandson'. Also a brief way of stating a genealogy (a
not uncommon linguistic act of Icelanders to this day) used a running genitive: *Uðr
. . . var . . . dóttir Ketils Flatnefs, Bjarnar **sonar** Bunu, Grims **sonar** Hersis ór Sogni
. . .*[15] 'U was the daughter of KF, son of BB, son of GH of Sogn' (emphasis mine). A
count of the frequency of the case forms of *sonr* in *Hrafnkels Saga* (Gordon 1957)
suggests that it is not implausible that the genitive singular was even the most frequent case form of *sonr* in Old Icelandic discourse:

Occurrences of inflectional forms of *sonr* 'son' in *Hrafnkels Saga*

Nom. Sg.   2
Acc. Sg.   3
Gen. Sg.   11
Dat. Sg.   —

Nom. Pl.   6
Acc. Pl.   5
Gen. Pl.   1
Dat. Pl.   2

Total: 30

3. Another putative exception is the OI gen. sg. *konar* 'kind's' which was quite
frequent in compounds, but not attested in other case forms, for example, OI *alls
konar* 'of all kinds', *hvers konar* 'of every kind', *margs konar* 'of many kinds' (Zoëga 1910: entry for *konar*). The PG antecedent for this form was most probably a neuter
ja-stem (cf. OI *kyn*, OHG *kunni*, OE *cynn*, Gothic *kuni* 'kind', all *ja*-stems). However the genitive singular ending *-ar* suggests *i*-stem rather than *ja*-stem class membership, and as noted above, the old *i*-stem genitive singular was a lowering environment.

Whilst in each of the three putative exceptions to raising, *holī*, *konr*, and *sonr*,
exceptional explanations can be found, the same kind of clear argument does not
emerge for all the much more frequent cases where original *u* unexpectedly fails to
lower to *o*.[16] If the phonemicization of *u* into *u* and *o* had predated the separation of
the dialects, arguments based on paradigmatic reanalysis could not explain why there
are so many cases of nonlowered *u,* but so few of nonraised *o*. Cercignani (1979:
77) makes a parallel argument against the complete merger account, for PG *i* and *e,*

pointing out that if particular *a*-stem case forms (e.g. vocative and locative) had blocked the lowering of PG *u* (and also, according to Hock 1973, *i*), then one would have expected parallel examples of *a*-stems with original PG *e* showing up as *i* in the same contexts. But this never happens. In general the rather numerous exceptions to the Germanic umlauts of short vowels are always conservative in terms of the old *i, *e, *u* vowel values: We find that cases of 'exceptional' *i > e, *e > i*, and *u > o* are very rare.

Our conclusion must be that the phonemic split of Germanic *u* into *u* and *o* post-dated the breakup of the dialects. So we have a case of a phonologically conditioned change, *u > o*, which applied in only approximately 80% of cases and which had different exceptions in each of OI, OHG, and OE.

The next step must be to ask whether there was any other conditioning environment that might account for the exceptions. Tables 5-1 to 5-3 provide a summary of the distribution of stems with *u* in lowering environments in OI, OHG, and OE, respectively, distinguished according to the following and preceding consonants. There are many examples from early Germanic where neighbouring consonants conditioned vowel height changes, so this is a logical place to look for conditioning of this change (cf. Van Coetsem 1968). In a cell of the table, 5/8 indicates that, of 13 cases of PG *u* in this phonological environment, 5 were regularly lowered to *o*, and 8 were 'irregularly' not lowered. D_ = dental obstruents,[17] V_ = velars (except *x*), and L_ = labials. *x, r* and *l* were separated out because of their relatively high frequency and also because evidence from other changes in early Germanic suggests they may be expected to have distinct effects on changes in the height of a neighbouring vowel.[18] The symbol *x* actually represents Germanic *x*, which is mostly reflected by *h* in the daughter languages. The symbol # represents the absence of a consonant in its position.

Tables 5-1, 5-2, and 5-3 give us no reason to suppose that the exceptional non-lowering cases can be accounted for by a *regular* conditioning environment. However the preceding and following consonants do seem to play a role, velars and labials[19] having a more strongly inhibiting effect on lowering than other consonants. In the majority of cases where lowering fails, *u* occurs adjacent to a velar or labial. In OI and OE, where there is a combination of both a preceding *and* a following velar

TABLE 5-1
Frequency of *u* > o in Old Icelandic, in the environment _C₀[−high]
(each cell represents numbers of o/u)

Preceding Consonant								
		x_	r_	l_	D_	V_	L_	#_
	_x	—	—	—	1/—	—	1/—	—
	_r	3/—	—	—	7/—	2/—	13/2	1/—
	_l	4/—	—	—	2/—	1/1	5/3	—
Following								
Consonant	_D	1/—	7/2	4/—	1/—	5/—	1/2	1/—
	_V	—/1	1/—	4/—	5/1	—	1/4	—/1
	_L	1/1	1/1	2/1	4/2	1/2	—	1/1
								Total: 81/25

TABLE 5-2
Frequency of *u > o in Old High German, in the environment _C_0[−high]
(each cell represents numbers of o/u)

Preceding Consonant

		x_	r_	l_	D_	V_	L_	#_
	_x	—	—	—	1/—	—	1/—	—
	_r	3/—	1/—	—	5/—	1/—	12/2	1/—
	_l	1/—	—	—	1/—	1/—	7/—	—
Following	_D	2/—	5/—	2/2	—	2/1	2/—	1/—
Consonant	_V	1/—	1/1	3/3	3/1	—	4/1	—
	_L	1/—	2/1	1/2	1/3	2/1	—	1/1
								Total: 67/13

or labial, non-lowering is the much more frequent outcome. On the other hand, where
*u was both preceded *and* followed by a dental or *x, lowering to o was almost exceptionless. We can also observe that in OHG the influence of following consonants seems to be more important than that of preceding consonants.

I wish to formalize these observations, and propose that the neighbouring consonant had a conditioning effect upon the outcome of vowel lowering in a probabilistic rather than a categorical fashion. An appropriate statistical tool—variable rule analysis—exists to interpret this kind of data, where two or more distinct variables or *factor groups* compete to determine an outcome of a rule. In this study there are two factor groups only, the preceding and following consonants, and each of these factor groups comprise a number of distinct environments, or *factors*. For the analysis I had originally used a MS-DOS version of VARBRUL II, distributed by Ralph Fasold at the NWAV XV (New Ways of Analysing Variation) conference in October 1986. The analysis for this chapter thas been redone using GoldVarb 2.[20] Although variable rule analysis was initially developed for modelling speakers' knowledge of variable rules in the synchronic state (Cedergren and Sankoff 1974), as a mathematical tool it can

TABLE 5-3
Frequency of *u > o in Old English, in the environment _C_0[−high]
(each cell represents numbers of o/u)

Preceding Consonant

		x_	r_	l_	D_	V_	L_	#_
	_x	—	—	—	—	—	—	—
	_r	3/—	1/—	—	7/—	1/—	8/4	1/—
	_l	3/—	—	—	3/—	1/—	5/3	—
Following	_D	2/1	5/1	3/3	—	3/—	1/1	1/—
Consonant	_V	1/—	2/—	2/2	2/1	—	2/3	1/—
	_L	1/—	2/—	1/1	4/2	—/3	—	1/1
								Total: 68/20

equally well be applied to the diachronic results of a variable sound change, as long as there is an appropriate correlation observed between particular environments and the frequency of particular changes (see Kay and McDaniel 1977). As used here, variable rule analysis is simply a tool for describing correlations between environments and frequency of change. It does not imply a particular theory of how these correlations are achieved over time: In particular it implies nothing about the cognitive states of early Germanic speakers.

For the purpose of analyzing this particular data the GoldVarb program performs four distinct main tasks.

1. It calculates which combination of factor groups will give the best fit. Through stepwise (both step-up and step-down) regression, the program calculates whether including a particular factor group significantly ($p < 0.05$) improves the likelihood of the analysis. In this way it determines whether the data set is best accounted for by a variable rule analysis in which both preceding and following consonants are included as determinants of vowel lowering, or whether a statistically more significant analysis is provided by including just one of the factor groups, or none at all (the null hypothesis).

2. It estimates an *input probability*, a value between 0 and 1. This is a measure of the probability of the change applying, apart from the effect of consonantal environments (factors). This is represented by p_0 in the formula below.

3. It estimates the strength and direction of each factor's probabilistic contribution to the change, assigning a value between 0 and 1. These are the values p_i in the formula. A value of 0.5 for p_i indicates that, within the model, the factor had a neutral effect on the change. The higher the value of p_i, the greater the strengthening effect; the lower the value, the greater the inhibiting effect. In other words, values greater than 0.5 indicate a relatively lowering effect on the adjacent vowel, values less than 0.5 a relatively inhibiting of lowering effect (a raising effect). GoldVarb calculates the values of p_i (including the input probability) so that the weighted mean of $\ln\left(\dfrac{p_i}{1 - p_i}\right)$ within a factor group is zero. This is an empirically unmotivated mathematical assumption which makes it possible to obtain a unique solution to the formula. It has the effect of distributing values of p_i within a factor group fairly evenly about the value 0.5.

4. When both factor groups are included, GoldVarb calculates a χ^2 value, an estimate of the goodness of fit of the solution found by GoldVarb to the data set.

The formula for the mathematical model of the variable rule analysis is:

$$p = \frac{p_0 \times \ldots \times p_n}{[p_0 \times \ldots \times p_n] + [(1 - p_0) \times \ldots \times (1 - p_n)]}$$

where p is the probability of a 'rule' (e.g. a sound change) applying in each particular case. The value n is the number of factor groups: in this study it is 2.

I will illustrate how the rule applies in some specific cases, first of all in that of the environment D_L in Old English, taking data from Table 5-6. To determine from our model the likelihood of lowering in this cell we need to know three independent values:

$p_0 = 0.83$. This is the input probability of the rule: roughly speaking, the likelihood of the rule applying irrespective of particular environments.

$p_1 = 0.71$. This is the contribution to the rule of the preceding environment, D_. Since this value is above 0.5, this environment favours lowering.

$p_2 = 0.11$. This is the contribution to the rule of the following environment, _L. Since the value is below 0.5, this environment inhibits lowering.

So here we have three factors: the input probability which favours lowering, the preceding consonantal environment which also favours it, and the following consonantal environment which inhibits it. The three factors are combined by the formula given above to generate the likelihood of lowering, and in Old English, for the environment D_L we have a probability of the lowering taking place of:

$$p = \frac{0.83 \times 0.71 \times 0.11}{[0.83 \times 0.71 \times 0.11] + [(1 - 0.83) \times (1 - 0.71) \times (1 - 0.11)]} = 0.60$$

his value corresponds well with the observed fact that 4/6 Old English tokens exhibit lowering in this environment. Another example, Icelandic L_V involves two environments that both hinder lowering. This yields, from Table 5-4:

$p_0 = 0.85$ (the input probability)
$p_1 = 0.15$ (the effect of L_)
$p_2 = 0.20$ (the effect of _V)

which gives, by the formula, $p = 0.21$. Thus one would expect only about 20% of lowering of *u in this environment in Icelandic, and indeed our data shows 1/5 lowered tokens, or 20%. Finally, consider the case of D_r, again from Old Icelandic. Here we have:

$p_0 = 0.85$ (the input probability)
$p_1 = 0.79$ (the effect of D_)
$p_2 = 0.87$ (the effect of _r)

Here all factors favour lowering, and the net result is $p = 0.99$, or a 99% likelihood that lowering will take place. Indeed we observe that 7/7 tokens of *u are lowered in Old Icelandic in this environment.

In addition to the three standard calculations of the GoldVarb program, I have added a fifth calculation, the harmonic mean of ρ_i, where $\rho_i = 0.5 + |p_i - 0.5|$ for each factor group (environment type). This is termed the *mean effect* of an environment. It is a measure of the relative strength of each factor group's overall effect on lowering. The mean effect values range potentially from 0.5 to 1. A value closer to 0.5 indicates that the factor group had a less marked overall effect on vowel lowering. A higher value indicates a relatively stronger overall effect.

Because the number of tokens in the samples for this study is small, and the number of potentially significant environments rather large, the environments _x, _# (no following consonant) and #_ (no preceding consonant) had to be omitted altogether from the analysis because of their very low number of tokens. Where a factor had a categorical effect (all outcomes are the same), it had to be excluded from the analysis. This was necessary for OHG x_ and _l, which were 100% lowering in the data set.

The results of GoldVarb analysis are given in Tables 5-4 to 5-6. All values are reported by GoldVarb to three decimal places but reported here only to two decimal places: this is more consistent with the small size of the data set. The effect of consonant environments can be represented more suggestively by bar graphs, as in Figure 5-3.

For Old English and Old Icelandic cases the χ^2 result indicates that the goodness of fit is reasonable (the independence hypothesis could not be discounted at even the 10% level of uncertainty). A model in which preceding and following consonants compete independently to determine vowel height lowering fits the data better than ones in which lowering occurs under the influence of just one of these factors, or independent of consonantal influence. For Old High German the best model is one which discounts the influence of preceding consonants as insignificant.

One simple pan-Northwest-Germanic generalization that can be made on the basis of this variable rule analysis is a ranking of consonants in terms of their effect on lowering to *o*: *r* and *l* favour lowering of **u* most of all, dental obstruents are somewhat less strongly favourable to lowering, velars even less favourable (with the exception of PG **x*), and labials obstruct lowering most of all.[21] The hierarchy is thus: r,l > D > V > L.[22] This generalization applies across the three languages, and also, in most cases, across the distinction between preceding and final consonants within OE and OI. An interesting confirmation of the whole analysis can be found in numerous regular consonant-conditioned vowel changes in early Germanic in which this pattern is confirmed. For example, in Upper German, PG **eu > iu, except* that **eu > eo* before all dentals and PG **x* with a [−high] following vowel. In Old English PG **e > eo*, and PG **i > io* before *x, rC* and *lC* (as well as before *w*). In Gothic *u* and *i* were lowered before *r* and *h* (<**x*).

TABLE 5-4
**u > o* Old Icelandic

[i] The best model for Old Icelandic is achieved by including *both* factor groups in the variable rule analysis.

[ii] Input probability, $p_0 = 0.85$

[iii] Effect of environments (values of p_i):

Preceding consonant		Following consonant	
x_	0.57		
r_	0.47	_r	0.87
l_	0.88	_l	0.57
D_	0.79	_D	0.55
V_	0.47	_V	0.20
L_	0.15	_L	0.09

[iv] $\chi^2 = 9.93$

[v] Mean effect of preceding consonants: 0.69

Mean effect of following consonants: 0.74

TABLE 5-5
***u > o* Old High German**

---

[i] The best model for Old High German is achieved by including just the following consonants in the variable rule analysis. (That is, including the initial consonants does not significantly improve the likelihood of the analysis.)
[ii] Input probability, $p_0 = 0.83$
[iii] Effect of environments (values of p_i):

Following consonant	
_r	0.66
_D	0.69
_V	0.43
_L	0.17

[iv] —
[v] Mean effect of following consonants: 0.79

There are a small number of cells in the data that fit less well than others, and among tokens in these cells we may be justified in expecting a few that are clearly susceptible to special explanations. It is for example surprising that in OI the data cell r_D shows 2/9 cases of non-lowering, given that both r_ and _D favour lowering in the Germanic dialects, and at the same time the data cell V_D in OI, with a preceding velar that inhibits lowering, shows a full 5/5 cases of lowering. One should be careful not to try to explain away every such anomaly: Given the number of cells in the data and their smallness, we should expect a few 'anomalous' cells. However in this case of r_D the Icelandic *ruð* 'clearing in a forest' (cf. OHG *rod*) seems amenable to two possible explanations: (1) analogical influence of the verb *ryðja* 'to clear (land, forest)' with past form *ruddi* and past participle *ruddr*, and (2) influence of an earlier Germanic locative case form *-ī* (which later presumably gave rise to the regular OI *a*-stem dative singular ending -*i*). For a locational noun such as *ruð*, the loca-

TABLE 5-6
***u > o* Old English**

---

[i] The best model for Old English is achieved by including *both* factor groups in the variable rule analysis.
[ii] Input probability, $p_0 = 0.83$
[iii] Effect of environments (values of p_i):

Preceding consonant		Following consonant	
x_	0.71		
r_	0.82	_r	0.75
l_	0.78	_l	0.72
D_	0.71	_D	0.41
V_	0.44	_V	0.41
L_	0.13	_L	0.11

[iv] $\chi^2 = 12.89$
[v] Mean effect of preceding consonants: 0.74
Mean effect of following consonants: 0.71

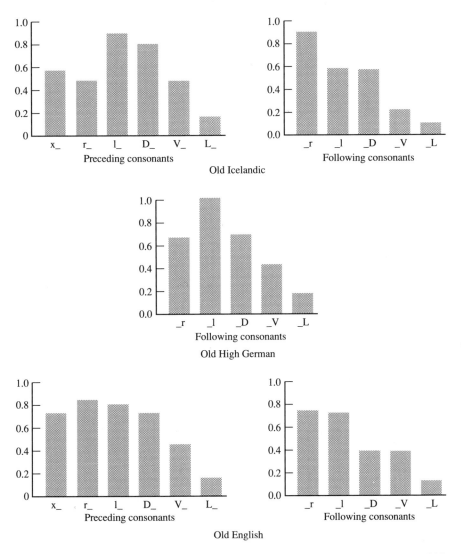

Figure 5-3. The effect of consonantal environment upon the change PG *u* > o. The value of p_i (y axis) is plotted against consonantal environment (x axis). A higher value for p_i indicates promotion of vowel lowering. A lower value indicates inhibition of lowering. A value of 0.5 is neutral in effect. The value of 1 for OHG _l indicates that the change was 100% effective in the sample (and therefore not included in the GoldVarb analysis).

tive singular ending may well have had a determinative influence against the lowering of *u* to *o*.

It is also interesting to reflect on the dialectal differences between the three languages included in the sample. The most striking effect is the already-noted divide between OHG, for which only the following consonants have a significant effect on vowel height, and OE/OI, for which preceding and following consonants are of similar 'strength'. This difference is reflected in other changes: OE and OI, but not OHG, show other vowel height changes that are conditioned by preceding consonants (that is, the breaking of vowels after palatal consonants in OE, and in OI the blocking of the change *e > ia after w, r and l). A minor difference between OI and OE is the slightly stronger relative effect of preceding consonants in OE. Another interesting effect is the difference between l_ and _l in OI: does this reflect an allophonic idiosyncrasy of OI l after *u? The relatively stronger lowering effect of the following velars in OE may be related to the general tendency for velars to be fronted in that language.

2.2 Germanic *i and *e

For Germanic *i and *e a problem exists which is similar to that for *u. We know that in all Germanic languages except Gothic, *i tended to be lowered before a [−high] vowel in the following syllable, and *e tended to be raised before a [+high] vowel (or semivowel) in the following syllable, with the qualification that, as with PG *u, there are a good number of exceptional cases, one of the most widely cited example is PG *fiskaz 'fish'. Since this is an a-stem, we might expect lowering of *i to e, but in every case we find i (OI fiskr, OR fisc, OFris, OS, OHG fisk). We have already briefly reviewed some of the literature and arguments which relate to the question of whether the umlaut processes affecting *i, *e, and *u are to be located in the common Germanic period, and whether they led to a complete phonemic merger in Proto-Germanic. Cercignani (1979, 1980) demonstrated convincingly both that the *i : *e opposition was never lost in any of the daughter languages except Gothic and that the umlaut processes must be attributed to the prehistory of the individual Germanic languages. His argument, in a nutshell, was that (i) the umlauts took place in partly different environments in the different languages and with partly different results, (ii) for each language except Gothic the *i : *e opposition was retained in some environments, and (iii) there were insuperable difficulties with arguments to the contrary that relied on processes of systematic analogy.

Let us consider these umlaut tendencies and their effects in the three languages of our sample. The situation for *e is rather simple. In all three languages, the following rule applies quite regularly:[23]

$$*e > i \ / \ \_C_0 \begin{Bmatrix} i \\ j \end{Bmatrix}$$

Examples:

OI hirðir, OHG hirdi, OE hierde 'herdsman' (< PG *herðjaz)
OI vist, OHG, OE wist 'sojourn, provisions' (< PG *westiz)
OI, OE, OHG gift 'gift' (< PG *geftiz)

In OHG (and also Old Saxon) there was, in addition, raising of *e > i in the environment $\_C_0u$. It is important to note that raising did not take place before -u in OE and OI, and this is one of the important pieces of evidence against the merger hypothesis: thus OI fjöl- 'much, many' and OE fela/feola beside OHG, Gothic filu

(< PG *felu) (cf. Cercignani 1979: 74–5). Some examples of u-stems are given below. A number of u-stems were changing or had changed their inflectional paradigm in all three languages:[24] where there is any uncertainty about the inflectional class membership of a reflex that may render it irrelevant as an example, I have included it in a footnote, with an explanation. Where information is available, I have given the Gothic as supporting evidence that the u-stem class membership is archaic.

OHG widar, OE weðer 'wether'[25]
OHG fihu, OE feo(h), Gothic faíhu 'cattle, money'[26] (< PG *fexu)
OI skjöldr,[27] Gothic skildus 'shield'[28] (< IE *skel-)
OI kvern,[29] OHG quirn, OE cweorn, Gothic -qaírnus 'mill'
OI mjöðr, OHG mitu/metu, OE meodo 'mead' (cf. Gk méthu 'wine')

In my database, the doublet mitu/metu provides the only exception to raising before -u in OHG, but see Braune and Eggers (1975: section 30) for some other possible exceptions.

Where raising to i might have led to paradigmatic alternations, it was almost always levelled. For example, the sg. pres. forms of OI gefa 'to give' were all levelled to e by analogy with the infinitive and pl. pres., thus for example PG *gebiz > *gibiz > OI gefr 'you sg. give'.[30] There is an interesting exception to this generalization in OI, where the u-stem paradigm included two archaic endings which constituted raising environments for PG *e: the dat. sg. -i < older loc. sg. *iu and the nom. pl. -ir < *-ius (cf. Szemerényi 1970: 162). The effect of i-umlaut was preserved in these case forms, thus we find dat. sg. miði 'mead', nom. pl. birnir 'bear',[31] dat. sg. skildi and nom. pl. skildir 'shield'. Here paradigmatic levelling of the old i : e contrast was apparently inhibited by the intervention of the effects of fracture and u-mutation, which changed all the expected retentions of *e, replacing them with jö (e.g. nom. sg. skjöldr) or ja (e.g. gen. sg. skjaldar).

Although PG *e undergoes quite regular raising umlaut, the change:

$$*i > e \quad / \quad \_C_0[-\text{high}],$$

like the lowering of *u > o, cannot be said to be regular in the normal sense: In my database it applied in OHG in about 50% of cases, in OI in about 20% of cases, and in only very few cases in OE.

Examples:

OI, OHG, OE gin 'mouth of a beast' (a-stem)
OI hlið, OHG lit, OE hlid 'gateway, space' (a-stem)
OI sleði, OHG slito, OE slide 'sledge' (an-stem)
OI seli/sili, OHG silo 'harness' (an-stem)
OI gleða, OE glida, 'kite, kind of bird' (ō-stem)
OI sin, OHG senwa, OE sinu 'sinew, tendon' (ō-stem)
OI klif, OHG klep, OE clif 'cliff' (a-stem)
OI neðarr/niðr, OHG nidar[i],[32] OE niðera/neoðera 'lower, down'
OI verr, OHG, OE wer 'man' (a-stem)

TABLE 5-7
Frequency of *i > e in Old Icelandic, in the environment _C₀[−high]
(each cell represents numbers of e/i)

Frequency of $*i > e$ in Old Icelandic, in the environment $\_C_0[-high]$
(each cell represents numbers of e/i)

Preceding Consonant		D_,r_, l_,x_	L_,V_
	_D,_r_l,_x	5/7	1/10
Following			
Consonant	_L,_V	1/12	—/5
			Total: 7/34

Although this change cannot be described as 'regular' in the normal sense of this term, I will demonstrate that it was also not random, contra Hock[33], Meillet, and others.

In OE there are only a very few examples of $*i > e$. In my database these are *wer* 'man', *nest* 'nest', *neoðera* 'nether, down' and the rare *spec* besides more common *spic* 'bacon' (see Flom 1930: sec. 260). Within OE these must be regarded as sporadic exceptions to the non-lowering of $*i$. For 'man' and 'nest' the argument for PG $*i$ is based only on external evidence from IE (e.g. Latin *vir* 'man' and *nīdus* 'nest'). Within Germanic only *e* or its derivatives is found in all attested reflexes, and this although lowering of $*i$ is generally the exception rather than the rule, and virtually unattested in OE except for a two or three forms. Therefore it is perhaps more plausible to reconstruct PG $*e$ for these forms, as Braune and Eggers (1975: §31, n. 1c) suggest.

For OI, the distribution of $*i$ in potentially lowering environments is represented in Table 5-7. Not as many cells are used as for $*u > o$, because of the smaller number of Germanic words with $*i$ in this environment. Variable rule analysis yields the results provided in Table 5-8. The statistical analysis supports the hypothesis that preceding and following consonants act independently to determine the probability of lowering. So we see here a similar pattern of consonantal influence to that observed for $*u > o$, with velars and labials favouring a high vowel, and dentals and $*x$ favouring a low vowel. One important difference is that whereas in the case of $*u$, the overall preference (the input probability) was strongly in favour of lowering, for $*i$ the preference is strongly against lowering.

TABLE 5-8
$*i > e$ Old Icelandic

[i] The best model for Old Icelandic is achieved by including *both* factor groups in the variable rule analysis.
[ii] Input probability, $p_0 = 0.11$
[iii] Effect of environments (values of p_i):

Preceding consonant		Following consonant	
D_,r_, l_,x	0.67	_D,_r, _l,_x	0.73
L_,V_	0.22	_L,_V	0.22

[iv] $\chi^2 = 0.108$
[v] Mean effect of preceding consonants: 0.73
Mean effect of following consonants: 0.76

TABLE 5-9
Frequency of *i > e in Old High German, in the environment _C_0[−high]
(each cell represents numbers of e/i)

Preceding Consonant			
	_D,_r,_l,_x	D_,r_,l_,x_ 5/13	L_,V_ 2/8
Following Consonant	_L,_V	12/-	7/3 Total: 26/24

For OHG, the distribution of *i in potentially lowering environments is represented in Table 5-9. The statistical analysis of Table 5-10 shows that, as for *u in OHG, the following consonants have a significant determinative effect on lowering of *i, but the preceding consonants have no significant effect.

There is a surprise in the OHG data: in this case it is the velars and labials which have the strongest lowering effect, whilst the dentals (including *r and *l) and *x are in comparison less favourable for lowering. This is the opposite of what might be expected, and provides something of a puzzle. The key can be found in the explanation that Cercignani offers for non-lowering of PG *i: [T]he extreme scarcity of forms with /e/ by a-umlaut of */i/ seems to imply that the assimilation exerted by *[-a] on */i/—being less powerful than that exerted by *[-i] on */e/—was resisted, with varying results, in order to avoid a merger of */i/ with */e/. . .' (1980: 131). The avoidance of merger, or 'phonemic clash' explanation can in fact account for three related facts: (1) lowering of *u before [−high] vowels is much more frequent than lowering of *i in the same environment, (2) raising of *e is much more frequent than lowering of *i, in all the Germanic dialects, and (3) lowering of *i is more frequent before labials and velars in OHG than before dentals and *x, but in OI the pattern is reversed. For (1) we can observe that since PG had no *o, the lowering of *u involved no potential for phonemic clash at all. For (2) we can note that PG *i was extremely rare before i or j of the following syllable, so *e could be raised in this environment with virtually no loss of functional contrast at all. For (3) we can note that in the en-

TABLE 5-10
*i > e Old High German

[i] The best model for Old High German is achieved by including just the preceding consonants in the variable rule analysis.
[ii] Input probability, $p_0 = 0.53$
[iii] Effect of environments (values of p_1):

Following consonant	
_D,_r,_ l,_x	0.20
_L,_V	0.85

[iv] —
[v] Mean effect of following consonants: 0.82

TABLE 5-11
Old High German: Distribution of *e Before a [−high] Vowel

Preceding Consonant			
	_D,_r,_l,_x	D_,r_, l_,x_ 28%	L_,V_ 44%
Following Consonant	_L,_V	11%	17%

vironment before [−high] vowels, *e was much more frequent with a following dental or *x, than with a following velar or labial (see Table 5-11). Indeed, in the context of a potential merger of *e and *i in Germanic by raising *e and lowering *i, the environment __{D,r,l,x}[−high] accounts for about 75% of the effective functional load of the *e : *i contrast. In OI, where *i > e was no more than a marginal change, the effect of a potential 'phonemic clash' is not significant, and the _D_r,_l,_x environments favour lowering according to the general Germanic tendency, but in OHG, where the lowering was a 50% likelihood, it is inhibited in this environment of maximum functional contrast.

3 CONCLUSION

The most important methodological conclusion to be drawn from this study is that it is not always necessary or even correct to divide cognate sets into 'regular cases' and 'exceptions'. If one allows conditioning factors which are probabilistic rather than categorical in their influence on a change—and this study shows that one must—then divergent outcomes can be evaluated in terms of their varying degrees of probability: a change which applies to 90% of cases can just be one that is highly probable, not one with 10% exceptions. That this is not just a matter of terminology is shown by the evidence of the development of PG *u and *i in Germanic languages, where neighbouring consonants contribute to determining the *likelihood* of lowering, but not whether it will happen in each individual case. Particularly strong evidence is the independence of the contribution of preceding and following consonants in OI and OE.

At the start of this chapter I noted that exceptional data are usually regarded as an unsolved problem in comparative reconstruction. The frequent appearance of such data in actual reconstruction is a phenomenon that can have many explanations, and no doubt in many cases it is reasonable to regard such data as an unsolved problem that a better analysis or new data might help to resolve. This study suggests that there is a place for application of statistical techniques such as variable rule analysis in historical linguistics to help resolve such cases.

A challenging aspect of the technique used in this study is the implication that a genuine sound change may be both subject to systematic phonological conditioning and yet not categorically regular. This is true, for example, of the lowering of *u, which is significantly influenced by neighbouring consonants, but only in such a way that an estimate of the probability of lowering can be derived from the effects of consonantal environment. This distinction allows an interpretation of the history of *i, *e, and *u which involves two stages. For each Germanic language, we can assume at an earlier stage that consonants had finely differentiated allophonic effects on the vowel height of neighbouring vowels. At the same time the height of the following vowel also had an allophonic effect on vowel height. Each of the affected phonemes thus had a number of allophonic distinctions, and there may have even been some overlap between *i and *e, with some low allophones of *i being lower than some high allophones of *e. These effects were low-level phonetic ones, and we can assume that they were quite regular. At a later stage there was attrition of the conditioning environments and concomitant abstract phonological change. For *u there was a split into two phonemes, and for *i and *e changes in phonemic identity. These abstract phonological changes were to some extent lexical and abrupt in nature, and thus not regular in the normal sense of this term in historical linguistics: The direction of change was significantly influenced by the effects of pre-existing allophonic conditioning, but only in a probabilistic way. It is not necessary to appeal to systematic analogy[34] to explain the divergent effects of the abstract change in particular cases: The element of unpredictability is not explained by the influence of analogy, but is, I would suggest, a potential inherent in the nature of abstract phonological sound change itself. For a discussion of similar phenomena in studies of sound change in progress, see Labov 1981. This study shows that lexically gradual yet phonologically conditioned sound change, as it has been observed in progress by Labov and others, will not necessarily be exceptionless in its final outcome. Such instances can be regarded as true cases of 'sound change', even if their final outcome is not categorically regular in the classical sense.

NOTES

1. In general, the only changes that are immune from exceptions are those involving restructuring of the phonological system, such as the complete loss of a phonemic contrast, or a change in phonotactic constraints, for instance, the loss of k before n in English words like *kneel* and *knob*.

2. PG also had a set of long vowels and diphthongs, these do not concern us here.

3. Within the Germanic philological tradition, the term *umlaut* is customarily used only for vowel changes under the influence of i, j, or u occurring in the next syllable. In this chapter, however, I use the term more generally to refer to changes which are conditioned by any vowel or semivowel of the next syllable.

4. Or *xurnan. No Germanic dialect has preserved a final -n, but this is suggested by other IE languages (Meillet 1970: 92).

5. So, for example, only Runic Norse preserved in the nom. sg. the -a- of a-stems and the -i- of i-stems (Meillet 1970: 92–3)

6. The Germanic philological tradition distinguishes *strong* from *weak* inflections of nouns, verbs, and adjectives. Verbs and nouns are classified lexically as either strong and weak: strong verbs are those that show the old ablaut alternations in their stem vowel (e.g. *sing-sang-sung*), and weak nouns are those belonging to an inflectional class characteristic of old -n-stems. In contrast, adjectives take both strong and weak endings, the weak forms being typically used after the definite article or a demonstrative (that is, in 'definite' syntactic contexts). Weak inflections typically preserve fewer morphological distinctions and have tended to be quite productive in the history of Germanic languages.

7. Some cases of raising of *e > i before 'aberrant' u-stem inflections are noted later. The discussion below of OI *sonr* 'son' provides a parallel case of non-levelling for *u.

8. These are both class III weak verbs in OI, OHG, and Gothic. In OE the weak classes are not so clearly distinguished, except by the vowel of the stem: the absence of i-mutation of *u to y, and the lowering

to *o* indicates that *þolian* was originally of class II or III in OE. (The form of the final syllable of the infinitive of class III weak verbs in PG is not quite clear; see Meillet 1970: 85).

9. The quite exceptional OI past part. *numinn* of *nema* 'to take' and the OE past part. *numen* of *niman* 'to take' (cf. the 'regular' OHG *neman, ginoman*) can be understood as resulting from the analogical influence of the numerous class III verbs with stems in -NC, which regularly had *$*u$* > u: compare, for example, OI *renna, runninn* and OE *rinnan, runnen* 'run'.

10. The fact that Gothic has only one phoneme *u* is of no account, because it has also merged the earlier *$*i$* and *$*e$*.

11. The data of the reference books concerning class membership must be treated with considerable caution. It can be very difficult to interpret. Sometimes, due to the reduction of inflectional forms, it is difficult to determine inflectional class. Thus, for example, in OHG the inflections of masculine *i*-stems and *a*-stems have fallen together in the singular, so nouns which are not attested in the plural cannot be certainly classified. In such cases scholars sometimes rely on class membership in related languages, or on the evidence of the stem vowel. Thus Braune and Eggers (1975: §216, n. 2) consider OHG *biȝ* 'bite', *grif* 'grip' and *zug* 'pull' to be *i*-stems, because of their high vowel. However, as this study shows, lowering of *$*u$* and *$*i$* before a low vowel in such words is by no means regular, and so non-lowering is not a reliable indicator of class membership in these cases. More telling is evidence of fronting in OE and OI before -*i* or -*j* of the inflection as for example in OE *lyft*. In the vast majority of cases the evidence of such fronting and non-lowering agree, but OI *kør* 'choice' shows a mixed history: It is an *a*-stem with a lowered vowel, but fronting reflects earlier *i*-stem class membership, as suggested by OHG and OE reflexes.

12. In some cases this variation was dialectal, as with OI *sonr* and East Norse *sunr*. Other cases involved paradigmatic alternations; thus in one text, the Edda, we find nom. sg. *sonr* (and most other case forms in *o*) alongside dat. sg. *syni* and nom. pl. *synir* (Kuhn 1968). This is one of the rare examples where levelling of the *u* : *o* contrast failed to take place within a paradigm. We can note the possible role of fronting umlaut (*$*u$* > *y*) in obstructing *u* : *o* levelling in this case. (On the other hand, the dat. sg. *søni* and nom. pl. *sønir* variants in other ON dialects are consistent with *u* : *o* levelling having preceded fronting.) Below we consider cases of *u*-stems in OI, where fracture and *u*-mutation of *e* also may have inhibited levelling of an older *i* : *e* alternation within the paradigm.

13. The acc. pl. doublets *syni* and *sonu* (Zoëga 1910) are 'regular' in the sense that the former is regular for an *i*-stem, the latter for a *u*-stem, in both the inflectional ending and stem vowel. From other Germanic and IE languages we would expect OI *sonr* to be a *u*-stem. In any case my argument is not affected: both -*i* and -*u* are raising environments for *$*u$*.

14. The gen. pl. *sona* also had no doublet, but this case form is not inherited directly from the PG *u*-stem case form: In OI the gen. pl. ending -*a* had become endemic to all nominal inflectional classes, replacing all the old inflections.

15. From *Brennu-Njáls Saga*, chapter 1.

16. The applicability to a particular word in question (or lack of it) of an 'explanatory' case form(s) (e.g. genitive singular for Icelandic *sonr*) must be taken into account in explaining an exceptional phonological treatment of that word. In discussing the parallel problem of Germanic *$*i$* and *$*e$*, Marchand (1957: 349) suggested that the nominative singular of *$*fiskaz$* 'fish' could have based its stem vowel upon that of a locative singular form *$*fiski$*:. This seems quite implausible, given the presumed rarity of the locative singular of 'fish' in actual discourse: Fish are not prototypical locations. The idea that the locative could have become the basis for the dative might improve Marchand's proposal, but he offers a distinct form for the Proto-Germanic dative and suggests the locative as the determinative case in the face of opposite pressure from the nominative, genitive, and dative. Hock (1973: 344–5) suggested that vocative singular forms such as *$*spik$* 'bacon', *$*berg$* 'mountain', and *$*wulf$* 'wolf' helped formed the motivation for such doublets as OHG *wolf*: OE *wulf* (and OI *úlfr*) 'wolf' or OHG *quec* : OE *cwic* 'alive' (to which might be added OHG *spek* 'bacon' : OI *spik* 'blubber'). Here again, vocative forms of 'bacon', 'mountain', and even 'wolf' must have been vanishingly infrequent in actual discourse, and thus, for these particular lexical items, quite improbable bases for morphological levelling. Of course there would be other nouns for which a vocative or locative might be expected to be more frequent (e.g. 'child' or 'place'), thus permitting some account of the exception; later in this chapter I suggest that the 'locative' hypothesis may provide an account for the rather irregular vowel of OI *ruð* 'clearing in a wood'. (If the hypotheses of Marchand and Hock were correct, then one would expect a statistically significant correlation between exceptional phonological treatment of a stem's vowel and a higher than normal likelihood for that stem to be used in an 'explanatory' case form.) In fairness to Marchand and Hock, one must acknowledge that their explanations were for them the most plausible ones available for otherwise inexplicable phenomena. Later in this chapter I provide an account for cases where *$*u$* is not lowered that treats the vast majority of exceptionally unlowered PG *$*u$* as not phonologically 'irregular' at all, so no morphological explanation is needed.

17. I use the term 'dental' because it is a traditional one in Germanic philology; of course the consonants may have been dental or alveolar.

18. One can note, incidentally, that there was a preference in Germanic against having $C_i uC_j$ syllable structures where C_i and C_j share the same place of articulation, and that this preference treated liquids together as one category and distinguished them from other dentals.

19. Cerciagnani (1980: 130) and others (e.g. Flom 1930: sec. 265) reported the effect of labials in inhibiting lowering, but not that of velars.

20. The analytical procedure is available on standard statistical computing packages under the name *logistic regression*. For information on the GoldVarb 2 program, contact D. Sankoff or D. Rand, Centre de recherces mathématiques, Université de Montréal, C.P. 6128, Succursale A, Montréal H3C 3J7, Canada. For further information on the statistical concepts used here, see Sankoff 1988. A copy of this article is also printed in the manual for GoldVarb 2.

21. Cercignani (1979) had already observed this effect of labials: 'the change */u/ > *[o] . . . appears to have been prevented, at least within certain dialects, by a neighbouring labial".

22. It must be stressed that this hierarchy defines relative, not absolute position: We cannot simply say that r_ is a lowering environment, rather that it is relatively more lowering than, say, V_. This is because the setting of the input probability p_0 determines the magnitude of p_i for particular factors.

23. But in OI *i, *e > e in the environment _x, e.g. PG *slixtaz > OI sléttr 'even'.

24. On the other hand the OI u-stem kviðr 'something spoken', which shows an exceptional reflex of Germanic *e, was originally an i-stem, as it is in OE and OHG. The rather unusual change from i-stem to u-stem was perhaps influenced by homophony with the u-stem kviðr 'womb'.

25. OI veðr 'whether' has become an exceptional a-stem: Its vowel is consistent with either a a-stem or u-stem. (The move away from the u-stem group accounts for the lack of fracture and labial mutation to jö in this form.)

26. OI fé 'cattle, money' had become an exceptional a-stem: in any case lowering to e before *x is quite regular in OI.

27. See Gordon (1957: 274) and Flom (1930: 25,30) regarding the fracture of earlier e in OI and OE.

28. OHG skild has changed to an i-stem (or a-stem, which perhaps explains scheld in the glossary of Braune and Ebbinghaus (1969), and OE scyld/scild is of unclear inflectional class.

29. In OI kvern 'mill' had become an i-stem, but the only explanation for the retention of *e is that the inflectional class change was ordered after i-umlaut of *e had run its course.

30. See Cercignani (1979: fn.14) regarding evidence from Runic for earlier i vowel in the present singular forms. Interestingly the fronting effect of i-mutation on the stem vowel of the present singular was not levelled, for example, the 3rd sg. grefr of grafa 'to dig', and 3rd sg. kømr of koma (< PG *kweman) 'to come'.

31. OI björn is a u-stem, but it may perhaps not be regarded as the best example of retention of *e before -u, because in other Germanic languages it is an -an stem (OHG bero, OE bera). Nevertheless the nom. pl. birnir suggests that its u-stem status is at least as old as the raising of PG *e before i, so for our purposes it is reasonable to regard björn as an example of non-raising of *e before u.

32. The OHG here may be a case or *i > i due the final -i.

33. ". . . there can be no doubt that the apparently random distribution of PIE *i and *e in environments other than before high front vocoid and nasal + consonant must have come about through analogical restructuring . . ." (Hock 1973: 321). This statement is wrong for two reasons: in this environment *e never shows up as i, and the lowering of *i is itself far from random.

34. See Labov 1981 for discussions of cases of 'irregular' abstract phonological change where morphological analogy is not a possible explanation.

REFERENCES

Antonsen, E. (1961). Germanic umlaut anew. *Language* 37: 215–30.

———. (1963). The Proto-Norse vowel system and the Younger Fuþark. *Scandinavian Studies* 35: 195-207.

————. (1964). Zum Umlaut im Deutschen. *Beiträge zur Geschichte der Deutschen Sprace und Literatur* (Tübingen) 86: 177–96.

————. (1965). On defining stages in prehistoric Germanic. *Language* 41: 19-36.

Beeler, M. S. (1966). Proto-Germanic [i] and [e]: one phoneme or two? *Language* 42: 473-4.

Benediktsson, H. (1967). The Proto-Germanic vowel system. In *To honor Roman Jakobson*, 1: 174-96. Mouton, the Hague.

Braune, W. and H. Eggers. (1975). *Althochdeutsche Grammatik*. Max Niemeyer Verlag, Tübingen.

Braune, W. and E. A. Ebbinghaus (1969) *Althochdeutsches Lesebuch*. Max Niemeyer Verlag, Tübingen.

Cedergren, H. and D. Sankoff. (1974). Variable rules: performance as a statistical reflection of competence. *Language* 50: 333–355.

Cercignani, F. (1979). Proto-Germanic */i/ and */e/ revisited. *Journal of English and Germanic Philology* 78: 72-82.

————. (1980). Early 'umlaut' phenomena in the Germanic languages. *Language* 56: 126-36.

Coetsem, Franz van (1968). A syntagmatic structure in development: 'umlaut' and 'consonantal influence' in Germanic. *Lingua* 21: 494-525.

Flom, G. T. (1930). *Introductory Old English grammar and reader*. D. C. Heath and Co., Boston.

Gordon, E. V. (1957). *An introduction to Old Norse*. Oxford University Press, Oxford.

Hock, H. H. (1973). On the phonemic status of Germanic e and i. In B. B. Kachru et al, eds., *Issues in linguistics: Papers in honor of Henry and René Kahane*, 319-51. University of Illinois Press, Urbana.

Kay, P., and C. K. McDaniel (1977). *On the logic of variable rules*. Indiana University Linguistics Club.

Kuhn, H. (1968). *Edda: die Lieder des Codex Regius nebst verwandten Denkmälern*. II. *Kurzes Wörterbuch*. Carl Winter Universitätsverlag, Heidelberg.

Labov, W. (1981). Resolving the Neogrammarian controversy. *Language* 57: 267-308.

Lehmann, W. P. (1961). A definition of Proto-Germanic: A study in the chronological delimitation of languages. *Language* 37: 76-74.

Lloyd, A. L. (1966). Is there an *a*-umlaut of *i* in Germanic? *Language* 42: 738-45.

Marchand, J. W. (1957). Germanic short *i* and *e*: two phonemes or one? Language 33: 346-54.

Meillet, A. ([1926]1970). *General characteristics of the Germanic languages*. Translated by W. P. Dismukes. University of Miami Press, Coral Gables, Florida. Originally published as *Caractères Généraux des Langues Germaniques*.

Prokosch, E. (1939). *A comparative Germanic grammar*. Linguistics Society of America, Philadelphia.

Sankoff, D. (1988). Variable rules. In U. Ammon, N. Dittmar and K. J. Mattheier, eds., *Sociolinguistics: an international handbook of the science of language and society*, 984-997. De Gruyter, Berlin and New York.

Szemerényi, O. (1970). *Einführung in die vergleichende Sprachwissenschaft*. Wissenschaftliche Buchgesellschaft, Darmstadt.

Twaddell, W. F. (1948). The prehistoric Germanic short syllabics. *Language* 24: 139–51.

Zoëga, C. T. (1910). *A concise dictionary of Old Icelandic*. Oxford University Press, Oxford.

5 The Neogrammarian Hypothesis and Pandemic Irregularity

ROBERT BLUST

1 THE NEOGRAMMARIAN HYPOTHESIS

The formulation of a principle that sound change is *inherently* exceptionless, even when appearances may suggest otherwise, is commonly attributed to the *Junggrammatiker* or 'Neogrammarians'—a group of Indo-European comparativists who worked at the University of Leipzig in the 1870s.[1] In this historical context it is clear that the Neogrammarian hypothesis was inspired by the then recent successes of Hermann Grassmann (1863) and Karl Verner (1876) in explaining phonological changes which had long appeared to be exceptions to Grimm's Law. According to Lehmann (1967: 197) 'the central axiom, that sound laws have no exceptions, was first published by the oldest of the group, August Leskien in *Die Deklination im Slavisch-litauischen und Germanischen* (1876).' Two years later, in the preface to a new journal founded by Hermann Osthoff and Karl Brugmann, Brugmann wrote (and both founders signed) a statement of philosophical position which can, with some justification, be called the 'Neogrammarian manifesto'.[2]

The revolutionary fervor so often associated with the name of the Neogrammarians stems in large part from the reaction of younger scholars such as Osthoff and Brugmann to what they evidently perceived as the 'old order' of scholarship in the Indo-European field. Their aim was more than the simple presentation of new ideas: They wished to establish a new order of scholarship by fundamentally changing the thinking of the younger generation of scholars. Like many revolutionary ideas, those of the early Neogrammarians undoubtedly were made more adamant by their having been formulated in an emotional climate of confrontation and polarization.

In retrospect, the zeal of the early Neogrammarians in advocating the principle of exceptionless sound change is not difficult to understand. Grimm's Law had been formulated in 1819. It was more than four decades before Grassmann was able to eliminate the relatively marginal class of apparent exceptions that Grassmann's Law describes, and close to sixty years before Verner's more fundamental contribution appeared in print. To a younger generation of scholars who longed for scientific precision in the study of language, the time must have seemed more than ripe for the introduction of new and more rigorous methods of analysis. Moreover, it must not be forgotten that between the formulation of Grimm's Law in 1819 and Verner's Law in 1875 science and technology as a whole had experienced enormous progress. In England Charles Lyell had founded the science of geology, laying the groundwork for the development of an evolutionary approach to the life sciences. In 1859 and 1871 Charles Darwin published his revolutionary *The Origin of Species* and *The Descent of Man*. In the 1870s the Scottish physicist James Clerk Maxwell published his equations on electromagnetism, the first major advance in physical theory since Newton. The first telegraph message had been sent in 1844, the telephone invented early in 1876, and the Industrial Revolution was in full swing. Finally, great progress had been made in phonetics since the time of Grimm. As a consequence of these ideas, inventions, and discoveries the general intellectual climate of Europe in the 1870s was attuned to a renewed belief in the rule of natural law and the ultimate triumph of technology.

In this chapter I will maintain that excessive enthusiasm for the insights of Grassmann and Verner caused the Neogrammarians to create what Vaihinger (1911) later called a 'fiction': a heuristically useful device which serves to simplify man's picture of nature and so accelerate the rate of scientific progress even while misrepresenting the reality it attempts to order and explain. In the context of their time the Neogrammarians perhaps could not have done otherwise. In part, Verner was able to formulate his 'law' because of the enormous advances that had taken place in phonetics since 1819, when Grimm spoke of 'letters' (*Buchstaben*) and 'sounds' (*Laute*) as fully equivalent entities. It would have been almost irresponsible for young scholars such as Osthoff and Brugmann to admit the successes of Grassmann and Verner and yet continue to believe that some sound changes may be sporadic. In advocating the absolute regularity of sound change, Osthoff, Brugmann, and their like-minded contemporaries had every reason to believe that they themselves or their successors eventually would be able to explain other apparent exceptions to absolute regularity. Moreover, even if they were wrong, the *belief* that sound change knows no exceptions was sure to have far greater value in uncovering previously unrecognized phonetic conditions than the seemingly defeatist view that irregularity was possible, and this alone was justification for maintaining that faith.

Almost from the beginning the Neogrammarian position flew in the face of well-known linguistic facts, as witnessed by the opposition of Schuchardt (1842–1927) and of the French and German dialectologists who followed him (most notably Jules Gilliéron, who commenced work on the *Atlas linguistique de la France* in 1897). Yet the success of the Neogrammarians in propagandizing their views was noteworthy. In 1913–14 the American linguist Leonard Bloomfield pursued postdoctoral studies in Leipzig and Göttingen, where he worked with the then aging Leskien and Brugmann (Bloch 1967: 509). Some fifteen years later Bloomfield confirmed the importance and universality of the Neogrammarian hypothesis in his work on the reconstruction of Proto-Central Algonquian (Bloomfield 1928). More recent writers such as Dyen

(1963) continue to state the Neogrammarian hypothesis more as a matter of ideology than as an empirically vulnerable position to be tested and, if necessary, modified.

To a large extent the success of the Neogrammarian hypothesis has stemmed from the apparent fact that sound change *is* overwhelmingly regular. Where irregularities exist it has generally been found possible to explain them (or, all too often, 'explain them away') as products of borrowing, analogy, or some other mechanism of secondary change. At the same time the problems associated with the Neogrammarian hypothesis stem from two apparent facts which may conflict with it: (1) The regularity of phonological change is an epiphenomenon rather than a primary datum, and (2) despite its overwhelming regularity, not *all* sound change is regular.[3]

2 PANDEMIC IRREGULARITY

In typical treatments of diachronic irregularity the phonological development of a single language or close-knit subgroup is examined and deviations from the expected reflexes are scrutinized in relation to borrowing, fossilized morphology, and various mechanisms of secondary change (metathesis, assimilation, etc.). The kinds of diachronic irregularities discussed in this chapter do not readily lend themselves to such conventional explanations, since they recur (independently, in different lexical items) throughout an entire language family or major subgroup. Like diseases which are characteristic of large human populations, such apparent abnormalities of phonological development which are characteristic of large populations of languages can be called 'pandemic'.

Pandemic irregularities resist a plausible explanation through borrowing, analogy or other mechanisms of secondary change and hence are particularly difficult to reconcile with the Neogrammarian position that all apparent diachronic rule violations are due to secondary factors which interfere with the perfect regularity of primary sound change. Two types of pandemic irregularity in the Austronesian languages of island Southeast Asia will be examined in this chapter: (1) medial prenasalization, and (2) voicing crossover in the velar stops. It is concluded that some types of pandemic irregularity, of which voicing crossover in the velar stops is an instance, are actually motivated by universal perceptual constraints.[4]

Finally, like recurrent regular changes, pandemic irregularities have the character of a drift—that is, they appear to be indicative of some persistent property either of their common parent or of the human *faculté de langage*.

3 AUSTRONESIAN COMPARATIVE LINGUISTICS: A BIRD'S-EYE VIEW

A critical interpretation of Wurm and Hattori 1981, supplemented in a few cases by additional sources, suggests that there are about 930 Austronesian languages scattered through island Southeast Asia (including Taiwan) and the Pacific, with outliers on the Asian mainland and the island of Madagascar. This figure agrees closely with that of Ruhlen (1987), who lists 945 names of Austronesian languages, but sometimes conflates language and dialect.⁵ Most comparativists have little knowledge of these languages or of the linguistic literature concerning them. The first question that probably will occur to the general reader, then, is 'How well studied is the Austronesian language family?'

Any comparison of the level of advancement of scholarship in one language family with that of another is a difficult matter, and one that runs the risk of bruising scholarly egos. Language families differ in size and internal complexity, in time-depth of historical attestation for given member languages, in time-depth for the language family as a whole, and in the degree to which the comparative material lends itself to systematic treatment. Nonetheless, I venture the following remarks in the hope that they will serve the constructive purpose of providing a perspective on the level of advancement of comparative Austronesian linguistics.

To choose only well-established language families in which traditional reconstruction is feasible, even the scholar with a vested interest in the matter probably would agree that, for example, comparative Algonquian is well in advance of, say, comparative Siouan, or that comparative Bantu has made much greater progress than, say, comparative Nilotic. In terms of having a well-established core phonological system, a large body of precisely reconstructed lexical items that are widely distributed in the language family, and a generally accepted and well-supported subgrouping at the higher levels, the comparative study of Austronesian languages certainly appears to be substantially in advance of such large and internally complex language families as Sino-Tibetan, Austroasiatic or Niger-Congo, or even such branches of putative larger language families as Chadic (part of Afroasiatic), Arawakan (part of Macro-Arawakan), or Yuman (part of Hokan). The Austronesian languages have, moreover, been the subject of more systematic comparative treatment than such smaller, comparatively well-studied groups as Dravidian, since Burrow and Emeneau (1961) simply assemble cognate sets without explicit reconstructions. On an admittedly impressionistic basis I would compare the level of advancement of comparative work in Austronesian to that in Algonquian (Goddard 1979), Mayan (Campbell and Kaufman 1985), or perhaps Semitic. In other words, it probably is as well-studied as any major language family apart from Indo-European.

The starting point for Austronesian comparative linguistics is Dempwolff 1934–38. Volume 1 (1934) is an 'inductive' comparison of three "Indonesian" languages: Tagalog of the Philippines, and Toba Batak and Javanese of western Indonesia. Volume 2 (1937) is a 'deductive' application of the reconstruction arrived at in volume 1 to three other 'Indonesian' languages (Malay, Ngaju Dayak of southeast Borneo, and Malagasy), two 'Melanesian' languages (Sa'a of the southeast Solomons and Fijian), and three Polynesian languages (Tongan, Futunan, and Samoan). Volume 3 (1938) is an Austronesian-German comparative dictionary.

Although much new comparative material has become available since the appearance of Dempwolff 1938, I will generally restrict my citations to this work so that the interested reader can more readily check my data and raw statistics. Dempwolff's phonological system and orthography underwent important modifications in the 1940s, 1950s, and 1960s, largely through the work of Isidore Dyen. The resulting system that is generally accepted today for the ancestor of all non-Formosan Austronesian languages includes twenty-one consonants and four vowels, as follows: consonants *p, *t, *c, *k, *q, *b, *d, *z (a palatal affricate), *g, *j (a palatalized velar), *m, *n, *ñ, *ŋ, *s, *h, *l, *r, *ʀ, *w, and *y; vowels *i, *u, *e (=[ə]), and *a. In addition, prenasalized obstruents are typically listed separately since their reflexes often differ from those of the corresponding oral segments. These are: *mp, *nt, *nc, *ŋk, *mb, *nd, *nz, *ŋg, *njj, and *ns.[6] Although the point is somewhat obscured by Dyen's orthography, Dempwolff regarded the preconsonantal nasal in CVNCVC and CV(N)CVC forms as homorganic with the obstruent that follows it. However, in some daughter languages such as Malay and Javanese, *ns is reflected as velar nasal + /s/.

Dempwolff 1938 contains 2,216 lexical reconstructions, including some 39 known loan words from non-Austronesian sources (mostly Sanskrit) which were incorporated for methodological reasons. According to Chrétien (1965) 2,081 of these, or 94%, are disyllabic. Of this number 130 items are reduplicated monosyllables (e.g. *butbut* 'pluck, pull out'). The remaining 1,950 disyllables conform to one of three canonical shapes: '(1) CVCVC, which is self-explanatory; (2) CVNCVC, where medial C is a stop and N the nasal homorganic to it; and 3) CV(N)CVC, which is the same as (2) except that whereas in (2) all reflexes testify to the nasal, in (3) some reflexes do and some do not' (Chrétien 1965: 245).

Although he reached a major subgrouping conclusion in volume 2 (1937), Dempwolff approached his data without a linguistically justified subgrouping theory. Rather he resorted to the use of geographical labels: 'Indonesian', 'Melanesian', and Polynesian, only the last of which corresponds to a valid linguistic subgroup.

Among Dempwolff's major conclusions are the following: (1) all phonological distinctions that must be posited for 'Uraustronesisch' can be reconstructed through a comparison of just three 'Indonesian' languages (Tagalog, Toba Batak, and Javanese); (2) the statement that Dempwolff's reconstruction is based on three languages is to be understood as a 'fiction' in the sense of Vaihinger (1911); (3) there is a large *melanesisch* subgroup which includes the Polynesian languages, most of the languages of Micronesia, and the languages of Melanesia exclusive of some non-Austronesian languages in the Solomon Islands chain and other parts of western Melanesia. This subgroup, which includes more than half of all Austronesian languages, is known today as 'Oceanic.'

4 DEMPWOLFF'S 'FACULTATIVE' NASAL

Dempwolff called the nasal of CV(N)CVC reconstructions a 'facultative' nasal. It is important to recognize that he distinguished between such nasals, which he enclosed in parentheses, and ambiguous segments, which he enclosed in square brackets. Rather than being ambiguous, the facultative nasal represents a contradiction which permits no immediate resolution: Some languages unambiguously indicate a simple medial consonant, while others unambiguously indicate a prenasalized stop. Dempwolff's parenthesis convention is often taken to imply that the nasal may or may not have been present in the etymon. Those who read Dempwolff's reconstructions in this way, however, simply sidestep the issue of regularity in sound change, as the notation was clearly intended to be a concise means of representing contradictory reflexes involving a nasal segment and zero.

Chrétien (1965) has assembled a number of frequency values and correlations from a statistical study of Dempwolff 1938. Because he does not distinguish Dempwolff's facultative nasal from his obligatory nasal, however, his results cannot be used to assess the frequent disagreements in the prenasalization of medial obstruents.

Allowing for the conflation of around a dozen doublets that Dyen (1953) showed to be unjustified, I count 193 examples of facultative nasals and 283 examples of obligatory preconsonantal nasals in Dempwolff 1938. This count does not include reduplicated monosyllables such as *banban 'bast fibre', in which the nasal is part of a reduplicated syllable, nor does it include loan words. Facultative nasals thus make up slightly over 40% of the 476 nasals that occur preconsonantally in Dempwolff's corpus of non-reduplicated reconstructions.

Although Dempwolff used material from eleven languages in his comparative dictionary, he never allowed the shape of a reconstruction to be determined by a reflex in an Oceanic language (e.g. *tamburi 'conch shell trumpet' was reconstructed with an obligatory nasal despite the disagreement of Sa'a ehuri and Fijian ndavui, both of which suggest an etymon with simple *b). All distinctions between -NC- and -(N)C- in Dempwolff (1938) are thus based on the comparison of just six languages: Tagalog (TAG), Toba Batak (TB), Javanese (JAV), Malay (MAL), Ngaju Dayak NgD), and Malagasy (MLG).

To make it easier for the general reader to appreciate the nature and pervasive scope of the facultative nasal problem in Austronesian linguistics, the following facts should be kept in mind: (1) Tagalog, Toba Batak, Javanese, Malay, Ngaju Dayak, and Malagasy are all, in Dempwolff's terminology, 'test languages' (*Test-Sprachen*) for the *-NC-: *-C- distinction; that is, the reconstructed distinction of simple and prenasalized obstruents has not been lost by merger; (2) any one or more of these six languages may show a simple/prenasalized disagreement in relation to the others; (3) in a number of cases the same language has doublets, one variant having and the other variant lacking the preconsonantal nasal. Sample comparisons appear below:[7]

(1a) *qa(n)dep 'front; facing'
   TAG haráp 'front, facade'; TB adop 'in front, before, facing'; JAV arep-an 'opposite, facing'; ŋ-arep 'front, that which is in front'; MAL hadap 'position facing'; NgD ta-harep 'in front, in sight of'; MLG t-andrif-y 'opposite to, before' (only Malagasy has a prenasalized reflex)

(1b) *gu(n)ci 'earthenware jar or jug'
   TAG gúsiʔ (-ʔ unexpl.) 'large China vase or pottery', TB gunsi 'earthen jug'; JAV goci, guci 'large earthenware jug'; MAL guci 'a water vessel' (only Toba Batak has a prenasalized reflex)

(2a) *hi(n)zam 'borrow, lend'
   TAG hirám 'borrowed; adapted', TB injam 'lend, borrow'; MAL p-injam 'borrowing'; NgD injam 'lend, borrow, what is lent or borrowed'; MLG indrana 'borrowed'; indram-ina 'used of the thing which is to be borrowed' (only Toba Batak has a simple reflex)

(2b) *ra(m)but 'head hair'
   TB rabut 'rough, hairy, of the skin'; JAV, MAL rambut 'hair on the human

head', NgD *rambut* 'thick thread on a fish hook' (only Tagalog has a simple reflex)

(3a) **ta(ŋ)gal* 'loosened, detached'
TAG *taŋgál* 'unfastened, dismantled', Tb *taŋgal* 'detached, unraveled', MAL *taŋgal* 'dropping, falling off', *tagal* 'large stones washed up on the beach by a storm' (only Malay has prenasalized/simple doublets)

(3b) **qi(n)tem* 'black'
TAG *itím* 'blackness', *ma-itím* 'black', Tb *itom* 'dark blue, indigo', *l-intom* 'deep black', JAV *batu-item* ('black stone'=) 'tooth decay', MAL *hitam* 'black', MLG *voa-ìtina* 'blackened', *ma-ìnty* 'black' (both Toba Batak *l-intom* and Malagasy *ma-ìnty* indicate **nt*; other reflexes contrarily indicate **t*)

Nasal/oral values for the reflexes of Dempwolff's 193 examples of **-(N)C-* have been tabulated. Although space does not permit the full set of values to be displayed here, some useful correlations can be given. Table 6-1 shows the distribution of facultative nasalization among the six 'Indonesian' languages in Dempwolff 1934–38. Presence of the facultative nasal in a language is indicated by +, absence by –, and nasal/oral doublets by +/–.

Thus in Tagalog, reflexes are found for 118 of Dempwolff's 193 reconstructions with a facultative nasal. In 27 of these, or 23% of the total number of reflexes, Tagalog has a prenasalized obstruent corresponding to a simple obstruent in at least one of the other five languages. In 78, or 66% of the total number of reflexes, Tagalog has a simple obstruent corresponding to a prenasalized obstruent in at least one of the other five languages, and in 13, or 11% of the reflexes, Tagalog has simple/prenasalized doublets.

The figures in Table 6-1 are summations of various distribution types which cannot be presented in full here, although the original data are available in Dempwolff 1938. Even without a full presentation of the supporting data, however, it should be evident that the problem of the facultative nasal in Austronesian linguistics presents a major challenge to the Neogrammarian hypothesis. It is thus imperative that we make every effort to find an explanation for the facts which will not require us to abandon the view that sound change is entirely regular. I will now consider a number of potential explanations for the facultative nasal correspondences, and argue that none of them can satisfactorily deal with the difficulties they present.

TABLE 6-1
Reflexes of Dempwolff's **-(N)C-* in six languages

	TAG	TB	JAV	MAL	NgD	MLG
+	27 (23%)	66 (50%)	53 (38%)	74 (51%)	52 (43%)	42 (55%)
−	78 (66%)	51 (39%)	68 (49%)	52 (36%)	52 (43%)	27 (36%)
+/−	13 (11%)	14 (11%)	18 (13%)	19 (13%)	17 (14%)	7 (9%)
TOTAL	118 (100%)	131 (100%)	139 (100%)	145 (100%)	121 (100%)	76 (100%)

4.1   The Facultative Nasal As a Product of Affixation

One transparent and intuitively satisfying alternative to the recognition of sporadic sound change would be to identify the facultative nasal with a fossilized affix. A solution of this kind is proposed by Dempwolff (1922: 180), who argues for an infixed *-m-. And a similar solution is implied by Blust (1970a), where the medial nasal is written *-ŋ-. The problems with this interpretation are nonetheless formidable.

If the facultative nasal is a product of infixation, it should be possible to find a meaning or grammatical function associated with it in at least a few languages. This expectation has never been fulfilled and is indeed contradicted by those languages with simple/prenasalized doublets, as these either show idiosyncratic differences of meaning or are nearly or fully synonymous. Moreover, the facultative nasal may appear in morphemes which belong to almost any word class.[8]

4.2   The Facultative Nasal As a Product of Conditioned Sound Change

An alternative to the foregoing explanation which avoids the problem of sound-meaning association is a hypothesis of conditioned sound change. Adelaar (1992: 103) has argued that original *e (schwa) followed by a simple obstruent was regularly prenasalized in Malay, as in PMP *hepat > Malay empat 'four'. Even if this is granted, such a change would account for only a very small portion of the facultative nasals reflected in Malay, and in many other cases prenasalized obstruents occur in the same segmental environment as simple obstruents (e.g. *ma-qa(n)taq > Malay mentah 'raw' versus *mata > Malay mata 'eye', or *bu(ŋ)su > Malay bu(ŋ)su 'youngest child' versus *susu > Malay susu 'female breast').

4.3   The Facultative Nasal As a Product of Borrowing

Malay has been an important trade language in western Indonesia and a source of numerous loanwords in other languages of island Southeast Asia for centuries. In a number of cases where there is reason to suspect that Toba Batak has borrowed a lexical item from Malay, the latter language has a simple medial obstruent and the former the reflex of a prenasalized obstruent, while Karo Batak (KB)generally agrees with Malay in having a simple obstruent: *gu(n)ci 'earthenware pot' (MAL, KB guci; TB gunsi), *Ra(ŋ)kit 'raft' (MAL, KB rakit, TB raŋkit); *ka(n)caŋ 'bean, peanut' (MAL, KB kacaŋ,;TB hansaŋ), *ki(n)su 'cheat, swindle' (MAL kicu; KB kicuk (-k unexpl.); TB hinsu), *cu(ŋ)kur 'shave' (MAL cukur; TB suŋkur), *la(m)pis 'layer' (MAL, KB lapis, TB lampis), *tu(ŋ)kaŋ 'craftsman, artisan' (MAL tukaŋ; TB tuŋkaŋ), *tu(ŋ)kup 'cover, lid' (MAL, KB tukup; TB tuŋkup), *salu(m)buŋ 'cape, cloth that is wrapped around' (MAL seluboŋ 'veil'; TB salumbuŋ 'cape'), *su(ŋ)kar 'difficult' (MAL sukar 'difficult'; KB sukar 'rude, uncivil', TB suŋkar 'difficult'), *cu(n)ci 'wash clothes' (MAL cuci; TB sunsi).

The foregoing examples suggest that in adapting Malay loanwords Toba Batak often (regularly?) altered a simple medial obstruent through prenasalization (with subsequent assimilation of the nasal to a following voiceless stop and change of *ns to [ts]). The motivation for this change is unclear, but our recognition of the phenomenon serves to explain a few examples of facultative nasals where Toba Batak is the sole offending language. Unfortunately, nothing similar appears to have operated in any of the other languages examined by Dempwolff.

4.4   The Facultative Nasal As a Sound Change in Progress

In opposition to the Neogrammarians, Wang (1969) has argued that sound change is not phonetically gradual and lexically abrupt, but is phonetically abrupt and lexically gradual. Wang's position is a modern adaptation of ideas expressed by Schuchardt (1885), and by a number of other linguists in this century (see n. 3). If sound change is in fact lexically gradual, Dempwolff's facultative nasal could reflect a sound change in progress. The advocate of this position, however, would be forced to assume that the *same sound change* is in progress simultaneously in many different languages and has not yet been completed in any of them. It is this pandemic character of the facultative nasal which makes it a problem not only for the Neogrammarian hypothesis but also for theories such as Wang's which seek to remedy problems with the Neogrammarian position.

4.5   Denasalization

To the extent that the question has been addressed at all in Austronesian linguistics, it generally has been assumed without argument that comparative disagreements relating to the facultative nasal are products of prenasalization rather than of denasalization. Such an assumption can be justified by an appeal to Occam's razor in comparisons such as (1a) and (1b), in which only one witness reflects a prenasalized obstruent.

In comparisons such as (2a) and (2b), on the other hand, in which only one witness reflects a simple obstruent, Occam's razor favors a hypothesis of denasalization. This type of correspondence is particularly frequent where Tagalog is the anomalous language (66% of all instances of PAN facultative nasals have a simple obstruent in Tagalog; cf. Table 6-1). Although many instances of homorganically prenasalized obstruents remain in Tagalog, the simplest explanation of these correspondences is that Tagalog has been gradually denasalizing medial clusters of nasal + homorganic obstruent one lexical item at a time. Such a tendency appears to have been carried much further in northern Philippine languages such as Ilokano or Bontok, where homorganically prenasalized obstruents are rare.[9]

4.6   The Facultative Nasal in Other Languages
of Island Southeast Asia

Dempwolff (1938) cites material from only six languages representing island Southeast Asia (including Madagascar). The problem of the facultative, however, is truly pandemic in this region. To illustrate, Dempwolff (1938) cites *betuŋ 'large bamboo species', with cognates in Malay and Ngaju Dayak. However, by adding Western Bukidnon Manobo (southern Philippines) bentuŋ (expected **betuŋ) 'large bamboo sp.' we are required by Dempwolff's procedures of reconstruction to introduce a facultative nasal in this etymon: *be(n)tuŋ*. Similarly, although scores of languages throughout the Philippines and Indonesia reflect *bitis* 'calf of the leg', *pija* 'how much, how many?', and *pusej* 'navel' with simple medial obstruents *t, *j, and *s, these show reflexes with a prenasalized reflex in Maloh (Borneo) *intis* 'calf of the leg', Maloh *insa* 'how many?', and Low Balinese *puŋsed* (cf. Refined Balinese *puser*) 'navel'. Given these observations it is clear that the number of reconstructed forms that ultimately will require a facultative nasal is largely a function of the number of languages included in any given cognate set.

4.7   The Problem of the Facultative Nasal in Oceanic Languages

The problem of the facultative nasal in Oceanic languages differs from that in the Austronesian languages of island Southeast Asia in two principle respects: (1) The 'nasal grade' reflex is often not phonetically a prenasalized obstruent, but rather a simple obstruent with greater articulatory constriction than the corresponding oral grade reflex, and (2) facultative nasals are not exclusively medial, but also appear in initial position. Space does not permit more than passing mention of a complex situation, but Lynch (1975) and Geraghty (1983) contain important discussions of the role of unstressed grammatical markers in creating secondary prenasalization of stem-initial obstruents in various Oceanic languages. Neither of these writers, however, can account for the facultative nasal in medial position in Oceanic languages. A thorough discussion of the major issues connected with consonant grade in Oceanic languages is found in Ross (1988, 1990).

4.8   Direct Evidence for Secondary Prenasalization

Under certain circumstances there is fairly direct evidence for sporadic prenasalization of earlier simple stops in the languages of island Southeast Asia. Gonda (1950) has pointed out the secondary prenasalization of, for instance, Malay *umpana* 'example' (from Sanskrit *upamā* 'resemblance'), and Malay *tembakau* (from Portugese *tabaco*) 'tobacco', but irregular consonant insertions in loanwords are less likely to occasion surprise than the similar changes in directly inherited vocabulary since the assimilation of loanwords is not, strictly speaking, a type of sound change. In forms such as Tagalog *taŋgíŋgi* (from *taŋgiʀi) 'a fish: Spanish mackerel', Iban *bumbus* 'perforated' (from *busbus) and Maloh *iŋko* '2sg. nominative' (from *i kaSu) prenasalization could not have taken place until after (1) the change of *ʀ to Tagalog /g/, (2) the reduction of medial reduplicative clusters in Iban, and (3) the loss of the morpheme boundary separating the old person marker *i and the pronominal stem *kaSu in Maloh. Examples such as these, then, provide direct evidence for historically secondary sporadic prenasalization in native vocabulary.

4.9   Conclusion

The problem of the 'facultative nasal' in Austronesian languages continues to resist any fully satisfactory solution within the Neogrammarian framework. Although particular instances of simple/prenasalized disagreements may be due to conditioned sound change, borrowing, or even sound change in progress, the phenomenon of the facultative nasal as a whole remains unexplained.

5 VOICING CROSSOVER IN THE VELAR STOPS

The second challenge to the Neogrammarian hypothesis that I wish to pose differs from the first in a number of particulars. Dempwolff (1934–38) reconstructed two 'Original Austronesian' velar stops, *g and *k, which have remained phonemically distinct (generally as /g/, /k/) in the majority of languages in the Philippines and Indonesia as well as in several of the languages of southern Taiwan. However, in a rather substantial number of cases, the reflex of *g or *k in one member of a cognate set exhibits a contrary value for voicing, a phenomenon that I will call 'voicing crossover'. In this section, I will endeavour to make the following points: (1) voicing cross-over among stops in Austronesian languages is confined almost exclusively to the velars in morpheme-initial position, and (2) these irregularities almost certainly are consequences of the nature of stop production and perception in human languages generally.

5.1 Irregular Reflexes of *g and *k in Dempwolff (1938)

Among the 2,216 reconstructed forms in Dempwolff (1938) word-initial *g is found 106 times and word-initial *k 214 times. Among the eleven languages that Dempwolff compared, five are 'test languages' for the *g/k distinction—that is, languages in which the reflexes of these phones have not unconditionally merged. These languages and their reflexes of *g and *k are: (1) Tagalog (*g became /g/ and *k became /k/ unconditionally), (2) Toba Batak (*g became /k/ word-finally, but /g/ elsewhere; *k became /h/ before a vowel and /k/ elsewhere), (3) Javanese (*g became /g/; *k became /k/, realized phonetically as a glottal stop in final position following any vowel except schwa, and as [k] elsewhere), (4) Malay (*g became /k/ word-finally, but /g/ elsewhere; *k became /k/, realized phonetically as a glottal stop in final position after all vowels), and (5) Ngaju Dayak (*g became /k/ in final position, but /g/ elsewhere; *k became /k/).

Despite these regular conditioned and unconditioned developments, for approximately 6% of Dempwolff's reconstructions that begin with a velar stop at least one reflex among these five languages exhibits an unexpected value for voicing. A fairly complete list of exceptions follows. The number of test languages for which a regular reflex is cited is given in parentheses, for example, *galiŋ (2) 'to roll', but TB haliŋ 'turned' indicates that two test languages on Dempwolff's proposed cognate set have the expected reflex of *g, while TB has the expected reflex of *k:

1. *galiŋ (2) 'to roll', but TB haliŋ 'turned'
2. *ganti (4), but NgD ganti, kanti 'substitute, replacement'[10]
3. *gatel (4), but TAG katí 'to itch'
4. *geli (2) 'incite to laughter', but NgD kali-en 'tickle'
5. *genDaŋ (3), but JAV keṇḍaŋ 'kettle drum'

6. *genDit* (2), but JAV *keṇḍit* 'girdle'

7. *gitik* (2), but NgD *kitik* 'tickle'

8. *gugut* (3) 'nibble off', but TAG *kukót* 'eat slowly, grain by grain (peanuts, dried seeds, etc.)'

9. *guntiŋ* (5), but NgD *guntiŋ, kuntiŋ* 'scissors'[10]

10. *gusuk* (4) 'to rub', but NgD *kusok* 'grated'

11. *kabal* (3) 'invulnerable', but NgD *gabal, kabal* 'thick-skinned'

12. *kali* (3), but MAL *gali* 'to dig'

13. *kaʀat* (2) 'to bite', but MAL *garat* 'grind the teeth'[11]

14. *kenTer* (4), but MAL *getar, gentar, g-el-etar, g-em-etar* 'tremble', *ketar* 'quiver', *buŋa ketar* 'artificial flowers on wires worn in a headdress'

15. *kesaq* (2) 'breathe loud', but JAV *gesah, g-er-esah* 'to sigh'

16. *kumis* (3), but TB *gumis* 'beard'

17. *kundur* (2) 'gourd, calabash', but TB *gundur* 'pumpkin sp.'

18. *kurap* (2), but TB *gurap* 'skin disease'

19. *kurapu* (3), but TB *gurapu* 'fish sp.'

20. *kuʀita* (2), but JAV *gerita*, MAL *gurita* 'octopus'[12]

In addition to these examples of voicing crossover among initial velar stops, Dempwolff (1938) contains one instance of voicing cross-over in a medial velar stop:

21. *bekas* (4) 'trace', but TB *bogas* 'footprint'

5.2 The Exceptional Instability of Velar Voicing

Among word-initial stops or affricates in Dempwolff 1938 *b* occurs 280 times, *p* 208 times, *d* and *D* 112 times, *t* and *T* 302 times, *z* 71 times, and *c* 48 times. In striking contrast with the velars, I have not found a single instance of voicing crossover in the pre-velar stops.[13] This distinctive instability in the voicing of velar, as opposed to pre-velar stops, is readily confirmed by a comparative examination of languages or cognate sets not considered by Dempwolff. The following cognate sets, which are found in Dempwolff 1938, show voicing irregularities in languages other than those used in that work:

22. *garis* (4), but Kayan *karih* (expected **garih) 'to scratch

23. *garus* (4), but Western Budiknon Manobo *karus* (expected **garus) 'to scratch'

24. *garut* (5), but Mansaka *karut* (expected **garut) 'to scratch'

25. *gasiŋ* (3), but Western Budiknon Manobo *kasiŋ* 'spinning top'

26. *gelap* (3) 'storm, darkness', but Cebuano Bisayan *kuláp, kúlap* (expected **gulap) 'dim, not affording much light'

27. *genep* (5) 'complete; every', but Bario Kelabit *kenep* (expected **genep*) 'each, every'

28. *gigit* (2) 'bite off', but Ilokano *kitkít* (expected **gitgít*) 'gnaw, nibble, as ants do'

29. *guham* (5) 'mouth sore', but Kadazan *kuam* (expected **guam*) 'sickness of the tongue in young animals'

30. *gumi* (2), but Sangir *kumi* (expected **gumi*) 'beard'

31. *kapas* (4), but Maranao *gapas* (expected **kapas*) 'cotton'

32. *kaya* (3), but Maranao *gaya* (expected **kaya*) 'rich'

33. *kazaŋ* (4), but Karo Batak *ganjaŋ* (expected **kanjaŋ*) 'long'

34. *kembar* (4), but Iban *gembar* (expected **kembar*) 'twin'

35. *kilala* (2) 'recognize', but Tiruray *gilolo-n* (expected **kilolo-n*) 'recognizable'

36. *kiTa* (2) 'see', but Tiruray *gito-n* (expected **kito-n*) 'visible'

37. *kutu* (4), but Miri *gutauh* (expected **hutauh*), Tapuh, Lundu *gutu* (expected **kutu*) 'louse'[14]

The following cognate sets do not appear in Dempwolff 1938, but are based entirely on the comparison of Tagalog and Malay, and so could in principle have been used to support reconstructions in that work had Dempwolff taken greater account of voicing crossover in cognate searching:[15]

38. TAG *galás* 'of taste: tartness; of wood: knottiness, roughness; of manners: harshness, gruffness', MAL *keras* 'hard, stiff, inelastic; (fig.) obstinate'

39. TAG *galót* 'crumpled', MAL *kerut* 'crease, furrow, deep line of the face'

40. TAG *gusót* 'crumpled, entangled, confused', MAL *kusut* 'tangled or disordered (of hair); difficult to unravel (of a situation)'

41. TAG *kalapáy* 'wing movements', MAL *gelapai* 'fight feebly (of cocks)'

42. TAG *kalatóg* 'knocking sound', MAL *gelatok* 'chatter (of the teeth)'

43. TAG *kamál* 'large handful', MAL *gemal* 'handful'

44. TAG *kilitíʔ*, MAL *geliték* 'tickle' (final is irregular: only -ʔ: -h and -k: -k are recurrent correspondences)

45. TAG *kimpál* 'lump, clod', MAL (Bahasa Indonesia) *gempal* 'clod, clot, lump'

46. TAG *kulóg* 'thunder', MAL *gerok-gerak* 'rumbling noises of all sorts'[16]

47. TAG *kulúmot* 'jamming of a crowd upon (something or someone)', MAL *gerumut/geremut* 'to swarm, as a moving mass of ants'

However, a number of the above Tagalog forms probably are Malay loans. Tagalog reflects PAN *e* (schwa) as /a/, /i/ and /u/ or /o/,[17] but reflexes with /a/ generally are regarded today as loans from neighboring Kapampangan, and reflexes with /u/ or /o/ are conditioned by a rounded vowel in an adjacent syllable. If they were directly inherited, we would thus expect /i/ rather than /a/ in *kamál* 'large handful' and *galás* 'tartness; knottiness, roughness', and /u/ rather than /a/ in *galót* 'crumpled'. Since Malay schwa generally is borrowed as Tagalog /a/ (Wolff 1976: 351), a hypothesis of borrowing would account for the vocalic irregularities in these forms. Similarly, a hypothesis of borrowing would explain the irregular final stop in TAG *kilití?*, since MAL /k/ is realized as glottal stop in final position.

A second observation which suggests that at least some of the above forms are loans in Tagalog is their limited distribution. Many probable loans nonetheless are attested in other (particularly lowland) Philippine languages, and it therefore would be puzzling if the above items should prove to be restricted to Tagalog and Malay. However, there is known evidence for a particularly intense Malay linguistic presence in the Tagalog-speaking region around Manila Bay. Wolff (1976) has even maintained (I believe correctly) that Malay was once spoken in the Manila region as a prestige language, much as English is today.

Finally, it is clear that Malay loanwords in some other languages were borrowed with the wrong value for voicing in a velar stop, as with Iban *gerena* 'cause, reason', from Malay *karena, kerena* (ultimately from Sanskrit *karna*). Whatever the explanation for the irregular Tagalog-Malay comparisons, (38)–(47) in particular cases, the problem is the same: Why do velar stops in borrowed or in cognate forms so often disagree in voicing?

5.3 Artifices for Salvaging the Neogrammarian Hypothesis

The foregoing data clearly illustrate the pervasive tendency for **g* and **k* in Austronesian languages to be reflected unpredictably with the wrong value for voicing in particular morphemes. They pose a particularly acute challenge to the Neogrammarian hypothesis for the following reasons: (1) although certain irregularities reported by Dempwolff are more common in *individual* languages (e.g. unexpected final glottal stop in Tagalog), voicing crossover in the velar stops is one of the most frequent types of irregularity in any given language, (2) like the problem of the facultative nasal, the problem of voicing crossover is rather evenly distributed over *all* of the languages compared, and (3) these irregularities work in *both* directions (**g* to /k/ and **k* to /g/).

To explain such correspondences we might reconstruct doublets. Despite the inevitable methodological questions that such a procedure raises, Dempwolff posited many doublets as unavoidable inferences from the data he considered: **abuk/ʀabuk* 'dust', **akar/wakar* 'root', **beli/bili* 'buy', and **tiDuʀ/tuDuʀ* 'sleep. Some of Dempwolff's doublets have turned out to be consequences of his inadequate treatment of the Proto-Austronesian 'laryngeals' (Dyen 1953). Others are resolvable as noncognate forms that contain a common submorphemic 'root' (Blust 1988a). Still others probably are consequences of voicing instability among velar stops, as with **gemgem* 'make a fist' (supported by reflexes in TB, JAV, MAL, and NgD) and **kemkem* 'keep closed, as the fist' (supported by reflexes in TAG, TB, and Ng D), **gilap* 'lustre' (supported by reflexes in JAV, MAL, and NgD) and **kilap* 'lustre' (supported by reflexes in TAG, TB, and MAL), **taNgap* 'seize, take hold of' (supported by reflexes in TAG and JAV) and **taNkap* 'seize, take hold of' (supported by reflexes in TB, MAL, and NgD). A number of true lexical doublets nonetheless must be acknowledged for earlier stages of Austronesian. These involve many different patterns of segmental variation, and are not readily explainable as products of prehistoric dialect borrowing. But doubleting would be a poor explanation of the facts in the present case since (a) in general the available comparative data support only one reconstruction for (1)–(47), and (b) if the forms with incompatible velar reflexes in (1)–(47) all derive from variant protoforms, the number of *g/k doublets that must be reconstructed would reach proportions that would raise serious questions of method.

Alternatively, we might consider the reconstruction of new protophonemes. But this clearly is an explanatory dead-end, since the first fifteen comparisons alone involve eight distinct velar correspondences and would consequently require the reconstruction of eight new velar stops distinct from *g and *k. How, then, can we explain the phenomenon of sporadic voicing crossover in comparisons (1)–(47)?

5.4   Voice Onset Time in Velar and Pre-velar Stops

The comparative data considered so far leads to an inescapable conclusion: In many of the languages of island Southeast Asia the voicing distinction in velar stops has historically been less stable than the similar distinction in pre-velar stops. What could be the basis for such a phenomenon in language change? To answer this question it will be necessary to integrate insights from two often semi-autonomous subfields of linguistics: phonetics and historical linguistics. The phonetic basis for my theory of voicing crossover was first suggested to me in conversation with Chin-wu Kim when he was a visiting professor in Hawaii in 1973.[18]

Voiced stops are produced by allowing egressive pulmonic air to pass through the narrowed vocal cords into a *closed* supraglottal cavity. Once the supraglottal cavity is filled, the pressure differential across the vocal cords is neutralized, thereby suppressing vocal cord vibration (= voicing). The space in the oral cavity which is available for continuing airflow before release of the closure is greater for labials than for dentals, and greater for dentals than for velars. This can be tested impressionistically by attempting to prolong a voiced stop without releasing the closure: [b] permits the greatest duration of prevoicing (as the cheeks expand to accomodate the continuing airflow through the vocal cords), [d] permits a shorter duration, and [g] a still shorter voicing duration.

Lisker and Abramson (1964) examined voicing in initial stops for a sample of eleven globally distributed languages, but their work relates only indirectly to the present problem. In 1973, then, the general phonetic observations provided by Kim were all I could find to help account for the puzzling velar correspondences in Austronesian languages.

However, reflection showed that these observations alone were insufficient to provide a complete explanation. Attention to the phonetic mechanism used in the production of voiced stops showed only that the *potential* duration of voicing for velar stops is shorter than the potential duration of voicing for pre-velar stops. This, undoubtedly, is why voicing contrasts are extremely rare in post-velar stops.[19] Whether the *actual* duration of voicing is shorter for velar than for pre-velar stops is, of course, a separate (though clearly related) question.

Smith (1977) reports a study of voice onset time in initial voiced labial, alveolar and velar stop consonants in English. The following findings are of potential relevance to the issues at hand:

1. The average prevoicing duration for initial voiced stops in Smith's experiments was: labials 74 msec.; alveolars 71 msec.; velars 65 msec.;

2. The average prevoicing duration for voiced stops was greater before high vowels than before low vowels;

3. Combining the foregoing, the longest prevoicing duration for English voiced stops occurs with the syllable onsets bu-, bi, and the shortest with the syllable onset ga-.

In considering his results Smith asks rhetorically "Now, what do all of these findings mean and how do they relate?". In answer to this question he replies:

> I am inclined to believe that these findings regarding voicing and place of articulation probably relate to the observation that certain languages have 'missing velars' in their stop inventories. Since voicing during stop occlusion is aerodynamically more difficult to maintain for velars than for alveolars and labials, this may explain why Dutch and Thai, for instance, lack voiced velar stops in their systems, when they do contrast voicing for labial and alveolar stops (6).

Smith's study carries us one step closer to an explanation for the widespread irregular velar stop correspondences in Austronesian languages. But it, too, falls short of completeness. The establishment of a greater duration of voicing for English /b/ than for English /d/ and for English /d/ than for English /g/ does not automatically establish the same relations for other languages. Moreover, Smith's study is concerned solely with *production*. To understand historical irregularities in the voicing value of stops it is important that we also consider *perception*. Smith's study does predict that whether a historical change involving initial velar stops is regular or sporadic, *g>/k/ is more likely to occur than *k>/g/, and furthermore that such changes, are most likely before low vowels. For purposes of historical change, Smith's conclusions regarding gender differences (longer duration of prevoicing for men than for women) need not concern us here.

5.5   Matching Phonetic Theory with Comparative Data

How well are the predictions of Smith's theory of voice onset time supported by the pattern of velar stop correspondences examined above?

The first point to note is that virtually all voicing irregularities in velar stops among cognate Austronesian forms appear in *initial* position. Irregularities in medial position are rare, and irregularities in final position are to date unknown. Both Lisker and Abramson (1964) and Smith (1977) are concerned exclusively with voicing onset time for initial stops, since the majority of voiced stops in other positions would follow a (voiced) vowel, and the issue of onset time could not arise.

The second point concerns Smith's statement (6) that voicing during stop occlu-
sion is "aerodynamically more difficult to maintain for velars than for alveolars and
labials." If true, and if the historical voicing irregularities we have seen have their origin in production rather than perception error, we would expect the change *g>/k/ to
be far more common than the change *k>/g/ in initial position. But this is not the case
in the sample at hand, and does not appear to be the case in Austronesian languages
generally.

Comparisons (1)–(37) involve nineteen cases of irregular initial *g>/k/ and seventeen cases of irregular initial *k>/g/. Not surprisingly, the one known case of voicing crossover in medial position is from voiceless to voiced (item 21). If the exceptionally high incidence of voicing irregularity among velar stops in Austronesian
languages is to be attributed to the relative brevity of voicing duration for velar as
against pre-velar stops, voicing crossover must begin as a perception error which
gives rise to variants, one of which is favored to the gradual exclusion of the other.
When the favored variant has the historically correct value for voicing, the misper-
ception is corrected and no lasting comparative irregularity results; but when the favored variant has the historically incorrect value for voicing, the result is a cognate
set with a voicing irregularity such as we have seen.[20]

6 WIDER IMPLICATIONS

Our attempt to correlate voicing anomalies in the comparative phonology of the Austronesian languages with an aspect of general phonetic theory inevitably raises questions of wider import. If voicing crossover in Austronesian is a by-product of phonetic universals, a similar voicing crossover in the velar stops would be expected in
other language families. To date I have not had an opportunity to determine whether
this is in fact the case. However, the analysis proposed here explicitly predicts that in
many language families voicing cross-over will be found in the sound correspondences holding among velar stops, but not in those holding in pre-velar stops.

The second of the wider implications suggested by our analysis of the Austronesian data concerns the nature of sound change in general. Ever since the Neogrammarians the regularity of sound change has been a basic tenet of historical linguistics.
Indeed, without such a tenet it is difficult to imagine how the progress that we have
observed in linguistic classification and in the reconstruction of protolanguages over
the past century would have been possible.

Why is sound change overwhelmingly regular? The most frequent answer to this
question is expressed in its best-known form by Hermann Paul (1978). Paul's discussion of sound change revolves about two concepts: (1) *Bewegungsgefühl* and (2)
Lautbild. Unfortunately, the most widely-used English translations of these terms
("motor sensation" and "memory-picture") leave much to be desired. I prefer the
translations "articulatory gesture" and "articulatory target" as being more readily
comprehensible to modern readers.[21]

In Paul's view the articulatory target leads and the articulatory gesture follows in
the implementation of sound change. But the articulatory target of any given speak-

er is a composite image made up of his perception of the articulatory gestures of others in the same speech community. Moreover, articulatory gestures are inherently unstable: the same speaker will not reproduce the same gesture every time he aims at a given articulatory target. Instead, there will be a scatter about a target which is held within limits by the need to maintain communication. Despite these constraints on change the target itself may drift in absolute physical terms. When speech communities separate this drift of articulatory targets leads to sound change.

Paul (p.18) suggests a physiological explanation for the regularity of sound change:[22] 'It must be plain to everyone who acknowledges in all phenomena the operation of general laws that the process of development works uniformly to its fulfillment. A motor sensation does not form itself specially for every word, but in every case where the same elements recur in language their production is guided by the same sensation. . . '

To Paul sound change is unconscious and gradual. Its regularity is a function of its independence from meaning. The speaker does not single out individual words in aiming at an articulatory target, and if the articulatory target drifts it will drift without regard to semantics. In an important sense, then, Paul maintains that the regularity of sound change is a by-product of the physiology of speech.

The experience of comparativists working in many different language families has shown that sound change does appear to be overwhelmingly regular. Its general regularity may, indeed, be physiologically motivated. However, the velar correspondences examined in this chapter suggest that the physiology of the speech organs may be equally responsible for certain types of universal *exceptions* to the regularity of sound change. These exceptions need not be limited to the voicing distinctions for velar stops. More generally, whenever a phonemic contrast involves a phonetic distinction that is perceptually difficult, there is a greater likelihood that the phonemes in question will be interchanged in some lexical items, probably by first passing through a stage in which the problematic item has variant pronunciations. But why should perceptually motivated changes affect some lexical items and not others?

If a phonemic distinction is relatively difficult to perceive in a given position, why not simply eliminate it by merger? The answer to this question is not yet clear to me, but it may involve the interplay of production and perception in phonological change. It is possible that regular sound change is basically a matter of production: Consciously or otherwise speakers alter a phonemic norm in a given environment or unconditionally. Voicing crossover in the velar stops probably has nothing to do with production. Rather, speakers mishear the voicing distinction for velars sufficiently often that doubts arise as to the correct form of a particular lexical item. By their nature, errors of perception are more likely to be random than changes in production. This is especially clear in the case of loanwords, where random phonetic substitutions are commonplace. In a sense, like sporadic metatheses or assimilations, one might wish to exclude changes such as those discussed here from the category of 'sound change' since what is involved is not a change of articulatory norms or of phonemes at all, but rather a change in the phonetic composition of morphemes based on a high incidence of mishearing and consequent reinterpretation. But under this interpretation not all phonetic change is sound change, and the regularity of sound change would become little more than a matter of definition.

7 EPILOGUE: THE REGULARITY HYPOTHESIS AND THE INTEGRITY OF SCIENCE

Some scholars surely will object that the admission of irregularity into the theory of language change will destroy the applicability of the comparative method. I take a less pessimistic view of the integrity and viability of science. Historical reconstructions do not presuppose absolute regularity in sound change. They presuppose only (1) recurrent sound correspondences, and (2) the need for independent evidence in support of each reconstructed distinction. In the cases at hand Dempwolff was able to reconstruct for example *gatel* 'itch' or *gusuk* 'rub' despite nonconforming reflexes in Tagalog and Ngaju Dayak, respectively. This was possible because he had already established a recurrent correspondence of $g : g : g : g : g$ in Tagalog, Toba Batak, Javanese, Malay, and Ngaju Dayak. Comparisons such as TAG *kalapáy* 'wing movements', MAL *gelapai* 'fight feebly (of cocks)' are more difficult to use in reconstruction, since the sound correspondence is recurrent, and distinct from that normally assigned to *g or *k, but is not supported by independent evidence (viz. a third witness which reflects the same lexical items with a reflex distinct from that normally assigned to either *g or *k). If a reconstruction is proposed it must be ambiguous: *(gk)alapay.

Finally, despite the fears of some, neither of the deviations from the Neogrammarian hypothesis that I have discussed in this chapter creates a situation in which genetically related forms are indistinguishable from similarities produced by chance. For such a situation to result, one would have to abandon the requirement of recurrence in sound correspondences. Lest I be misread, let me emphasize in the strongest terms that I do not advocate a facile acceptance of irregularity in sound change. Every effort should be made to find rule-governed explanations for the primary observations. But when plausible explanations for irregularity cannot be stated it is pointless to resort to mechanical contrivances out of fear that the only alternative to such ad hoc solutions is to open a Pandora's box of methodological chaos. Irregularity is not mere chaos. Rather, as I hope to have shown here, irregularity appears to be an integral part of the natural process of language change.

NOTES

1. Jankowsky (1972:108) includes in the "original group": (a) August Leskien (1840–1916), (b) Berthold Delbrück (1842–1922), (c) Hermann Osthoff (1847–1909), and (d) Karl Brugmann (1849–1919). He laments the extension of the term 'Neogrammarian' to later scholars who did not always hold the same set of views. As late as the 1930s the German comparativist Otto Dempwolff regarded himself as a 'Neogrammarian', but explicitly recognized and listed irregularities (*'unerklärte Ausnahmen'*) in sound change (Dahl 1976: 9; Blust 1988b: 173).

2. The publication date of Verner's celebrated article gives the misleading impression of an almost instantaneous response on the part of Leskien. According to Jankowsky (1972: 104, n.61) the piece actually "is dated July 1875. Its contents seem to have been made known through discussions with friends, notably Vilhelm Thomsen, Karl Brugmann, Hermann Osthoff, several years before."

3. Both of these views were held by Schuchhardt (1885). The belief that regularity is the end product of changes which are not regular in their inception has been expressed by many others since, including Sturtevant (1917: 78–81), Sapir (1921: 178), Labov (1963) and most recently Wang (1969).

4. The examples of pandemic irregularity cited in this chapter are not unique. Many Austronesian languages exhibit multiple reflexes of *R* (probably a voiced uvular trill) which cannot easily be explained as products of conditioned change or of borrowing, while a number of others both in island Southeast Asia and in the Pacific show sporadic fronting of *u* to /i/ (Blust 1970b).

5. My own earlier estimates (e.g. Blust 1990) have been lower than this, at around 825. A preliminary attempt to generate a complete list of Austronesian language names from a critical examination of Wurm and Hattori, however, appears to justify the higher figure.

6. Dempwolff (1934–38) also constructed retroflex stops that Dyen writes *D, *T, together with their prenasalized forms *nD, *nT. Many Austronesian comparativists now ignore these distinctions, which were only weakly supported by Dempwolff's evidence and which have received no additional support from further comparative work in the ensuing half century.

7. The prenasalized reflex is phonetically a nasal-obstruent cluster in all languages except Toba Batak, where /mp/, /nt/ and /ŋk/ are [pp], [tt], and [kk] (though written as prenasalized stops in the traditional Batak syllabary). Toba Batak /ns/ is [ts], but /mb/, /nd/, /nj/, and /ŋg/ are [mb], [nd], [nj], and [ŋg] respectively.

8. For examples in nouns, active verbs, and stative verbs/adjectives, see (1a) through (3b). Most prepositions are too short to contain an intervocalic obstruent, and only two numerals (*esa/isa 'one', *pitu 'seven') are reconstructed with consonants that can be prenasalized, but the facultative nasal is attested both in personal and demonstrative pronouns, as with Toba Batak *indi* 'that, that one there' next to Tagalog *irí* (earlier *idi) 'this', and Taman *iŋko* '2 sg. nominative' (earlier *iko).

9. The issue of prenasalization versus denasalization here is, of course, crucially dependent on subgrouping. If it should turn out that the five 'Indonesian' languages compared by Dempwolff belong to a subgroup apart from Tagalog, the weight of the evidence in such comparisons would be markedly altered, as one witness (represented by Tagalog) would indicate a simple obstruent, and a second witness (represented by the other five languages) would indicate a prenasalized obstruent. In such circumstances the direction of change could no longer be determined by simple appeal to a principal of parsimony.

10. Dempwolff (1938) gives only the Ngaju Dayak form with *g-; Dempwolff's source for Ngaju Dayak (Hardeland 1859) gives both variants.

11. Dempwolff (1938) assigns MAL *karat* 'rust' to *kaRat, but *garat* clearly provides a semantically more persuasive comparison.

12. Dempwolff (1938) avoided the reconstruction of an initial consonant in this form, since the initial of TAG *pugíta?* could not be reconciled with the initial segment in other languages. However, there is now abundant comparative evidence in support of *kuRita.

13. A handful of *doublets* differs in initial *b- versus *p- and the like, as with *biqak 'to split' (supported by reflexes in TAG and JAV) versus *piqak 'to split' (supported by reflexes in TAG, TB, JAV, NgD, and MLG). However, in these cases the evidence points to phonologically and semantically similar forms which coexisted in an earlier language. By contrast, instances of voicing crossover involve a single reconstructed shape with isolated irregularities in the value for voicing in particular morphemes. For pre-velar obstruents such correspondences appear to be entirely lacking.

14. Dempwolff (1938) also assigned NgD *guti* 'louse' to *kutu, but the double irregularity raises questions about cognation.

15. Dempwolff's principal source for Tagalog was Laktaw (1914). The forms cited here are from Panganiban (1966). Curiously, apart from *galás* none of the items taken from the latter source appears in the former. I have not had an opportunity to examine earlier Tagalog dictionaries to determine how far back in time the lexicographical attestation of any of these words can be traced.

16. Dempwolff (1938) assigns TAG *kulóg* to *kuDug 'rumble'. Even if his cognate association is accepted in preference to that suggested here, however, we must deal with voicing crossover, since the Tagalog form is compared with Javanese *k/r/udug, g/r/udug* 'rumble'.

17. The phones [u] and [o] are virtually in complementary distribution in native Tagalog forms (where [o] is found only in final syllables). As a result of the introduction of Spanish loans these sounds now contrast.

18. Due to the pressure of other commitments, this matter lay dormant for many years. I now wish to make use of Kim's insight and to extend to him my sincere, if somewhat belated thanks for his assistance. Iovanna Condax supplied the reference to Smith (1977). Neither she nor Kim is responsible for any of my conclusions based on this material.

19. Hockett (1955) reports no examples of voicing contrasts in post-velar stops. Maddieson (1984) lists

only four language with such a contrast in a sample of 317 (Awiya, Tlingit, Klamath, and Lak), although a voicing contrast for post-velar fricatives appears to be considerably more common.

20. Smith's correlation of the duration of voicing with the height of the following vowel also makes a testable diachronic prediction: Voicing crossover in stem-initial velars should be greatest before the low vowel /a/. Because it is not always possible to infer the relative chronology of sound changes that interact, the correlation of consonant and vowel sequences is more difficult in diachronic than in synchronic studies. Nonetheless, there is little evidence to suggest a greater tendency for voicing crossover to occur before low vowels than before non-low vowels. While the *absolute* frequency of voicing crossover for velars is greater before **a* (the most frequent vowel) than before other vowels, the relative frequency of voicing crossover for velar stops does not appear to correlate in any way with the following vowel.

21. Paul (1978 3) distinguishes between 'the movements of the organs of language' and 'the series of sensations by which these movements are necessarily accompanied', reserving the term *Bewegungsgefühl* for the latter. The *Bewegungsgefühl* is thus the psychological counterpart in the speaker of the Lautbild in the hearer. The English translation 'articulatory gesture', which is ordinarily understood in a purely physical sense, must therefore be understood in the present context as including concurrent physical and psychological components.

22. In the English translation of Paul which is used by Baldi and Werth (H.A. Armstrong 1891) *Bewegungsgefühl* is rendered 'motory sensation'. Here and elsewhere I have altered this to 'motor sensation'.

REFERENCES

Adelaar, K. A. (1992). *Proto-Malayic. Pacific Linguistics* C119. Australian National University, Canberra.

Bloch, B. (1967). Leonard Bloomfield. In T. A. Sebeok, ed., *Portraits of Linguists*, vol. 2, 508–18. Indiana University Press, Bloomington.

Bloomfield, L. (1928). A note on sound change. *Language* 4: 99–100.

Blust, R. (1970a). Proto-Austronesian addenda. *Oceanic Linguistics* 9: 104–62.

———. (1970b). *i* and *u* in the Austronesian languages. *Working Papers in Linguistics* 2.6: 113–45. Department of Linguistics, University of Hawaii, Honolulu.

———. (1988a). *Austronesian root theory: An essay on the limits of morphology.* Studies in Language Companion Series, no.19. Benjamins, Amsterdam.

———. (1988b). Dempwolff's contributions to Austronesian linguistics. *Afrika und Übersee* 71: 167–76.

———. (1990). Summary report: Linguistic change and reconstruction methodology in the Austronesian language family. In P. Baldi, ed., *Linguistic change and reconstruction methodology* 33–53. Trends in Linguistics Studies and Monographs, no. 45. Mouton de Gruyter, Berlin.

Burrow, T., and M. B. Emeneau. (1961). *A Dravidian etymological dictionary.* Clarendon Press, Oxford.

Campbell, L. and T. Kaufman. (1985). Mayan linguistics: Where are we now? *Annual Review of Anthropology* 14: 187–98.

Chrétien, C. D. (1965). The statistical structure of the Proto-Austronesian morph. *Lingua* 14: 243–70.

Dahl, O. C. (1976). 2nd ed. *Proto-Austronesian.* Scandinavian Institute of Asian Studies monograph series, no. 15. Curzon Press, London.

Dempwolff, O. (1922). Entstehung von Nasalen und Nasalverbindungen im Ngadju (Dajak). *Zeitschrift für Eingeborenen-Sprachen* 13: 161–205.

———. (1934–38). *Vergleichende Lautlehre des austronesischen Wortschatzes.* 3 vols. Beihefte zur Zeitschrift für Eingeborenen-Sprachen Vol. 1, *Induktiver Aufbau einer indonesischen Ursprache* Beiheft 15 (1934); vol. 2, *Deduktive Anwendung des Urindonesischen auf austronesische Einzelsprachen* Beiheft 17 (1937); vol. 3, *Austronesisches Wörterverzeichnis* Beiheft 19 (1938). Reimer, Berlin.

Dyen, I. (1953). *The Proto-Malayo-Polynesian laryngeals.* Linguistic Society of America, Baltimore.

———. (1963). Why phonetic change is regular. *Language* 39: 631–37.

Geraghty, P. A. (1983). *The history of the Fijian languages.* Oceanic Linguistics Special Publication, no. 19. University of Hawaii Press, Honolulu.

Goddard, I. (1979). Comparative Algonquian. In L. Campbell and M. Mithun, eds., *The languages of Native America: Historical and comparative assessment* 70–132. University of Texas Press, Austin.

Gonda, J. (1950). Indonesian linguistics and general linguistics I. *Lingua* 3: 308–39.

Grassmann, H. (1863). Über die Aspiration und ihr gleichzeitiges Vorhandensein im An- und Auslaute der Wurzeln. *Zeitschrift für vergleichende Sprachforschung* 12: 81–138.

Hardeland, A. (1859). *Dajaksch-Deutsches Wörterbuch*. Frederik Muller, Amsterdam.

Hockett, C. F. (1955). *A manual of phonology*. International Journal of American Linguistics, memoir 11. Waverly Press, Baltimore.

———. (1958). *A course in modern linguistics*. Macmillan, New York.

———. (1965). Sound change. *Language* 41: 185–204.

Jankowsky, K. R. (1972). *The Neogrammarians: A re-evaluation of their place in the development of linguistic science*. Republication edition. Georgetown University, Washington, D.C.

Labov, W. (1963). The social motivation of a sound change. *Word* 19: 273–319.

Laktaw, P. S. (1914). *Diccionario Tagálog-Hispano*. Manila.

Lehmann, W. P. (1967). Introduction to Hermann Osthoff and Karl Brugmann, Preface to *morphological investigation in the sphere of the indo-european languages* I. In W. Lehmann, ed., *A reader in nineteenth-century historical Indo-European linguistics* 197. Indiana University Press, Bloomington.

Lisker, L., and A. S. Abramson. (1964). A cross-language study of voicing in initial stops: acoustical measurements. *Word* 20: 384–422.

Lynch, J. (1975). Oral/nasal alternation and the realis/irrealis distinction in Oceanic languages. *Oceanic Linguistics* 14: 87–99.

Maddieson, I. (1984). *Patterns of sounds*. Cambridge University Press, Cambridge.

Panganiban, J. V. (1966). *Talahuluganang Pilipino-Ingles*. Government Printing Office, Manila.

Paul, H. ([1886]1978). On sound change. In P. Baldi and R. N. Werth, eds., *Readings in historical phonology: Chapters in the theory of sound change* 3–22. Pennsylvania State University Press, University Park.

Ross, M. D. (1988). Proto Oceanic and the Austronesian languages of western Melanesia. *Pacific Linguistics* C98. Australian National University, Canberra.

———. (1990). Proto-Oceanic consonant grade and Milke's *nj. In R. Harlow and R. Hooper, eds., *VICAL I: Papers from the Fifth International Conference on Austronesian Linguistics*. Part II, 433–95. Linguistic Society of New Zealand, Auckland.

Ruhlen, M. (1987). *A guide to the world's languages*. Vol. 1: *Classification*. Stanford University Press, Stanford.

Sapir, E. (1921). *Language*. Harcourt, Brace & World, New York.

Schuchardt, H. (1885). Über die Lautgesetze; gegen die Junggrammatiker. Berlin. (Reprinted with English translation in T. Vennemann and T. H. Wilbur, eds. (1972). *Schuchardt, the neogrammarians and the transformational theory of phonological change*. Athenäum, Frankfurt.)

Smith, B. L. (1977). Effects of vocalic context, place of articulation and speaker's sex on 'voiced' stop consonant production. Paper presented at the West Coast Phonetics Symposium, March 26–28, 1977, Santa Barbara, California.

Sturtevant, E. (1917). *Linguistic change: An introduction to the historical study of language*. University of Chicago Press, Chicago.

Vaihinger, H. (1911). *Die Philosophie des Als Ob*. Berlin.

Verner, K. (1876). Eine Ausnahme der ersten Lautverschiebung. *Zeitschrift für vergleichende Sprachforschung* 23: 97–130.

Wang, W. S-Y. (1969). Competing changes as a cause of residue. *Language* 45: 9–25.

Wolff, J. (1976). Malay borrowings in Tagalog. In C. D. Cowan and O. W. Wolters, eds., *Southeast Asian history and historiography: Essays presented to D. G. E. Hall* 345–67. Cornell University Press, Ithaca and London.

Wurm, S. A., and S. Hattori, eds. (1981). *Language atlas of the Pacific area, part 1: New Guinea area, Oceania, Australia*. The Australian Academy of the Humanities, in collaboration with the Japan Academy, Canberra.

7 Regularity of Change in What?

GEORGE W. GRACE

1 INTRODUCTION

Two of the fundamental assumptions of historical linguistics, I believe, have been (1) what one might call the "once a language boundary, always a language boundary" assumption (that is, the assumption that language boundaries, and hence languages, maintain their integrity over time) and (2) an assumption that the changes (at least phonological changes) which these long-persisting languages undergo are regular.

What I want to do here is describe my experience in applying the comparative method in one particular case and use that case to raise some questions about these assumptions—especially about the quite special role we have assigned to the individual language as the locus of diachronic processes and about the locus and source of regularity.

The case that I want to discuss here is one in which the comparative method failed. Or perhaps it would be more accurate to say that it succeeded only to a quite limited extent. Or more accurate yet to say that *I* failed, or largely failed, in my attempt to apply it in the particular case.

It is important to point out at once that I expected the case to be difficult—in fact, that this expectation was an important part of my motivation in undertaking it. I am convinced that the existence of such cases is a matter of considerable interest for the comparative method and for diachronic linguistics in general. Each successful application of the comparative method may be regarded as (incidentally) a confirmation of the correctness of our assumptions about the processes of linguistic change. Any failure, by the same token, is likely to be evidence of something wrong in our assumptions. In short, I believe that we cannot be sure why the comparative method works when it does work until we also know why it does not work when it does not. It is for that reason that I first decided to work on this particular case.

The languages involved are spoken on the island of New Caledonia at the southern end of the Melanesian chain of islands in the South Pacific Ocean. The languages in question and, in fact, all of the languages of New Caledonia, are generally acknowledged to be members of the Austronesian language family, and more specifically of a particular subgroup—Oceanic—of Austronesian.

2 "EXEMPLARY" AND "ABERRANT" AUSTRONESIAN LANGUAGES

Now, the comparative method has generally produced good results in Austronesian. In fact, among the language families of the world to which the method has now been applied, surely Austronesian would be regarded as one of its more noteworthy successes. And yet the degree of success which it has had in Austronesian has been very variable. There are, in fact, many languages in the family whose history is very difficult to reconstruct. Such evidence as these languages provide contributes little to the reconstruction of Proto-Austronesian or of the protolanguages of any of its subgroups, and even after the reconstructions have been made on the basis of other languages in the family, the position of these languages and the changes which they have undergone are difficult to establish with certainty.

I have come to speak of these languages as the "aberrant"[1] ones and to contrast them with the "exemplary" languages.

Exemplary Austronesian languages can be well illustrated from Otto Dempwolff's *Vergleichende Lautlehre des austronesischen Wortschatzes* (Dempwolff 1934–38—henceforth *VL*). This work has long been recognized as the cornerstone of comparative Austronesian linguistics. Although there have been substantial advances since its publication, all of these acknowledged and built upon the foundation of *VL*. There were also predecessors to *VL*, among the most notable being earlier works by Dempwolff himself. However, *VL* is generally thought of as superseding everything that went before.

Anyway, a remarkable feature of *VL* is that its first volume presents a step-by-step reconstruction of the phonemic inventory of Proto Austronesian from the evidence of just three languages. The three are Tagalog, Toba-Batak, and Javanese. In fact, of course, Dempwolff had done extensive previous research in which he examined the available evidence for a very large number of Austronesian languages, and, except for a few details, he had completed his reconstruction of the Proto-Austronesian sound system in those earlier works. Nevertheless, *VL* was intended as the definitive systematic presentation of his method and results (and the presentation is indeed systematic, not to say didactic). Furthermore, it provides a considerably larger reconstructed vocabulary than did any of his previous works. He made it quite clear that his reason for working from just three languages was that it simplified the presentation of his argument and that it was only on the basis of his extensive prior research that he was able to choose three languages which, among them, provided all of the phonemic distinctions required for the protolanguage.

But the point which I want to emphasize here is that from the perspective of my contrast between aberrant and exemplary languages, these three languages which Dempwolff used are clearly exemplary. Whether or not he actually did make a reconstruction of Proto-Austronesian which was adequate to account for the several hundred Austronesian languages—or at least what was known of them at the time—from the evidence of only these three languages is beside the point. What is to the point is that he demonstrated that it would have been possible to do so. That is tantamount to saying that if all of the Austronesian languages except three had disappeared without a trace, he would still have been able to make as complete and accurate a reconstruction of Proto-Austronesian phonology as he was able to make with the evidence of hundreds of them—provided, of course, that the three which had survived had been the right three.

But if these three are "right," there are others which are equally "wrong." There are, as I said earlier, many languages in the family whose history is very difficult to reconstruct. Many of them are difficult to place within the Austronesian family tree because their sound correspondences with other Austronesian languages are difficult to establish since they share relatively few cognates—or few cognates which can be identified as such with any certainty—with these other languages. (Or perhaps the causality goes the other way around—we cannot identify many cognates because we cannot figure out the sound correspondences). Anyway, such evidence as these languages provide has been virtually useless for the reconstruction of Proto-Austronesian or of the protolanguages of any of its subgroups.

Of course, I do not want to suggest that the Austronesian languages divide neatly into an aberrant set and an exemplary one. Some are more aberrant or exemplary than others, and furthermore I would not like to appear to assume that all aberrant languages are aberrant in the same way or for the same reasons.

The problem of the aberrant languages has bothered me since I began working in comparative Austronesian linguistics. I felt that no genetic classification of the family as a whole could be very trustworthy as long as there were a large number of languages in the family whose exact position could not be determined. Any one of them might potentially, if ever its history were fully revealed, require serious revisions in the family tree with which we were working. And by the same token, any one of them might potentially, once more of its history became clear, require substantial revisions in the reconstructed protolanguage. I was also concerned with the very fact of their aberrancy (whatever aberrancy was) because it suggested that the changes which they had undergone were somehow different from what historical linguistics expected—that they did not conform to the processes of linguistic change as we understood those processes.

The conventional problems of comparative linguistics—subgrouping and the reconstruction of the protolanguages of the family as a whole and of the more prominent subgroups—have provided Austronesianists with more than enough challenges. However, I eventually came to feel that in the long run perhaps the most important thing to be learned from Austronesian comparative linguistics was what these aberrant languages had to teach us—that is, to teach historical linguistics and perhaps linguistics in general. I felt that a particular effort should be made to solve one of these puzzles—to reconstruct the main lines of the history of one of these aberrant languages. I hoped that doing so would provide at least a clue to the other cases.

I eventually decided to pursue the problem with languages of the southern (more accurately, southeastern) end of New Caledonia as a site for research. I chose these languages for two reasons. First, the languages of that area have quite generally been recognized as being very problematic—"aberrant," as I am using the term—in fact, among the most aberrant of all Austronesian languages. They have very few recognizable cognates with other Austronesian languages, sound correspondences are not self-evidently regular, and they are structurally quite atypical of Oceanic languages or of the languages of any other Austronesian subgroup. Their phoneme inventories are unusually large, and the canonical forms are unusual, with numerous monosyllables.

Second—and this was a particularly important consideration—the languages of southern New Caledonia all seem to be quite closely related to one another. I thought that this should make possible a strategy of reconstructing their history back from a very recent stage to successively earlier stages. I intended to make a careful analysis of sound correspondences between neighboring languages; I hoped that this would reveal that the sound changes had been regular, even though no doubt quite complicated, and that at this level there would be large numbers of cognates to work with.

3 THE NEW CALEDONIA RESEARCH

I first collected data in New Caledonia in 1955, then returned on several occasions in the early 1970's. In 1955 I collected vocabularies of some 400 words for a number of New Caledonia languages, several of them members of the southern group. In 1970 I decided to concentrate on working out the history of one of the languages of the southern group, and eventually chose the Xārācїi (henceforth, X) language of the Canala area. In 1970–1973 I collected data on it (cf. Grace 1975). However, during the last two of these years, I also collected a considerable vocabulary for the neighboring language spoken at Grand Couli (henceforth GC; cf. Grace 1976).[2]

I tried two approaches to working out the phonological history of X. First, I looked in X for reflexes of lexical items which had been reconstructed for Proto-Oceanic (POC) and attempted to determine the sound correspondences between Proto-Oceanic and X. This might be described as a "top-down" approach. Second, I attempted to work back from X to an intermediate stage in its history by reconstructing a stage ancestral to X and just its closest relatives. This would be the "bottom-up" approach. For the "bottom-up" approach I relied primarily on the evidence of X and GC.

3.1 The Top-down Approach

The consonants of X are the following:

voiceless fricatives:		f	š	ç	x	x^w
voiceless stops:	p^w	p	t	c	k	k^w
prenasalized stops:	b^w	b	d	j	g	g^w
nasals:	m^w	m	n	ñ	ŋ	

Other: w, v, y, r

The vowels are:

i	ɨ	u		ī	ɨ̄	ū
e	ə	o			ɔ̄	
ɛ	ʌ	ɔ		ɛ̃	ʌ̃	ɔ̃
a				ã		

Note that I interpret phonetically long vowels as sequences of like vowels. However, it should be noted that all vowels can occur in such sequences (That is, phonetically all vowels occur short and long). I count all words with two vowels (whether the two are like or unlike) as disyllabic.

I have discussed my attempt to apply the top-down approach in Grace 1986. One principal problem was that the longest plausible X reflexes of POC reconstructions had the form CVCV, but most were shorter, either CVV or CV, whereas POC had characteristically disyllabic CVCV(C) root forms, with some trisyllabic roots. I began with the CVCV forms, which preserved the greatest amount of information, and then on the basis of the few of these which seemed reasonably plausible, went on to the CVV and then the CV forms. The full evidence is presented in Grace 1986. However, the following are the best examples of the CVCV forms and also three GC CVCV forms whose X cognates (if indeed they are cognate) are reduced in form:

POC	X		
*kutu	kiti	'louse'	(N.B.: GC əʀə)
*patu	pɛti	'weave mat'	(N.B.: GC veʀu)
*mata	mata	'new, unripe'	
*quda	kura	'shrimp'	
*kudo	kirɛ	'pot'	(N.B.: GC ɔ)
*manu	mãrã	'bird'	
*matudu	mɛti	'lying down'	(N.B.: GC meʀɔ)
*kuʀita	kətɛ	'octopus'	
*maqudi	muru	'alive'	(N.B.: GC mɔʀɔ)

See also:

POC	GC		
*tuda	ʈuʀɔ	'stand'	(X tãã)
*taŋi	ɖãʀĩ	'weep'	(X tɛ̃ĩ)
*patu	veʀe	'stone'	(X pɛ- [combining form])

Briefly, I proposed (cf. Grace 1986) the following hypotheses (which cannot claim to be more than that—hypotheses):

1. POC final consonants are always lost in X.

2. The CVV shape results from the loss (or original absence) of a POC medial consonant. Most POC consonants are regularly lost in medial position in X. All of the exceptions are consonants whose X reflexes are apicals.

3. No POC consonant, not even *t, *d, or *n, is unconditionally retained in medial position in X. Even *t, *d, and *n are often lost under conditions which I am unable to specify.

4. The CV forms result from a single development which may have involved a grammatical function such as the Rotuman "phases."[3]

5. The conditions that determine which manner of articulation (voiceless fricative, voiceless stop, prenasalized stop, nasal) will be represented in a X reflex of a POC initial obstruent cannot be determined in detail at present. Some choices seem

to be inherited from an earlier stage, but most apparently are not. It seems clear that manner changes in the initial consonants of some words are fairly recent since apparent cognates in closely related languages disagree.

6. POC initial nasals are always reflected as nasals in X.

7. Other initial reflexes are as follows:

    i. POC *w is reflected as X k^w, otherwise POC labials are reflected as X labials.

    ii. POC *t, *d, and *n are reflected as X apicals.

    iii. POC *ñ is reflected as X n.

    iv. POC *s seems to be the source for the X retroflex consonant, š; otherwise, *s is reflected as a palatal.

    v. POC *k and possibly *q are reflected as velars. However, X appears to insert a velar before initial vowels. Therefore, it is possible that *q has been lost in initial position as elsewhere and a velar has subsequently been inserted.

    vi. POC *l becomes X n.

    vii. POC *R is lost.

    viii. I have found no evidence on POC *ŋ or *y.

8. In addition to *t and *d, the only POC medial consonants which can be overtly reflected in X are *n, *l, and probably *ŋ. All except *t are reflected as X r.

These hypotheses were based on eighty-one tentative (some of which were very tentative indeed) etymologies which were cited in Grace 1986. Although I believe that the general picture presented here is probably valid, it is only a very general picture. I was not able to propose any hypotheses about the vowels, and of course, no specific details about the development of individual POC consonants could be provided. In fact, the hypotheses tacitly recognize a number of phonemic splits but make no attempt to state conditions for them. The following list of consonant reflexes found in initial position in the tentative etymologies appeared in Grace 1986: 64 (note that oral/nasal and velarized/nonvelarized distinctions were omitted from the POC reconstructions on which these reflexes are based):

POC	X		POC	X	
*p	p	(4 cases)	*k	k^w	(1 case)
*p	p^w	(1 case)	*k	g	(1 case)
*p	f	(3 cases)	*k	x	(5 cases)
*p	b	(5 cases)	*k	ŋ	(1 case)
*t	t	(3 cases)	*q	k	(1 case)
*t	j	(1 case)	*q	k^w	(1 case)
*d	d	(5 cases)	*m	m	(5 cases)
*d	t	(1 case)	*m	m^w	(3 cases)
*d	n	(1 case)	*n	n	(1 case)
*s	ç	(1 case)	*ñ	n	(1 case)

*s	y	(1 case)	*ŋ		(no examples)	
*s	c	(2 cases)	*w	kʷ	(4 cases)	
*s	j	(7 cases)	*l	n	(5 cases)	
*s	š	(5 cases)	*R	Ø	(2 cases)	
*s	ñ	(2 cases)	*y		(no examples)	
*k	k	(5 cases)	*Ø	kʷ	(2 cases)	

Although I was able to make no specific suggestions about the vowels, I did observe (1986: 66n) in relation to one problem—the source of the nasalized vowels—that they seemed to be associated with nasal consonants, especially POC medial consonants, and that POC *l (which regularly becomes n in New Caledonian languages) counted as a nasal consonant.

This is as far as I have been able to get with the top down approach.

3.2 The Bottom-Up Approach

I explained earlier that one of my main reasons for choosing southern New Caledonia languages for my attempt to solve the problem of "aberrancy" was that the languages of that area all seemed to be quite closely related to one another—a fact which I hoped would make it possible to do some reconstructing from the bottom up. That is, I hoped to be able to apply the comparative method to whichever language I eventually focussed on (X, as it turned out) and one or more of its nearest relatives, thereby arriving at a reconstruction (or perhaps I should be careful to say a tentative reconstruction at the stage I am discussing here) of their latest common ancestor. Anyway, once I had established a sufficiently clear and detailed account of this most recent reconstructible stage in the the the history of X, the plan called for reconstructing back to successively earlier stages and eventually arriving back at POC.

When the time came, I began with the two languages with which I was most familiar—X and GC. To begin with just these two seemed justified. Each is at least very nearly the closest relative of the other. And even if they were not the only surviving descendants of their most recent common ancestor, it appeared reasonable to expect that at least a very significant portion of those details of that protolanguage that would be reconstructible at all—that is, that would be reconstructible from the evidence of all surviving descendants—should be reconstructible on the basis of just these two. In short, although there would surely be details still to be filled in, the two should provide the main lines of the picture. And working with the data of two languages to begin with was considerably simpler than trying to juggle more. Such, anyway, was my reasoning.

The GC sound system resembles that of X. The consonants are:

voiceless fricatives:	fʷ	f			š	h	hʷ
voiced continuants:	w	v	ð	r	ɣ		
voiceless stops:	pʷ	p	t	ṭ	k		
prenasalized stops:	bʷ	b	d	ḍ	g		
nasals:	mʷ	m	n	ṇ	ŋ		

Other: y, ř

The vowels are:

i	ɨ	u	ī	ɨ̄	ū
e	ə	o		ə̄	
ɛ	ʌ	ɔ	ɛ̃	ʌ̃	ɔ̃
a			ã		

Note that GC, like X, has phonetically long vowels which are here interpreted as sequences of like vowels.

As may be seen from the top-down hypotheses presented in the previous section, in my search for X reflexes of POC reconstructions I came to the tentative conclusion that POC morphemes, whatever their length, can be reflected in X only in the canonical form (c)v(c)(v), where the second c can be only X t or r. Therefore, I hypothesize that, except for t and r, any medial consonant found in contemporary X lexical items marks an old morpheme boundary. Although I have not made as serious a search in the GC lexicon for reflexes of POC reconstructions as I did for X, what I have done leads me to an almost identical tentative conclusion about the reflexes of POC morphemes in GC. The one difference is that in the formula as it applies to GC the only permissible second c (that is, the only medial consonant which reflects a POC medial consonant) is ř.

It seems, then, that most of the POC morphemes which have been retained in X or GC have been shortened. As far as I have been able to tell, trisyllabic or longer words have regularly been shortened to disyllables (at longest), many (if not most) disyllables have become monosyllables, and many (no doubt most) of those disyllables which have remained disyllabic have lost their medial consonants). Such shortening, if it occurred without some compensation, would be expected to result in the loss of much information—in a proliferation of homophones, in fact. However, the shortening has been compensated for by two developments.

First, the phoneme inventories—both consonant and vowel—of both languages (and, in fact, of all New Caledonia languages) are substantially larger than those of POC. How this expansion has come about is precisely the question to be answered, but the implication that it must have involved numerous phonemic splits seems inescapable.

Second, much of the vocabulary of both languages seems to consist of (what are at least historically) compounds—that is, words made up of two or more elements, each of which was formerly (probably at least as recently as POC times, in most cases) an independent morpheme. Nevertheless, many homophones, and especially many monosyllabic homophones, remain.

I began the comparison of the two languages by compiling a list of possible cognates—i.e., lexical items in the two languages which were well matched in meaning and which phonetically resembled each other sufficiently to justify, in my opinion, an initial hypothesis that they were cognate. I was able to compile a list of over nine hundred such lexical pairs.

Some of these pairs are, of course, much more convincing than others. Among the more convincing ones are a few cases included in the top-down comparisons where both X and GC appear to have retained a medial consonant. These were:

X	GC		
kɨtɨ	ɔr̃ə	'louse'	(attr. to POC *kutu)
pɛtɨ	ver̃u	'weave mat'	(attr. to POC *patu)
mɛtɨ	mer̃ɔ	'lying down'	(attr. to POC *matudu)
muru	mɔr̃ɔ	'alive'	(attr. to POC *maqudi)

Not only do these pairs look relatively convincing ("relatively" by Southern New Caledonian standards, that is) on the face of them, but as it turned out later, all, or almost all, of the specific X-GC sound correspondences implied in them appear to be valid ones (see Appendix). However, that is getting ahead of the story. A major problem confronting the bottom-up approach once the initial list of tentative cognates had been compiled was that there were very few pairs in the list which consisted of (or contained) such disyllabic morphemes. Many of the other pairs consisted of monosyllables (generally cv in X, (c)v in GC). In the case of such short forms it is difficult, even when the sound correspondences involved are very firmly established ones, to be at all certain that we are dealing with true cognates and not simply accidental resemblances. And, of course, at this stage of the investigation there are no sound correspondences which have been established, firmly or at all.

The situation, then, was that although I had a list of tentative cognates, this list did not lead in any direct way to an inventory of the regular sound correspondences between the two languages. The status (cognate or not) of the items on the list was far too uncertain for that. But at the same time I had no criteria for culling the list. What is the next step in such a case?

It is probably worthwhile at this point to take a moment to consider the process of doing comparative reconstruction as it usually works. This process, as I understand it, involves an interplay between hypotheses about what items are cognate and hypotheses about what sound correspondences between the languages are regular, with the hypotheses of each kind depending on those of the other for their confirmation. That is, a crucial part of the evidence establishing the validity of a sound correspondence is that it is found in a sufficient number of (what appear to be) cognates, and a crucial part of the evidence establishing forms as cognate is that they are related by (what appear to be) regular sound correspondences. The process of comparative reconstruction therefore may be thought of as a going-back-and-forth between the task of identifying cognates and that of identifying sound correspondences, although of course the two tasks are not kept as separate as that description makes it sound.

One might think in terms of the following schematization of the process for two languages, A and B:

Step 1: Compile a list of tentative cognates. Assuming nothing else is available at this juncture, this would be done by simple inspection. That is, the list would be based essentially on close likeness of meaning and of form.

Step 2: From these tentative cognates, make a set of hypotheses about the sound correspondences between the languages. These hypotheses would take into account the number of examples of each correspondence. I would expect both the absolute number of cases and the number of cases relative to the overall lexical frequency of the A phoneme and of the B phoneme to be considered.

The absolute number of cases should be taken into account since a large number of cases of the same correspondence must almost certainly have some historical explanation in terms of either genetic relationship or extensive borrowing. This is all the more true if (and to the extent that) the corresponding phonemes are phonetically dissimilar.

However the number of cases relative to the lexical frequency of the phonemes figuring in the correspondence also needs to be taken into account because if a particular phoneme occurs only relatively infrequently in the lexicon of the language as a whole, its regular correspondences may be manifested in only a small number of cognates. Thus, as a general rule, one would probably want to include at least one correspondence for each phoneme in each language.

Steps 3–n: Revise the set of hypothesized cognates, rejecting those which are not confirmed by the hypothesized sound correspondences, and adding whatever new cognates were originally missed because they involve sounds which are phonetically dissimilar, but which have now been shown to correspond regularly.

Then, on the basis of the revised cognate list, further refine the set of hypothesized sound correspondences, and so on back and forth.

In the X-GC comparison I was never able to get beyond Step 2. In Step 1, as I mentioned above, I was able to compile a list of over nine hundred possible cognate sets. These consisted of lexical items in the two languages which were well matched in meaning and which, in my opinion, showed sufficient phonetic similarity to justify an initial hypothesis that they were cognate. I entered these hypothetical cognates into computer storage in a format designed by my colleague, Bob Hsu. This format made it possible for the computer to identify the sound correspondences upon which each hypothesis depended. We were thus able to list all of the correspondences so hypothesized and to count the number of occurrences of each.

I expected that the number of valid correspondences for any phoneme in either language would almost always be quite small—probably one or two in most cases. I further expected that any correspondence which was found in more than a few items would be a valid one—that is, it would reflect either direct inheritance or a pattern of heavy borrowing from a single source. In short, I expected that most of the valid correspondences would be quite conspicuous and also that the invalid hypotheses would generally be so infrequent as to be clearly implausible. I realized that borrowing might complicate the picture somewhat, but I expected the number of problematic correspondences to be quite small.

In sum, I anticipated a number of valid correspondences not much greater than the number of phonemes in either language, and expected that most of these would be more or less self-evident. In addition, I expected a sizable, but random, collection of invalid correspondences which had gotten included simply because they had at the outset appeared plausible on purely phonetic grounds. I supposed that the invalidity of these would generally be self-evident. Finally, I was prepared for a few problematic correspondences, correspondences appearing frequently enough not to be discarded out of hand, and yet doubtful because they were in competition with other correspondences purporting to account for the same phoneme in each language. It might be expected that some such problematic correspondences might have been produced by borrowing and others by phonemic splits whose conditions had been obscured by subsequent developments.

These expectations bore little resemblance to the actual results. Each language, as we have seen, has 26 consonants (not counting probably borrowed ones in Grand Couli); each also has 18 vowels (10 are oral and 8 nasalized in each language; however, it should also be noted that two of the 18 in Grand Couli are rare and probably to be regarded as suspect). However I found 140 consonant correspondences (counting 24 in which a consonant in one language corresponded with zero in the other) and 172 vowel correspondences (counting 26 in which a vowel in one language corresponded with zero in the other). These figures, of course, include many correspondences which occurred only once and others which occurred only two or three times. However, it seems reasonable to assume that correspondences which occur as often as 10 times in the list probably require some historical explanation, and there were 36 consonant correspondences and 32 vowel correspondences which occurred at least 10 times. These are all shown in the Appendix. Furthermore, there are 4 X consonants (x^w, η, g^w, v), 6 GC consonants (p^w, h^w, f^w, k^w, g^w, $\eth$), 3 X vowels (Λ, $\dot{\dot{i}}$, ∂), and 3 GC vowels (∂, Λ, $\bar{\Lambda}$) which are not accounted for in any of these 68 correspondences. The most frequent correspondences for each of these are also shown in the Appendix.

Finally, there were 56 consonant correspondences and 67 vowel correspondences which occurred at least five times. It was remarkably difficult to find even the approximate place to draw the line between clearly valid and clearly invalid correspondences. What was particularly discouraging was that no obvious conditioning—no indications of complementation among any of these correspondences—was apparent.

There were some regularities which might be mentioned. For example, consonant point of articulation seems to correspond more regularly than manner. I even considered the possibility of trying to make a start toward reconstructing the last common protolanguage of these two languages by accepting the most frequently occurring correspondences as hypothetically valid and assigning a symbol to represent each (or if complementary distribution could be found between any, to represent each complementary set). This would have required a large number of symbols, but might have led to an overdifferentiated sort of reconstructed vocabulary, I thought. As long as I considered only the consonants, the idea seemed to have some attractiveness. However, when I turned to the vowels, it seemed clearly hopeless. I could not imagine that it could ever lead to my being able to carry out my original program. That is, I could not imagine ever being able to reconstruct such recent protolanguages in enough detail that they could be used as the basis for reconstructing the next earlier stage in a process that would lead eventually back to Proto Oceanic. What makes these results particularly discouraging is that these languages appear on other criteria to be very closely related.

3.3 Conclusions from the New Caledonia Research

It seems that the principal result that I have to offer is precisely my failure to achieve results. I did not succeed in applying the comparative method to X and GC—at least I did not succeed in realizing my objectives—in getting the kind of reconstructions that would permit further stages of reconstruction leading back to POC. What I have offered as a conclusion so far, then, is that in this particular application, the comparative method failed to achieve the desired results.

Of course, the possibility remains that the program I undertook might be workable with more or better data or with a more skillful application of the comparative method. However, whether or not the comparative method itself, in sufficiently skillful hands and with adequate data, might eventually be capable of producing the desired results, the fact remains that the case presents particular difficulties. In other words, I might claim to have achieved one result: a demonstration that these languages are indeed aberrant in the sense which I have given that term (a claim to which an expected reply might be that everyone already knew that anyway!).

However, there might be some ground for claiming that the research accomplished a bit more than simply confirming a state of affairs of which everyone was already aware. It might be claimed that it has also given a more complete account of aberrancy, or at least of this one case of aberrancy. Although it would be foolhardy to make any categorical claims about what future research might or might not reveal, the aberrancy in the case of X and of GC seems to have the following characteristics:

1. There must surely be more valid correspondences (that is, nonaccidental correspondences, by which I mean correspondences with a historical explanation) between X and GC than there are phonemes in either language.

2. These surely must not represent that many different phonemes in a common (to X and GC) protolanguage.

3. There are surely many more valid correspondences between POC and X than there are phonemes in POC, or indeed in X.

4. The excess of valid correspondences over phonemes of either proto language surely cannot be accounted for in terms of (that is, surely cannot be mainly due to) phonologically conditioned phonemic splits.

5. There are no obvious patterns of extensive borrowing by either of these languages from an identifiable source. (In this case I cannot claim to have made a thorough examination of the vocabularies with this possibility in mind, but nothing I have seen has suggested any pattern of this sort).

4 DISCUSSION

This whole enterprise began, it will be recalled, with my idea that there was something unexpected about the aberrant languages—that there was something in the processes by which they had developed that was different from what historical linguistics had come to regard as normal. If this was true, it suggested that our general theory (if "theory" is not too exalted a label) of linguistic change was incomplete or otherwise wrong in some way. The aberrant Austronesian languages thus seemed to present an opportunity to complete or correct, or at least to make progress toward correcting, our theory of linguistic change.

I have already attempted once (in Grace 1981b) to describe my impression of the linguistic situation in southern New Caledonia and my speculations on how it might have arisen. I would like to return to what I said there and attempt to identify some of its theoretical implications. In that work (1981b: 260) I made the following statement:

> One is tempted to suggest that the languages of the area as a whole might be made the object of a single linguistic description—that those languages have a single grammatical system (with no variation greater than might be expected of dialects of the same language), a single phonological system (with each language operating with a selection from the phoneme inventory of the system as a whole), and a single vocabulary except for a proliferation of synonyms (with each language, again, operating with a selection from the inventory of synonymous forms).
>
> The foregoing remarks might seem to suggest that we are dealing with a single dialectally differentiated language. But on the other hand, all observers agree in identifying a number of different languages, cognate counts among them are surprisingly low. . . .

I now realize that what I was really saying there—rather clumsily, I am afraid—was that there is a very obvious *Sprachbund* in southern New Caledonia which includes X and GC and much more. I probably should say a little more about the idea of coincident *Sprachfamilien* and *Sprachbünde*.

4.1 *Sprachfamilie* and *Sprachbund*

The point to be made here is that genetic relationship and membership in the same linguistic area or sprachbund are entirely independent of each other; what needs to be *particularly* emphasized is that both relationships can exist simultaneously between the same languages.

The most famous linguistic areas, of course, are those which include different languages which are not genetically related, or are only distantly related, to one another. However, although those cases are particularly striking, they are not different in kind from less striking ones.

I would like to propose that a linguistic area is simply an area within which linguistic features diffuse. Surely genetic relatedness itself poses no obstacle to the diffusion of areal features. Indeed, the mutual compatibility of structure which usually accompanies close genetic relationship must surely facilitate diffusion rather than pose obstacles to it. In sum, the coincidence of genetic relationship and sprachbund is surely common (however much it may have been ignored).

But the development of an areal sprachbund depends on the existence of communication on a significant scale between speakers of different languages. In other words, there must exist a community, even though a more or less attenuated one, embracing the entire area. However, such communities seem generally not to have been acknowledged in the assumptions with which historical linguistics has traditionally operated.

Of course, the underlying assumptions of historical linguistics (like those of any other comparable field) have for the most part never been explicitly stated, and it is therefore difficult to specify exactly what they are. However, if I am to discuss the implications of my New Caledonia research for the assumptions of the field, I will need to do so from some understanding of (some assumptions about) what those assumptions are. I am, therefore, obliged here to undertake the imposing task of attempting to formulate some of the more relevant ones.

4.2   Assumptions About Language and Community

The assumptions in which I am particularly interested here are those dealing with individual languages and communities of language-users and the relations between the two—especially as they are related to the processes of linguistic change. These assumptions might, I believe, be formulated in something like the following terms:

1. Each language defines a speech community; the speech community consists of those people who communicate with one another by means of the language in question or are connected to one another by chains of speakers who communicate with one another by means of that language.

2. A language has split into more than one just when such intercommunication is no longer *linguistically* possible—that is, when mutual intelligibility has been lost. Since, by the first assumption, the speech community is defined by the language, the community is assumed necessarily to have undergone a comparable split at the same time (if not before).

3. Conversely, one cause of language splits can be the interruption of a chain of intercommunicating speakers by the denial of physical access—as in the case of a migration or the installation of a political boundary. Presumably this might, in fact, result in a situation in which, according to linguistic criteria (e.g. mutual intelligibility), what would still be a single language might be associated with two distinct communities. However, it is assumed that such a situation could never be more than transitory as the language would be expected to change differentially in the two communities and soon to become two different languages.

4. The interruption of communication within a community is not necessarily abrupt. Obstacles to communication sometimes develop gradually, so that the links between some parts of the community are weaker than those between others. While such conditions exist, some changes may be expected to affect the language as a whole, while others affect it only as it is spoken in one or another part of the community (that is, affect only one or another dialect).

5. Otherwise (that is, as long as the community remains intact), the language would be expected to change as a unit.

In fact, one of the assumptions of the theory of linguistic change of which I have been speaking is that the domain of a linguistic change—the entity that changes—is a system. And it is assumed that the system in question is this unit which we have been calling the "language". In short, historical linguistics is primarily concerned with linguistic change and with reconstruction, and linguistic change is conceived of as the changes undergone by these entities—languages—while reconstruction is reconstructing the history—the changes and splits—of such languages. Therefore the language has traditionally been a critical concept in historical linguistics.

4.3   Some Recent Developments

But to what extent do languages ever actually change as units? Recently there have been a number of studies of linguistic change in progress, especially in English-speaking communities such as Martha's Vineyard and New York City (see Labov 1972), and local communities within Belfast (for example Milroy and Milroy 1985). These studies give additional prominence to the fact, which was already known from the entire recorded history of the language, that the English language does not function as a single unit in linguistic change. Has the English language, in fact, ever changed as a unit at any time in its recorded history?

Each of the studies of change in progress has focused on a more narrowly defined community (or more than one) within the English-speaking community as a whole, and each has found the pattern of changes in progress in the community in question to be to some extent peculiar to that community. What is more, some of these communities (e.g. Martha's Vineyard, Ballymacarrett) are more narrowly defined than others (e.g. New York City). In short, there seems to be a complex pattern of communities within communities, with even the most narrowly defined ones having their own linguistic individuality.

This suggests that the familiar linguistic map—a map which depicts the region being mapped as divided up into linguistic domains, one for each language (that is, with the domain of the language being the area occupied by its community of speakers)—is misleading. At least it is misleading if it is taken to represent the *linguistically effective* communities of the region. The kind of mapping of linguistic communities which the studies of change in progress suggest is quite different. This mapping would show not a single exhaustive partition of the world of language-speakers into communities, but rather a system of communities nested one inside the other, with the degree of internal consistency increasing step by step.

But there is a further point. Even the most narrowly defined communities in the studies to which I have been referring do not behave as diachronic units. Even within these most restricted communities changes may be seen to take place not by a uniform shift but by a process of diffusion. There is likely to be diffusion through the community, through the lexicon, and through the stylistic repertoire—perhaps all going on at the same time.

But there have been other developments which further modify the picture. Sociolinguists have pointed out, and provided many examples, that actual communities are often not monolingual. In fact, it has often been asserted that multilingualism, rather than monolingualism, is the normal human state. Thus, the linguistically-relevant community can no longer be thought of as corresponding to a specific single language, but rather to a linguistic repertoire which may include resources from several languages.

These developments all seem to indicate that the individual language and the linguistic community vary independently (rather than essentially defining each other as suggested by the assumptions stated above). On the one hand they show that the speakers of a particular language may be formed into a complex pattern of larger and smaller communities through which innovations may diffuse along complex routes (cf. Milroy and Milroy 1985). On the other hand they also show that regular and frequent communication among a particular group of people does not necessarily imply that there is a single language which serves as the vehicle of that communication.

The first of what I proposed above as traditional assumptions of historical linguistics was: "Each language defines a speech community; the speech community consists of those people who communicate with one another by means of the language in question or are connected to one another by chains of speakers who communicate with one another by means of that language." However, the developments to which I am referring suggest a modification of that assumption to omit the requirement that only one language can be used. In its modified form it might read: "A speech community consists of those people who communicate with one another or are connected to one another by chains of speakers who communicate with one another." But to be entirely satisfactory it would also need to recognize that community is a matter of degree—more narrowly-defined communities involving more frequent intercommunication and, in the case of individual members who do not communicate directly with one another, shorter chains of interconnecting speakers.

Finally, diffusion through the affected community would be a part of the process typically involved in each change. That would be true whether the diffusion remained internal to what, by linguistic criteria, was a single language or proceeded from one language to another.

In fact, I would like to go so far as to propose that wherever there is linguistic community in the sense given above (that is, a chain of intercommunicating speakers), no matter how tightly or loosely constituted that community may be, the sprachbund phenomenon will be present in some measure. This means incidentally that even a monolingual community speaking a dialectally complex language (such as English today or apparently throughout most of its history) constitutes, or participates in, a sprachbund.

It will no doubt be apparent that part of what I am proposing is precisely that the very special status that historical linguistics has given to language boundaries, as contrasted with all other linguistic boundaries (e.g. dialect boundaries), or for that matter to transitions without clear boundaries, is misconceived. That is, I am proposing that the difference between differences of dialect, on the one hand, and differences of language, on the other, is actually just one of degree rather than of kind. In fact, I believe that the unique place accorded by linguistics to the individual language (the *langue*), making it the exclusive preoccupation of both synchronic and diachronic linguistics, is becoming an increasingly serious obstacle to progress in many directions. But that is a longer story for which there is no room here.

5 CONCLUDING REMARKS

5.1 Communities

In southern New Caledonia we find a whole array of structural characteristics that are widely shared among the languages of the area. Most of these characteristics are unique to the area (and to these we might add some others which are shared only with the languages of the rest of New Caledonia). Although it is clear that all of the languages are genetically related, this genetic relationship does not seem sufficient to account for the similarities. In fact, that might be taken as exactly what the research that I have reported here has shown. For example, does it seem quite realistic to imagine that the genetic relationship between X and GC is close enough to be the entire explanation for their approximately morpheme-for-morpheme intertranslatability[4] when I was not even able to provide a reasonable account of the sound correspondences between them?

What I am proposing here is that the features shared by X and GC, and indeed by southern New Caledonia languages generally, are attributable only in part to their genetic relationship but also in part to their constituting a sprachbund. This proposal implies that two opposing tendencies have been operating. First, divergent changes were necessary to produce many languages out of one to begin with (and, in fact, the evidence is that there was a single ancestor for all of the languages of southern New Caledonia—that the languages of the area do constitute a separate genetic subgroup within Oceanic[5]). But secondly, there have also necessarily been parallel (and perhaps even convergent) changes—that is, the changes which produced the areal features of which we have been speaking.

But, then, what is it that changes in a linguistic change? Is it a language, or a dialect, or could it even be a sprachbund? I think that a part of the answer is that the unit which changes is not linguistically defined, but defined in terms of the linguistic community. That is, it is not so much such-and-such language (or linguistically defined dialect) which changes, but that language (or even two or more different languages) *as spoken by* such-and-such community of speakers.

Each of the studies of linguistic change in progress mentioned earlier focused on communities. And these were always more narrowly defined communities within the English-speaking community as a whole. Thus we saw what might be called "local" linguistic communities which have their own particular places within a larger linguistic community. These local communities are partially—but only partially, of course—independent of the larger community.

This larger-community/local-community picture is, of course, considerably oversimplified. First, there are likely to be not just two, but in fact several layers of community structure which might be distinguished. Second, communities are often not sufficiently well defined to be unambiguously countable anyway. However, since a very rough model of the situation is all I need for immediate purposes, I will not attempt to specify a more exact model.

The precolonial situation in southern New Caledonia is difficult to reconstruct after the extensive resettlement of the people which occurred under colonial rule, but I am inclined to believe that in that situation there was no particular role that could be attributed to communities defined on the basis of particular languages. I am influenced in this belief not only by reports about early colonial New Caledonia itself but also by reports from various other parts of Melanesia where there are many languages with few speakers. These reports indicate that in many such areas, even though a particular language (as linguistically defined) was spoken in more than one village, there was no sense of community among those villages or any other indication that they in some way constituted a community.

If I try to interpret the linguistic situation in precolonial southern New Caledonia in terms of my larger-community/local-community model, it seems to me that the relevant community, the larger community as well as the local, generally did not correspond to a linguistically-defined unit—that is, a language, a dialect, or a genetic subgroup. In fact, the best choice for the larger-community role seems to be the whole linguistic area. Of course, as in the case of English it would surely have been possible to recognize communities of intermediate size (and also probably one or more of even greater size).

The individual villages would presumably have been the best choice for the local-community role. Whether or not there was any notion of community based on particular languages, there do seem to be indications (although it is hard to know how to confirm this) that villages usually accorded a special status to a single language, which was recognized as the language of the village, at least for emblematic purposes. However, because of intermarriage, war captives, trade networks, ceremonial interaction, etc., a number of different languages would typically have been in the repertoire of individual villagers. And often there were probably two or more which were known by virtually everyone in the village.[6] (Villages are reported to have sometimes abruptly changed their emblematic language).

Thus the local communities were (from all accounts) typically multilingual, although it is quite possible that they usually recognized a particular language as having a special emblematic status. The larger community of course included villages with a number of different emblematic languages.

Now, what is a linguistic change in such a situation? What is the unit that changes? The answer that I proposed above was that the unit that changes is not a linguistically defined one at all, but rather a language (or possibly even two or more languages) as spoken by a particular community of speakers. If this answer is valid, then the locus of a change would be the linguistic repertoire of a linguistic community. And to the extent that the larger-community/local-community model proposed above accurately represents the state of affairs in precolonial New Caledonia, the locus of a change would be the repertoire of the entire sprachbund or that of a village. However, I would certainly not want to insist on the details of that model; it is only the general idea that is important.

5.2   Regularity

We are accustomed to thinking of "regularity" as a relation between linguistically defined entities—especially between languages, or more precisely, between states of language. Thus, regularity between an earlier and later state of the same language is regularity of *change* (for example, regular sound change); regularity between two related languages is regularity of *correspondence* (for example, regular sound correspondences).

We expect both sound correspondences and sound change to exhibit regularity. In fact, it is generally assumed that they are simply two faces of the same phenomenon, that regular sound correspondences are produced by—that they in fact presuppose— regular sound change. However, I would like to propose that regular sound correspondences do not necessarily presuppose regular sound change; they may also be independent of it or even prior to it.

Consider, for example, that in dialectally complex languages speakers from one dialect area are often familiar enough with the dialect of another area that signantia can readily diffuse from one area to the other with the pronunciation being automatically converted to fit the receiving dialect. The same kind of conversion formula has also regularly been used between different languages; one familiar example is the regular conversion from one European language to another of the pronunciation (and spelling) of learned words coined from Latin or Greek elements.

To state the matter more generally, let us use the term "phonological dialect" to label the complete set of articulatory subroutines used by a fluent speaker to speak a language which s/he speaks fluently (or at least to pronounce the particular expressions that s/he pronounces fluently).[7] What I want to propose is that to the extent that there is diffusion of signantia[8] from any particular phonological dialect to any other, there will be regular sound correspondences which provide the basis for the conversion of such signantia from one to the other. And this will be true either if the two phonological dialects are virtually indistinguishable ones spoken, say, by next-door neighbors or if they are fundamentally different ones—for example, belonging to mutually unintelligible languages.

It should be kept in mind that there were certainly regular sound correspondences between X and GC. The problem was that while some were more clearly regular than others, it was ultimately impossible to decide exactly which correspondences should be accepted as regular and which should not. As a consequence of this uncertainty, it was impossible to give anything like a precise historical interpretation to even the most clearly regular ones.

In any case, the regular correspondences did not have such a focus as to project a single protosystem; they do not seem all to have arisen from two linguistic systems each evolving in isolation. On the contrary, I imagine them to be the result not only of the interplay between differentiating and parallel development during the earlier stages of X and GC themselves, but also of various patterns of diffusion—surely involving other languages as well—over the period of centuries in which they were developing. In any case, successful application of the comparative method depends on regular sound correspondences which pattern in a particular way, and these do not pattern in that way.

What I would like to suggest here is that the kind of regularity of sound change that makes possible successful reconstruction by means of the comparative method depends on particular conditions. In particular, it depends on congruence between, on the one hand, relevant linguistic communities and, on the other hand, linguistically defined units—that is, linguistically defined languages or dialects. To the extent that the linguistically relevant communities (i.e., the networks of intercommunicating speakers) fail to correspond to what according to strictly linguistic criteria are individual languages (or dialects, etc.), the sound changes will appear to lack regularity.

Therefore, my hypothesis is that the aberrancy (which is to say the relative intractability by the comparative method) of the languages of southern New Caledonia comes precisely from such a lack of correspondence between the languages themselves and the associated linguistically relevant communities.

Finally, I would like to suggest that the main lesson to be drawn from this study is that we do not know enough about diachronic processes in situations where there is not a close association between linguistically defined units and communities. As long as this gap in our knowledge persists, our reconstructive efforts must be limited largely to what can be accomplished with the evidence of (relatively) exemplary languages. In Austronesian we are fortunate in having a very large number of languages which provide much more useful evidence than the languages of which I have been speaking here. But, although resort to the exemplary languages permits us—Austronesianists at any rate—largely to by-pass the problem of the aberrant languages, the gap in our knowledge of linguistic diachrony remains, and is troublesome.[9]

APPENDIX TABLE 7.1
Consonant correspondences occurring at least ten times in the cognate list

Correspondence		Number of Instances		
X	GC	Correspondence	X Phoneme	GC Phoneme
m	m	85	96	92
mʷ	mʷ	27	29	30
b	b	32	54	45
b	p	15	54	48
bʷ	bʷ	20	31	25
p	v	26	80	47
p	p	30	80	48
p	Ø	15	80	73
pʷ	w	20	35	88
f	f	21	23	30
w	w	23	33	88
x	h	59	73	73
k	k	35	84	45
k	Ø	26	84	73
k	ɣ	16	84	28
kʷ	w	15	20	88
g	g	14	28	25
ñ	n	15	24	28
j	d	31	55	44
j	t	13	55	99
ç	t	65	75	99
c	t	15	48	99
c	y	13	48	38
y	y	12	13	38
š	š	63	68	73
r	ř	153	179	205
t	ř	27	83	205
t	r	25	83	48
t	ţ	24	83	42
d	ḍ	61	96	73
d	ţ	18	96	42
d	r	10	96	48
n	ṇ	85	94	92
Ø	ř	21	66	205
Ø	w	12	66	88
Ø	h	10	66	73

Maximum number of occurrences in a single correspondence of consonants having no correspondences occurring as many as ten times in the cognate list:

v	v	4	4	47
xʷ	f	9	21	30
gʷ	w	2	3	88
ŋ	g	8	13	25
pʷ	pʷ	9	35	13
xʷ	fʷ	5	21	5
xʷ	hʷ	6	21	9
kʷ	kʷ	1	20	1
gʷ	gʷ	1	3	1
c	ð	7	48	9

APPENDIX TABLE 7.2

Vowel correspondences occurring at least ten times in the cognate list

Correspondence		Number of Instances		
X	GC	Correspondence	X Phoneme	GC Phoneme
i	i	192	255	273
e	i	42	86	273
e	e	19	86	154
e	ə	12	86	120
ɛ	e	97	195	154
ɛ	ɛ	24	195	24
ɛ	a	13	195	351
ɛ	ɔ	11	195	112
ɛ	i	10	195	273
a	a	286	339	351
a	ã	17	339	138
a	Ø	13	339	68
ɨ	ə	24	64	120
ɨ	ɔ	15	64	112
ə	ə	50	74	120
u	u	95	140	141
u	ɔ	19	140	112
o	o	28	42	170
o	u	13	42	141
ɔ	o	94	159	170
ɔ	ɔ	17	159	112
ɔ	a	16	159	351
ɔ	Ø	11	159	68
ĩ	ĩ	44	81	71
ɛ̃	ɛ̃	49	83	81
ã	ã	93	138	138
ã	ɔ	11	138	112
Ã	ɔ̃	16	30	76
ũ	ũ	21	42	37
ɔ̃	ɔ̃	25	38	76
a	Ø	13	339	68
ɔ	Ø	11	159	68

Maximum number of occurences in a single correspondence of vowels having no correspondences occurring as many as ten times in the cognate list:

ʌ	o	7	23	170
ɨ	ɔ̃	4	8	22
ɔ̃	ɔ̃	1	2	22
ɔ̃	ɔ̃	1	2	76
Ø	i	9	51	273
ʌ	ʌ	1	23	2
a	ʌ	1	339	2
ɛ̃	ɔ̃	4	83	22
i	ɔ̃	4	255	22
ɔ	Ã	1	159	2
Ã	Ã	1	30	2

NOTES

1. It would obviously not be possible to list the aberrant Austronesian languages. However, the reader might find it helpful if I point out that the languages that were found to have low "critical percentages" (that is, low cognate percentages with all the other languages of the study) in Isidore Dyen's (1965) lexicostatistical classification of the Austronesian languages constitute a fairly representative sample of the languages which I would call aberrant.

2. I should point out here that the population of the Grand Couli reserve at one time spoke two different dialects, Tîrî and Mea. My informant occasionally identified particular items as belonging specifically to one or the other of the dialects, but most of the vocabulary which I got from him was supposed to belong to the common speech of GC. This apparently is based in what was shared by the two dialects to begin with and probably further extended through subsequent leveling. The fact that the GC material does derive from two originally distinguishable dialects probably contributes in some measure to the complexity of the sound correspondences which I found (I think especially that one or two rare vowels may occur only in Mea forms). However, every indication that I have is that any distortion that it may introduce into the results is relatively insignificant.

3. In Rotuman, most words occur in two forms, which Churchward (1940) referred to as the "complete" and "incomplete" "phases". The complete phase is definite and specific; the incomplete is indefinite and/or unspecific (see Besnier 1987). The complete phase ends in a vowel. In the incomplete phase a final CV sequence is metathesized, and either (1) the two vowels thus juxtaposed merge as one or (2) one loses its syllabicity. Thus the incomplete phase is generally shorter by one syllable than the complete phase, a disyllable becoming a monosyllable.

4. This morpheme-for-morpheme intertranslatability is precisely what is produced by what in Grace 1981a I called convergence of content form and cited as one of the most conspicuous indicators of the sprachbund phenomenon.

5. One quite independent indication that the languages of southern New Caledonia constitute a genetic subgroup is provided by lexicostatistics; cf. Dyen 1965.

6. Observers in various parts of Melanesia have commented that languages with small numbers of speakers find themselves in a situation reminiscent of border areas in Europe. That is, most speakers are multilingual, language switching is common, and interference of one language on another is often observable. Of course, in Europe and other such parts of the world (at least wherever standard languages on the European model have become established), such situations are regarded as abnormal, or at least marginal. But whether it is the great monolingual heartland or the multilingual border situation that is more typical of the entire human experience seems less than certain.

7. I do not think it matters for present purposes whether we think of every individual as having his or her own unique phonological dialect or imagine phonological dialects to be shared by numbers of individuals.

8. In addition to the "change from above" in which signantia diffuse, there is also change from below in which signata and articulatory subroutines diffuse. Change from below (which, by the way, I think is much more revealing of the nature of language) is particularly characteristic of the sprachbund situation. I discussed this in Grace 1981a.

9. It seems to me that we consistently give priority to genetic relationship over contact as an explanation for similarities of all kinds and that this leads to a constant bias in our perceptions. For example, how many times have you heard linguists casually suggest that some similarity between particular European languages was "presumably" due to their "both being Indo-European" in cases where Indo-Europeanness was obviously not the explanation? And do you ever get the impression that regular sound correspondences are regarded almost as a touchstone for genetic relatedness?

REFERENCES

Besnier, N. (1987). An autosegmental approach to metathesis in Rotuman. *Lingua* 73: 201–23.

Churchward, C. M. (1940). *Rotuman grammar and dictionary*. Australasian Medical Publishing Company, Sydney.

Dempwolff, O. (1934–38). *Vergleichende Lautlehre des austronesischen Wortschatzes*. 3 vols. Beihefte zur

Zeitschrift für Eingeborenen-Sprachen. Vol. 1, *Induktiver Aufbau einer indonesischen Ursprache* Beiheft 15 (1934); vol. 2, *Deduktive Anwendung des Urindonesischen auf austronesische Einzelsprachen* Beiheft 17 (1937); vol. 3, *Austronesisches Wörterverzeichnis*, Beiheft 19 (1938). Reimer, Berlin.

Dyen, I. (1965). *A lexicostatistical classification of the Austronesian languages.* International Journal of American Linguistics, Memoir 19.

Grace, G. W. (1975). *Canala dictionary (New Caledonia). Pacific Linguistics* C2. Pacific Linguistics, Canberra.

———. (1976). *Grand Couli dictionary (New Caledonia). Pacific Linguistics* C–12. Pacific Linguistics, Canberra.

———. (1981a). *An essay on language.* Hornbeam Press, Columbia S.C.

———. (1981b). Indirect inheritance and the aberrant Melanesian languages. In J. Hollyman and A. Pawley, eds., *Studies in Pacific languages and cultures in honour of Bruce Biggs* 255–68. Linguistic Society of New Zealand, Auckland.

———. (1986). Hypotheses about the phonological history of the language of Canala, New Caledonia. In C. Corne and A. Pawley, eds., *Le coq et le cagou: Essays on French and Pacific languages in honour of Jim Hollyman. Te Reo* 29: 55–76.

Labov, W. (1972). *Sociolinguistic patterns.* University of Pennsylvania Press, Philadelphia.

Milroy, J., and L. Milroy. (1985). Linguistic change, social network and speaker innovation. *Journal of Linguistics* 21: 339–84.

8 Contact-induced Change and the Comparative Method: Cases from Papua New Guinea[1]

MALCOLM D. ROSS

1 INTRODUCTION

The overriding goal of the comparative method is to reconstruct linguistic prehistory and thereby to contribute to human culture history. Unfortunately, the method is blinkered in this endeavour by its prerequisites. It deals only with genetically related languages, and then only with regular correspondences among them. Yet the history of almost every language entails contact between its speakers and those of other languages, contact which often impairs the language's correspondences with its kin. Whether the languages in contact are genetically related or not, or so closely related that one should more accurately speak of dialects, the comparative method usually leaves this noncorresponding material unaccounted for, either by ignoring it or by labelling it 'borrowed'.

This blinkeredness is perhaps less limiting in the study of the Indo-European language family (where, after all, the comparative method came into being) than in the study of, say, the Austronesian languages of New Guinea.[2] As far as we can tell, contact with non-Indo-European languages has done little to impair correspondences among Indo-European languages throughout much of their history, and the traces of contact between, for example, Germanic and Romance languages are often obvious enough to be set aside without much ado. Szemerényi (1990), introducing the study of Indo-European comparative linguistics, makes no mention of borrowing. He limits his discussion (24) of contact between dialects to a statement that irregular sound correspondences occur only in transitional zones between dialects, but not in their nuclear zones, where sound change operates regularly. The implication is clear: We can ignore transitional zones, and take our data from the nuclear zone of each dialect (although this begs the question of whether, say, the dialects of German can realistically be treated as having nuclear and transitional zones). Such a procedure may be possible for Indo-European because its dialects and languages are apparently consistent over fairly large areas. But it is not possible for a region like New Guinea, where the area of each language is usually tiny, embraces just a few villages, and has no nuclear zone protected from contact with its neighbours.

The difference between the sociolinguistic history of the Indo-European region and of New Guinea reflects the distinction between a 'spread zone' and a 'residual zone' formulated by Nichols (1992: 13–24). As she points out (4–5), historical linguistics has typically been concerned with spreading language families like Indo-European. The comparative method is designed to deal with the problems presented by large language families, and it accords no theoretical status to genetically diverse linguistic areas. Yet such areas are a recurrent phenomenon even today, and their significance probably increases the further back we delve into prehistory.

Typically, residual zones—areas of structural and genetic linguistic diversity like New Guinea[3]—tend to be mountainous and to serve as a refuge, attracting intrusive languages from outside. Since new languages tend not to replace the old, diversity increases over time. Within the whole New Guinea residual zone we find perhaps a thousand languages among a population of around five million. About a quarter of these languages are Austronesian, the remainder 'Papuan'. 'Papuan' is a cover-term for the non-Austronesian languages of eastern Indonesia and western Melanesia, which belong to perhaps fifty or sixty different genetic groups (Foley 1986), some of which may be related to each other. In the premodern era a residual zone was not served by just a single lingua franca. Instead, there were various local bilingualisms, whereby communities knew each other's languages. In New Guinea, many languages were spoken by the people of only a few villages, so that, before the spread of modern *lingue franche* in the last years of the nineteenth century,[4] bi- and multilingualism were the norm (as in many places they still are).

Before European contact in the nineteenth and twentieth centuries, the largest sociopolicial unit in New Guinea was the village, and a person's ethnic identity was tied to his village.[5] For many New Guinea bilinguals ('bilingual' here also subsumes 'multilingual'), one of their languages is emblematic of that ethnicity—it is their 'emblematic language' (Grace 1975, 1981:155-156; Laycock 1982). The other is the emblematic language of a nearby village which serves as a means of intergroup communication, a sort of local *lingua franca*. However, it is vacuous to describe a bilingual group's emblematic language as its native language: Both the emblematic and the intergroup languages are 'native' in the sense that they are acquired together in infancy. Ironically, many speakers are more at home in the intergroup language than in their emblematic language: They use the intergroup language more often, and maintain their emblematic language principally as marker of their ethnicity and for (often limited) use within the village community.[6]

The functional asymmetry of these local bilingualisms can have significant effects on the history of the languages which participate in them. Often, the majority of (at least) the males in a New Guinea village are bilingual in the same languages. Where the 'other' language is an intergroup language, the stage is set for contact-induced change of the kind described in Weinreich's landmark *Languages in contact* [1953]1963. Speakers progressively adapt the semantic and morphosyntactic structures of their emblematic language to the model of the more often spoken intergroup language. At the same time, they may speak the intergroup language with a phonology which approximates that of their emblematic language. This process has two alternative outcomes. One is that bilingualism continues, and the emblematic language survives in its restructured version. The other is that the emblematic language is eventually abandoned in favour of the speakers' version of the intergroup language. These are the outcomes which Thomason and Kaufman (1988: chap. 3) call 'borrowing' and 'interference through shift'. I find the term 'borrowing' somewhat unfortunate in this context, however, as it does not capture the thoroughness with which contact-induced change may restructure an emblematic language. Since this restructuring involves changes in structural typology, I will coin for it the term 'metatypy'.

Metatypy and language shift both interfere with a language's correspondences with its genetic kin, and many of the Austronesian languages of Papua New Guinea display this interference to a marked degree. It is true that almost every application of the comparative method leaves a certain amount of data unaccounted for: irregular correspondences in phonology, morphology or syntax, unexplained semantic changes, or noncogate lexical items. However, when I applied the comparative method to reconstructing the prehistory of Papua New Guinea's Austronesian languages (as reported in Ross 1988), I felt quite often that this residue was unsatisfactorily large—as if the data had a story to tell which I could not read. Subsequently, I have learnt to read parts of the story and to see that some features of this residue are attributable to metatypy (Ross 1985, 1987) and others to language shift (Ross 1994a). Clearly, if we apply the comparative method to the data which are amenable to it and leave the rest, we have probably given a very biased account of the prehistory of the languages under study. Indeed, we will have left much of their story untold. An aim of this chapter, then, is to accord to this 'residual' material a theoretical status which approaches that allowed to the correspondences identified by the comparative method, and to achieve some theoretical integration of the two.

Under the comparative method, evidence of genetic relatedness between languages consists in (i) cognate paradigms of grammatical morphemes and (ii) sets of cognate lexical items. 'Cognate' means that the items resemble each other both in form and in meaning. But, as I will show below, when a language has undergone metatypy, this evidence is distorted. The 'metatypised' (restructured) language maintains forms resembling those in its genetic relatives, but the meanings of these forms have changed. In the case of grammatical morphemes, this change in meaning often entails not only the restructuring of the paradigm to which the morpheme belongs, but also rearrangement of the morphosyntactic structures in which the members of the paradigm occur. For the comparative method, these 'distortions' are just unexplained residue. But when we compare the restructured material with its functional equivalents in the language which has provided the model for metatypy, we find that the model language and the metatypised language often resemble each other quite systematically in their semantic organisation, in the structures of their paradigms, and in their morphosyntax. Hence a metatypised language participates in two kinds of resemblance. It shows correspondences in form and partial resemblances in meaning to its genetic relatives. And it shows more precise correspondences in meaning and resemblances in morphosyntax to its metatypic model.

Just as metatypy leaves its marks on a language's semantic and morphosyntactic structure, so language shift leaves its marks, if at all, on the phonology of the adopted language. If there are still speakers of the old emblematic language (or of a language closely related to it), then there is a possibility that this and the adopted intergroup language will show enough resemblances in their phonological systems to provide evidence of the shift. As a result, the adopted language may, like a metatypised language, display two sets of resemblances. It continues to manifest form/meaning correspondences with its genetic relatives, but its phonological system resembles that of the old emblematic language and/or of the latter's close genetic relatives.

Nichols (this volume) coins the term 'individual-identifying' to characterise the evidence which is used to diagnose genetic relatedness under the comparative method: 'its probability of multiple independent occurrence among the world's languages is so low that for practical purposes it can be regarded as unique and individual' (48). The theoretical status of the form/meaning correspondences diagnostic of genetic relatedness lies in their individual-identifying nature, that is, in the fact that they can be reckoned to identify just one individual protolanguage. Note, however, that it is generally not single form/meaning correspondences which meet the individual-identifying criterion, but whole paradigms or sets which correspond.

A similar theoretical status can be accorded to resemblances in semantic organisation, paradigmatic structures, and morphosyntax between a metatypised language and its putative model. Although a single resemblance will rarely reach the individual-identifying criterion, a *collection* of such resemblances (as I will exemplify below) may do so, identifying just one language or one set of similarly structured languages as the model for metatypy.

Less commonly perhaps, a collection of resemblances between the phonology of a language adopted by shift and the phonology of its speakers' old emblematic language may also meet the individual-identifying criterion, identifying just the latter as the source of phonological features of the adopted language. However, because phonological systems are closed and small in size, these resemblances will only be individual-identifying if they entail enough phonemes and/or phonological rules which are either universally uncommon or unusual in the geographic region of the two languages.

There is another dimension of change which may occur alongside metatypy or language shift and which may also interfere with a language's correspondences with its genetic kin. This consists of the processes which Thurston (1989: 556–57), seeking to account for the linguistic history of northwestern New Britain (Papua New Guinea), calls 'esoterogeny' and 'exoterogeny'. Esoterogeny is the process which operates on a group's emblematic language so that it becomes an 'in-group' code from whose use outsiders are excluded, an 'esoteric' language in Thurston's terms. The language becomes increasingly complicated and increasingly difficult for one's neighbours to understand. Processes of elision and assimilation result in phonological compactness, in allophony and in allomorphy (Thurston 1987: 56–60). There is an accumulation of irregular variants; Thurston (1987: 55) calls them 'grammatical baggage'. The lexicon is elaborated with numerous near synonyms, often by borrowing, and there is an increase in the frequency of opaque idioms (Thurston 1989: 556). Metatypy may co-occur with esoterogeny in a group's emblematic language, but there is no necessary reason for it to do so. Metatypy is the product of bilingualism; esoterogeny arises through a group's desire for exclusiveness.

Exoterogeny is the opposite process, operating on an intergroup language to make it simpler, more regular, more understandable and learnable, and to keep it this way (to make it, in Thurston's terms, 'exoteric'). Exoterogeny results from the use of the language with and by people for whom it is an intergroup language but not their emblematic language. In these circumstances there is a constant pressure towards simplification. An inter-group language may be affected by the processes of both exoterogeny and language shift. Thurston (1994) suggests that when a group shifts to an inter-group language, their somewhat simplified version of it may in the next generation replace the 'standard' version. However, language shift does not necessarily entail exoterogeny.

Unlike metatypy and language shift, the processes of esoterogeny and exoterogeny do not result in resemblances between languages. On the contrary, their products—complication and simplification—are recognisable precisely because they do *not* correspond with either their relatives or their neighbours. They are important in an extended application of the comparative method, however, because they give rise to 'residues' which are also amenable to historical interpretation.

The main focus of this chapter is on contact-induced change in a residual zone, New Guinea, but the phenomena described in the case studies here also occur, albeit more rarely, in spead zones like the Indo-European region. Case studies of two Austronesian languages of Papua New Guinea are sketched below: one has undergone metatypy, the other metatypy and esoterogeny. These sketches are followed by a discussion of the issues they raise and of some of the rather programmatic statements in this introduction. I shall not deal further with language shift here, as I have shown elsewhere (Ross 1994a) how a resemblance between phonological systems may be used to infer earlier language shift. On the subject of exoterogeny, the reader is referred to Thurston (1987, 1989).

2 CASE STUDIES

One of the most successful applications of the comparative method outside the Indo-European language family has been to the vast Austronesian family of languages in the Pacific Basin and on parts of the Pacific Rim. Comparative work on the Austronesian family began in the eighteenth century, but the foundations of modern work on the family were laid by Otto Dempwolff (1934, 1937, 1938), who used a representative sample of languages to establish phonological and lexical correspondences and to reconstruct the phonological system and a large number of etyma in the protolanguage which is today known as 'Proto-Malayo-Polynesian'.[7] Among other things, Dempwolff (1937) demonstrated the existence within Austronesian of the large Oceanic subgroup, embracing most of the languages of Melanesia, Micronesia, and Polynesia. He reconstructed the phonological system of Proto-Oceanic, showing that it manifested a set of innovations relative to the Proto Malayo-Polynesian system, innovations which are reflected in all Oceanic languages.[8]

Although the languages of Oceania can be conveniently divided on a geographical basis into those of Melanesia, Micronesia, and Polynesia, only the languages of the latter two regions form genetic subgroups within Oceanic.[9] There is no 'Melanesian' genetic group of Oceanic Austronesian languages. Instead, we find a large number of smaller groups of Oceanic languages within the Melanesian region, scattered over an area embracing the north coast of the Indonesian province of Irian Jaya, the mainland coasts and smaller islands of Papua New Guinea, and the island groups of the Solomons, Vanuatu, New Caledonia, and Fiji (Pawley & Ross 1993). Especially in the western portion of this region (Irian Jaya, Papua New Guinea and the western Solomons), the Oceanic languages of Melanesia display enormous structural and lexical diversity. This diversity has long posed a problem for historical Austronesian linguistics. In Dyen's (1965) classic lexicostatistical study of the Austronesian language family, three-quarters of the first-order subgroups of the family are in Melanesia. That is, the Oceanic subgroup, so clearly established on the basis of shared innovations, seemingly has no lexical foundation. Two earlier researchers (Capell 1943, Ray 1926) and a more recent one (Thurston 1982, 1987), faced with the diversity of the Austronesian languages of western Melanesia, observe that these languages have been in intense contact with Papuan languages. They seek to explain this diversity through the hypothesis that the Austronesian languages of western Melanesia are hybrids—not truly Austronesian—produced by contact between a variety of Papuan languages and various immigrant Austronesian languages, presumably from Indonesia. Pawley (1981) defends the comparative method and the integrity of the Oceanic subgroup against the hybridisation hypothesis. He proposes instead a model whereby Melanesian diversity has been internally generated over time by sociolinguistic factors. Lynch (1981) points out that it is possible to attribute a measure of Melanesian diversity to Austronesian/Papuan contact without throwing out Dempwolff's Oceanic theory.

The position adopted here is essentially Lynch's. The Austronesian languages of western Melanesia are demonstrably members of the Oceanic subgroup of Austronesian, that is, they reflect the innovations which had occurred before the breakup of Proto-Oceanic. Indeed, many of them are descended from a dialect network, labelled 'Proto Western Oceanic' (PWOc), a continuation of Proto Oceanic in the Bismarck Achipelago of Papua New Guinea after Proto Oceanic itself had broken up (Ross 1988). The diversity of these languages has arisen since that breakup (around 1600 B.C.[10]) and is attributable to metatypy, language shift, and to eso- and exoterogeny.

The case studies of contact-induced change sketched here are from two Western Oceanic (WOc) languages, Takia and Maisin. The two languages are in widely separated parts of Papua New Guinea and belong to different primary subgroups of WOc—Takia to the North New Guinea cluster, Maisin to the Papuan Tip cluster (Ross 1988). Both have Papuan neighbours which are potential sources of contact-induced change, and they have in a number of respects undergone parallel changes.

It will be convenient here to consider these changes relative to the lowest-order proto language ancestral to both languages, that is, PWOc. Table 8-1 gives some typological context for the accounts below, and the major typological features of PWOc are listed in its second column. Many of New Guinea's Papuan languages share a set of typological features. I will use McElhanon and Voorhoeve's (1970) term 'Trans-New Guinea' to refer to this areal grouping, but with no implication that its members

TABLE 8.1

A typological comparison of (Austronesian) Proto-Western-Oceanic
and the (Papuan) Trans New Guinea type

	Austronesian: Proto-Western-Oceanic	Papuan: Trans New Guinea type
Unmarked Clause Order	Subject—Verb—Object	Subject—Object—Verb
Noun Phrase: article	preposed article with common/personal distinction	no article
adjective	postposed adjective	
adjective agreement	possessor pronoun suffixed to adjective agrees in person and number with head noun	none
Possession System	alienable/inalienable distinction	
possessor NP	postposed	preposed
possessor pronoun: with inalienables	suffixed to possessed noun	prefixed/infixed to possessed noun
possessor pronoun: with alienables	suffixed to a classifier	independent, preposed
Verb Complex Distinctions	mood/aspect	tense/mood/aspect
subject referencing pronoun	prefix or proclitic	portmanteau suffix
(tense/)aspect/mood	prefix or proclitic, reduplication for continuative	portmanteau suffix
object referencing pronoun	suffix	prefix or suffix (preceding portmanteau)
Pronoun System	inclusive/exclusive distinction	no inclusive/exclusive distinction
Adpositional Phrases	prepositional	postpositional
Clause Linkage	co-ordinate, subordinate	co-ordinate, cosubordinate, subordinate
linking devices	parataxis, independent conjunctions	suffixation (often part of portmanteau suffix)

are all genetically related.[11] The Papuan neighbours of Maisin and Takia all belong to this grouping, whose major features are listed in the third column of Table 8-1. For the sake of brevity, I use the term 'Papuan' interchangeably with 'Trans New Guinea' in the remainder of this chapter.

Table 8-1 largely speaks for itself. It is clear that PWOc and the Trans New Guinea languages are rather different typologically. Trans New Guinea bound morphemes tend to behave inflectionally, whilst those in PWOc are readily analysable. PWOc had four sets of pronoun morphemes, each distinguishing at least two numbers, three persons, and inclusive and exclusive in the first person plural:

i. independent;
ii. a proclitic or prefix to the verb referencing the person and number of the subject;
iii. an enclitic to the verb referencing the person and number of the object;
iv. suffixes on inalienably possessed nouns referencing the person and number of the possessor; if the possessed noun was alienable, the possessor suffix was attached to a classifier.

In Trans New Guinea languages, nonindependent pronouns tend to be inflectional and therefore difficult to segment from their heads.

The PWOc mood/aspect system was simple (there was no tense as such), distinguishing an unmarked realis from an irrealis marked by a morpheme preceding the verb phrase, and an unmarked punctual from a durative marked by reduplication of the verb stem. The Trans New Guinea tense/mood/aspect system is often more complex and is marked by a portmanteau suffix on the verb stem which also references the person and number of the subject. In the Papuan languages which concern us here, the object is referenced, if at all, by a suffix preceding the portmanteau suffix.

Clause linkage in Trans New Guinea languages is of three kinds (Foley 1986: 175–205):

i. coordinate (each clause is fully marked for aspect and mood);
ii. subordinate dependent (the subordinate clause is formally independent, with a subordinating enclitic added, and functions as complement or relative clause);
iii. coordinate dependent (clauses participate in a clause chain, in which all clauses except the last are incompletely marked for aspect and mood; the final [independent] clause is marked for the aspect and mood of the whole chain).

The three categories are marked by a suffix (or the absence thereof) on the (clause-final) verb phrase; this suffix is sometimes part of the portmanteau tense/mood/aspect suffix.

PWOc was not a clause-chaining language, and had only coordinate and subordinate linkage, expressed either by independent conjunctions or by simple parataxis.

2.1 Takia

The fifteen thousand or so speakers of Takia occupy the southern half of Karkar Island, a large volcanic island near Madang on the north coast of Papua New Guinea, as well as smaller Bagabag Island and a coastal enclave where the Megiar dialect is spoken.[12] Takia is a member of the Bel family of the North New Guinea cluster (Ross

1988:161, 180), closely related to Gedaged, which was the *lingua franca* of the Lutheran Church in the area for several decades.[13] Gedaged and Takia's other sister languages in the Bel family often have 'Papuan' features which match Takia's in structure and sometimes in form. This suggests that at least a portion of these features is reconstructible for Proto Bel or one of its early daughters. Discussion of some of these features is found in Ross (1987, 1994b).

The northern half of Karkar Island is the domain of the speakers of Papuan Waskia, which is related to languages on the nearby mainland. However, the relationship between Waskia and its closest relatives is much more distant than that between Takia and the other Bel languages. This suggests that the Waskia have been on the island for much longer than the Takia. Waskia and its relatives are languages of the Trans New Guinea type.[14]

Although Takia elders claim that they had little contact with the Waskia at the time of first European contact (in the 1890s), McSwain's (1977) study reports that ethnographically it is impossible to tell the Takia and the Waskia apart, indicating a close relationship for a long period of time sometime in the past. However, it is not certain that Waskia is the main or the only source of Takia Papuanisation.

The Takia pronominal system is as outlined for WOc above, with all that this implies categorically and morphosyntactically. Takia pronominal forms all have cognates in other WOc languages. Takia also retains the PWOc structure whereby an attributive adjective has a possessor pronominal suffix agreeing in person and number with the head noun. In other respects Takia is markedly Papuan in its typology (and markedly un-Oceanic—see Table 8-1): clause order is strictly verb-final; the noun phrase lacks an article; in possessive noun phrases the possessor is preposed; adpositional phrases have postpositions; aspect, mood, and clause linkage are marked by enclitics on the predicate, and there are chains of coordinate dependent clauses terminating with an independent clause.

It is important to note here that all the Papuan features of Takia have to do with morphosyntactic *structures*. Where grammatical morphemes participating in these structures can be sourced (by way of cognates in other languages), their *forms* are invariably WOc. This is true of possessor pronominal suffixes in possessive noun phrases, of predicate enclitics encoding the mood of coordinate dependent clauses, and of postpositions.

I have shown elsewhere (Ross 1987) that, although the structure of coordinate dependent clauses in Takia and other Bel languages is Papuan, every coordinate dependent clause in Takia ends with one of the predicate enclitics /-go/ 'realis' and /-pe/ 'irrealis', derived respectively from PWO *ga* 'realis conjunction' and *be* 'irrealis conjunction'.

The postpositions of Takia and Waskia are set out below:

(1) | | **Takia** | **Waskia** |
|---|---|---|
| location | na, te | se, te |
| location 'in' | lo | i, nuŋi |
| location 'on' | fo, fufo | kuali |
| ablative | — | ko |

instrument	nam (= na-mi)	se
referential	o	ko
manner	mi	wam
accompaniment	da	karo

The categories of Takia postpositions match those of Waskia with just one exception, the Waskia ablative. The forms, however, do not match each other. The only possible borrowing is the form *te*, serving as a location postposition in both Takia and Waskia. But given the simple consonant systems and phonotactics of both languages, this could well be a chance resemblance—the more so as Waskia *te* has only limited use, as an allative with human and some other nouns.

Two of the Takia postpositions, *lo* 'in' and *fo/fufo* 'on' have known origins in inalienably possessed PWOc 'part nouns', that is, nouns like *inside*, *side*, or *top* which denote part of an object. A possessive noun phrase with an inalienably possessed head noun had the following structure in PWOc:[15]

(2) **ŋuju-ña a   manuk*
   beak-its ART bird
   'the bird's beak'

Locations were often expressed in PWOc by a prepositional phrase with such a possessive noun phrase as its governee:

(3) **i   lalo-ña   a   Rumaq*   **i   papo-ña a   Rumaq*
   PREP inside-its ART house   PREP top-its   ART house
   'inside the house'   'on top of the house'

The head of the noun phrase **lalo-ña a Rumaq* '(the) inside of the house' is **lalo-ña* 'its inside'; **a Rumaq* 'the house' is the possessor. In languages like most of those of the North New Guinea cluster of WOc, in which the article is lost and the possessor preposed, the first result was apparently the following structure:

(4) **Rumaq i   lalo-ña*   **Rumaq i   papo-ña*
   house PREP inside-its   house PREP top-its
   'inside the house'   'on top of the house'

It may well be objected that the preposition would have shifted to the front of the possessive phrase (i.e. **i Rumaq lalo-ña*), but two facts speak against this: (i) in the WOc Papuan Tip languages Wedau and Tawala, in which a parallel development has occurred, a preposition remains in the middle of the phrase; and (ii) the Takia reflex of **lalo-ña* is *i-lo-n*, with fossilised *i-* (there is no directly corresponding Takia reflex of **papo-ña*).

With the shift in Proto Bel to verb-final syntax, this structure underwent a further change: Prepositions were lost or ceased to be productive. The first syllable of the part noun was (optionally?) deleted, resulting in structures somewhat as follows:

(5) *ɣaba   ilo-n   *ɣaba   [fu]fo-n
    house   inside-its   house   top-its
    'inside the house'   'on top of the house'

Next came the reinterpretation of the part nouns as postpositions, and their concomitant reduction in form. Gedaged, with the postposition *lon* 'in', represents this stage. Takia and the other western Bel languages have lost the now redundant *-n*, so that Takia has

(6) *ab   lo*   *ab   [fu]fo*
    house in   house on
    'in the house'   'on top of the house'

When a Takia speaker wishes to be precise about the location, one hears *ab ilo-n lo* 'in the house's inside'.

There is evidence that the motivation of this process in Takia was not purely internal, but was metatypic. In a Waskia phrase like *kar kuali* 'on the fence', *kuali* 'on' is derived from *k<u>al + i*, where the infix *<u>* marks a third person possessor (corresponding to PWOc *-ña*, Takia *-n*), *-i* is the location postposition (corresponding functionally to the PWOc preposition *i*—the formal correspondence is chance), and *kal* was a now-lost part noun meaning 'top' (corresponding to PWOc *papo-*). The Waskia postposition *nuŋi* 'in' has a similar history, derived from an earlier part noun *niŋ* 'inside'; this inference is supported by the dialectal variant *niŋi*.

The process I have just outlined is typical of metatypy. The semantic and syntactic structures of Takia have been restructured on the model provided by Waskia (or a typologically similar language), but the forms are inherited.

There is enough information available from both Takia and Waskia to see that metatypy has also affected the lexicon. That is, the semantic ranges of equivalent items have converged, or perhaps more accurately Takia items have shifted their range to correspond with Waskia. An item's semantic range is a function of its collocations (and vice versa), and these are often exactly parallel in Takia and Waskia, as we see in expressions involving body-parts. In both languages, the palm of my hand is my 'hand's liver': Takia *bani-g ate-n*, Waskia *a-gitiŋ gomaŋ*. If I am dizzy, my 'eye goes round': Takia *mala-g i-kilani*, Waskia *motam gerago-so*. If I am waiting for someone, I am 'putting my eye': Takia *mala-g ŋi-ga*, Waskia *motam bete-so* (Takia *-ga* and Waskia *bete-* share the range of meaning 'put, do, make'). The expression for 'first' (as in 'do something first') in both languages is 'his eye + his eye': Takia *mala-n + mala-n*, Waskia *motam + motam*. Expressions of obeying and disobeying in both languages have the 'mouth' of the authority as their object. If I obey a person, 'I hear his mouth' (Takia *awa-n ŋa-loŋ*, Waskia *kuriŋ iki-so*) or, alternatively, 'I give him I follow his mouth' (Takia *awa-n ŋa-li ŋu-pani*, Waskia *kuriŋ karo tu-so*). Likewise, if I disobey him, 'I cut his mouth': Takia *awa-n ŋu-tale*, Waskia *kuriŋ batugar-so*.

And where a lexical item consists of more than one morpheme, Takia has tended to shift from the Oceanic pattern to the Papuan. For example, 'person' in both languages is a compound of 'man' and 'woman': Takia *tamolpein* (from *tamol* 'man' and *pein* 'woman') and Waskia *kadimet* (from *kadi* 'man' and *imet* 'woman'). The Takia components reflect respectively PWOc *tam^wata* 'man' and *papine* 'woman', but there is no evidence that they formed a compound in PWOc, in which the lexeme for 'person' was *tau*. Similarly, 'animal(s)' in both languages is a compound of 'pig' and 'dog': Takia *bor-goun*, Waskia *buruk-kasik*. And 'his parents' is a compound of 'his mother' and 'his father': Takia *tinan-taman*, Waskia *niam-niet*. There is a long list of phrasal lexemes in Takia and Waskia which use Takia *ilo-* 'inside' and Waskia *gemaŋ* 'liver' to express feelings and attitudes. For example, Takia *ilo-g saen/uyan* (inside-my bad/good) and Waskia *a-gemaŋ memek/yawarakala* (my-liver bad/good) both have the basic meaning 'my internal organs are bad/good', expressing 'I am angry/ happy'.

We do not have enough detailed lexica of Papua New Guinea languages to discern the geographical extent of these examples of lexical metatypy. Some of them certainly reach well beyond Takia and Waskia, but this is not surprising, considering the millenia of contact between languages of different families in this region. What is significant is that we have such close lexical parallels between languages which are genetically unrelated. That is, the parallels must be the result of metatypy.

The examples below show that structural parallels between Takia and Waskia are quite pervasive, except at the level of bound morphology.

(7) Takia: *Waskia tamol an*
    Waskia: *Waskia kadi mu*
                Waskia man   DETERMINER
                'the Waskia man'
    Takia: *tamol   tubun   uraru en*
    Waskia: *kadi   bi-biga   itelala pamu*
                man   (PLURAL-) big two   this
                'these two big men'
    Takia: *Kai   sa-n   ab*
    Waskia: *Kai   ko   kawam*
                Kai   CLASSIFIER-his house
                              POSTPOSITION
                'Kai's house'
    Takia: *ŋai   tamol   an   ida*
    Waskia: *ane   kadi   mu   ili*
                I   man   DETERMINER with-him
                'the man and I'

The direction of convergence here is Oceanic to Papuan, as Waskia phrase structure is typical of the Papuan languages of the area.

The clause structures of Takia and Waskia are also very similar:

(8) Takia: *tamol an   ŋai   i-fun-ag-da*
                man   DETERMINER me   he-hit-me-IMPERFECTIVE
    Waskia: *kadi mu   aga   umo-so*
                man   DETERMINER me   hit-PRESENT-he
                'The man is hitting me.'

The Takia verb *ifunagda* is characteristically Oceanic Austronesian in having a preposed subject marker and a postposed object marker, but unusual in having a postposed tense/aspect marker, whilst the Waskia verb is typically Papuan with its postposed portmanteau marking of tense/aspect and subject.

We could continue this catalogue of syntactic parallels further by noting interclausal parallels. Both languages, for example, mark various subordinate clauses with a clause-final determiner (for Takia, see Ross 1994b; for Waskia, see Ross 1978). However, it is more important to conclude by pointing out what has *not* occurred in Takia. There has not been much lexical borrowing from Waskia (or any other Papuan language). And there is no sign that Takia phonology has undergone any major changes relative to its closest 'un-Papuanised' kin—not that there is any pressing reason to expect this, since Waskia and the Papuan languages of the nearby mainland have phonological systems fairly similar to those of Takia and its relatives.

2.2 Maisin

Maisin probably has between two and three thousand speakers, who live in the Kosirava swamp lands inland from Dyke Ackland Bay and in several coastal enclaves on Collingwood Bay on the north coast of Papua's Oro (formerly Northern) Province. The Maisin claim Kosirava as their homeland; coastal settlement seems to have occurred in the last few generations before European contact in the 1880s.[16] Kosirava Maisin is completely surrounded by languages of the Papuan Binandere family, whilst the coastal villages have neighbours from the Oceanic Papuan Tip cluster. Papuan languages of the Koiarian, Yareban, and Dagan families occupy the hinterland a few kilometres from the various Maisin enclaves. A short description of Maisin has appeared as Ross (1984), and notes on various Maisin features occur in Ray (1911), Strong (1911), Capell (1976), and Lynch (1977).

The metatypic processes which have occurred in Maisin often run parallel to those which have occurred in Takia, but in some cases have gone much further. This, together with extensive lexical borrowing and opaque allomorphy, has made its prehistory a matter of controversy. Indeed, the following paragraphs are the first published justification of its Austronesian status. This controversy will be summarised and evaluated in section 2.3, after the features of the language and their metatypic origins have been sketched.

Maisin is a member of the (WOc) Papuan Tip cluster (Ross 1988:chap. 6). The reader is asked to beware of the unfortunate collocation of terms here: 'Papuan Tip' (PT) languages are *not* Papuan languages but members of the WOc subgroup of Austronesian.

Proto–Papuan Tip (PPT), spoken perhaps around 800 B.C., itself underwent metatypy as the result of contact with languages of the Trans New Guinea type (Lynch 1981: 110–11; Ross 1988: 208). Most PT languages, including Maisin, reflect this metatypy, which resulted in verb-final clause order, loss of the article, preposed possessors, and postpositional phrases. In other areas of grammar PPT retained its WOc features (see Table 8-1), and was less Papuanised than Takia is today. Maisin, however, underwent a 'second Papuanisation', and the features originating during this second metatypy, combined with its allomorphy and borrowed lexicon, have resulted in a language which stands out as quite different from its PT relatives. The postposition system was expanded. As in Takia, predicate enclitics mark aspect, mood, and clause linkage, and coordinate dependent clauses form chains ending with an independent clause. In order to distinguish between PPT metatypy and Maisin metatypy, Maisin forms are compared here with reconstructed PPT forms.

Like Takia, Maisin retains the WOc pronominal system. The reconstructed forms for the four PPT pronominal paradigms are set out in Table 8-2 with their Maisin equivalents.[17] Maisin morphemes are cited in their underlying forms, as morphophonemic rules result in various allomorphs. It is clear that most, if not all, the of Maisin morphemes are reflexes of the PPT forms. The sound correspondences they exemplify—initial devoicing and medial loss of the reflexes of the PPT voiced stops *d-, *-d- and *-g-—allow us to place Maisin in the Are-Taupota subgroup of the PT cluster.[18] Non-corresponding segments in the Maisin forms are attributable to four causes:

(9) a. The PPT possessor/object suffix *-da 'first person plural inclusive' has been replaced by forms derived from the independent pronoun aiti. The latter is derived, with unexplained preposed a-, from PPT *qita (*-a is regularly replaced by -i in directly inherited forms).

b. Reanalysis and generalisation have resulted in the insertion of a consonant or a consonant–vowel sequence between the verb stem and object suffix in all except certain third person forms. Before non-third person forms, /-re-/ is inserted; before some instances of third person plural /-i/, the insertion is /-ri-/; and before third person singular /-i/, it is /-s-/. (It is tempting to see Maisin/-rii/ 'third person plural object suffix' as a reflex of PPT *-dia, but intervocalic*-d- is lost before *-i in Maisin, and Maisin /r/ reflects PPT *r and *ñ.)

TABLE 8.2
The Reconstructed Pronominal Morphemes of Proto-Papuan Tip and Their Maisin Reflexes

		Possessor Suffixes		Subject Prefixes		Object Suffixes		Independent Pronouns	
		PPT	Maisin	PPT	Maisin	PPT	Maisin	PPT	Maisin
Singular	1	*-gu	-u	*a-	a-	*-gu	-ren	*yau	au
	2	*-m	-m	*ku-	ku-	*-m	-ren	*qoi	ai
	3	*-ña	-r	*i-	i-	*-na, -i	-n, -si	*ia	ari
Plural	1 incl	*-da	-ati	*ta-	ta-	*-da	-reti	*qita	aiti
	1 excl	*-ma	-m	*ka-	ka-	*-ma	-ren	*qama	am
	2	*-mi	-m	*ko-	ku-	*-mi	-ren	*qomi	em
	3	*-di	-i	*di-	ti-	*-dia	-rii, -i	*iti	ei

c. All final nasals surface as [-ŋ] in Maisin, and this has led to conflation of object suffix forms. We would expect PPT *-gu to be reflected in Maisin by the final consonant /-ŋ/, *-m, *-ma, and *-mi by /-m/, but instead all are reflected by /-n/. (We know that the segment is /-n/, not /-m/, because the distinction between them is maintained when the following morpheme begins with a vowel.)

d. Maisin /ari/ 'third person singular independent pronoun' is derived not from PPT *ia, but apparently (by regular changes) from demonstrative *aña, the neutral member of a three-way set *iña 'this one', *aña 'that one', *oña 'the one over there.'

The important point about the Maisin pronominal paradigm in Table 8-2 is that, despite its superficial strangeness, it shows systematic form/meaning correspondences with the equivalent paradigms of other PT languages. That is, we have clear individual-identifying evidence that Maisin is a member of the PT cluster (and is therefore an Oceanic Austronesian language).

Extensive though the Papuanisation of Maisin has been, its Papuan features (like those in Takia) are all morphosyntactic *structures*. Careful reconstruction reveals that their *forms* are of PT origin.

Maisin has three predicate enclitics which mark coordinate dependent clauses, each of which has a possible source in a PPT conjunction:[19]

(10) **PPT conjunction**   **Maisin enclitic**

    ma 'coordinating'   -n 'simultaneous'
    na 'realis'   -na 'durative'
    be 'irrealis'   -fe 'irrealis'

There is not enough morphological material here to be certain about these derivations. Nonetheless, the semantic correspondences are good. PWOc *ma* was apparently used to tie serialised verbs together into a semantic unit, and this is the function of Maisin -n. Maisin /-fe/ IRREALIS is with reasonable certainty derived from PWOc *be* IRREALIS CONJUNCTION (as is the functionally equivalent Takia form /-pe/).

As in Takia, the paradigm of postpositions is a fruitful source of evidence. Under (11) are listed the underlying forms of Maisin postpositions (Ross 1984:30–34), along with those from Arifama (Maisin's nearest PT neighbour) and Yamalele, another PT language, and from Maisin's immediate neighbour Baruga, a member of the Papuan Binandere family:[20]

(11)

	Maisin	**Yamalele**	**Arifama**	**Baruga**
location	-e	-ye	-ai	-re
source	-efe	-yega	-ai	-reta
instrument	-em, -sem	-amo	-mai	-mi
referential	-so	—	—	-du
attributive possessor	-ar	—	—	-da
predicate possessor	-kam	—	—	-da
accompaniment	-tom	—	airu	-de
future time	-fe	—	—	—

Again we see that the postposition categories of the metatypised WOc language, Maisin, match those of its possible Papuan metatypic model, Baruga, far more closely that those of its WOc relatives Yamalele and Arifama. Maisin and Baruga have a larger number of postpositions, and they resemble each other functionally. Particularly striking is that Maisin -*em* 'instrument' is also attached to an agentive subject:

(12) *tamateseŋ*   *sikōka*   *tifunesi*
     tamāti-e-sem   sikō-ka   ti-fune-si
     man-PLURAL-INSTRUMENT   pig-TOPIC   they-cut-it
     'The men cut up the pig.'

Significantly, this pattern of using the same postposition to mark an instrument and an agentive subject also occurs nearby in the Papuan languages Baruga, Korafe, Yareba and Ömie.[21] It does not occur in Yamalele, Arifama, or elsewhere in Oceanic languages.

However, although the categories of Maisin postpositions are founded on a Papuan model, those postposition forms which we can source are of PT origin, and none is recognisably Papuan. It is fascinating to review the various processes which have conspired to align PT forms with the Papuan model.

Two postpositions appear to be directly inherited from PPT. Maisin /-e/ 'location' reflects PPT *-[i]ai*, as do Yamalele -*ye* and Arifama -*ai*. Maisin /-em/ 'instrument' may reflect PPT *-mai*, as does Arifama -*mai* [22] (the Maisin alternant /-sem/ contains inserted /-s-/ analogous to that in (9a)).

The origin of /-fe/ 'future time' and /-efe/ 'source' is rather more complex. The postposition /-fe/ 'future time' occurs in contexts like

(13) *Bendō* *foiŋfe*   *irāna*
     Bendō   foim-fe   i-ra-anan
     Bendo   night-FUTURE   he-come-will
     'Bendo will come tonight.'

However, it has a much broader usage. As noted in (10), the enclitic /-fe/ also marks a coordinate dependent clause as irrealis (Ross 1984: 49):

(14) *imāmatufe*   *ayēana*
     i-mā-matu-fe   a-yē-anan
     he-REDUPLICATION-sleep-IRREALIS I-swim-will
     'While he is asleep I shall swim.'

The postpositional use of /-fe/ is clearly derived from its coordinate dependent usage. It is quite common in Papua New Guinea discourse to treat a temporal as a separate chain-initial clause ('When it is night, I will . . .'/'It will be night and I will . . .'), and it is only a short step to reinterpret a chain-initial one-word clause as a chain-initial one-word postpositional phrase.

Maisin /-efe/ 'source' is derived from a sequence /-e/ 'location' and /-fe/ 'irrealis coordinate dependent', that is, '. . .-at + -and . . .', by a mechanism similar to that just described. Papua New Guineans commonly express 'from . . . to . . .' sequences with two clauses: 'I was at X and I came to Y', or, as a Papuanised WOc structure, 'I X-at and Y-to I-came.' This provides a ready context for the reinterpretation of the sequence '. . . -at and . . .' as a source postposition. This etymology has exact parallels in Yamalele *-yega* and Baruga *-reta*, where the first element is the location postposition and the second a conjunction (PPT **ga* 'realis conjunction'; Baruga *eta* 'conjunction').

The attributive possessor postposition /-ar/ in (15) results from a reinterpretation of the PPT possessive noun phrase structure on a Papuan model. In Maisin's Papuan neighbours, possession is expressed by attaching a postposition to the preposed possessor, for example, Korafe *Dafini-da nati* 'Daphne's house', where the postposition *-da* marks the genitive. Maisin uses the postposition /-ar/ similarly:

(15) *Borebā*   *vā*   *tamata*   *vā*
      boreba-ar   var   tamāti-ar   var
      Boreba-POSSESSOR   house man-POSSESSOR   house
      'Boreba's house'   'the man's house'

In PPT, as in other Oceanic languages, if the possessed noun was alienable a possessor suffix was attached to a possessive classifier. Reconstructed PPT forms are:

(16) **tamʷata a-ña*   *ruma*   **tamʷata a-di*   *ruma*
      man   CLASSIFIER-his   house   man   CLASSIFIER-their   house
      'the man's house'   'the men's house'

The possessor suffixes here are **-ña* and **-di*, whilst *a-* is the general possessive classifier. The Maisin possessor postposition /-ar/ has been derived by regular sound change from the PPT sequence **a-ña* (CLASSIFIER-his), reinterpreted as a postposition, and generalised across the semantic range of the possessor postposition in nearby Papuan languages. It has ousted the PPT plural sequence **a-di* (CLASSIFIER-their) (which would have become Maisin ***ai*).

There are several areas of morphology where Maisin departs from the PPT and PWO pattern, but is less obviously Papuan-like. The languages of the PT cluster, like Oceanic languages generally, do not mark tense. They do mark mood (realis/irrealis), but do so with prefixes. But in Maisin tense, mood and aspect are marked by an enclitic on the predicate (usually a verb phrase). Maisin has /-anan/ 'future', /-me/ 'past', /-aka/ 'potential', and several more complex markers. For example:

(17) *tamenana*
      ta-me-n-anan
      we(INCL.)-give-it-FUTURE
      'we will give it'

Here /-anan/ occurs in the position of a Papuan tense/aspect/mood marker. But in a Papuan language the marker here would be a portmanteau also referencing the person and number of the subject. In Maisin the PT subject prefix (here *ta-*) retains this function. The Maisin set has no obvious cognates in any of these languages, but it is possible that /-anan/ 'future' and /-me/ 'past' are derived from auxiliary uses of, respectively, PWOc *lako* 'go' and *mai* 'come'. This suggestion is not as far-fetched as it might seem: tense/aspect markers in other metatypised WOc languages (including Takia's close relative Gedaged) are derived from motion verbs (Ross 1982, Ross 1987).

In PWO and PPT, an attributive adjective took a *possessor* suffix agreeing in person and number with its head. For PPT we may reconstruct:

(18) *ruma*   *vau-ña*   *ruma*   *vau-di*
       house   new-its   house   new-their
       'a/the new house'   'a/the new houses'

These structures are reflected in nearby PT Arifama as *sisi bobu-na* 'new house' and *sisi bobu-i* 'new houses' (where *-na* and *-i* are regular reflexes of PPT *-ña* and *-di*). In neighbouring Papuan languages, adjectives are unmarked for number except for occasional reduplication to mark the plural. Here again Maisin departs from the PT pattern but does not adopt the Papuan one. The Maisin structures equivalent to those in (18) are:

(19) *va*   *wauŋ*   *va*   *waun-a*   OR *vā*   *waun-ari*
      var   waun   var   waun-ar   var   waun-ari
      house   new   house   new-PLURAL   house   new-PLURAL
      'a/the new house'   'a/the new houses'   'a/the new houses'

There are two forms of the plural morpheme, /-ar/ and /-ari/ (the conditions, if any, of their alternation are not known). The forms in (19) are not directly inherited reflexes of those in (18). Final /-n/ of /waun/ 'new' is apparently a fossilised irregular reflex of the PPT possessor suffix *-ña, indicating that /waun/ is a borrowing from another PT language. The expected Maisin reflex of the PPT possessor pronominal suffix *-di 'third person plural' is /-i/ (see Table 8-2), not /-ar/ or /-ari/.

A speculative history of these forms in (19) runs as follows. Maisin roots may be either vowel-final or consonant-final, whereas PPT adjective roots were always vowel-final. The adjective /waun/ 'new' has a final consonant. The phonotactic changes which gave rise to final consonants may have motivated enclitic-initial /-a-/ of /-ar/ and /-ari/: an epenthetic vowel inserted between a root-final consonant and an earlier suffix /-ri/. The form /-ri/ is derived by analogy from the object pronominal suffix /-rii/ 'third person plural' (discussed in (9b) above). The variation between /-ar/ and /-ari/ simply entails the deletion of /-i/, whose original plural function is here long forgotten.

The point of this speculative and *ad hoc* history is not that it necessarily represents the truth. It is rather that in the course of metatypy the earlier functions of morphemes can readily be forgotten before the goal provided by the model (in this case the elimination of plural marking on adjectives) is reached. The present state of this portion of Maisin grammar is rather messy, such that a few Maisin adjectives follow another pattern, and have unpredictable or suppletive plural forms, for example, *rāti* 'small' (plural *rāte*), *taubaŋ* 'good' (plural *boregī*), which almost certainly do not have a PT origin.

Most of what has been said here about the development of Maisin suggests that it simply represents a more extreme metatypy than that which affected the development of Takia. In two areas, however, Maisin has developed quite differently from Takia. These areas are its phonology and its lexicon.

Maisin has quite a complex set of morphophonemic rules, as one can see in some of the examples above. These rules are sketched by Ross (1984: 11–22). They include the deletion of all word-final non-nasal consonants, with compensatory lengthening of the preceding vowel, and the neutralisation of word-final nasal consonants to [-ŋ]. Both these processes result in allomorphy. The verbal system in particular is also affected by allomorphy arising from assimilation across morpheme boundaries and from the exigencies of mora-timing which may degeminate both vowels and consonants. Neither Maisin's Oceanic relatives nor, as far as I can ascertain, any nearby Papuan language has such a set of features.

Everyone who has studied Maisin has been struck by the presence of more non-Austronesian lexicon than they would expect in an Oceanic language, but this lexicon has yet to be carefully sourced. A number of common words are clearly from a Binandere language, as they have cognates in Korafe, a member of that family:[23]

(20)	**Maisin**	**Korafe**	**'gloss'**
	birī	biria	'lightning'
	damana	damana	'star'
	fonji	fonja	'dust'
	jameŋ 'child'	jamena	'younger siblings'
	janjāki 'rib'	janje	'chest cavity'
	kūta 'yam'	kuta	'sweet potato'
	kaifi	kaifa	'waiting'
	kamora 'money'	kamora	'rock used as anchor'
	kasaŋ	kasama	'knowledge'
	keisi	keisa	'no'
	munju	munju	'egg'
	sikō 'pig'	sikogo	'black (used only of pigs)'
	tambuŋ	tambuno	'moon'

This is apparently not the only non-Oceanic source, as there are still numerous unsourced words of basic vocabulary. There are, for example, many words of apparently non-Oceanic origin with geminate consonants in Maisin. None has a Korafe cognate.

An interesting semantic field is the numerals:

(21)	1	sesei
	2	sandei
	3	sinati
	4	fūsese
	5	faketi-tarosi 'hand, one side'
	10	faketi-tautau 'hand, both sides'
	20	tamati-sesei 'one man'

As Ray (1911) points out, the *meanings* of the items for '5', '10', and '20' resemble those of Oceanic numerals rather than Papuan, but the only recognisable Oceanic *form* here is *tamati* (PPT *$tam^{w}ata$* 'man'). On the other hand *sandei* '3' is related to (Papuan) Yareba *sadei* '3'. Otherwise the numerals are so far unsourced.

Ray also draws attention to Maisin compounds like *nomba-fafusi* 'jealous person', *nane-fafusi* 'worker' (his data) and *būro tamāti* (work + man) 'worker' with the same structure as 'Binandele' *ainda-embo* 'servant' and *beonoari-embo* 'thief' (*fafusi*, *embo* are 'person', according to Ray), where nearby PT languages use other structures.[24]

2.3 The Maisin Controversy

In the previous section I have shown, among other things, that there is sufficient individual-identifying evidence to determine that Maisin is an Austronesian language (and none to suggest that it is Papuan). Yet Maisin is the one language out of a thousand or so in Melanesia which the contributors to Wurm and Hattori 1981 label as 'unclassified'. This label reflects the fact that the genealogy of Maisin has been a matter of dispute since linguists first went to Papua. It is instructive to see (i) what methodological issues underlie the controversy and (ii) why Maisin (but not, for example, similarly Papuanised Gedaged) has been the subject of genealogical controversy.

The controversy has its roots in 1911, when the *Journal of the Royal Anthropological Institute* published two short articles on Maisin side by side. One of the authors, Strong (1911), claimed it as a 'Melanesian', that is an Austronesian, language, whilst the other, Ray (1911), identified it as Papuan. Each, however, agreed that it had admixture from the other source. Both use materials from nearby languages as their benchmarks of what is Austronesian and what is Papuan, so that Strong effectively classifies Maisin as a PT language, Ray as a Trans New Guinea language.

Not surprisingly, since there was so little systematic knowledge of either Austronesian or Papuan languages, the argument lay dormant for a number of years. It was taken up again by Capell (1943: 77), who regarded Maisin as Papuan with largescale borrowing from Austronesian languages.

By the 1970s, Dempwolff's (1937) work establishing Oceanic was well known and widely accepted, and a good deal was known about Papuan languages. Interestingly, however, the dispute was not resolved. Capell continued to support Ray: 'Strong overestimated the Melanesian resemblances of Maisin very seriously; Ray was much closer to the truth. It seems very definitely a case in which a true mixture has taken place. . . .' (1976: 571). Dutton (1971), on the other hand, writes in his survey of the languages of southeast Papua, 'My hunch . . . is that Strong is probably correct'. An unpublished paper by Lynch (1977) is the one systematic attempt to compare Maisin with its neighbours and also concludes that Strong is basically right, 'The evidence . . . fairly clearly indicates that Maisin is an Austronesian language— one which may well have undergone considerable influence from Papuan languages, but an Austronesian language nevertheless'.

Strong had at least an intuitive grasp of the comparative method. The features he recognises as PT are in the main form/meaning correspondences, and those he recognises as Papuan are structural. He writes, 'It is [the pronouns and their derivatives] which give the clearest proof of the close relationship between the Maisin and the Melanesian languages generally'. The grammatical features he lists as PT are form/meaning correspondences between cognate paradigms of grammatical morphemes: three pronominal paradigms (possessor suffixes on inalienably possessed nouns; subject prefixes and object suffixes on verbs—cf Table 8-2) and the locative postposition /-e/. He also recognised lexical cognates in Maisin and other PT languages.

Strong (1911: 382) cites only two Papuan characteristics of Maisin:

(22) (a) 'a complete set of suffixes which are used to decline the noun' (and pronoun and adjective);
      (b) tense/aspect enclitics on the verb phrase.

In (a), Strong is referring to the enclitic postpositions listed in (11). As a result of allomorphy he understandably views them as an inflectional paradigm rather than as a set of postpositions. He correctly identifies both the structure and the set of categories as Papuan.[25] In the case of (b), it is evidently the structure which he recognises as Papuan.

Strong's interpretation of the material he presents is that Maisin may be 'a Melanesian [i.e. PT] language which has been modified, as is to be expected if a Melanesian language was imperfectly learnt by a non-Melanesian [i.e. Papuan] speaking people.' He notes (i) that one form covers several slots in the possessor and object pronominal paradigms (cf. Table 8-2) and (ii) that the set of inalienable nouns (that is, those taking possessor suffixes) is much smaller in Maisin than in other Oceanic languages. He attributes these features to poor learning.

Ray disagrees with Strong, maintaining that Maisin is basically Papuan because, he says, Papuan languages may borrow both syntax and grammatical morphemes from Oceanic languages, but Oceanic languages never borrow Papuan grammatical morphemes, only Papuan syntax. Even if we set aside the question of what motivated Ray's generalisation, his argumentation remains odd, since neither Strong nor Ray himself claims to find Papuan forms among Maisin grammatical morphemes; both find only Papuan categories. Strong apparently assumes that the Maisin grammatical morphemes whose forms he cannot recognise must be Papuan. It follows from his generalisation that since Maisin also has PT forms (he recognises the possessor suffixes and subject prefixes), it must be Papuan!

Ray supports this claim by listing both morphosyntactic and phonological features of Maisin which he considers to be Papuan. The morphosyntactic features include:

(23) (a) The Maisin adjective follows the noun, as in Papuan languages. (It also does so in PT languages, as Ray admits.)
      (b) There are 'case inflections' on the noun (cf. 22a). Ray, whose models were classical Indo-European languages, found it curious that when a noun is followed by an adjective, the 'case particle' occurs on the adjective, but not the noun. (Since the 'case particles' are enclitic postpositions, the structure is predictable, and in any case occurs in both Papuan and PT languages.)

(c) Ray correctly recognises the Papuan structure of Maisin compounds like *nomba-fafusi* 'jealous person' (see section 2.2).

(d) Ray writes that the independent pronouns 'show no likeness to any of the neighbouring languages, either Papuan or Melanesian. . . . This shows clearly the separation of the Maisin from the Melanesian, as well as its position as an independent Papuan language.' (This is a direct—and incorrect—contradiction of Strong, who recognised the independent pronouns as PT forms; see Table 8-2).

(e) Ray compares the person and number distribution of the object referencing suffix /-ren/ to a similar distribution of the object *prefixes* in the Papuan Kiwai languages.

These features are interesting not for their correctness or otherwise, but for what they tell us about Ray's methodological assumptions. Features (a), (b), (c), and especially (e) suggest that he regarded syntactic structure and paradigmatic organisation as far more important than form in diagnosing genetic relationship. This inference is confirmed by the fact that Ray noted regular sound correspondences between Maisin and nearby PT languages both in the lexicon and in some pronominal paradigms, yet did not recognise them as markers of Maisin's PT affiliation.

Space does not permit detailed consideration of Capell's (1976) discussion. He had a better knowledge of the WOc languages of Papua New Guinea than his predecessors, and observes that Maisin syntactic features—verb-final clause order, postpositional phrases—are shared by both Trans New Guinea and PT languages. His remarks about the Maisin reflexes of Austronesian words and various grammatical topics indicate that he understood little of Maisin morphophonemics. Like Strong and Ray, he misinterprets the Maisin postposition paradigm as inflectional. He does not recognise the Oceanic origin of the independent pronouns and object suffixes (see Table 8-2),[26] but does attribute the possessor suffixes and subject prefixes to Oceanic. Like Strong, he finds the tense/aspect markers closer to the Papuan pattern.

Given Capell's knowledge of Austronesian languages, it seems surprising that he missed many of the Oceanic reflexes in Maisin grammatical paradigms. But the reason for this emerges indirectly when he remarks, 'The evidence from structure cited up to this point suggests that in all really diagnostic features, Maisin is NAN [non-Austronesian, i.e. Papuan], with some penetration of Austronesian features' (1976: 562). Capell evidently regarded structural features as diagnostic of genetic relationship, and was not looking particularly attentively for the form/meaning correspondences which the comparative method treats as diagnostic of relatedness.

This brief summary reveals that the three protagonists are agreed about the facts of Maisin. Their controversy over its origins is in reality a conflict of methodologies. Strong, albeit informally, applies the comparative method, recognises the form/meaning correspondences between certain Maisin paradigms and those in other PT languages, makes a correct diagnosis of the origins of Maisin, but attributes the effects of metatypy to language shift. Ray and Capell, on the other hand, treat Maisin's *structural* features as diagnostic of its origin (note that neither of them identifies a single grammatical morpheme with a Papuan cognate *form*). Although they recognise some form/meaning correspondences between Maisin and other PT languages, they see them as resulting from contact.

It is also noteworthy that both Ray and Capell failed to recognise many WOc reflexes in Maisin, including the forms in the paradigms of independent pronouns and object suffixes. There are two apparent reasons for this. The first is the opaque allomorphy which results from the Maisin morphophonemic system (see Ross 1984). The second is the large quantity of non-WO lexical material in Maisin, which complicates the search for reflexes of WOc items and makes it easy to miss them. These are the reasons why Maisin has been a subject of controversy. In other Papuanised WOc languages, like Takia or Gedaged, most inherited WOc paradigms and lexical items are easily recognised and there are fewer non-WO distractors.

This brings us to the question of how the similarities and differences between Maisin and Takia are to be explained. In their bound morphology they share a number of characteristically WOc features: possessor pronominal suffixes on inalienably possessed nouns, subject prefixes and object suffixes on the verb, and an inclusive/exclusive distinction in the first person plural. In their typology they share a number of markedly Papuan (and markedly un-Oceanic features): lack of an article in the noun phrase, strict verb-final clause order, postpositional phrases, preposing of a possessor noun phrase, and chains of coordinate dependent clauses terminating with an independent clause. The WOc features are form/meaning correspondences reflecting inheritance from PWOc. The Papuan features are structural correspondences reflecting the metatypy which has resulted from contact with languages of the Trans New Guinea type.

The differences between Maisin and Takia (and the sources of the Maisin controversy) lie in those features of Maisin which have been generated by esoterogeny: complex morphophonemics and a large amount of non-WO vocabulary. These are attributable neither to inheritance nor to metatypy. None of Maisin's Papuan neighbours shares its morphophonemics, so these cannot be directly due to contact. Both morphophonemic complexity and lexical borrowing, however, are typical outcomes of esoterogeny (Thurston 1987: 56–60, 1989: 556), and this motivation is very much in accord with what is known about the social situation of the Kosirava Maisin, a group who (before European contact) were faced with ongoing hostility from neighbouring speakers of Binandere family languages (James and Cynthia Farr, personal communication). The process of lexical borrowing has continued to be reinforced by the practice of intensive word taboo in a small community: words wholly or partially homophonous with the names of the recently deceased are replaced, often by borrowings.

3 AN INFORMAL ACCOUNT OF METATYPIC CHANGE

Thus far metatypy has been described in terms of its externals (semantic and morphosyntactic restructuring). We turn now to the internal features of metatypy, to how it is motivated and how it arises. The account is inevitably informal: my insights are based partly on the data of languages such as Takia and Maisin, and partly on my observations of metatypy in WOc languages where the metatypic model is now Tok Pisin (New Guinea Pidgin), the Papua New Guinea's major lingua franca (Ross 1985).

When PNG bilinguals first acquire their second language, they are confronted not only by new lexical forms and new morphosyntax but also by new semantic organisation and new ways of construing reality.[27] The extent of the novelty depends, of course, on whether their two languages are genetically related and how much contact there has been between them directly or indirectly in the past.

Pawley sums up nicely what is involved in construing reality (1991a: 342):

> . . . even the most descriptive things we say, the 'just-the-bare-facts' reports of events and situations, are of necessity caricatures, extremely simplified sketches or interpretations. When people utter a sentence that purports to describe an event they have witnessed, they do not (and cannot) describe everything that happened in an objective and exhaustive manner. They must put a construction on what they observed.

He pursues the different ways in which languages may construe reality in two papers (Pawley 1987, 1991b) which describe how Kalam speakers construe events far more explicitly than speakers of English (Kalam is a Papuan language located in the highlands of Papua New Guinea). An English speaker might say that he 'went hunting', but a Kalam speaker would conventionally construe the 'same' event as an event sequence in which he goes to the hunting location, finds the animal, kills it, brings it to camp/home, cooks it and eats it. This, 'the linguistic construction of reality', is analysed in some depth by Grace in the book of that name (1987).

Conventional construals are reflected in the huge collection of entrenched[28] collocations which speakers appear to store as wholes. These are effectively phrase- and clause-sized entries in the speaker's lexicon (Pawley 1985, Pawley & Syder 1983). Such entrenchments include (i) particular designations, for example, *newsagent* rather than something like *newspaper dealer* (Harris 1981: 79–80), (ii) irreversible binomials like *black and white* (Grace 1981: 48), (iii) conventionalised ranges of referents, as in General American *ham and cheese sandwich* (but not *cheese and ham sandwich*), which refers to a narrower range of referents than it might potentially designate (Grace 1987: 87), (iv) borderline phenomena like the singular in 'a fifty-*cent* cigar', which are exceptions to generalisations and thereby complicate the morphosyntax (Grace 1981: 47–8), (v) generalised choices of pattern in expressing an event, for example the German preference for nouns in *vor seiner Ankunft* versus the English verb of *before he came*, (vi) 'speech formulae' or 'sentence stems' both in everyday conversation (e.g. *Come to think of it, . . .* or NP *have*–TENSE *a* ADJECTIVE *time*, Pawley 1985:92–3) and in specialised discourse genres (Pawley 1991a: 359–62).

Entrenchments are not simply conventionalised sequences of words in particular morphosyntactic structures. By incorporating imagery, they impinge on the semantic organisation of the language. To take a somewhat banal example, speakers of different languages in what seems objectively to be the same simple experience may say (cf. Langacker 1988: 11):[29]

(24) English: I am cold
     Buru: *yako*   *bridi-n*
               I   cold-its

or 'my body is cold':

(25) Balinese: *dingin*   *awak-é*
           cold   body-the

or 'I have cold' (or something similar):

(26) French: *j'* *ai*   *froid*
              I   have cold
     Dutch: *ik* *heb* *het*   *koud*
             I   have it   cold

or something like 'it is cold to me':

(27) German: *mir*   *ist* *kalt*
            me.DATIVE is   cold
     Russian: *mne*   *xolodno*
            me.DATIVE   cold.NEUTER SINGULAR

or use a verb like 'I am freezing':

(28) Tokelauan: *ko*   *au* *e*   *makalili*
                TOPIC I   PRESENT feel.cold
     Norwegian: *jeg* *fryser*
                I   freeze. PRESENT

or conceive of 'cold' as a force which 'hits', 'bites', or 'does' me:

(29) Takia: *madid* *i-fin-ag-da*
             cold   it-hit-me-IMPERFECTIVE
     Koiari: *ribiri-vare*   *da*   *vani-ma*
             cold-SPECIFIER me   hit-PRESENT
     Lewo: *miava* *kar-nu*
             cold   bite-me
     Korafe: *na* *yaura* *erira*
             me   cold   it.does

An interesting feature of these examples is that there is no particular correlation between genetic relationship and similarity of image.

For first-time bilinguals, mastery not only of different lexicon and grammar but also of different semantics and different reality construal conventions poses a considerable processing burden on their cognitive and linguistic faculties. Papua New Guinea cases, however, indicate that bilinguals shed much of the burden by bringing the semantic organisations and reality construals of their two languages into line with each other. Since the emblematic language by definition belongs to a smaller group of people than the intergroup language, it is the emblematic language whose semantic organisation and reality construal conventions are restructured on the model of the intergroup language. This observation is not new. Weinreich ([1953]1963: 7–11) wrote of the 'coexistence of merging [semantic] systems', and Sasse (1985: 84) remarks pithily, 'gemeinsamen Denken folgt gemeinsames Ausdrucksbedürfnis.'[30]

In the discussion section 2.1 of lexical metatypy in Takia, we saw that Takia items have acquired the same range of meaning as their Waskia counterparts. Indeed there is a sense in which we can say, for example, that the Takia and Waskia body-part expressions presented earlier are different phonological realisations for the same lexical items.[31]

Semantic organisation is also a parameter of morphological paradigms. In the Maisin postposition paradigm, the semantic organisation of a morphological paradigm has been restructured on the model of a Papuan language. This has had consequences not only for semantics (the instrument postposition also acquires the meaning of agentivity) but also for morphosyntax (an agentive subject is marked by the 'instrument' postposition) and for form (a source postposition is formed from two other morphemes). When the semantic organisation of an emblematic language is restructured on the model of an intergroup language, metatypy is liable to follow.

Other examples in the research literature also reflect metatypy. In his account of the restructuring of Arvanitic (the dialects of Albanian spoken in central Greece) along Greek lines, Sasse (1985: 84) describes how the Arvanitic categories have come increasingly to match the Greek. Morphosyntax has been remodelled in the direction of morpheme-for-morpheme translatability. Here, too, indigenous forms continue to be used in the acquired categories. In the well known Indian case at Kupwar, the local varieties of (Indo-European) Marathi and Urdu have undergone metatypy on the model of (Dravidian) Kannada. Here is just one example from Kupwar Urdu (Gumperz and Wilson 1971:165):

(30) Kupwar Urdu:

	o	*gəe*	*t-a*		*bhæs*	*carn-e-ko*		

Kupwar Kannada

	aw	*hog*	*id-a*		*yəmmi*	*mes-Ø-k*		
	he	go	PAST-MASC		buffalo	graze-OBLIQUE-to		

Standard Hindi-Urdu:

	wo	*bhæs*	*cərane-ke*	*liye*	*gəy-a*	*th-a*
	he	buffalo	graze-OBLIQUE	to	go-MASC	PAST-MASC

'He went to graze the buffalo.'

Restructuring does not always proceed this far. Thurston (1987) provides a well researched case from northwestern New Britain where speakers of a Papuan language, Anêm, are bilingual in the Oceanic intergroup language Lusi. Like Takia and Waskia, these languages show similar semantic organisation, but differences in morphosyntax, as in the examples below (from Thurston 1987: 82):

(31) Anêm: *gêt-î*   *ia*
                      ear-his   fish

Lusi:	*iha*	*ai-taŋa*	
	fish	his-ear	
	'lateral fin of a fish'		
Anêm:	*eil-îm*	*te*	
	eye-his	knife	
Lusi:	*uzage*	*ai-mata*	
	knife	his-eye	
	'knife blade'		
Anêm:	*agîm-k-i*		*tiga*
	neck-LIGATURE-his		foot
Lusi:	*ahe-gu*	*ai-gauli*	
	foot-my	his-neck	
	'my ankle'		

In each example the two languages show differing phrase structure (Anêm HEAD + POSSESSOR vs. Lusi POSSESSOR + HEAD)[32] and differing word structure (Anêm suffixes the possessive marker, Lusi prefixes it), but their semantic organisation is exactly parallel. For example, both Anêm and Lusi speakers assign the semantic structure 'ear of fish' to what English speakers call 'a lateral fin'.

The implications of sameness or difference in semantic organisation and reality construal become more significant when we look at clause-sized cases. In the example below an English construal would be roughly 'hand me some tobacco to smoke', but in both Anêm and Lusi one says roughly 'Let some tobacco come (and) I will eat it'. Although the phrase structures of the two languages differ, their clause structures are quite similar:[33]

(32) Anêm:	*uas*	*gox*	*o-mên*	*da-t*
	tobacco	some	HORTATIVE.it-come	IRREALIS. I-(eat-)it[34]
Lusi:	*uasi*	*eta*	*i-nama*	*ŋa-ani-Ø*
	tobacco	some	it-come	I-eat-it

As illustrated in (7) and (8), the metatypy of Takia morphosyntax goes one step further. The two languages match each other not only in semantic organisation and in clause structure, but also in phrase syntax. Even the structures of compound lexemes like Takia *tamolpein* and Waskia *kadimet* 'person' are matched. Only the domain of bound morphemes remains relatively untouched in Takia.

To sum up, then, bilinguals tend first to restructure the entrenched ways of saying things and the semantic organisation of their emblematic language on the model of their intergroup language. This semantic restructuring leads easily to morphosyntactic restructuring, and metatypy has begun. In the Papua New Guinea cases, metatypy seems generally to affect the clause first,[35] then the phrase, and finally the structure of words. And as syntactic structures are reinterpreted and reorganised, so the functions of grammatical morphemes shift (e.g. conjunctions to coordinate dependent markers) and new grammaticalisations occur (e.g. nouns become postpositions).

4 DISCUSSION

The topics of this discussion are (i) the theoretical status of the structural correspondences between a metatypised language and its putative model (henceforth 'metatypic correspondences'); (ii) the implications of this for the comparative method; and (iii) features which are often mentioned in the literature on contact but have received no attention here.

The informal psycholinguistic account in section 3 shows how metatypic correspondences arise. It thereby provides a somewhat more principled basis for examining their theoretical status and how this relates to the status of form/meaning correspondences.

The form/meaning correspondences between two (or more) languages are diagnostic of genetic relatedness because, mediated by the regularity of sound change, the forms in both languages reflect the forms of a single protolanguage. Metatypic correspondences are diagnostic of metatypy because the stages of restructuring also proceed in a regular manner. This regularity is discernible in the fact that Takia and Maisin have both undergone similar metatypic change: The two languages share a WOc origin, have both had metatypic models of the Trans New Guinea type, and as a result have undergone strikingly similar changes (the most striking is that the irrealis coordinate dependent marker in both languages is a reflex of the PWOc irrealis conjunction *be*). Indeed, the similarity between Takia and Maisin invites at first glance a hypothesis of close genetic relationship. However, the form/meaning correspondences which Takia displays with other languages of the Bel family (of the North New Guinea cluster) and Maisin with the Are-Taupota subgroup (of the PT cluster) show unambiguously that Takia and Maisin are not closely related and that the structural resemblances between the two languages are due to parallel but independent metatypy.[36] The fact that independently occurring cases of metatypy can proceed along such similar lines confirms that metatypy is governed by regular processes. Because contact-induced change has generally lacked a firm theoretical foundation, descriptions of it often resemble incomplete jigsaw puzzles and give the impression that no regularity is involved.

The foregoing paragraph illustrates the fact that metatypic correspondences are in a particular kind of dependency relationship to form/meaning correspondences. Metatypic correspondences cause 'interference' with form/meaning correspondences and are discernible as the result of metatypy precisely because of this interference. This is what Boas (1917) refers to when he writes that historical linguists should enquire into 'the possibility of mutual influences [between languages], which will be revealed, in part at least, by lack of correspondence between lexicographic, phonetic, and detailed morphological classifications.' The interference is of a quite specific kind. Where a form/meaning correspondence is expected, we do indeed find a correspondence in form with genetically related languages, but only an incomplete correspondence in meaning; instead, we find a precise correspondence in meaning with a putative metatypic model. Thus Takia *mala-* 'eye' no longer has the same range of uses as WOc *mata-* but instead corresponds semantically with Waskia *motam*. And Takia /-pe/ is no longer a conjunction, but a coordinate dependent marker on the Waskia model.

This dependency of structural correspondences on form/meaning correspondences is not merely an artefact of method. It reflects the interaction between the processes which give rise to the two kinds of correspondence. Thomason and Kaufman (1988) draw a line between languages which have been 'normally transmitted' from generation to generation and those which have not: The latter include, in my terms, metatypised languages. They take 'normal transmission' to be synonymous with 'genetic relationship' (1988: 8–10). Ultimately, their criterion is that normal transmission is considered to be broken if the resulting language cannot be used for comparative reconstruction (1988: 200–01). This criterion is problematic: How do we know which languages to exclude from our reconstructive data before we have done the reconstruction? And, given that almost every language shows some residue of noncorresponding material, where does one draw the line between genetic relationship and its absence? I have tried to show here not only that several different processes may be involved in the history of a single language, but also how these processes can (and, because of the dependency relationship between the two kinds of correspondence, must) be investigated through an integrated methodology.

In section 1 the possibility was noted that metatypic correspondences between a metatypised language and its putative model might singly or collectively have such a low probability of multiple independent occurrence that they could be regarded as identifying just one language or set of similarly structured languages as the metatypic model. It is not clear to me how this probability can be given a formal mathematical foundation such as Nichols (this volume) provides for form/meaning correspondences. But intuitively at least, it is clear that the semantic and structural correspondences between Takia and Waskia are greater than can be attributed to chance. The correspondence of the Maisin postposition system with those of its Papuan neighbours, including the double-morpheme source postposition and the distribution of the instrumental/agentive postposition, is also surely not a product of independent development.

There is an important difference between the identifying potentials of form/meaning correspondences and of metatypic correspondences. Form/meaning correspondences are individual-identifying in that they identify a single protolanguage, that is, an entity separate from (but ancestral to) the languages being compared. Metatypic correspondences, on the other hand, identify a single *type* of metatypic model. Thus there is no necessary reason why Waskia (or an earlier stage thereof) should have been *the* (or the only) metatypic model for Takia. Nearby mainland Papuan languages may also have provided a model. In the case of Maisin, we cannot at present tell which of several typologically very similar Papuan languages has/have provided a metatypic model (although there is in principle no reason why further research should not provide an answer). The Balkan *Sprachbund* has long been recognised as a result of what I have called metatypy, but here it has been even more difficult to identify the model language(s) (Joseph 1983) because all are Indo-European.

Time-depth has quite different effects on form/meaning correspondences and on metatypic correspondences. Whereas form/meaning correspondences peter out at the time-depth where lexical replacement becomes close to total (and this time-depth covaries with sociolinguistic factors), metatypy often ensures that particular semantic and structural features continue in a particular area over seemingly immense periods of time. This is presumably why Nichols (1992: 167, 183, 193) finds that basic clause order has little genetic stability, but considerable areal stability. Obviously, as semantic and structural features become more and more generalised across a region through metatypy, it is decreasingly feasible to sort out the detailed contact histories of the languages in which these features occur. The Trans New Guinea language area is probably the result of repeated metatypy rather than of common genetic origin. It has been suggested that the 'Altaic' languages form such an area (or a part of such an area), containing three genetic groups (Turkic, Mongolian, and Tungusic).

The thrust of this chapter is that the comparative method can take cognisance of the effects of metatypy. This is, of course, a rather different position from Meillet's ([19141948]: 87) formulation that grammatical borrowing can only occur among closely related languages. Unfortunately, this formulation still enjoys currency (e.g. Appel & Muysken 1987: 162; see also the sources cited by Thomason & Kaufman 1988: 14), and creates a problem for linguists seeking to understand the history of languages like Maisin. For the diagnosis of genetic relationship they are forced to choose between (i) form/meaning correspondences (the orthodox and proper choice) and (ii) structural features (which allegedly cannot have been borrowed and must therefore have been inherited). Small wonder that Ray and Capell treated structural evidence as diagnostic of genetic relationship, form/meaning correspondences as diagnostic of contact.

Meillet's formulation reflects the extreme Neo-grammarian position formulated by Osthoff and Brugmann (1878) of the utter regularity of sound change, seemingly allowing no place at all for contact-induced change. Schuchardt responded with a critique of that hypothesis (1884) and a demonstration of contact-induced change which laid the foundations of creolistics (Schuchardt 1885). Thus historical linguistics diverged along two separate and seemingly incompatible paths. The enforced choice between them surfaces again in the proposal that the family tree model be replaced by one which treats all languages as creoles, that is, as the products of contact-induced change (Bailey 1973: 35–7, Mühlhäusler 1985, Thurston 1987: 35–6).

Neither position alone accounts for the data of Takia and Maisin. These languages require us to recognise that several kinds of process have intersected in their genesis. The form/meaning correspondences which they share with each other and with other Oceanic languages *are* best explained by a version of the regularity hypothesis (indeed, I know of no other explanation), and the relationships reflected in the correspondences *are* best modelled as some kind of genetic tree.[37] At the same time, the structural correspondences between each and its Papuan neighbours require the hypothesis of metatypy, a specific contact-induced process which we cannot ignore if we are serious about the reconstruction of culture history.

It may seem surprising that in section 3, there was no discussion of lexical borrowing or of phonology. This is because neither of them plays a necessary role in metatypy. Contrary to received wisdom (e.g. Moravcsik 1978, Thomason & Kaufman 1988: 21), it is not the case that substantial lexical borrowing always precedes other kinds of contact-induced change.[38] Conversely, extensive lexical borrowing may occur without widespread bilingual contact, as in the cases of modern Japanese (from English) (Thomason & Kaufman 1976: 169) and Middle English (from French) (Thomason & Kaufman 1988: 314–15). Thus although lexical borrowing and other kinds of contact-induced change may occur simultaneously, they are separate phenomena. In cases where the emblematic function of the lexicon is particularly significant, lexical borrowing is especially limited (as Gumperz and Wilson 1971 observe).

Where extensive borrowing does take place, it may bring with it enough instances of non-native phones to bring about changes in the phonological system. Again, as the Japanese example shows (Thomason & Kaufman 1988: 54), this does not depend on bilingualism. This seems to be quite a common phenomenon.[39] Extensive lexical borrowing may also effectively result in the borrowing of bound morphemes. However, the productiveness of such a morpheme in the borrower language arises because speakers make an induction about its function from its occurrences in a number of borrowings. English *-tion*, which has entered the language through Latin and French borrowings, is a classic case. Although now clearly an element of the language, it was not borrowed as a discrete element.

Following Weinreich (1963[1953]: 1), I prefer to reserve the term 'language contact' for cases which entail bilingualism. The modern Japanese case is one of culture contact, not language contact, and highlights the need to distinguish between processes which are the result of contact and processes which do not necessarily entail contact.[40]

The model and methodology presented in this chapter were devised to deal with a limited range of cases. However, if the diachronic processes described here are indeed systematic, we should be able to detect them in data from other places and other language families. The major difficulty in doing this is that many published accounts of contact-induced change have little theoretical underpinning, and are particularly deficient in describing semantic reorganisation, a crucial component of metatypy. I have endeavoured to test the model of metatypy by applying it to published accounts of contact-induced change. Space contraints prohibit an account of these tests here. Suffice it to say that, just as it is necessary to posit esoterogeny as an additional factor in the Maisin case, so other additional factors must be posited in other cases. These include lexical borrowing widespread enough to introduce bound morphemes and new phonemes into the language. It is also clear that structural similarities and differences between a metatypised language and its metatypic model play a role in contact-induced processes. No phonological change has occurred in Takia, but in cases of metatypy elsewhere, phonological simplification has occurred which is attibutable neither to extensive lexical borrowing nor to impending language death (Sasse 1985: 58). This simplification entails the loss (by merger with other phonemes) of segments such as pharyngeal fricatives, labialised dorsal stops, ejectives, retroflexes, and velarised consonants, that is, of phonemes which are recognisable as universally 'marked' (difficult though this concept is to define). In such cases these phonemes are absent from the model language.[41] There are just a few morphological borrowings where a morphological paradigm has been borrowed complete with its forms. For example, some Rumanian dialects have acquired Bulgarian verbal inflections. Křepinský (1949) believes these were introduced by bilingual Slavs, eased by the formal and categorial similarity of the two languages.

The factors described in the previous paragraph clearly warrant further research. However, none of them speaks against the conclusions drawn on the basis of Takia and Maisin. Instead, they suggest (i) that contact-induced change entails a number of discrete linguistic processes, each with its own sociolinguistic correlates; (ii) that metatypic processes are affected by the structures of the languages involved; and (iii) that the comparative method requires principled augmentation to interpret (i) and (ii).

NOTES

1. Much of the work on this chapter was done during a visiting professorship in the Southeast Asian Studies Department of the Johann Wolfgang Goethe University in Frankfurt, supported by a grant from the *Deutsche Forschungsgemeinschaft*. I am grateful to the *Forschungsgemeinschaft*, and especially to Bernd Nothofer, who initiated my stay and has given so much encouragement to my research activities.

I am grateful to Mark Durie, Peter Mühlhäusler, and William Thurston for comments on earlier versions of this chapter.

2. The term 'Papua New Guinea' refers to the political entity, whilst 'New Guinea' refers to the linguistic area which also embraces the Indonesian province of Irian Jaya. The cases presented in this chapter are from Papua New Guinea, but the sociolinguistic conditions described apply over the larger New Guinea region.

3. Nichols' (1992) prototype for a residual zone is the Caucasus, located on the edge of the Eurasian spread zone. Analogously, the New Guinea residual zone sits on the edge of the Austronesian spread zone. The features of residual zones listed in the text are based on Nichols' (1992: 13–15, 21–23) account of the Caucasus and augmented from my own acquaintance with New Guinea.

4. The modern *lingue franche* of New Guinea are (in Irian Jaya) Indonesian, (in Papua New Guinea) Tok Pisin (New Guinea Pidgin), Hiri Motu, and English.

5. 'Village' is not a very precise term for pre-contact New Guinea. A 'village' was often a network of scattered hamlets or homesteads, but this does not affect the argument of this paragraph.

6. Tok Pisin has progressively replaced other inter-group languages in many areas of Papua New Guinea. Sankoff (1972) describes the division of usage between an emblematic language and Tok Pisin in one village. Ross (1985) describes something of the effects of such bilingualism on some emblematic Austronesian languages.

7. Many Austronesianists today make a terminological distinction between 'Proto-Malayo-Polynesian' (Dempwolff's *Uraustronesisch*), the language ancestral to all Austronesian languages outside the island of Taiwan, and the highest-order 'Proto-Austronesian', ancestral to all Austronesian languages, whether they are on or outside Taiwan (Dempwolff did not use any data from Taiwan). It is beyond the scope of this chapter even to summarise the vast amount of comparative work on the Austronesian language family which has been done since Dempwolff's foundational publications. An important milestone was Dahl (1976), who *inter alia* proposed the existence of the Malayo-Polynesian subgroup within Austronesian. This hypothesis received support from Blust (1977). Available lexical comparisons have been vastly expanded by Blust (1980, 1984, 1986, 1989). Ross (1995a) provides a survey of work in Austronesian comparative linguistics.

8. Since the Second World War, Dempwolff's reconstruction of Proto-Oceanic (his *Urmelanesisch*) has continued to receive support (see, for example, Milke 1958, 1961; Grace 1959, 1961, 1964; Pawley 1973; Pawley and Reid 1980) and has also undergone some modification (Blust 1978; Lichtenberk 1978; Ross 1988, 1989). But it remains at least as clearly defined as it was for Dempwolff.

9. The innovations of the Polynesian subgroup were established by Dempwolff (1937). The criteria defining the Micronesian group are somewhat less clear, but still quite convincing (Jackson 1986).

10. This date is based on the correlation of linguistic with archaeological findings (Pawley and Ross 1993).

11. The assumption has been made that the Trans New Guinea languages form a genetic group (McElhanon and Voorhoeve 1970), but this has not been verified by the comparative method and has been called into question (Foley 1986).

12. The locations of Takia and Megiar are shown on Map 7 of Wurm and Hattori (1981) and on the map in Ross (1988: 123).

13. Materials describing Takia are Hubers (n.d.), Rehburg and Tuominen (1978), and Ross (1994a, 1994b). Gedaged attracted linguists' attention because of its more widespread use: there is a brief grammar by Dempwolff (n.d.) and a dictionary by Mager (1952).

14. Ross with Paol (1978) gives a sketch of Waskia grammar, Barker and Lee (1985) a basic dictionary.

15. Since Proto-Western-Oceanic was a dialect network rather than a unitary language, I take something of a liberty in reconstructing its forms, since these can be expected to have varied somewhat across the network. In the present context this does not matter, however, since very similar (or identical) forms are reconstructable for its parent, POC.

16. The locations of Maisin are shown on Map 9 of Wurm and Hattori (1981) and on the map in Ross (1988: 194). The claim that Kosirava is the homeland is mentioned by Strong (1911) and Dutton (1971: 8), and is also confirmed by the oral history I collected from a Maisin speaker.

17. The reconstructed forms are from the investigations reported in Ross (1988); the subject pronominal prefixes were published on page 364 of that work.

18. This is a more precise subgrouping of Maisin than was provided by Ross (1988: 191). For PT sound correspondences, see Ross (1988: 198–202).

19. I am grateful to David Lithgow for pointing out to me the functions of reflexes of *be in several PT languages.

20. Maisin data are from Ross (1984) and my fieldnotes, Yamalele and Arifama from my fieldnotes, and Baruga from James and Cynthia Farr (personal communication).
Strong (1911) also refers to the case markers 'objective' -nq and 'vocative' -e/-be. His 'objective' is a misinterpretation of the focus marker -na (Ross 1984: 34; the dialect from which my data come has sporadic loss of - from enclitics). His 'vocative' seems to be the predicate marker -e, as in au-e 'it's me!' (Ross 1984: 34).

21. Sources for Ömie are Austing and Upia (1975) and Austing and Austing (1977); for Yareba, Weimer and Weimer (1975). Korafe data come in part from Farr and Farr (1975), but in part from James and Cynthia Farr (personal communication).

22. Proto–Papuan Tip *-mai is also reflected in Tubetube -me .

23. I am grateful to James and Cynthia Farr for a Korafe dictionary on disk and for help in sourcing some items. Ray (1911) also lists a number of Papuan cognates of Maisin words. Those which are convincing are all from member languages (like Korafe) of the Binandere family.

24. Ray's other examples have two structures, both common in PT languages. In one tau- 'person' is prefixed to a verb, as in Wedau tau-noða 'worker'.The other has the structure of inalienable possession: Are ('Mukawa') giugiu bita-na (teach person-its) 'teacher'. (Ray's first PT example, from Ubir, agir orot 'servant', has the same structure as his Maisin and 'Binandele' examples (orot 'person'), but he seems not to have recognised this.)
Ray is probably wrong in saying that fafusi means 'person': there is no Maisin noun with this form and meaning, and Strong records such compounds as viso-fafusi 'fleshy thing'.

25. There is some confusion in Strong's thinking here. He recognises the 'case inflections' as Papuan, but sees no particular connection with neighbouring Baruga (his 'Binadele'), commenting—wrongly—that Maisin has case inflections where Baruga has postpositions.

26. A little later (561) Capell writes, '. . . the whole Maisin pronominal system, apart from cardinal pronouns, seems to have come from Austronesian sources'. Whether he includes the forms of the object suffixes in 'the whole . . . pronominal system', or just the categories of the paradigm, is not clear.

27. The present account owes much to Grace (1981), who captures the relationship between a language's semantic organisation and how its speakers construe reality by referring to both together as 'content form' (Grace 1981: 24), a term he adopts from Hjelmslev (1961: 50–52).

28. I owe the term 'entrenched' to Langacker (1991: 2, 195).

29. I am grateful to Alexander Adelaar, Adrian Clynes, Tom Dutton, Robert Early, Cynthia Farr, Charles Grimes, and Arnfinn Vonen who helped me assemble this example. Balinese, Buru, Lewo, and Tokelauan are all Austronesian languages, spoken respectively on the islands of Bali (western Indonesia), Buru (eastern Indonesia), Epi (Vanuatu), and Tokelau (Polynesia). Koiari is a Papuan language of the Koiarian family.

30. 'Common thought is followed by common expressive needs'.

31. In the terminology of Grace (1981: 24), the members of these pairs are different lexifications of a single content form.

32. Where Lusi has only a single possessive construction, Anêm has two constructions: (i) HEAD +

POSSESSOR, akin to a compounding construction ('fish-ear' = 'lateral fin'), and (ii) POSSESSOR + HEAD, the standard possessive construction ('fish's ear') (William Thurston, personal communication).

33. Weinreich ([1953]1963: 50) provides an example of the same kind from the Balkans, where Aromanian, Albanian, Greek, Bulgarian, and Serbocroation both express 'may God punish you' with their equivalents of 'may you find it from God'.

34. The example is from Thurston (1987: 69), with additional glossing provided by Thurston (personal communication). The verb 'eat' in Anêm has no segmentable stem (Thurston 1987: 57).

35. Lincoln (1977) shows that basic clause order may vary even between quite closely related languages, and their are indications among the Oceanic languages of the north coast of Papua New Guinea that there have been changes from SVO to SOV and back again.

36. Another case of parallel but independent metatypy is provided by Proto PT, Proto Ngero (the Ngero languages are spoken on both sides of the Vitiaz Strait between New Britain and mainland New Guinea), and Torau (on Bougainville Island). All are WOc languages, but each belongs to a different cluster of WOc. All three have acquired verb-final clause order and postpositions, and the default postposition in all three cases is derived from the Proto Oceanic oblique proto-form *iai.

37. Note that the conventions for drawing genetic trees can be formulated so as to allow the depiction of various kinds of relationship. For a discussion, see Ross (1988: chap. 1).

38. Writers who make this kind of claim usually formulate it along the lines that lexical borrowing must precede other kinds of transfer. But such formulations are almost vacuous, given that *some* words are bound to be borrowed in contact situations such as those discussed here.

39. Other examples of phonological change resulting from extensive lexical borrowing are English (Thomason and Kaufman 1988: 54, 124), West Uvean (Ozanne-Rivierre f.c.), Asiatic Eskimo (Thomason and Kaufman 1988: 33), Tagalog (where the vowel system has been restructured under the pressure of English loanwords), the Nguni and Sotho-Tswana groups of Bantu languages (which have acquired Khoisan clicks through borrowing; Alexandre 1972: 35; Thomason & Kaufman 1988: 60).

40. Because of this distinction, I have avoided the use of the term 'calque', which may refer to metatypic restructuring (a language contact phenomenon) or to loan translation (in German and Russian, for example, an outcome of culture contact *without* language contact). I have also avoided 'substrate', 'superstrate' and 'adstrate' because they straddle the same divide and because, where language contact is involved, they tend to presuppose that contact-induced change is the result of elite dominance—and this is clearly not the case in a residual zone.

41. Cases are Ma'a, described by Thomason (1983) and Kormatiki Arabic, described by Newton (1964) and Tsiapera (1969).

REFERENCES

Alexandre, P. (1977). *An introduction to languages and language in Africa*, trans. by F. A. Leary. Heinemann, London.
Appel, R., and P. Muysken. (1987). *Language contact and bilingualism*. Edward Arnold, London.
Austing, J., and J. Austing. (1977). *Semantics of Ömie discourse*. Language data, Asia-Pacific Series, no. 11. Summer Institute of Linguistics, Huntington Beach, Calif.
Austing, J., and R. Upia. (1975). Highlights of Ömie morphology. In T. E. Dutton, ed.), *Studies in languages of central and southeast Papua* 513–97. Pacific Linguistics C-29. Australian National University, Canberra.
Bailey, C.-J. N. (1973). *Variation and linguistic theory*. Center for Applied Linguistics, Arlington, Va.
Barker, F., and J. Lee. (1985). *Waskia diksenari*. Dictionaries of Papua New Guinea, no. 7. Summer Institute of Linguistics, Ukarumpa.
Blust, R. A. (1977). The Proto-Austronesian pronouns and Austronesian subgrouping: A preliminary report. *University of Hawaii Working Papers in Linguistics* 9: 1–15.
———. (1978). *The Proto-Oceanic palatals*. JPS Monograph, no. 43. Polynesian Society, Auckland.
———. (1980). Austronesian etymologies. *Oceanic Linguistics* 19: 1–182.
———. (1984). Austronesian etymologies II. *Oceanic Linguistics* 22–23: 29–149.
———. (1986). Austronesian etymologies III. *Oceanic Linguistics* 25: 1–123.

————. (1989). Austronesian etymologies IV. *Oceanic Linguistics* 28: 111–80.

Boas, F. (1917). Introductory. *International Journal of American Linguistics* 1: 1–8.

Capell, A. (1943). *The linguistic position of South-Eastern Papua*. Australasian Medical Publishing Company, Sydney.

————. (1976). Austronesian and Papuan 'mixed' languages: General remarks. In S. A. Wurm, ed., *New Guinea area languages and language study 2: Austronesian language* 527–79. *Pacific Linguistics* C-39. Australian National University, Canberra.

Dahl, O. C. (1976). *Proto-Austronesian*. 2nd, rev., ed. Curzon Press, London.

Dempwolff, O. (1934). *Vergleichende Lautlehre des Austronesischen Wortschatzes*, Vol. 1: *Induktiver Aufbau einer indonesischen Ursprache. Beihefte zur Zeitschrift für Eingeborenen-Sprachen* no. 15. Dietrich Reimer, Berlin.

————. (1937). *Vergleichende Lautlehre des Austronesischen Wortschatzes*, Vol. 2: *Deduktive Anwendung des Urindonesischen auf Austronesische Einzelsprachen. Beihefte zur Zeitschrift für Eingeborenen-Sprachen* no. 17. Dietrich Reimer, Berlin.

————. (1938). *Vergleichende Lautlehre des Austronesischen Wortschatzes*, Vol. 3: *Austronesisches Wörterverzeichnis. Beihefte zur Zeitschrift für Eingeborenen-Sprachen* no. 19. Dietrich Reimer, Berlin.

————. (n.d.) Grammar of the Graged language. Mimeo. Lutheran Mission, Narer, Karkar Island.

Dutton, T. E. (1971). Languages of south-east Papua: A preliminary report. In T. E. Dutton, C. L. Voorhoeve, and S. A. Wurm (ed.), *Papers in New Guinea linguistics* no. 14. *Pacific Linguistics* A-28, 1–46. Australian National University, Canberra.

Dyen, I. (1965). *A lexicostatistical classification of the Austronesian languages. International Journal of American Linguistics Memoir* no. 19. Waverly Press, Baltimore.

Farr, J., and C. Farr. (1975). Some features of Korafe morphology. In T. E. Dutton, ed., *Studies in languages of central and south-east Papua* 731–69. *Pacific Linguistics* C-29. Australian National University, Canberra.

Foley, W. A. (1986). *The Papuan languages of New Guinea*. Cambridge University Press, Cambridge.

Grace, G. W. (1959). *The position of the Polynesian languages within the Austronesian (Malayo-Polynesian) language family. International Journal of American Linguistics Memoir*, no. 16.

————. (1961). Austronesian linguistics and culture history. *American Anthropologist* 63: 359–68.

————. (1964). Movement of the Malayo-Polynesians 1500 B.C. to A.D. 500: The linguistic evidence. *Current Anthropology*, 5: 361–68, 403–04.

————. (1975). Linguistic diversity in the Pacific: On the sources of diversity. Paper presented to the 13th Pacific Science Congres, Vancouver.

————. (1981). *An essay on language*. Hornbeam, Columbia, S.C.

————. (1987). *The linguistic construction of reality*. Croom Helm, London.

Gumperz, J. J., and R. Wilson. (1971). Convergence and creolization: A case from the Indo-Aryan/Dravidian border. In D. Hymes, ed., *Pidginization and creolization of languages* 151–68. Cambridge University Press, Cambridge.

Harris, R. (1981). *The language myth*. Duckworth, London.

Hjelmslev, L. (1961). *Prologomena to a theory of language*. Trans. F. J. Whitfield. 2nd ed. University of Wisconsin Press, Madison.

Hubers, H. (n.d.) Takia-English dictionary. Typescript.

Jackson, F. H. (1986). On determining the external relationships of the Micronesian languages. In P. Geraghty, L. Carrington, and S. A. Wurm, eds., *FOCAL II: Papers from the Fourth International Conference on Austronesian Linguistics* 201–38. *Pacific Linguistics* C-94. Australian National University, Canberra.

Joseph, B. D. (1983). *The synchrony and diachrony of the Balkan infinitive: A study in areal, general and historical linguistics*. Cambridge University Press, Cambridge.

Křepinský, M. (1949). Réponse à la Question IV. In *Actes du Sixième Congrès International des Linguistes* 317–24. Klincksieck, Paris.

Langacker, R. W. (1988). An overview of cognitive grammar. In B. Rudza-Ostyn, ed., *Topics in cognitive linguistics* 3–48. Benjamins, Amsterdam.

————. (1991). *Concept, image and symbol: the cognitive basis of grammar*. Mouton de Gruyter, Berlin.

Laycock, D. C. (1982). Melanesian linguistic diversity: a Melanesian choice? In R. J. May and H. Nelson, eds., *Melanesia: Beyond diversity* 1: 33–8. Research School of Pacific Studies, Australian National University, Canberra.

Lichtenberk, F. (1978). A third palatal reflex in Manam. *University of Hawaii Working Papers in Linguistics* 10/1: 183–90.

Lincoln, P. C. (1977). Subgrouping across a syntactic isogloss. Mimeo.

Lynch, J. (1977). Notes on Maisin—an Austronesian language of the Northern Province of Papua New Guinea. Mimeo. University of Papua New Guinea.

———. (1981). Melanesian diversity and Polynesian homogeneity: The other side of the coin. *Oceanic Linguistics* 20: 95–129.

Mager, J. F. (1952). *Gedaged-English dictionary.* Board of Foreign Missions, American Lutheran Church, Columbus, Ohio.

McElhanon, K. A., and C. L. Voorhoeve. (1970). *The Trans-New Guinea phylum: explorations in deep level genetic relationships.* Pacific Linguistics B-16. Australian National University, Canberra.

McSwain, R. (1977). *The past and future people.* Oxford University Press, Melbourne.

Meillet, A. ([1914]1948). *Linguistique historique et linguistique générale.* Champion, Paris.

Milke, W. (1958). Zur inneren Gliederung und geschichtlichen Stellung der Ozeanisch-Austronesischen Sprachen. *Zeitschrift für Ethnologie* 83: 58–62.

———. (1961). Beiträge zur ozeanischen Linguistik. *Zeitschrift für Ethnologie* 86: 162–82.

Moravcsik, E. A. (1978). Language contact. In J. H. Greenberg, C. A. Ferguson, and E. A. Moravcsik, eds., *Universals of human language* 1: *Theory* 93–122. Stanford University Press, Stanford.

Mühlhäusler, P. (1985). Patterns of contact, mixture, creation and nativization: Their contribution to a general theory of language. In C.-J. N. Bailey and R. Harris, eds., *Developmental mechanisms of language* 51–88. Pergamon Press, Oxford.

Newton, B. (1964). An Arabic-Greek dialect. In R. Austerlitz, ed., *Papers in memory of George C. Pappageotes* 43–52. *Word* 20 (Supplement). Linguistic Circle of New York, New York.

Nichols, J. (1992). *Linguistic diversity in space and time.* University of Chicago Press, Chicago.

Osthoff, H., and K. Brugmann. (1878). *Morphologische Untersuchungen auf dem Gebiete der indogermanischen Sprachen.* S. Hirzel, Leipzig.

Ozanne-Rivierre, F. (1994). Iaai loanwords and phonemic changes in Fagauvea. In T. E. Dutton and D. Tryon eds., *Language contact and change in the Austronesian world* 523–49. Mouton de Gruyter, Berlin.

Pawley, A. K. (1973). Some problems in Proto Oceanic grammar. *Oceanic Linguistics* 12: 103–88.

———. (1981). Melanesian diversity and Polynesian homogeneity: a unified explanation for language. In Jim Hollyman and Andrew Pawley, eds., *Studies in Pacific Languages and cultures in honour of Bruce Biggs* 269–309. Linguistic Society of New Zealand, Auckland.

———. (1985). On speech formulas and linguistic competence. *Lenguas modernas (Universidad de Chile)* 12: 84–104.

———. (1987). Encoding events in Kalam and English: Different logics for reporting experience. In R. S. Tomlin, ed., *Coherence and grounding in discourse* 329–60. Benjamins, Amsterdam.

———. (1991a). How to talk cricket: On linguistic competence in a subject matter. In R. A. Blust, ed., *Currents in Pacific linguistics: Papers on Austronesian languages and ethnolinguistics in honour of George W. Grace* 339–68. Pacific Linguistics C-117. Australian National University, Canberra.

———. (1991b). Saying things in Kalam: Reflections on language and translation. In A. K. Pawley, ed., *Man and a half: Essays in Pacific anthropology and ethnobiology in honour of Ralph Bulmer* 432–44. Polynesian Society Memoirs no. 48. The Polynesian Society, Auckland.

Pawley, A. K., and L. A. Reid. (1980). The evolution of transitive constructions in Austronesian. In P. B. Naylor, ed., *Austronesian studies: Papers from the Second Eastern Conference on Austronesian Languages* 103–30. Center for South and Southeast Asian Studies, University of Michigan, Ann Arbor.

Pawley, A. K., and M. D. Ross. (1993). Austronesian historical linguistics and culture history. *Annual Review of Anthropology* 22: 523–59.

———. (1995). The prehistory of Oceanic languages: A current view. In P. Bellwood, J. Fox, and D. Tryon, eds., *The Austronesians: Historical and comparative perspectives* 39–74. Department of Anthropology, Research School of Pacific and Asian Studies, Australian National University, Canberra.

Pawley, A. K., and F. Syder. (1983). Two puzzles for linguistic theory: nativelike selection and nativelike fluency. In J. Richards and R. Schmidt, eds., *Language and communication* 191–225. Longman, London.

Ray, S. H. (1911). Comparative notes on Maisin and other languages of eastern Papua. *Journal of the Royal Anthropological Institute* 41: 397–405.

———. (1926). *A comparative study of the Melanesian island languages.* Cambridge University Press, Cambridge.

Rehburg, J., and S. Tuominen. (1978). Takia grammar essentials. Typescript. Summer Institute of Linguistics, Ukarumpa.

Ross, M. D. (1982). The development of the verb phrase in the Oceanic languages of the Bougainville region. In A. Halim, L. Carrington, and S. A. Wurm. eds., *Papers from the Third International Conference on Austronesian Linguistics* 1: *Currents in Oceanic* 1–52. Pacific Linguistics C-74. Australian National University, Canberra.

———. (1984). Maisin: A preliminary sketch. In *Papers in New Guinea linguistics No. 23* 1–82. Pacific Linguistics A-63. Australian National University, Canberra.

———. (1985). Current use and expansion of Tok Pisin: effects of Tok Pisin on some vernacular languages. In S. A. Wurm and P. Mühlhäusler, eds., *Handbook of Tok Pisin (New Guinea Pidgin),* 539–56. Pacific Linguistics C-70. Australian National University, Canberra.

———. (1987). A contact-induced morphosyntactic change in the Bel languages of Papua New Guinea. In D. C. Laycock and W. Winter, eds., *A world of language: Papers presented to Professor S. A. Wurm on his 65th birthday* 583–601. Pacific Linguistics C-100. Australian National University, Canberra.

———. (1988). *Proto Oceanic and the Austronesian languages of western Melanesia.* Pacific Linguistics C-98. Australian National University, Canberra.

———. (1989). Proto-Oceanic consonant grade and Milke's */nj/.* In R. Harlow and R. Hooper, eds., *VICAL 1: Oceanic languages. Papers from the Fifth International Conference on Austronesian Linguistics* 433–95. Linguistic Society of New Zealand, Auckland.

———. In 1994a. Areal phonological features in north central New Ireland. In T. E. Dutton and D. T. Tryon, eds., *Language contact and change in the Austronesian world* 551–72. Mouton de Gruyter, Berlin.

———. In 1994b. Describing inter-clausal relations in Takia. In G. P. Reesink, ed., *Topics in descriptive Austronesian linguistics.* Semaian 11: 40–85. Vakgroep Talen en Culturen van Zuidoost-Azië en Oceanië, Leiden University, Leiden.

———. In 1995a. Some current issues in Austronesian linguistics. In D. T. Tryon, ed., *Comparative Austronesian Dictionary.* Part 1: Fascicle 1, 45–120. Mouton de Gruyter, Berlin.

———. (1995b). Takia. In D. T. Tryon, ed., *Comparative Austronesian Dictionary.* Part 1: Fascicle 2, 677–685. Mouton de Gruyter, Berlin.

Ross, M., with J. N. Paol. (1978). *A Waskia grammar sketch and vocabulary. Pacific Linguistics* B-56. Pacific Linguistics, Canberra.

Sankoff, G. (1972). Language use in multilingual societies: Some alternative approaches. In J. B. Pride and J. Holmes, eds., *Sociolinguistics: Selected readings* 33–51. Penguin, Harmondsworth.

Sasse, H.-J. (1985). Sprachkontakt und Sprachwandel: Die Gräzisierung der albanischen Mundarten Griechenlands. *Papiere zur Linguistik* 32: 37–95.

Schuchardt, H. (1884). *Slawo-deutsches und Slawo-italienisches.* Leuschner und Lubensky, Graz.

———. (1885). *Über die Lautgesetze; gegen die Junggrammatiker.* Reprinted with English translation in T. Vennemann and T. H. Wilbur (1972), Berlin.

Strong, W. M. (1911). The Maisin language. *Journal of the Royal Anthropological Institute* 41: 381–96.

Szemerényi, O. (1990). *Einführung in die vergleichende Sprachwissenschaft* 4th, rev. ed. Wissenschaftliche Buchgesellschaft, Darmstadt.

Thomason, S. G. (1983). Genetic relationship and the case of Ma'a (Mbugu). *Studies in African Linguistics* 14: 195–231.

Thomason, S. G., and T. S. Kaufman. (1976). Contact-induced language change: Loanwords and the borrowing language's pre-borrowing phonology. In W. M. Christie, ed., *Current progress in historical linguistics: Proceedings of the Second International Conference on Historical Linguistics, Tucson, Arizona, 12–16 January 1976,* 167–79. North Holland, Amsterdam.

———. (1988). *Language contact, creolization and genetic linguistics.* University of California Press, Berkeley.

Thurston, W. R. (1982). *A comparative study of Anêm and Lusi. Pacific Linguistics* B-83. Australian National University, Canberra.

———. (1987). *Processes of change in the languages of north-western New Britain. Pacific Linguistics* B-99. Australian National University, Canberra.

———. (1989). How exoteric languages build a lexicon: Esoterogeny in West New Britain. In R. Harlow and R. Hooper, eds., *VICAL 1, Oceanic languages: Papers from the Fifth International Conference on Austronesian Linguistics* 555–79. Linguistic Society of New Zealand, Auckland.

———. (1994). Renovation and innovation in the languages of north-western New Britain. In T. Dutton and D. Tryon, eds., *Language contact and change in the Austronesian world* 573–609. Mouton de Gruyter, Berlin.

Tsiapera, Maria. (1969). *A descriptive analysis of Cypriot Maronite Arabic.* Mouton, The Hague.

Vennemann, T., and T. H. Wilbur. (1972). *Schuchardt, the neogrammarians and the transformational theory of phonological change.* Athenäum, Frankfurt.

Weimer, H., and N. Weimer. (1975). A short sketch of Yareba grammar. In T. E. Dutton, ed., *Studies in languages of central and south-east Papua* 667–729. *Pacific Linguistics* C-29. Australian National University, Canberra.

Weinreich, U. ([1953]1963). *Languages in contact.* Mouton, The Hague. Originally published 1953 by the Linguistic Circle of New York.

Wurm, S. A., and S. Hattori, eds., (1981). *Language atlas of the Pacific area,* Part 1: *Pacific Linguistics* C-66. Australian National University, Canberra.

9 Reconstruction in Morphology

HAROLD KOCH

1 INTRODUCTION

The linguistic literature gives little guidance on how to do morphological reconstruction. I propose a few basic procedures for morphological reconstruction
and compare them to procedures needed for other kinds of linguistic reconstruction.
Since so much of morphological reconstruction depends on knowing what morphological changes are possible, I present a typology of morphological change with comments on the reconstruction procedures that follow from each. Finally I illustrate the
methodology in a few case studies where aspects of the morphology of Australian
languages, principally of the Arandic subgroup[1] of Central Australia, are reconstructed.

1.1   Current Literature on Reconstruction Methodology

The comparative linguist who wants to do morphological reconstruction will not find
much guidance in the existing literature on how to go about the task. This stands in
sharp contrast to the copious discussions available on the comparative method for reconstructing phonology. On the other hand, we find statements acknowledging that
nonphonological reconstruction is more difficult than phonological reconstruction
because of the lack of regularity in changes and our more limited understanding of
what kinds of changes are natural or common (Hock 1991: 609 f, 592).

It has been claimed that "comparative morphology is simply applied phonology"
(Anttila 1989: 351). According to this view one arrives at aspects of the morphology
of the protolanguage by simply performing synchronic morphological analysis on a
set of morphologically related words that have been reconstructed by the methods of
comparative phonological reconstruction. While this is a feasible procedure where

morphologically complex words, especially members of a protoparadigm, can be reconstructed by phonological comparison, one would hardly want to limit the possibility of morphological reconstruction to situations where these conditions are met.

At the same time it is recognised that some members of an inflectional paradigm in a given language may violate established sound correspondences; these occurrences are regarded as resulting from analogical levellings and other processes of regularisation and are consequently ignored in reconstruction (Anttila 1989: 358 f). The widespread prevalence of analogical change increases the difficulty of morphological reconstruction. 'In morphology, . . . and especially in inflection, the factor of analogy enters—often extensively—into their distribution throughout the system. Considerable caution is therefore advisable in ascribing to a protolanguage any features of inflection which do not show wide-spread correspondences throughout the group of related langues' (Hall 1983:3).

While not offering a method or set of procedures for morphological reconstruction, some textbooks do provide instructive examples of morphological reconstruction; for example, Haas (1969:51–8, 62–4) from Muskogean, and Anttila (1989) from Finno-Ugric.

Furthermore the literature does provide a certain amount of guidance in the form of **principles** that should be observed in doing morphological reconstruction. It is agreed that reconstruction should proceed by comparing **archaic** patterns. If these provide cumulative and convergent evidence from different languages, one can use them as the basis for reconstructing patterns in the protolanguage (Hock 1991: 610 f). Here the initial problem is how to recognise which of the variant patterns represent archaisms and which are the result of innovations. Archaisms are known to survive in less basic functions (English *brethren* versus. the normal plural *brothers*, *elder* versus the regular comparative *older*), and in certain discourse (or textual) contexts such as idiomatic expressions (French *sans mot dire*, with OV word order and no article), traditional folk poetry, proverbs, nursery rhymes, e.g. "*Pease porridge..*" (Lehmann 1992: 223; see also 5.2 of this chapter)

Another principle is that one should begin from synchronically **irregular** or **anomalous** forms since regular forms can easily result from regularising or simplifying processes at some time during the history of the language. "[P]ay special attention to those forms that appear **anomalous** and could not possibly be the result of analogy" (Arlotto 1972: 143). Hall, following Bloomfield (1935: 318), claims that 'if a given form shows a particular irregularity which is shared by corresponding forms in a group of related languages, this is a good indication that the irregularity was present in the proto-language as well' (Hall 1983: 3). For a textbook application see Anttila (1989: 358).

Hetzron (1976: 93) has expressed this insight as the "principle of archaic heterogeneity":

> If a number of cognate languages each have a system similar to its homologues in the other languages in some respects, but different in other respects–unless one can find a clear conditioning factor for differentiation–the relatively most heterogeneous system might be considered the most archaic, the closest to the ancestor, and the more homogeneous ones might be assumed to have arisen as a result of simplification.

TABLE 9-1
Semitic verb inflection. The direction of analogical influence is
indicated by a dotted line with an arrow ($\rightarrow$ and $\leftarrow$).

	1Sg.		2Sg.M.
Akkadian	-ku		-ta
Arabic	-tu	$\leftarrow$	-ta
Ethiopic	-ku	$\rightarrow$	-ka
Proto-Semitic	*-ku		*-ta

As an example he gives the Semitic verb person/number suffixes shown on Table 9-1. Here Akkadian is taken to reflect the Proto-Semitic situation since its paradigm is the most heterogeneous. The suffixes *-tu* of Arabic and *-ka* of Ethiopic are each assumed to have altered their consonant by analogy with the other member of their respective paradigms.

Hoenigswald (1991) gives a method for reconstructing syncretism in morphosyntactic paradigms (comparable to the reconstruction of phonemic merger) and identifying analogical extensions.

2 PROPOSED METHODOLOGY

In this section I outline the methods of morphological and phonological reconstruction. I also contrast the reconstruction of morphology with the reconstruction of phonology, semantics, syntax, and lexicon (etymology). Finally I describe common features of all types of reconstruction.

2.1 Procedures for Morphological Reconstruction

I propose that the method of morphological reconstruction consists basically of applying the following general procedures:

1. Match tentative morphs, that is, formal bits that are potentially cognate according to established phoneme correspondences and changes. These matches may be found in the same language (so we have internal reconstruction), in different but related languages (so we have comparative reconstruction), or in different but not necessarily related languages (so we have an analysis of borrowing). Note that this assumes the prior establishment of phonological changes on the basis of lexical cognates.

2. Assess the relative likelihood of each of the compared forms and/or paradigmatic patterns being archaic or innovative.

3. Posit an appropriate protoform and a series of plausible processes of morphological change that (in combination with phonetic and semantic changes) would transform the protoform into each of the attested forms.

These procedures, however, will not in themselves be very helpful unless they are supplemented by a knowledge of what is worth comparing, which in turn depends on a knowledge of what diachronic changes are likely. Before we survey these, however, it will be useful to review the methodology of phonological reconstruction. In the next section a set of procedures is presented that in my opinion encapsulates the traditional comparative method of phonological reconstruction.

2.2   Procedures for Comparative Reconstruction in Phonology

1. Assemble a set of tentative cognates in a group of languages assumed to be genetically related. Begin with lexemes which belong to relatively basic vocabulary. To qualify as tentative cognates the words must exhibit similarities in both their semantic and their phonological make-up that could be accounted for by a combination of phonetic and semantic changes.

2. Match the tentative cognates segment by phonological segment.

3. List the sets of matched phonological segments which recur in the matched cognates. These are correspondence sets.

4. For each group of two or more overlapping correspondence sets (that is, sets that share a phoneme in any one of the languages), check whether the sets occur in the same phonological environment (defined in terms of other correspondence sets or boundaries).

5. Group together the correspondence sets which occur in mutually exclusive environments, that is, which occur in complementary or noncontrastive distribution with one another, bearing in mind that there may be more than one possible way to group them.

6. For each such group of noncontrasting correspondence sets, posit (i) a phoneme in the protolanguage and (ii) a chronologically ordered set of changes which will transform the protophoneme into the attested phoneme in each of the languages under comparison.

7. Where two or more languages have undergone the same change—and this change must be ordered chronologically before other changes which are not shared by the languages in question—posit (i) an intermediate protolanguage ancestral to just the languages in question (which are thus defined as a subgroup) and (ii) a single change that took place only once at some time intermediate between the protolanguage and the intermediate protolanguage.

8. When all the correspondence sets have been accounted for in terms of a protophoneme and associated changes, indicate the phonological system of the protolanguage; that is, the inventory of phonemes and the features that distinguish phonemes from one another and characterise their pronunciation.

9. Check the reconstructed phonological system for plausibility according to what is known from the typology of synchronic systems. If more plausible solutions are consistent with the comparative data, try them.

10. Give the reconstructed form of all the words that have reflexes in the daughter languages.

11. From the list of protowords that are reconstructed, it is possible to describe the phonotactics of the protolanguage, that is the distribution of the protophonemes.

Criteria for choosing between alternative workable solutions:

Economy. Prefer the most economical solution, that is, the solution which involves the fewest elements in the protosystem and/or the fewest changes between the protolanguage and each of the descendant languages. (Hock (1991) calls this the Occam's Razor Principle.)

Plausibility. Prefer the most plausible solution for both the protosystem and the sequence of changes. The evidence for plausibility comes from typology: The plausibility of the protosystem is judged by the evidence of synchronic typology; the plausibility of the changes is judged by the evidence of diachronic typology. (Cf. Hock's principle : "Given two otherwise acceptable competing analyses, we prefer the one which postulates more natural or more common processes" (Hock 1991: 535)) The criterion of plausibility should take precedence over the criterion of economy.

In the following sections I contrast morphological reconstruction with other kinds of reconstruction.

2.3   Morphological Reconstruction and Phonological Reconstruction

There is no analogue in morphological change to regular sound change. **Regularity** is, however, taken into account in phonological reconstruction not by the core reconstruction procedure (step 6) but in the correspondence sets which are the input to this core reconstruction procedure. The set of corresponding phonemes is established by extracting phonemes from the same relative position in (tentative) cognate words or morphemes, that is, in words that are similar enough in both phonological form and meaning to be considered possible reflexes of the same original word. The comparative method is applied to such sets of phonemes only if they recur in numbers of cognate sets. This recurrence follows from the basic regularity of sound change. Morphological change is not regular in the same sense, and therefore does not lead to recurrent correspondences between tentative morphs.

The units matched in morphological reconstruction are linguistic signs, whereas the units of phonological reconstruction (phonemes) are meaningless diacritic marks that serve to differentiate the signs. Each morphological unit consists of both a stretch of phonological substance (form) and an associated grammatical or derivational meaning (function). Like phonological units, however, morphological formatives are characterised by certain combinatorial possibilities; thus morphotactics is comparable to phonotactics.

Like phonological reconstruction, morphological reconstruction basically starts with matchings. For each set of matched formatives there is posited an original formative, that is, a phonological form, meaning/function, and distribution, together with a set of morphological changes leading to each of the attested formatives.

The same criteria of economy and plausibility are relevant to morphological reconstruction. The problem is that diachronic morphology provides considerably less guidance than diachronic phonology because the typological study of morphological change has not progressed as far as that of phonological change.

The prospects of reconstructing the whole of the (morphological) system of a protolanguage are not as good for morphology as for phonology. This is because the number of inflectional and derivational formatives is typically greater, hence the frequency less, than that of phonemes. Furthermore, for many languages, there are many more possible morphological changes than phonological, since in principle each inflectional paradigm or each derived word can undergo its own changes.

2.4 Morphological Reconstruction and Semantic Reconstruction

Change in the content side of morphology is similar to that in semantics, except that there is probably more use of grammaticalisation and degrammaticalisation in morphological change. Since much of morphology has to do with inflectional paradigms and derivational pseudoparadigms, the semantic side of morphological reconstruction will be similar to the reconstruction of semantic fields.

2.5 Morphological Reconstruction and Syntactic Reconstruction

Both require the linguist to posit reanalyses and to look for contexts of reanalysis. Both may involve the recognition of grammaticalisation processes. Morphological reconstruction allows greater confidence in recovering the earlier order of elements since the order of bound morphemes in words is more fixed than that of phrases and clauses.

2.6 Morphological Reconstruction and Etymology

The etymology of affixes is in principle no different from that of lexemes; there is a similar need to have regard to change in each of: phonology, semantics, distribution, etc. Formatives, however, are probably more liable than lexical morphemes to suffer reanalyses that affect their external boundaries. On the other hand, since formatives (especially those used in inflectional morphology) occur much more frequently than most lexical morphemes, and occur in sets, it should be possible to reconstruct a greater proportion of inflectional morphology than of general vocabulary.

2.7 Common Features of all Reconstruction

Reconstruction in all domains of language has the following features in common. Both comparative and internal reconstruction are possible. The comparativist needs to find the elements that can be compared. Appeal must be made to directionality, plausibility of changes as established by diachronic typology, as well as to a general principle of economy. In all reconstruction except phonology it is useful to rely on synchronically archaic features of the languages.

Much of morphological reconstruction depends on judgements regarding the plausibility of particular morphological changes. This is important for judging between alternative hypotheses for reconstructing particular formatives. It also comes into play in decisions about what might be compared as tentative cognate morphs in the first place. For these reasons I shall present a typology of morphological changes, with comments on the implications of each type for reconstruction. This will be followed, in section 11, by a number of case studies which illustrate the application of the methods of morphological reconstruction. (For another typology of morphological change, organised along different lines, see Andersen 1980.) The following sections classify morphological change into the following categories: They are given in order of their sections within this chapter.

- morph replacement (3)
- change in the formal realization of a morpheme (allomorphic change) (4)
- change in the place of a boundary (5)
- change in content/meaning/function (6)
- change in morphosyntactic status (7)
- reordering of morphemes (8)
- morpheme doubling (9)

3 MORPH REPLACEMENT

A simple form of morphological change consists of the replacement of one exponent of a grammatical meaning by another exponent. If the earlier and later exponents differ only in terms of phonemes that are relatable by regular sound change, this is not considered to be an instance of morphological change, but merely of sound change. If the replacement morph was formerly the exponent of a different grammatical or lexical meaning, this may be described as content change (possibly grammaticalisation). Hardest to classify is a replacement where there is no obvious source in the language for the new exponent: It may simply have been borrowed from the equivalent exponent in another language or dialect. (For constraints on the borrowing of morphemes, see Heath 1978.)

4 CHANGE IN THE FORMAL REALIZATION OF A MORPHEME (ALLOMORPHIC CHANGE)

There are several subcategories of allomorphic change. These are discussed under the headings of:

- development of allomorphy (4.1)
- change in relationship between basic/underlying and derived allomorphs (4.2)
- change in conditioning of allomorphy (4.3)
- loss of allomorphy (4.4)
- redistribution of allomorphs (4.5)

4.1 Development of Allomorphy

Allormophy can develop through sound change or through analogical change, and analogical change may involve a change in stem or a change in inflectional affix.

Perhaps the simplest type of morphological change consists of the development of new allomorphs as the result of sound change. Where a sound change affects a morpheme differently in different environments, a situation arises where a given morpheme is realised by means of formally different morphic shapes in different grammatical words. The choice of allomorph is determined on purely phonological grounds at first, but with subsequent phonological change the allomorphy may come to be conditioned partly or wholly by nonphonological (morphological, syntactic, semantic, or lexical) factors.

Where the original phonological conditioning is largely preserved, the **method of internal reconstruction** can be used to restore the earlier phonological shape of the morpheme. The method consists of reducing the variation to a set of alternating phonemes, each of which occurs in a different allomorph, noting the phonological environment where each occurs and positing for each alternating set an invariant earlier phoneme and a phonological change (or if necessary a chronologically ordered set of phonological changes) that produced the phonemic variants.

For example, in Kaytetye the present imperfective of transitive verbs is marked by two allomorphs, *-rranytye* and *-ranytye*. Sample verb stems with which they co-occur are given in Table 9-2. We note that the variation is localised in the alternation between *rr* (an apical trill/tap) and *r* (an apico-postalveolar, i.e. retroflex approximant). We can discern a phonological environment for the alternation. The former occurs where the nearest consonant to the left is a velar, labial, laminal, or palatal; the latter occurs only where it is preceded by an apical consonant (whether alveolar, retroflex, or prepalatalised) except the approximant *r*; that is, by an apical obstruent. We consider the alternative hypotheses that (1) the suffix had an earlier invariant *rr* and a change took place whereby *rr* was altered to *r* after a preceding apical obstruent (with an intervening vowel), and (2) that the consonant was originally *r*, which was replaced by *rr* after a preceding labial, velar, laminal, or palatal consonant. The first of the two hypotheses, a change $rr > r / C_{\text{ap obst}} \text{ v}+\_\_$, is chosen on the grounds of (a) economy— the environment of the change can be described in terms of a single class of phonemes, apical obstruents—and (b) phonetic plausibility—that is, since *rr* itself is an apical obstruent, this change may be understood as a kind of dissimilation. A further consideration of generality supports this choice: There is another synchronic process whereby all apical consonants are backed to the corresponding retroflex consonant in the same environment, after a preceding apical obstruent. The

TABLE 9-2
Kaytetye present imperfective allomorphs

-rranytye		-ranytye	
ange-	'scoop'	ate-	'press with foot'
pwe-	'cook'	arte-	'chop'
apme-	'dig'	aynte-	'eat'
athe-	'excrete'	erntwe-	'break'
etye-	'hang up'	ayle-	'sing'
etnye-	'give'	arre-	'put'
are-	'see'		

change under consideration may be seen as a manifestation of the same general process.

This procedure, it should be noted, is not **morphological** reconstruction, but is rather one of the two established methods of **phonological** reconstruction, one which nevertheless takes morphological (or, more stricly, morphophonemic) data as its input and results in the reconstruction of invariant morphemes.

Morphs may also undergo changes to their phonological shape that are not caused by sound change but by analogical processes. These may affect lexical morphs or affixes.

In Spanish, as a result of sound changes that affected the different members of the paradigm differentially, many verbs of the -er and -ir inflectional classes came to have two stem alternants in the present tense, one of which occurs in the 1st person singular of the indicative mood and in all person-numbers of the subjunctive mood: the other occurs in the remaining person-number forms of the indicative. Thus the verb *dezir* 'say' had stem allomorphs *dig-* and *diz-*. According to Malkiel (1968), *fazer* (later *hacer*) 'do' likewise had alternants **faç-* and *faz-* (where ç stands for [tʃ]), but its alternation *ç : z* was replaced by an alternation *g : z* under the influence of the *dezir*. Similar remodelling of alternation patterns under the influence of other lexemes from the same inflectional class is discussed in connection with Italian data by Maiden (1992) under the term 'novel allomorphy'. There are even cases where allomorphy is introduced into stems that were formally invariant. Italian *fuggire* 'flee' in this way acquired an alternant *fugg-* (in the 1Sg and 3Pl indicative and all persons of the subjunctive) beside the formerly invariant *fuddʒ-*, a pattern that was present in other -*ire/-ere* class verbs like *legg-/leddʒ* 'read'. As Maiden emphasises, these extensions of alternation patterns do not result in, and are not motivated by, an improvement in the coding of inflectional categories (see the discussion of allomorphy redistribution in stems in 4.5).

The reconstruction of such allomorphic change is difficult. One should first look for an explanation of such allomorphy in terms of phonological conditioning within the word forms of the particular lexeme, either in the present distribution of the allomorphs or in another distribution if one can plausibly invoke a redistribution that is motivated by the morphological categories (see 4.5). If there is no other explanation, one is justified in looking for influences from other lexemes in the same inflectional class.

Grammatical formatives may also undergo phonological changes for analogical reasons. This source of the analogy may be another formative in the same paradigm, as in the Arabic and Ethiopic examples in Table 9-1. Alternatively, in a language that has inflectional classes, formatives may be influenced by the shape of other formatives that mark the same property in another, but related, inflectional class. In the pre-Latin nominal declension system Masculine *o*-stems and Feminine *a:*-stems were closely associated, since both were productive and complementary adjectives (and some nouns) were formed on these bases. Through mutual influences certain case-number forms in each paradigm were reshaped to resemble more closely the form of the complementary gender class (Palmer 1954: 241 ff), as is shown in Table 9-3.

In situations like this the earlier form of the affix is recoverable only by comparison with other languages and/or by the recognition of relic forms (for example, in

TABLE 9-3
Pre-Latin *a:*-stem and *o*-stem nominals. New endings are shown in boldface. The
direction of influence is indicated by a dotted line with an arrow.

	Fem earlier	Masc earlier	Fem later		Masc later
Sg Nom	fi:lia	fi:lios	fi:lia		fi:lios
Sg Gen	fi:lia:s	fi:lii:	fi:lia**:i:**	- - < - -	fi:lii:
Pl Nom	fi:lia:s	fi:lioi	fi:lia**:i**	- - < - -	fi:lioi
Pl Gen	fi:lia:so:m	fi:lio:m	fi:lia:so:m	- - > - -	fi:lio**:so:m**

Latin there are some residual masculine plural genitive forms in *-um* < * *o:m*, and a
feminine genitive singular in *-a:s* that are used in archaic legal or religious phrases).
Successful reconstruction requires that the source and mechanism of such analogical
reformations be identified.

4.2 Change in Relations Between Basic/Underlying and Derived Allomorphs

This process is referred to in the literature as rule inversion (Vennemann 1972). The
change follows a sound change applying in a particular phonological context, which
creates allomorphs that occur in different contexts and consists of a reanalysis whereby the newly created allomorph is treated as the basic form of a morpheme and the
old allomorph is treated as conditioned by an environment that is complementary to
that of the original change. If the allomorphy is stated in terms of a rule that derives
one of the alternating phonemes from the other, the effect of inversion is to replace a
rule of the form A$\Rightarrow$B/Z with one of the form B$\Rightarrow$A/~Z. An easy example of inversion can be seen in the English indefinite article. Of the allomorphs *an* and *a*, *an* was
formerly the basic form, with *a* being derived by the loss of *n* before a following consonant (a change that was also responsible for producing the variants *mine* versus *my*
and *thine* versus *thy*). Now, however, their relation is reversed: *a* is treated as the basic form and *n* is derived by a process of insertion before a following word that begins with a vowel.

The reconstruction method used for such cases is as follows. Given an alternation
whose synchronic direction lacks phonetic motivation, consider whether a historical
change in the opposite direction, and with an environment complementary, to that of
the synchronic derivation makes more phonetic sense and is supported by relics.

4.3 Change in Conditioning of Allomorphy

As a result of the accumulation of phonological changes, the original phonological
conditioning of allomorphy may become opaque. This may result in a reinterpretation on the basis of lexical or morphological conditioning, or there may be a loss of
conditioning.

A change to lexical conditioning can occur when the allomorphy is reinterpreted
as determined by the particular lexical morpheme that it co-occurs with. For exam-

ple, in the speech of some older speakers of Kaytetye, the locative/ergative case of
weye 'meat', *wepe* 'spider', *kayle* 'boomerang' uses the allomorph *-nge*, as a lexically conditioned allomorph, instead of the form *-le* which is specified by the general
rule whereby the choice of allomorph is conditioned phonologically by the length of
the nominal stem (see 11.2):

-nge after v(c)cv_
-le after . .cv(c)cv_

Here cognates suggest earlier short nominal stems **uye*, **upe*, **ayle*, which would
determine the *-nge* allomorph. When the stems were lengthened, acquiring an additional consonant by phonological change (*u* > *we*) or contact-induced change (**ayle*
reformed to *kayle* under the influence of *karli* in the neighbouring Warlpiri language),
the conditioning of the allomorph no longer fitted the allomorphy rule, since they now
had the structure cvcv; so they became lexically determined. (In the speech of most
Kaytetye people, these irregular forms have now been replaced by the new combinations *weye-le*, *wepe-le*, *kayle-le* which are produced by the allomorphy rule; that is,
they have lost their exceptional conditioning.)

More characteristically, allomorphy comes to be reinterpreted as partly or wholly determined by the morphological category of the word in which it appears. Viewed
differently, the morphophonemic process that can be abstracted from the allomorphs
can be seen as a (partial) signal or marker of the morphological category. Thus the
English verb *sleep* formerly formed its past tense simply by the addition of a suffix
-t(e). As a result of two changes—the shortening of a long vowel before a consonant
cluster, which affected the past form, and the raising of *e:* to *i:*, which affected the
present tense form—we now have an alternation of *i:* to *e* in the past tense form—
which is conditioned not by the presence of a following consonant (since the alternation does not occur in *sleeps*, where the root vowel also precedes two consonants),
but by the morphosyntactic category PAST TENSE. In fact the replacement of *i:* by *e*
can be described as a subsidiary marker or cosignal (beside the suffixation of *t*) of the
past tense.

Where the erstwhile allomorph ceases to have any phonological conditioning, it
becomes the sole marker of a morphological category. Here it is no longer a matter
of allomorphy, but of a new morphological marker. The alternation process itself is a
morphological (or morpholexical in the terminology of Matthews 1972, 1991) rule.
Thus, for example, in English *foot* versus *feet*, which continues an earlier phonological change of vowel fronting before a front vowel suffix in the following syllable,
the replacement *u* ⇒ *i:* is now the sole marker of plural.

Changes in conditioning of the type just discussed form part of a long diachronic pathway that leads from phonetics to morphology. This was already discussed in
the nineteenth century by Kruszewski (1881) and Baudouin de Courtenay (1895).
More recently it has been discussed as the morphologisation of phonological rules by
phonologists in the naturalist tradition (Vennemann 1972; Hooper 1976; Dressler
1977, 1985; Klausenburger 1979; Wurzel 1980, 1981). What begins as the creation
of a new allophone may lead to the rise of a new phonemic contrast which may survive as morphophonemic alternation—automatic at first, then later conditioned in

part by nonphonological factors—which takes on a (in the first instance partial) morphological role (that is, it becomes a cosignal of a grammatical property), and eventually becomes the sole marker of a grammatical property. For example the vowel distinction which now serves as the only marker of the plural in *mice* (versus *mouse*) began as an allophone of *u:* that was conditioned by a following *i* in the plural suffix.

Reconstruction involving the effects of the morphologisation of phonology belongs to phonological reconstruction in so far as the goal is to establish the original phonological form of the morphs and/or to identify phonological changes. Inasmuch as morphological factors are involved in the changes which need to be unraveled, this is morphological reconstruction. Reconstruction here begins by examining alternations that (co)signal morphological categories. The linguist will assume that the alternation was originally conditioned phonologically, but will bear in mind the possibility that one or more of the following developments may have occurred.

1. The phonological environment of the change may have changed or been lost through subsequent changes.

2. One or both of the alternating phonemes may have undergone changes subsequent to the change which caused their original divergence. Hence the current alternation may represent the telescoping of several earlier processes (Wurzel 1980).

3. A morphological environment may have supplemented or replaced the original phonological environment.

4. The directional process relating the phonemes may have been reversed.

5. The original process may have split into several different processes, which may be inverted or noninverted, morphologised or nonmorphologised (Dressler 1985).

6. Many words which formerly participated in the alternation may have lost it through lexical fading of the process (Dressler 1985).

7. Some words which now have the alternation may not have had it originally, but gained it through the extension of a morphologised alternation pattern (see 4.5 and Maiden 1992). For example, a morpholexical rule, like an inflectional affix, may spread to new stems as a cosignal of a morphological property. Thus, whereas the effects of umlaut (vowel fronting) have been largely lost in the English inflectional system, except for a few irregular plurals like *feet*, *teeth*, *geese*, *mice*, *lice*, *men*, the alternations resulting from a similar change in German have been extended to a great many new words as a subsidiary marker (with *-e* or *-er*) of the the plural.

4.4 Loss of Allomorphy

Loss of allomorphy is an extreme effect of the redistribution of allomorphs. Either stems or affixes may be affected. The loss of allomorphy in stems may be due to paradigm levelling or to paradigm split.

The loss of one alternant with generalisation of another is called **paradigm lev-**

elling if it affects the allomorphy of lexical morphs. Thus Old English had root variants of the verb 'ride' such that *ra:d*-occurred in the past singular and *rid*-in the past plural. The *ra:d* (> *rode*) alternant was generalised at the expense of *rid*. In German, on the other hand, it was the variant occurring in the past plural which was generalised (Modern German *rit*).

Where levelling extends to and changes the basic form of a paradigm, **restructuring** is said to have taken place (Vennemann 1974). Thus in Latin, as a result of a change of *s* to *r* between vowels, many nouns ending in *s* in the nominative singular developed allomorphs ending in *r* in the other members of the paradigm (where suffixes started with a vowel). In the words for 'honour' and 'tree' (see Table 9-4), however, the stem was eventually levelled in favour of the *r*-form. Thereby the lexeme was restructured as *honor-*, *arbor-* (and the derivatives *honestus* 'honest' and *arbustus* 'covered with trees', if derived by a rule, would have involved an inverted rule r ⇒ s / _t). Levelling, which does not necessarily involve a total loss of allomorphy, is discussed further in 4.5.

Where comparison yields paradigms in different languages that are similar enough on grounds of the semantics, inflection, and phonological shape to be considered cognate, but whose stems do not fully match phonologically, the comparativist is justified in suggesting a plausible scenario involving the generalisation of one allomorph and the elimination of another. Thus Indo-Europeanists, faced with comparative paradigms such as that of 'foot' (Table 9-5), reconstruct a protoparadigm with alternating vowels *o:*, *o,* and *e*. Where the attested vowels of particular languages are not the expected reflexes (according to the usual sound changes) of the originals, they are explained in terms of levelling. Greek has generalised the *o*-vocalism from both the Nominatives and from the accusative singular, keeping the lengthening process in the nominative singular; Germanic (represented here by Old Norse) has generalised the *o:* of the nominative singular, and Latin has generalised the *e*-vocalism from the oblique cases (Ernout-Meillet 1985: 502). These levelling patterns recur in other lexemes, such as 'tooth', where the stems of Greek *odont-* and Latin *dent-* result from the generalisation of different alternants.

Internal reconstruction of paradigm levelling is sometimes possible; it depends on finding a relic which is an offshoot from a generalised paradigm. Thus in the Latin case-number paradigm of *parvus* 'little', *v* (pronounced [w]) disappeared by sound change before certain inflections but not others; *v* was restored to the whole paradigm

TABLE 9-4
Latin singular case paradigms of 'honour' and 'tree' (levelled phonemes are in boldface).

	'honour' I	'honour' II	'tree' I	'tree' II
Nom	hono:s	hono:**r**	arbos	arbo**r**
Acc	hono:rem	hono:rem	arborem	arborem
Gen	hono:ris	hono:ris	arboris	arboris
Dat	hono:ri:	hono:ri:	arbori:	arbori:
Abl	hono:re	hono:re	arbore	arbore

TABLE 9-5
Partial paradigms of 'foot' in Indo-European languages. Replaced stem allomorphs
are in boldface. (Relevant phonology: Sanskrit *a:* reflects PIE *o, o:, e:, a:;* Sanskrit
a reflects PIE *e* or *a;* Old Norse *ó* reflects PIE *o:* or *a:,* *ǿ* is a later fronting of *ó*
before *i* or *j*.)

	Nom	Acc	Gen	Dat	Loc	PlNom
Sanskrit	pá:t	pá:d-am	pad-ás	pad-é	pad-í	pá:d-as
Doric Greek	pó:-s	pód-a	**pod-ós**		**pod-í**	pód-es
Cl. Armenian		ot-n				ot-kh
Old Norse	fót-r	**fót**	fót-ar	fǿt-e		fǿt-r
Latin	**pe:-s**	**ped-em**	ped-is	ped-i:	ped-e	**ped-e:s**
pIE	*pó:d-s	*pód-m	*ped-ós	*ped-éi	*ped-i	*pód-es

by levelling from the unaffected wordforms such as the Genitive Singular *parvi:*.
However the adverb *parum* 'too little', which was in origin an offshoot of this paradigm, allows us to see the effect of the sound change (Anttila 1989: 95).

Another kind of reduction of allomorphy involves **paradigm split**, in which a paradigm is split through a semantic/functional differentiation of the allomorphs, each
becoming a separate lexeme, which may then be inflected for the full set of morphosyntactic properties. Thus Latin *deus* 'god' and *di:vus* 'divine', English *shade* and
shadow, *mead* and *meadow*, *staff* and *stave* are examples of pairs of lexemes that result from paradigm split (Anttila 1989: 95,96). Here a kind of internal reconstruction
method can be applied: Given two semantically related lexical morphemes which are
phonologically similar, posit an earlier single paradigm with two variant forms of the
stem morpheme, plus plausible extensions and semantic differentiation.

For the loss of allomorphy in affixes, see the discussion of allomorph redistribution in affixes in the latter half of the next section.

4.5   Redistribution of Allomorphs

The distribution of co-allomorphs may be altered, one allomorph replacing another
in certain contexts. This replacement results in the creation of new morph combinations, and may cause the elimination of certain allomorphs and hence lead to a reduction in the number of allomorphs of a particular morpheme. If all but one allomorph are eliminated, the result is the total loss of allomorphy, and the achievement
of the ideal of one meaning being expressed by just one form. Here it is useful to distinguish between allomorph redistribution in a lexical stem and in affixes. (I shall confine my discussion to inflectional affixes. Much the same principles apply to derivational affixes and to modificatory morphological processes.)

Reduction of allomorphy in stems is traditionally called paradigm levelling (4.4).
In fact, reduction of allomorphy is more likely to take place within inflectional paradigms than across derivationally related forms. Within paradigms, levelling affects
(sub)paradigms that are more closely related in meaning before those that are less
closely related in meaning (Bybee 1985: 64 f). Thus levelling may affect the grammatical words expressing all the person-number combinations in a given tense before

it affects other tenses, or all tenses of one aspect before other aspects, or all cases in the plural before similar cases in the singular, etc. The expanding allomorph may be either the newer one (typically created by sound change) or the older one. It is not possible to give a general rule which predicts which allomorph will prevail in such levelling. A number of factors have been suggested. A combination of several factors may be responsible in many cases.

1. Paradigm frequency: The variant occurring in the most forms in the paradigm prevails.

2. The variant occurring in the word form that expresses the semantically most basic category in the paradigm prevails. Basic forms express singular number, nominative case, third person, present tense, indicative mood, etc.

3. The variant occurring in the word form that occurs most frequently for the particular lexeme. Thus the plural allomorph prevails in words typically used in the plural in Frisian, where 'tooth'/'teeth' *kies* /*kjizz-en* is replaced by *kjizze* /*kjizze-n* (Tiersma 1982). Similarly, in Polish place names, the stem allomorph of the local cases has penetrated to other word forms of the paradigm (Mańczak 1957–58: 396 ff.).

4. The variant that most closely resembles invariant morphemes that occur in related paradigms.

For example, in Latin many lexical stems contained allomorphs with an alternation of *s* word-finally and *r* elsewhere (resulting from a sound change s > z/V_V followed by z > r; see 4.4). Since all case-number suffixes began with a vowel except the nominative (and accusative for nouns in the neuter gender) singular, the resulting paradigm had *s* in only one (or two for neuters) of nine forms. While largely preserved in neuter nouns and monosyllabic non-neuters, the alternation was levelled for polysyllabic masculine and feminine nouns, with *r* prevailing. The prevalence of the *r*-forms, in spite of its nonoccurrence in the nominative singular basic form, can be attributed to the numerical preponderance of *r* in the paradigm—factor (1)—and also to the influence of many paradigms with invariant *r* (Schindler 1974)—factor (4). In the one monosyllabic non-neuter stem that generalised the *r*-form, *las* / *lar-* 'household deity', it is the greater frequency of usage of the noun in the plural which is supposedly responsible (Schindler 1974)—factor (3).

In prehistoric Greek a sound change m > n /_#, which affected only the nominative singular, led to the alternations shown on Table 9-6. Here the alternant with *n*, which occurred only in the semantically basic nominative singular, prevailed over the

TABLE 9-6
Prehistoric Greek nasal alternations

	'snow'	'earth'	'one' (neuter)
Nom Sg	khio:n	khtho:n	hen
other case-number	khiom-	khthom-	hem-

TABLE 9-7
Middle High German 'guest' and Old Norse 'to sacrifice'

	'guest' I	'guest' II		'to sacrifice' I	'to sacrifice' II
Sg Nom/Acc	gast	gast	Infinitive	blo:ta(n)	blo:ta(n)
Sg Gen	gastes	gastes	Pres 1 Sg	blo:tu	blø:tu
Sg Dat	gaste	gaste	Pres 2 Sg	blø:tiR	blø:tiR
Sg Inst	gestiu	gastiu	Pres 3 Sg	blø:tiR	blø:tiR
Pl Nom/Acc	gesti	gesti	Pres 1 Pl	blo:tum	blo:tum
Pl Gen	gestio	gestio	Pres 2 Pl	blo:teð	blo:teð
Pl Dat	gestim	gestim	Pres 3 Pl	blo:ta(n)	blo:ta(n)

m which occurred in the other seven or more forms—factor (2). (The modification of vowel lengthening, however, continued to mark nominative singular alone.) But here the influence of numerous other paradigms with invariant *n* may have also been a factor in the generalisation of the *n*-form (Schindler 1974)—factor (3).

Allomorph redistribution does not always involve the elimination of one of the alternants. Sometimes the distribution is adjusted so that one allomorph consistently occurs in word forms expressing a semantically unitary subset of the paradigm and hence comes to function as a cosignal, with affixation, of that semantic category. The paradigms of Middle High German 'guest' and Old Norse 'to sacrifice' (Table 9-7) furnish examples (taken from Wurzel 1981).

In Middle Hight German 'guest' the alternant with vowel *e* (which arose by sound change before a vowel *i* in the following syllable) was replaced by *a* in the instrumental singular, with a resulting distribution of *a* in all singular forms and *e* in all plural forms. In the Old Norse verb the stem allomorph with a front vowel caused by umlaut was generalised from the second and third person singular to the first person, with the result that the vowel of the stem correlates with the number of the subject. In the former case the new alternant became more restricted in its distribution, while in the latter case the new allomorph expanded. In both instances, the variants came to be distributed according to the singular/plural category distinction in the word.

Another kind of rearrangement of allomorphs results in a pattern of distribution that resembles a pattern found in other paradigms, even though it does not correspond to a unified content. Thus Modern Standard German has replaced, in the present tense of the verb 'give' and several others, the alternation pattern I of Table 9-8 with that

TABLE 9-8
Modern Standard German 'give'

	'give' I	'give' II
Sg 1	gib	geb-e
Sg 2	gib-st	gib-st
Sg 3	gib-t	gib-t
P l1	geb-en	geb-en
P l2	geb-t	geb-t
P l3	geb-en	geb-en

of II, where the vowels are no longer distributed according to a unified morphological category (singular versus plural), but according to a pattern occurring in another large class of verbs where the basic vowel is altered only in the second and third persons of the singular (Keller 1978: 424).

Reconstruction involving stem allomorphy must take these kinds of redistribution into consideration. While it is likely that most of the stem allomorphy of a given language is the result of sound changes, these sound changes may not have taken place in the same stem-affix combinations which now occur. The stem allomorphs may have been redistributed in the paradigm for one reason or another. Furthermore, the affixes occurring in particular paradigmatic positions may have changed in various ways (see later discussion). Hence the stem allomorphs may have resulted from regular sound changes, but in combination with affixes different from those with which they now occur. This points to the danger of using stems of a variable inflectional paradigm for the purposes of phonological reconstruction. It is better to base this on invariant words, or even on words that are related derivationally, where redistribution of the results of sound change is less prevalent.

Where the sound changes are known and the comparison of paradigms across languages shows certain inflectional forms to have nonhistorical reflexes of the stem, the comparativist should reconstruct a protoparadigm, consistent with the historical phonology, which will serve as a starting point from which plausible redistributions of allomorphs can be posited for each of the relevant languages(see the example of Indo-European 'foot', Table 9-5).

Allomorph redistribution involving affixes is probably a more common type of change than that involving stems. In the case of affixes, allomorph redistribution results in the creation of new stem-plus-affix combinations, with one allomorph of an affix replacing another in the context of certain stems. This may lead to the elimination of one variant of an affix or simply to a reduction in the number of stems it co-occurs with. Where sets of affix allomorphs have parallel conditioning, we have to do with morphological classes. With morphological classes, the choice of inflectional affix may be conditioned by the semantic features of the lexical stem (animacy, gender, or proper noun status of nouns, active versus stative in the verb), by co-occurring morphosyntactic features (number, definiteness), by phonological features of the adjacent stem (number of syllables, vowel versus consonant). Where there are no extramorphological features that determine the choice of inflectional markers, we have arbitrary inflectional classes; the term morphological class is often restricted to situations where this kind of conditioning holds. Here the allomorph replacement can be seen as the encroachment of the marker appropriate to one class on the domain of another class. Where the whole set of inflectional affixes of one morphological class replaces those of another class, this process can be seen as the transfer of lexical items from one class to another; and if all lexemes are so transferred, the result is the merger of two morphological classes.

The domain of affix replacement is typically between morphological classes that have in common one or more of these extramorphological allomorph-conditioning features and/or which already have partly overlapping inflectional markers. Thus in Latin case-number paradigms there was affix replacement between the first and fifth declensions, both of which contained predominantly feminine nouns and had stems ending in long vowels; between the second and fourth declensions, which contained mainly masculine nouns, and whose nominative and accusative singular markers were both *-us* and *-um* respectively; or between the 3A and 3B declensions, both of which contained nouns of either masculine or feminine gender and whose nominative singular inflections were identical. What factors influence which affix will prevail in these replacements?

1. The variant which is numerically predominant, that is, which occurs with the most stems. Where the conditioning factor is a single extramorphological feature, the predominant affix will be that one which occurs with stems containing that feature. For example, I hypothesise (see 11.2) that in Arrernte the locative allomorph *-le* replaced *-nge*; *-nge* formerly occurred only after short nominal stems of the structure vcv, which were fewer in number than the longer stems that conditioned the choice of *-le*.

2. Where there are inflectional classes, the predominant allomorph is one which occurs in the class which has the greatest number of members (the stable class of Wurzel (1984) or is the allomorph which occurs in the greatest number of inflectional classes (Wurzel's super-stable marker).

3. The variant which can better maintain a distinction from the markers of other morphological categories. Thus in Arrernte *-nge*, being an allomorph of locative, was also the marker for ablative; hence the co-allomorph *-le* was better suited to maintain the distinction between locative and ablative.

4. The variant which is most convenient for phonotactic reasons. In Latin the dative/ablative suffix *-ibus* of the 3B declension replaced the *-bus* of class 3A. Since the former began with a vowel, it avoided the consonant clusters that resulted from the suffixation of *-bus* to consonant-final stems.

5. The variant which is most iconic, that is, which allows for a better diagramming of the semantic relations between categories by the formal relations between the markers of those categories. This relation of form to meaning, called constructional iconicity by Mayerthaler (1981), is generally referred to as diagrammaticity (Andersen 1980, Bybee 1985, Dressler 1985). In most of the Slavic languages the Ø suffix of the genitive plural which resulted from sound change has been replaced by overt allomorphs, predominantly *-ov*. On the other hand, in the nominative singular of masculine nouns, it is the Ø allomorph which has been consistently replacing overt variants (Greenberg 1969: 186 ff). Semantically, the nominative singular is unmarked for both number and case, and hence should ideally be coded by a zero marker, whereas the genitive plural is marked for both categories and should accordingly have an overt exponent. Other allomorph replacements in the Russian noun declension system have involved the generalisation of shorter suffixes in the dative and instrumental singular and longer suffixes in the instrumental plural, resulting in a situation where the semantically marked plural forms are each one phoneme longer than the corresponding singular suffixes—a more diagrammatic construction (Andersen 1980: 39 f). This is illustrated in Table 9-9.

6. The one that is the most congruent with major structural properties of the morphological system at the time (for system congruency see Wurzel 1984). One can interpret in these terms a lovely example adduced by Watkins (1985: xiii) as an illustration of the comparative method. For the Indo-European term for 'daughter-in-law',

TABLE 9-9
Number of segments in Russian case-number suffixes
(based on Andersen 1980: 40)

	Middle Russian	Modern Russian
Sg Dat	1/3	1
Pl Dat	2	2
Sg Inst	2/3	2
Pl Inst	1/2/3	3

the comparison of cognates in several languages yields two different prehistoric forms, *snusós* and *snusá:*, each supported by three languages. The earliest form must have been *snusós*, because a language-particular transfer of a feminine noun to the -*a:* class, which came to be the feminine class par excellence, is easy to motivate. The transfer makes this word more system-congruous, whereas *snusós* was anomalous in a class which included predominantly masculine nouns.

In trying to do reconstruction involving stem-affix combinations, it is important to realise that the attested combinations may be the result of various changes. Where affixes are well suited to their function in terms of syntagmatic separability, paradigmatic distinctiveness, and diagrammaticity, this situation may not be original but may be the result of therapeutic changes in the direction of increased morphotactic transparency, morphosemantic transparency, and diagrammaticity, respectively. Furthermore, where there are inflectional classes, one must not forget that it is normal for the dominant classes to exert constant influence on their complementary classes— in terms of affecting the form of affixes (see the discussion of changes in inflectional affixes in 4.1) and replacing affixes, and attracting lexemes into their own class (Wurzel 1984). But the dominance of particular classes, and their relation to other classes, is also subject to change through time as a result of factors outside morphology (in particular, phonological change). Consequently many lexemes that are found in a particular dominant (or formerly dominant) class will not be original members of this class, but will be there because of transfers. In comparisons between languages, therefore, not a great deal of reliance should be put on agreements in dominant class membership; the inflectional pattern can more reliably be reconstructed if the cognate lexemes belong to irregular or minor inflectional classes in their respective languages. If members of a cognate set belong to dominant inflectional classes in some languages and minor classes in others, more weight should be given to the latter, since they are less likely to be the result of language-particular normalisations. A kind of morphological internal reconstruction can then be applied to the forms that lack comparative support: By comparing the inflectional classes among themselves it may be possible to posit language-internal affix replacements or reformations and class transfers of lexemes that will account for the morphological facts that are not inherited (see 11.1 for application). Sometimes the irregular inflectional pattern of a few lexical items is the only remaining evidence of the presence of former inflectional classes in a language. Thus English *ox* with its isolated plural *oxen*, or German *Käse* 'cheese' with its unique case pattern—Genitive -*es*, Plural -*e*—(Wurzel 1989: 123) are remnants of once larger inflectional classes. One might posit that there were formerly other members of these classes, but it would be impossible to know without comparative evidence which lexemes belonged to these classes.

5 CHANGE IN PLACE OF BOUNDARY

A whole class of morphological changes consists in a change in the external dimensions of a morph, as one of the boundaries of a morph is shifted. (We are not discussing here the effects of phonological changes on the dimensions of a morph.) If the boundary is shifted outward, the new morph is bigger than the old and includes phonic material that was formerly part of another morph. If the boundary is shifted inward the new morph is smaller than the old, and material that was formerly part of the morph now belongs to another morph, or constitutes a morph of its own.

The mechanism that effects boundary change is reanalysis. The motivation for reanalysis is that an alternative analysis becomes possible and more plausible to speakers for various reasons. These may involve ambiguity or universal considerations of iconicity, etc. The possibility of the new analysis may depend on changes having occurred elsewhere in the system. For example, sound changes may have affected the relevant morphs, the meaning of the morph in other combinations may have changed, or the morph may have disappeared from other environments.

5.1   Loss of Morpheme Boundary

A morpheme boundary may be lost or erased. This results in the absorption of a morph into another inflectional, derivational, or lexical morph. Viewed differently, there is fusion between a morph and (a part of) another morph. Schematically,

abcd + efgh $\Rightarrow$ abcdefgh
abcd + ef + gh $\Rightarrow$ abcd + efgh

Boundary loss takes place by means of a reanalysis, motivated by the obscurity or the ambiguity of the boundary. A morpheme boundary may become **obscure** when there is no longer any motivation for viewing the material on each side of it as belonging to separate meaning-bearing elements. The position of the boundary becomes **ambiguous** when there is a competing analysis which appears more plausible to speakers. The loss of motivation of compounds and their reinterpretation as monomorphemic is familiar from the history of English (for example, *shepherd* is no longer analysable as 'sheep-herder'). Likewise numerous derived words have been reanalysed as monomorphemic (e.g. *filth* is no longer 'foul-th').

An example of the fusion of two derivational morphs resulting from ambiguity comes from Hittite (for a fuller discussion see Koch [1973]1977, chap. 1) Here -*n*-was originally an infix inserted before the final -*u*- of an adjective stem to derive a factitive verbal stem. Where the *u*-stem adjective was itself derived by suffixation from an intransitive verb stem, the transitive verb stem in -*nu*- was ambiguous in its derivation: Instead of being a derivative by infixation of -*n*- from the adjective, it could be viewed as derived directly from the intransitive verb stem by the addition of a unitary suffix -*nu*. The evidence for the new analysis comes from the fact that many new transitive verbs in -*nu*- were formed from intransitive verbs (and eventually even some transitive verbs) which did not provide adjectival derivatives in *u*-. Here the boundary between *n* and *u* was erased, and the infixed morpheme -*n*- fused with the final *u*- of an adjective stem into a new causative suffix. Schematically,

abcd + e + f $\Rightarrow$ abcd + ef.

A form like *huesnu*- changed in interpretation from Adjective-FACTITIVE ('make alive') to Verb-CAUSATIVE ('make live'), as illustrated in Table 9-10.

One subtype of boundary elimination occurs when a bimorphic sequence that realises an unmarked inflectional property (which universally tends to have zero expression) is reanalysed as a single morph in combination with a zero inflectional morph. Schematically,

abcd + ef $\Rightarrow$ abcdef + $\emptyset$

Several examples of this kind of change are given below (see 7.4).

The reconstruction method required for boundary loss changes consists of comparing **part of a morph** with a cognate found elsewhere in the same or a related language, finding a plausible source for the remainder (noncognate part) of the morph, and motivating the reanalysis which leads to the loss of the boundary.

5.2   Creation of Morpheme Boundary

A morpheme boundary may be created or inserted where none existed before. In the process part of a morph is split off from the rest and absorbed into another morph or comes to constitute by itself another morph. The original morph is thus diminished in its dimensions. In some instances the whole of an affix comes from a part of a lexical morph. Schematically,

abcdef $\Rightarrow$ abcd + ef.

In the history of erstwhile *s*-stem neuter nouns in German of the type *Kalb*, 'calf', plural *Kälb+er*, sound change involving the loss of final syllables led to a reanalysis

TABLE 9-10
Hittite reanalysis of -*n-u* as -*nu*

	Itr. verb	Adjective	Tr. verb
Original pattern		tep-u- 'little'	$\Rightarrow$ tep-n-u- 'diminish'
Ambiguous	(hues- 'live' $\Rightarrow$)	hues-u- 'alive'	$\Rightarrow$ hues-n-u- 'keep alive'
	hues- 'live'	(hues-u- 'alive')	$\Rightarrow$ hues-nu- 'keep alive'
New pattern	war- 'burn' (itr)		$\Rightarrow$ war-nu- 'burn' (tr)

TABLE 9-11
German *ir*-plural (here P stands for a segmental phoneme)

	Earlier analysis	Result of sound changes	Later analysis
Sg Nom/Acc	*PPPPes	> PPPP	PPPP
Pl Nom/Acc	*PPPPes-a	> PPPPir	PPPP-ir

whereby the final *es > ir > er* of the stem came to be interpreted as the marker of the plural (Lehmann 1992: 225, discussion Jeffers & Lehiste 1979: 64 f). This is represented schematically in Table 9-11.

The reanalysis was favoured by a universal preference for iconic marking. The earlier analysis after the sound changes would have required a subtractive process to mark the singular and zero to mark the plural. After the reanalysis the singular is marked by nothing (that is, it is identical to the stem) and the plural is marked additively, by the suffixation of *-ir*. The English plural *-en* in *oxen* has a similar origin.

In some instances a boundary is inserted because part of a morph is plausibly identified with another morph. Thus English *pea*, *riddle*, *cherry* all result from a "back-formation" whereby an earlier final *s* was analysed as the Plural suffix (since many nouns formed their plural in *-s*). As a result of the boundary insertion *pease > pea-s*, the lexical morph was shortened from *pease* to just *pea* (Lehmann 1992: 223).

Reconstruction in cases of boundary insertion requires the comparison of two adjacent morphs to a single morph elsewhere, or the identification of a morph with a part of a morph elsewhere. Thus the English plural form *ox-en* can be compared to Sanskrit *ukṣan-* a unitary lexical morph meaning 'bull'.

5.3 Shift of Boundary

This change involves the simultaneous loss of a boundary in one place and insertion of a boundary in another place. Boundary shift can apply to morpheme boundaries or word boundaries. (For exemplification from Indo-European languages, see Dunkel 1987)

A morpheme boundary may be shifted inward into a morph. Part of the morph is thereby shed and absorbed into the adjacent morph or comes to constitute a separate morph. The dimensions of the first morph are thereby diminished, while those of its neighbour are increased. Where the shift is between a lexical and an affixal morph, part of the lexical morph is absorbed into an affix, part of the new affix historically "comes from" a lexical morph (or class of lexical morphs). Schematically,

abcd + ef ⇒ abc + **d**ef

This process, when it results in longer suffixes, has been called "suffix accretion" or "suffix clipping" (Lehmann 1992: 224). Textbook examples are English *aethel-ing* vs. *dar-ling*, French *argent-ier* 'silversmith' versus *bijou-tier* 'jeweler'.

Word boundaries may also be shifted, as a result of reanalysis of the position of a word boundary in an ambiguous phrase. When boundaries are shifted inward, part of a lexical morpheme is lost to a separate word. When they are shifted outward, (part of) a separate word is absorbed into a morpheme. Classic examples from the history of English are, for the former process, *apron* (cf. *napery, napkin*), *auger, adder* (cf. German *Natter*) (Anttila 1989: 94), and for the latter process, *newt, nickname, nuncle < uncle* (Anttila 1989: 93). The ambiguous context was the preceding indefinite article, *a/an*, and in the case of *uncle*, the possessive adjective *my/mine*.

Reconstruction of boundary shifts involves comparing a lengthened morph to a shorter cognate, or a shortened morph to a longer cognate, and finding a likely source for extra material (in part of another morph). This means proposing a combination of morphs where a reanalysis could have taken place and, ideally, a motivation for the reanalysis.

6 CHANGE IN CONTENT/MEANING/FUNCTION OF MORPHEME

Morphemes may change in their semantic content or function. This is in principle a kind of semantic change. Several subtypes can be distinguished.

6.1 Lexical ⇒ Grammatical Meaning (Grammaticalisation)

The change from a lexical to a (more abstract) grammatical meaning is called grammaticisation or **grammaticalisation**. After some early discussion by Meillet (1912), this topic has received considerable attention recently (see Heine & Reh 1984; Traugott & Heine 1991; Hopper & Traugott 1993). Many typical grammaticalisation patterns, however, are not morphological changes, since they only involve changes in independent words, for example, body part > adposition, noun > classifier, verb > auxiliary, temporal adverb > tense marker. The term morphological change can only be applied to changes that produce or affect forms that are bound, that is, clitics and affixes. Often the shift to bound status accompanies the grammaticalisation of a lexical morph. Examples of grammaticalisation of bound morphs are found in the revaluing of members of lexical compounds as derivational affixes; for example, English *-shape > -ship, -dom, -hood, -like > -ly* (Lehmann 1992:224).

6.2 Regrammaticalisation

The semantic content of a morpheme may shift from one grammatical meaning to another grammatical meaning. This change can be called **regrammaticalisation** (cf. Jeffers & Lehiste 1979: 64 "regrammatization"—but their example is of grammaticalisation). The new meaning may be more abstract than the old. A nonmorphological example is the frequent shift from a deictic meaning ('that') to a definite meaning ('the'). A content shift may take place between different properties in the same category (to use the terminology of Matthews 1991): for example locative > allative case; plural > nonsingular number. A nonmorphological example is the shift of the Western Arrernte pronoun *nweke* from 1 pl gen > 1 sg gen (see 11.6). Alternatively, a grammatical meaning may shift to one in a different category, for example, perfect

Aspect > past tense; potential mood > future tense; dative case > purposive subordination.

There may be a shift from a productive derivational to an inflectional meaning (Panagl 1987), for example, collective > plural (Armenian, Sogdian), participle to tense, case form of a verbal noun to infinitive.

Shifts from inflectional to derivational meanings are hard to illustrate. According to L. Hercus (personal communication), the Wangkangurru (Australia) suffix -*li* has shifted from ergative case to an adverbialising function.

Syncretism is a particular kind of morphological change that involves "the functional merging of paradigmatic categories" (Meiser 1992: 186), that is, the loss of a contrast between grammatical meanings. This happens when the meaning of one morpheme is extended to cover that of another morpheme without the original meaning receiving a new expression. The morpheme that is thus made redundant may disappear, survive only in relic constructions, or persist as an allomorph of its replacement in free variation or conditioned by some new factor.

Certain dialects of Arrernte apparently syncretised the inclusive and exclusive meanings of first person nonsingular pronouns. In some dialects either form could be used in either value. In Western Arrernte only the formerly exclusive forms survived, except that the former first plural inclusive genitive *nweke* shifted to denote 1st Singular Genitive.

Partial syncretism, where a paradigmatic contrast is neutralised in only part of the inflectonal system, is sometimes motivated by the rest of the inflectional system. Thus in Old High German, feminine nouns of the 'gift' class, whose singular genitive was originally identical to the nominative and accusative, was restructured to become identical to the dative, following the dominant pattern of the 'favour' class, where genitive and dative were identical but different from nominative and accusative (Wurzel 1989: 76). This is illustrated in Table 9-12.

6.3   Degrammaticalisation

The loss of grammatical meaning, where a morph changes from a meaning-bearing unit to a contentless "empty morph", may be called **degrammaticalisation**. In English verbs such as *forget* and *forgive*, the element *for-* has lost any derivational meaning it once had, although many linguists would still want to say the verbs are bimorphemic. In Kaytetye all demonstratives end in an element -*arte*, which has no apparent meaning. Although it might have once indicated definiteness it can no longer

TABLE 9-12
Old High German feminine nouns

	'favour'	'tongue'	'gift' I	'gift' II
Sg Nom	anst	zung-a	geb-a	geb-a
Sg Acc	anst	zung-u:n	geb-a	geb-a
Sg Gem	enst-i	zung-u:n	geb-a	geb-**u**
Sg Dat	enst-i	zung-u:n	geb-u	geb-u

be said to have that function, since it also occurs now on interrogative indefinite pronouns (*want-arte* 'what') and some quantifiers (*atherr-arte* 'two'). Any grammatical meaning it once had has been bleached; nevertheless it must still be recognised as a separate morph, because the remainder of the word is analysable (e.g. *wante-l-arte* 'what-ERGATIVE-arte'). Reconstruction of degrammaticalisation requires the identification of the semantically bleached morph with a cognate that has actual content.

7 CHANGE IN MORPHOSYNTACTIC STATUS OF MORPHEME

A morph may change with respect to its status as a formal unit. That is, it may become a different kind of morph. It may change with respect to its independence, from free word to bound clitic, from clitic to affix, or from affix to simply a part of another morph. (The change in status from a free lexical morpheme to a free grammatical morpheme with no cliticisation is grammaticalisation; this is syntactic but not morphological change.)

7.1   Free Word Becomes Bound Word

A free word can become bound, becoming either a clitic or a lexical component.

Cliticisation is the change from an independent word to a phonologically bound word (a clitic). This status change typically occurs in conjunction with the content change of grammaticalisation. If, however, clitics are not considered part of morphology, this is only syntactic change and not morphological change.

Reconstruction of cliticisation involves identifying a clitic with a full word found elsewhere. For example, in Kaytetye an emphatic clitic =*mpele* may occur after imperative verbs (and elsewhere). This can be compared to the full word (*a*)*mpelarte* 'thus, like that'. The forms are identical except for the optional initial vowel and the -*arte* suffix that is included on most demonstratives. One can plausibly assume that =*mpele* originated as a cliticised form of 'thus' before the -*arte* suffix became fixed on (*a*)*mpelarte*.

Another change where an independent word becomes bound occurs in the formation of lexical compounds. (To accommodate for languages that have base form inflection instead of word inflection (see Wurzel 1984 for this typological distinction), it is more accurate to describe this change in terms of lexemes than independent words.) This does not involve concurrent grammaticalisation, but may confine the lexical morph (in this combination) to a more restrictive semantic interpretation. It is a kind of lexical change, since it involves the creation of new lexical items. But compounding is a part of word-formation, and if all word-formation is considered to be included within morphology, it is also morphological change.

Reconstruction involves identifying a component morph of a compound with an independent word. For example, in the Arandic languages edible grubs are typically named for the kind of tree or woody plant they inhabit. Thus a witchetty grub (*a*)*tnyem-ayte* (> (*a*)*tnyem-atye* in some dialects of Arrernte) is hosted in a witchetty bush (*a*)*tnyeme*. All grub terms consist of *X-ayte* (or *X-atye*), where X is usually the name of the host tree or shrub. We can therefore isolate a compounding morph -*ayte* 'grub'. The free form of 'grub' however is -*tyape* in Arrernte and *kayte* in Kaytetye. Languages further afield have a cognate *parti* 'grub', which by normal sound changes would have evolved into Arandic *ayte. We posit that this was the Proto-Arandic for 'grub', that it was compounded in this form with various tree names, that in Kaytetye the free form acquired an unetymological initial *k* (for reasons that remain uncertain), and that in Arrernte the free form was replaced by *tyape*, leaving -*ayte* as a "cranberry morph".

7.2   Bound Morpheme Becomes Affix (Affixisation)

A bound morph may become an affix. I shall call this process **affixisation**. (I assume that free words do not directly become affixes, but first go through a stage of being bound morphs.) There are two ways this may come about. A clitic, especially if it has already been grammaticalised, may evolve into a (typically inflectional) affix, or a lexical component in a compound may become reinterpreted as an affix.

Reconstructing the development of an inflectional affix from a clitic involves comparing an affix with a clitic or earlier independent word and positing the processes and motivation for cliticisation and subsequent affixisation. For example in Kaytetye the nominal dual number suffix -*therre*, as in *atye-le-therr-arte* 'this-ERGATIVE-DUAL-arte' is obviously relatable to *atherre*- in the independent word *atherr-arte* 'two'. One can infer that the word for 'two' was first encliticised after nominals then interpreted as a dual suffix. (See 11.7 for the reconstruction of person-marking affixes on Arandic kin nouns as affixised clitic forms of personal pronouns.)

A clitic that develops into an affix may itself have complex morphemic status. Thus Diyari and some other Karnic languages developed suffixes that mark a combination of gender, number, and case out of earlier third person pronouns. Similarly Polish developed a set of person-number markers on the verb out of an earlier 'be' auxiliary paradigm (Andersen 1987).

The second kind of affixisation takes place when a component morph of a lexical compound (7.1) comes to be analysed as a (typically derivational) affix. This happened in English with the suffixes -*shape*, -*like*, -*man* (accompanied by reduction in stress, and other phonological changes), -*do:m*, -*ha:d* (Lehmann 1992: 224).

Reconstruction involves comparing an affix with a bound or even free lexical morph of related form and meaning and positing plausible paths of semantic and morphological change. For example the English affix -*ly* can be compared both to the compounding -*like* and the free *like*.

7.3   Phrasal Becomes Affixal

We need to recognise a separate kind of morphological change whereby a phrase comes to be interpreted as a single word, without one of the words necessarily going through a clitic stage. This happens with words which end up being simple lexical items, for example, English *maybe* and its French counterpart *peut-être*, Latin *quam vi:s* 'as you wish' > *quamvis* 'however' (Anttila 1989: 356). Where a phrasal construction expresses a grammatical category or a meaning which grammaticalises to a morphosyntactic category the result may be a single word containing an affix. For example the imperfective aspect in (most) Kaytetye intransitive verbs is expressed by a suffix *-rrane*, for example, *ake-rrane-* 'cry-ing'. In origin this was probably a phrase consisting of a dependent form of the verb, *ake-rre* 'cry-ing' followed by a quasi-auxiliary verb *ane-* 'be, sit'. With fusion into a single word the whole form was reanalysed semantically as 'cry-IMPFV' and formally as *ake-rrane* with preservation of the integrity of the root morpheme but loss of the word boundary.

7.4 Absorption

An affix may cease to be interpreted as a separate morph and be reanalysed as merely a part of another (typically lexical) morph. The morph is absorbed into another morph and loses its morphic status altogether. This proceeds by means of boundary deletion, which has been discussed in 5.1. This kind of change in status of a morph has been called *demorphologization* by Hopper: "When a morpheme loses its grammatical-semantic contribution to a word, but retains some remnant of its original form, and thus becomes an indistinguishable part of a word's phonological construction, I shall speak of the resulting phonological material as *morphological residue*, and of the process itself as *demorphologization*" (Hopper 1990:-154).

Reconstruction involves identifying part of a morph as morphological residue, comparing it with a morph elsewhere that has full content, and proposing a plausible process whereby it lost its independence. For example Arrernte *(a)rrakerte* 'mouth' contains the material *akerte* which is formally identical to the HAVING suffix in the same language, while the remainder *(a)rr-* can be equated with Kaytetye *arre* 'mouth'. We can posit that in Arrernte as well 'mouth' was earlier *arre* but that the HAVING suffix *-akerte* was absorbed into the lexeme (the deletion of *e* before another vowel is regular). A parallel development is seen in Kaytetye *erlpe* vs. Arrernte *irlpakerte* 'ear'.

This absorption can occur with inflectional as well as derivational affixes. An example of the absorption of an inflectional affix is Kaytetye 'father', *arlweye*, where *-ye* in other kin terms is the marker of first person singular possessor, but has become a part of the lexeme in 'father' through reanalysis of 'my father' as just 'father'. Cognates suggest that the original form of 'father' was **kurla,* which by regular sound changes would have become Kaytetye *arlwe-*.

8 RE-ORDERING OF MORPHEMES

Although it is generally recognised that the order of elements is more rigid within a word than between words, it is nevertheless necessary to accept the possibility that morphemes can be reordered. In the first place, reordering may take place within sequences of clitics, and these clitics may later be reinterpreted as affixes. Secondly, there are documented instances (though relatively rare) of the the reordering of affixes within words. When functional change or morphosyntactic status change leads to affix sequences that are not congruent with preexisting patterns in the language and/or not iconic of the semantic relations among these affixes and their lexical host

TABLE 9-13
**Georgian and Latin reordering of case inflections. The new Latin stem *ips-* has been
extended from the nominative singular masculine.**

	Georgian 'anything'	Latin 'himself'
original	ra-s-me 'what-DAT-INDEF'	eum-pse 'he:ACC-self'
hybrid	ra-s-me-s 'what-DAT-INDEF-DAT'	eum-ps-um 'he:ACC-self-ACC'
final	ra-me-s 'what-INDEF-DAT'	ips-um 'himself-ACC'

(according to the relevance principle of Bybee 1985: 13 ff), the affixes may be reordered. It is also possible that in situations of bilingualism affix sequences in one language are adjusted to those of another language; this may be responsible for the dramatic congruence between Tlingit and Athapaskan-Eyak verbal prefix position classes (Thomason 1980). Haspelmath (1993) gives examples of the reordering of inflections to appear outside erstwhile clitics which have grammaticalised to postfixes. Table 9-13 indicates the progression whereby the case inflection occurs first inside the indefiniteness marker, then pleonastically on both sides of it, and finally at the external border of the word.

Examples of the reordering of case and possessive markers can be found in the Uralic languages (Comrie 1980b). Here the inherited order appears to be case-possessive, reflecting the more recent creation of possessive suffixes from clitic pronouns. In a number of northern languages, when new case suffixes arise from postpositions, the resulting order possessive-case is inverted under the structural pressure of the pattern in preexisting cases, for example, in Kil'din Lappish the new abessive case, marked by a suffix *-xa / -xɛn*, is in the process of being reordered from pattern (a) to pattern (b) in Table 9-14 (Comrie 1980b: 83).

In Hungarian, however, where most of the original cases have been replaced by new cases deriving from postpositions (and ultimately locational nouns): "[T]he new order possessive-case influenced the (few remaining) instances of the old order case-possessive (other than in frozen forms like the conjugated postpositions) to give the order possessive-case throughout (Comrie 1980b:83–4).

In the other Ugric languages the order possessive-case is found, although it cannot be attributed to the influence of a pattern found in new cases. Here we may speculate that motivation for the change to possessive-case order was either the universal principle of iconicity or perhaps influence from the Turkic languages, which prevailingly have this order (Comrie 1981: 75).

Where a new inflectional affix develops from an erstwhile derivational affix, a re-

TABLE 9-14
**Kil'din Lappish, reordering of possession
and case**

(a)	(b)
puaz-an-xa	*puaz-xɛn-an*
reindeer-my-without	reindeer-without-my

TABLE 9-15
Chukchi desiderative > future

(a) Desiderative	(b) Future
re-viri-ŋə-rk-ət	*re-viri-rkəni-ŋ-ət*
DES-descend-DES-CNT-3PL	FUT-descend-CNT-FUT-3PL
'they want to descend'	'they will descend'

ordering adjustment may likewise take place. Comrie (1985: 89 ff) shows that when in Chukchi a desiderative derivation, marked by both a prefix *re-* and suffix *-ŋ*, developed into a future tense inflection, the suffix *-ŋ* was repositioned outside of the continuous aspect marker *-rk(ən)*. The resulting forms conform to typological expectations of inflection outside (that is, further from the verb root than) derivation and tense outside aspect, both of which are explained by Bybee's principle of relevance. Compare the forms in Table 9-15.

Reconstuction of order changes requires an identification of morphs with elements that are found in a position other than the synchronically attested position, the positing of earlier order patterns, and a plausible scenario for reordering. Since reordering changes may produce a better fit between form and meaning, earlier orders may not be detectable unless relics survive (such as Hungarian *bennem* 'in me' < *bele-ne-m* 'inside-LOC-1SG', preserving the earlier order case-possessive (Comrie 1980a: 94). On the other hand, morphological patterns that are not iconic of their semantic relations may be explicable as young forms that have not yet been adjusted to their semantics and may thus be able to provide clues to their etymological sources. An example of reconstruction involving reordering is provided in 11.7.

In the preceding discussion we have assumed, with Bybee (1985), that the following (and their mirror images) are the preferred orders in language:

Lexical stem-dervational affixes-inflectional affixes

Verb stem-aspect-tense-person

Noun stem- number-possessor person/number-case

9 DOUBLING OF MORPHEMES

Another minor kind of morphological change is the doubling of morphological markers. This involves the addition of a productive affix onto the periphery of a word to make the analysis of the word more transparent, and typically occurs when the existing marker is obscure. Examples are:

English 'child-PLURAL' childer > childr-en
Vulgar Latin 'be:INFINITIVE' esse > esse-re
colloquial Spanish 'wash-2:SG:PAST' lava-ste > lava-ste-s

For a discussion of these examples and for further references, see Haspelmath (1993:297–8).

Reconstruction requires the identification of two different morphs in a word with (earlier) markers of the same inflectional or derivational meaning, and the positing of a plausible motivation and mechanism for the remarking. An example of reconstruction involving double marking in the context of reordering is given in 11.7.

10 GENERALISATIONS ON MORPHOLOGICAL CHANGE

Certain general and unidirectional developmental tendencies in morphological change can be described. Following Ferguson's (1990) terminology with respect to phonological change, I shall call these **pathways**. Hopper uses the term **trajectory** (Hopper 1990: 153). A pathway that leads from phonetics to morphology has already been mentioned (see 5.3). A different pathway leads into morphology from the lexicon. This long-range tendency can be described as a "diachronic trajectory for morphemes, which might start out as full words, become clitics and then affixes, and finally disappear from the scene" (Hopper 1990: 153). There are two variants of this pathway, one that leads through more grammatical territory, and one which remains in the lexical domain. In the first, an independent lexical word in certain contexts becomes a grammatical clitic and further develops into an inflectional affix, and finally disappears, perhaps being absorbed into a lexical stem. The other route involves the development from free lexemes through lexical components to derivational affixes and finally to disappearance into another morph. These might be summarised as displayed on Table 9-16. The columns of Table 9-17 give three examples of the former development and one of the latter.

Several kinds of change—according to the typology given above—may co-occur. Content change involving loss of lexical meaning—desemanticisation/grammaticalisation— is typically accompanied by reduction in the independence of the morph. Cliticisation involves loss of independent word stress; affixisation involves restriction of classes of lexemes with which a morph co-occurs. Concomitant with this loss of independence is often phonological change as well; the morph may be reduced in size through the loss of phoneme segments, shortening and neutralisation of vowels, etc. The absorption of one morph into another (typically lexical) morph involves simultaneously loss of independent status of the morph, erasure of a boundary, and reanalysis of word forms. All of the changes in morphic content, morphosyntactic status, and boundary position are effected by processes of reanalysis. Reconstruction of where these kinds of changes have taken place always requires comparisons that allow the linguist to identify the later morphic bits with earlier morphs of different content, boundaries and/or morphosyntactic status and to formulate of plausible scenarios of reanalysis. Successful reconstruction depends not only on the existence of "cognate"

TABLE 9-16
Pathways from lexicon to morphology

Lexeme	> grammatical clitic	> inflectional affix	> part of lexical morph
Lexeme	> lexical component	> derivational affix	> part of lexical morph

TABLE 9-17
Examples of morphological pathways

verb	demonstrative pronoun	body part noun	wi:f, mann
auxiliary verb (clitic)	anaphoric pronoun	adposition	wif#man
tense affix*	definite article/specific article[†]	case affix	wif+man
	class marker		woman
e.g. Romance future			

*Rimat 1987: 153 ff.
[†]Greenberg 1978; Uttan 1978

morphs elsewhere in the language or in related languages, but also on the linguist's understanding of what kinds of plausible changes can be expected in the particular domain of morphology at issue. In other words, knowing what to compare depends on knowing what kinds of morphological change are possible, typical, and expected.

To what extent do types of morphological change depend on the predominant morphological typology of the language? I believe it is premature to try to answer this question. A few things can be said, however. None of these changes will be relevant to languages that lack morphology. Nevertheless many so-called isolating langues have plenty of lexical compounds, some of which involve morphophonemic alternations (sometimes under the guise of unmotivated "tone sandhi"). Changes such as compound formation, boundary deletion, and perhaps even lexical component to derivational affixisation may be relevant, as well as the creation of new allomorphs. Languages that lack inflectional classes (noun declensions and verb conjugations) will not have much redistribution of affix allomorphs.

11 CASE STUDIES

In this section I provide a series of case studies of morphological reconstruction.

11.1 Walmajarri Verb Conjugations

This case study illustrates an approach to the reconstruction of changes involving inflectional classes. The data, taken from Hudson (1978), is from Walmajarri, a language of the Ngumpin subgroup of the Pama-Nyungan language family of Australia. Table 9-18 shows the inflectional system of the verb, illustrated with the paradigms of sample verbs. Here NOM indicates a nominal or gerund form of the verb used in dependent clauses; REP is a stem that forms a Repetitive Aspect which is further inflected for tense. Most of the forms have reliable cognates in the other Ngumpin languages and hence are probably inherited. CUST, the customary tense, unlike the other categories, appears to have been created within Walmajarri. The affixes of the 'go' and 'carry' classes appear to be built on the repetitive stem by the suffixation of a consonant *ny*. The customary of the 'fall' class could then have been taken over from the 'carry' class, with which it shares its past suffix. The 'cook' and 'eat' classes share a form -*lany*, which is not built on any other form in the paradigm. But certain other

TABLE 9-18
Walmajarri verb conjugations

	'carry'	'fall'	'cook'	'eat'	'leave'	'go'
NOM	ka-ngu	wanti-nyu	kampa-rnu	nga-rnu	wanyja-nu	ya-nu
REP	ka-nga-	wanti-nya-	kampa-rna-	nga-rna-	wanyja-na-	ya-na-
PAST	ka-nya	wanti-nya	kampa-rni	nga-rni	wanyja-ni	ya-ni
CUST	ka-ngany	wanti-ngany	kampa-lany	nga-lany	wanyja-rralany	ya-nany
IMPV	ka-ngka	wanti-Ø	kampa-Ø	nga-nyja	wanyja-rra	ya-nta
FUT	ka-ngku	wanti-wu	kampa-wu	nga-lku	wanyja-rrku	ya-nku

languages in the subgroup, Bilinara and Mudbura, do have a suffix -*la* in the 'eat' class with a meaning similar to the Walmajarri customary. It is reasonable to suggest that the suffix -*lany* was formed from this -*la* suffix in the 'eat' class and was extended to the 'cook' class by virtue of the fact that these two classes share three other inflections. Finally the suffix-*rralany* of the 'leave' class remains to be explained. It appears to contain the -*lany* of the 'eat' and 'cook' classes added to the -*rra* of its own Imperative. But there are otherwise no common inflections between that class and the latter which would motivate a spread of the affix between the classes. Nevertheless when one realises that the 'cook' class is by far the largest verbal class in the language, it makes sense to see the partial source of -*rralany* in this dominant class. The presumed development of the customary is summarised in Table 9-19. The suffixes -*ngany*, -*nany*, and -*lany* were formed first, in the classes of 'carry', 'go', and 'eat' respectively (these are in boldface). Then -*ngany* was extended from the 'carry' to the 'fall' class, and -*lany* from the 'eat' to the 'cook' class, because these pairs of classes shared other inflections. This extension is shown by a solid line containing an arrowhead. Finally, a suffix -*rralany* was created for the 'leave' class by adding the -*lany* from the dominant 'cook' class to the -*rra* inflection of the imperative; the influence of the 'leave' class is indicated by a line containing an arrowhead.

Note that we have used a kind of internal reconstruction to undo the presumed morphological changes that have occurred within Walmajarri. We have applied this internal reconstruction to forms which remain unexplained after (here, implicitly) applying comparative reconstruction. The internal reconstruction has been of a morphological kind; we have not resorted to phonological internal reconstruction. This approach is radically different from the methods applied to the same data by Dixon (1980: 385 ff), who posits earlier forms consisting of root plus conjugation-marking consonant plus inflectional suffix, which undergo only changes of a phonological na-

TABLE 9-19
Development of customary inflections in Walmajarri

	'carry'		'fall'	'eat'		'cook'		'leave'	'go'
REP	nga-		nya-	rna-		rna-		na-	na
CUST	**ngany**	—>—	ngany	**lany**	—>—	lany	- -> -	rralany	**nany**
IMPV	ngka		Ø	nyja		Ø		rra	nta

ture. For a criticism of this methodology, see Alpher (1990). In fact, one of the problems in reconstruction is to know whether a phonological or a morphological solution is to be preferred for a particular problem. There is no universally valid answer; it depends on which solution is more plausible overall.

11.2   Locative Case Suffixes in Arandic

The Arandic languages do not fully agree in their locative case suffixes. We find the forms given on Table 9-20. Here c stands for a consonant or consonant cluster, and v indicates a vowel. The choice of allomorph in Kaytetye is determined partially by the syntactic category of the stem (whether demonstrative or not) and is partially phonologically conditioned—determined by the phonotactic shape of the (nondemonstrative) stem. The phonologically conditioned allomorph, however, is not phonologically motivated, since there is no commonality between the phonemes of the suffix and those of the stem. The allomorphy does not appear to be the result of sound change in the recent past.

Comparing the Kaytetye and Arrernte allomorphs, we see that both languages have an exact match in -le, which must therefore be reconstructed for Proto-Arandic. But we need to determine whether the protosystem had a single allomorph and Kaytetye has then innovated by introducing another allomorph -nge, or whether Proto-Arandic had an allomorphic distribution like Kaytetye and Arrernte has eliminated the variant -nge. Taking the first alternative, it is difficult to imagine why Kaytetye would introduce an allomorph of totally different phonological shape from -le and restrict it to occurring after stems of the shape vcv. On the other hand, the elimination of allomorphic alternation is a common type of morphological change, and may be thought of as being especially favoured by the unnatural conditioning of the distribution. We conclude that it is more plausible that Kaytetye has preserved the earlier system and that Arrernte has innovated by eliminating the allomorph -nge and generalising the allomorph -le. This reconstruction can thus be considered an application of Hetzron's principle that the more heterogeneous pattern is the more archaic one. (Comparison with more distantly related languages, such as Warlpiri, confirms the reconstruction of two allomorphs.)

11.3   Ablative Case Suffixes in Arandic

Sample Ablative suffixes are given in Table 9-21. Here the dialects of Arrernte are not consistent. Alyawarre shares -theye with Kaytetye. Here the question is whether Eastern and Western Arrernte have innovated by replacing an original -theye with -nge, or whether Kaytetye and Alyawarre have innovated. (Since the latter two are

TABLE 9-20
Arandic locative case allomorphs

Kaytetye	-nge after stems in vcv
	-le after stems in (. . .)cvcv and all demonstrative stems
Arrernte	-le after all stems

TABLE 9-21
Arandic ablative case suffixes

Western Arrernte, Eastern Arrernte	-nge
Alyawarre	-theye
Kaytetye	-theye

adjacent, it is possible that only one of them may have introduced *-theye* and the other borrowed it.) Here the evidence from relics in Kaytetye leads us to posit **nge* as the original ablative suffix. Certain relative spatial nominals include a syllable *nge*. 'Behind' in Kaytetye is expressed by *antenge* or *antengetheye*, which explicitly includes the productive ablative suffix *-theye*. The actual inclusion of the ablative marker suggests that it is natural for a term of this meaning to occur with the ablative, and hence confirms as plausible the inference that the inherited ablative suffix *-nge* was absorbed into the stem. (For a parallel, cf. Latin *a: tergo:* 'behind', lit. 'from behind'). We therefore posit a diachronic development as shown in Table 9-22.

While this development is plausible, it is not necessary, especially in the absence of an etymology for the stem of *ante(nge)*. The *-nge* might equally well, from a sound-change perspective, continue an earlier locative suffix, since the stem was disyllabic and *-nge* would therefore have been the appropriate allomorph of the locative. Several other forms, however, point to the ablative. Beside *kwene* 'below, inside' we find a variant *kwenenge* 'below', and beside *errwele* '(on) top, above', we find *errwelenge*. Now, in both of these the stem is of a structure that would have required the *-le* allomorph of the locative. Hence the *-nge* cannot continue an earlier locative, and we are left with the hypothesis that it is a surviving relic of the original Ablative *-*nge*.

No sure etymology has yet been found for the new ablative *-theye*. Nevertheless it is possible to suggest a motive for the replacement of the Proto-Arandic ablative suffix *-nge* in Kaytetye. The same suffix *-nge* would have served both as the marker of the ablative case and as an allomorph of the locative case. After stems of the shape CVC the suffix *-nge* would have been ambiguous between the locative and the ablative meaning. The replacement of one or the other would have been motivated by the iconic principle of morphosemantic transparency (Dressler 1985, Mayerthaler 1981), whereby one form preferably serves as the marker for just one function. In fact this polyfunctionality of *-nge* is probably to be seen as providing the motivation for the generalisation of the *-le* allomorph of the locative in Arrernte as well. Arrernte has thus solved the polyfunctionality problem by eliminating the *-nge* allomorph of the locative, whereas Kaytetye has remedied the situation by replacing the *-nge* marker of the ablative. Alyawarre has eliminated *-nge* in both functions.

TABLE 9-22
Diachronic development of Kaytetye 'behind'

I	ante-nge	*back-ABL
II	antenge	behind
III	antenge-theye	behind-ABL
IV	antengethey	behind

TABLE 9-23

Arandic third person singular pronouns

	ERG	NOM	ACC	DAT
Alyawarre	re	re	renhe	ikwere
Eastern Arrernte	re	re	renhe	ikwere
Western Arrernte	ire	ire	irenhe	ikwere
proto-Arrernte	*re	*re	*renhe	*ikwere

11.4   Arandic Third Person Singular Personal Pronouns

Table 9-23 gives the first four case forms of the 3 Sg pronoun. The ergative and nominative case forms are identical for the 3 Sg and all nonsingular personal pronouns. Other case forms are built on the dative form.

Here reconstruction is easy, since all dialects agree for each case category. (The Western Arrernte initial *ir* corresponding to *r* in the other dialects can be explained phonologically.) We may note that in the Proto-Arrernte paradigm, as in that of each dialect, the ergative and nominative case forms are identical, that the Accusative form consists of this form plus a suffix -*nhe*, and that the dative form is suppletive.

11.5   Second Person Singular Personal Pronouns

Comparing the dialects, we note for the ergative case that Aliterre *nge* does not match the other two dialects, and for the nominative case that Western Arrernte *unte* does not match the form found elsewhere. We also observe that the nonmatching ergative *nge* of Aliterre is identical with the nominative form in the same dialect, and that the nonmatching nominative *unte* of Western Arrernte is identical with the ergative form in its dialect. In other words, no case distinction is made between ergative and nominative in these two dialects, whereas there are contrasting forms in Alyawarre. Alyawarre thus has the most heterogeneous paradigm, in the sense of Hetzron, and is thus likely to reflect the original situation, if we can motivate the differences in the paradigms of the other dialects. We note that case syncretism between the ergative and the nominative is found in all dialects in the third singular and all dual and plural personal pronouns (but not in the first person singular pronoun). Hence the identity of these two case forms in the second person singular can be explained as the result of a diachronic extension of this normal (for-personal pronouns) pattern to one of the two pronouns which had an abnormal pattern. This results in an increase in sys-

TABLE 9-24

Arandic second person singular pronouns

	ERG	NOM	ACC	DAT
Alyawarre	unte	nge	ngenhe	ngkwenge
Aliterre	nge	nge	ngenhe	ngkwenge
Western Arrernte	unte	unte	ngenhe	ngkwenge

TABLE 9-25
Arandic second person singular pronouns, inherited forms only

	ERG	NOM	ACC	DAT
Alyawarre	unte	nge	ngenhe	ngkwenge
Aliterre		nge	ngenhe	ngkwenge
Western Arrernte	unte		ngenhe	ungkenge
Proto-Arrernte	*unte	*nge	*ngenhe	*ungkenge

tem congruity (Wurzel 1984). We can safely assume then that the aberrant *nge* of the ERG column and the aberrant *unte* of the NOM column represent innovations. We might therefore remove them from the table, which results in Table 9-25. Here all columns agree. Hence we can reconstruct the Proto-Arrernte forms as morphologically identical to the remaining forms. (I assume that the phonological change uCe > Cwe in the Dative is post-proto-Arrernte, i.e. occurred only dialectally.)

11.6 First Person Singular

For the first person singular pronoun (Table 9-26), we note agreement between the dialects for the ergative case, and can thus reconstruct *(a)the*. Likewise, the consistency for the nominative case justifies reconstructing *(a)yenge*. For the accusative case, however, there is no agreement. How do we account for the attested forms? In the first place, we observe that in Eastern Arrernte the accusative form is identical to that of the nominative. Since we have already concluded that the nominative form was inherited, can we find a motive for deriving the accusative form from the nominative? There is in fact a model for this pattern: With most nonpronominal nominals the nominative and the accusative have identical form. We can therefore posit that Eastern Arrernte has extended this pattern to the first person singular pronoun. Next, we note that the Western Arrernte accusative form is identical to the nominative plus *-nhe*. Can we hypothesise that the accusative was built on the nominative? Yes, since there is a pattern in Arrernte whereby nominals (including interrogatives and demonstratives) which refer to humans have an inflectional suffix *-nhe* in the accusative case. In fact the pattern is found in Western Arrernte in the third person singular pronoun, and must have been present also in the second Person, before the replacement of nominative *nge* by *unte*. We can thus plausibly assume that Western Arrernte

TABLE 9-26
Arrernte first person singular pronouns

	ERG	NOM	ACC	DAT
Alyawarre	athe	ayenge	ayenhe	atyenge
Eastern Arrernte	the	yenge	yenge	atyenge
Western Arrernte	(a)the	yenge	yengenhe	nweke
Proto-Arrernte	*(a)the	*(a)yenge		

TABLE 9-27
Western Arrernte accusative of singular personal
pronouns

	ERG	NOM	ACC
3 Sg	ire	ire	ire-nhe
2 Sg	unte	*nge	nge-nhe
1 Sg	(a)the	yenge	yenge-nhe

yenge-nhe was constructed from the nominative according to this pattern (see Table 9-27).

The Alyawarre accusative form also resembles the nominative; it also includes the suffix *-nhe,* but this appears to be added to a truncated form of the nominative which lacks the syllable *nge.* Here, too, we can hypothesise that the accusative form was built on the nominative. The motivation for the syllable truncation may have been to keep the same number of syllables as in the accusative forms of the second and third Person pronouns. We have now found plausible dialect-specific explanations for all the accusative forms. Therefore no protoform can be reconstructed on the basis of these data.

For the dative case, the agreement of Alyawarre and Eastern Arrernte favours the reconstruction of *x(a)tyenge.* Nevertheless, since these dialects are contiguous, it is possible that they have jointly innovated. If we compare further afield, however, it immediately becomes clear which of the forms is inherited. In Table 9-28 we add the first person singular forms of the pronoun in the closely related Lower Aranda language and the slightly more distantly related Kaytetye, (the Lower Aranda accusative form is omitted, since it could not be verified at the time of writing).

Here we see that the Alyawarre and Eastern Arrernte form have further comparative support from the other two languages. This leaves the Western Arrernte *nweke.* Now, there is an identical form elsewhere in Arrernte, but with a different meaning. In Alyawarre it occurs (extended by a suffix that is irrelevant to the argument) in the dative of the first person plural inclusive. Is a shift in meaning from first person plural inclusive to first person singular plausible? Note firstly that Western Arrernte lacks the inclusive versus exclusive distinction in first person dual and plural pronouns that is found in Alyawarre and other northeastern dialects as well as in Kaytetye. There are a number of good reasons for assuming that Proto-Arrernte possessed the distinction and that it was lost in Western Arrernte. The undifferentiated forms of West-

TABLE 9-28
Arandic first person singular pronouns

	ERG	NOM	ACC	DAT
Alyawarre	athe	ayenge	ayenhe	atyenge
Eastern Arrernte	the	yenge	yenge	atyenge
Western Arrernte	(a)the	yenge	yengenhe	nweke
Lower Aranda	athe	yenge		atyenge
Kaytetye	atye	ayenge	atyenge	atyenge

TABLE 9-29
Arandic first person singular pronouns, showing identical and analogous forms

	ERG	NOM		ACC		DAT
Alyawarre	athe	ayenge	- - - - - -	ayenhe		atyenge
Eastern Arrernte	the	yenge	————	yenge		atyenge
Western Arrernte	(a)the	yenge	- - - - - -	yengenhe		nweke
Lower Aranda	athe	yenge				atyenge
Kaytetye	atye	ayenge		atyenge	————	atyenge

ern Arrernte continue the formerly exclusive forms. Thus the current first person plural dative form is *anwerneke*, which corresponds to the exclusive form in dialects that have the contrast. Hence the inherited first person plural inclusive form was no longer needed in the Plural; it apparently shifted semantically to the first perosn singular.

Returning to the accusative, we note that in Kaytetye it has the same form as the dative, which we have reconstructed as **(a)tyenge*. Now in Kaytetye all personal pronouns have identical forms in the accusative and dative. Hence one could explain the accusative *atyenge* as an extension of the inherited dative form on the basis of this general pattern. Such an extension of dative to cover accusative is widespread in languages, as witness English *him* and *them*, which were originally datives. Now if the Kaytetye accusative form is removed from consideration as inherited forms, we are left with no form that necessarily continues the Proto-Arandic accusative of the first person singular. This is what results from the comparative method. We cannot legitimately posit any form. The original form might conceivably have been identical to the dative; then Proto-Arrernte replaced it everywhere, and the extension of the accusative form to the dative just mentioned, took place not in Kaytetye but rather in Proto-Arandic. In this scenario it is difficult to see why *atyenge* should have been replaced in the accusative function. The other possibility is that Proto-Arandic had a separate form for the accusative, which was lost everywhere, possibly because it was too short phonetically.

We can illustrate the reconstruction procedures applied to the first person singular by means of a series of tables. The basic forms have been given above in Table 9-28. Within each language's paradigm, join identical forms with a solid line, analogous forms with a dotted line (Table 9-29). For each set of linked items, add an arrow showing the direction of replacement or analogical influence (Table 9-30). Remove the items for which a plausible language-internal genesis has been found (that is, those

TABLE 9-30
Arandic first person singular pronouns, showing extension and analogical creation of forms

	ERG	NOM		ACC		DAT
Alyawarre	athe	ayenge	- - > - -	ayenhe		atyenge
Eastern Arrernte	the	yenge	—>—	yenge		atyenge
Western Arrernte	(a)the	yenge	- - > - -	yengenhe		nweke —<—(1PL)
Lower Aranda	athe	yenge				atyenge
Kaytetye	atye	ayenge		atyenge	—<—	atyenge

TABLE 9-31
Arandic first person singular pronouns, inherited forms

	ERG	NOM	ACC	DAT
Alyawarre	athe	ayenge		atyenge
Eastern Arrernte	the	yenge		atyenge
Western Arrernte	(a)the	yenge		
Lower Aranda	athe	yenge		atyenge
Kaytetye	atye	ayenge		atyenge
Proto-Arandic	*(a)the	*(a)yenge		*(a)tyenge

forms which in Table 9-30 have an incoming arrowhead). What remains should include only the forms which are inherited (Table 9-31). The presumed Proto-Arandic forms are indicated in the last row of Table 9-31. (The *ty* of the Kaytetye ergative may perhaps be the result of an analogical influence of the consonant of the dative.)

11.7   Arandic Person Marking on Kinship Nouns

Kinship nouns in Arandic languages (except Western Arrernte) are inflected for the person of the singular possessor, or "propositus" (Heath et al. 1982). Arrernte uses suffixes for this purpose (Wilkins 1989, chap. 3.9), while Kaytetye has prefixes for the second and third person and a suffix for the first person. Examples from Kaytetye and Mparntwe Arrernte are given on Table 9-32.

Before attempting a reconstruction, we note a number of anomalies concerning this construction. In the first place, these are the only prefixes in Kaytetye morphology, which otherwise uses only suffixation. Secondly, the morphosyntactic category KIN POSSESSOR is expressed in two different positions in Kaytetye: second and third person possessors are prefixed, whereas the first person is indicated by a suffix. Thirdly, these kinship terms display peculiarities of inflection in Mparntwe Arrernte when combined with case suffixes. The order of person marking and case marking is variable, for example 'her mother ERG' can be expressed in three ways, as shown in table 9-33.

Here we have three anomalies: the fact of variability, the double case-marking of (3), and the antidiagrammatic ordering case-possessor in (1). The expected order is possessor-case, since this reflects the semantic relations, the possessor being more

TABLE 9-32
Kaytetye and Mparntwe Arrernte kin possession

	Kaytetye 'brother-in-law, spouse'	Mparntwe Arrernte 'brother-in-law'
'my'	mpwerne-ye	mpwerne-ye
'my'		mpwern-atye
'your'	ngke-mpwerne	mpwern-angkwe
'his/her'	kwe-mpwerne	mpwern-ikwe

TABLE 9-33
The order of case and person marking in
Mparntwe Arrernte. The morphemes are
m(e) **'mother',** *-l(e)* ERGATIVE, *-ikwe* **'3 SG**
kin possessor'.

(1)	me-l-ikwe
(2)	m-ikwe-le
(3)	me-l-ikwe-le

SOURCE: Data from Wilkins 1989: 134.

closely related semantically to the kinship relation than is the case, which merely relates the nominal to the rest of the sentence. The order possessor-case is in fact the usual order of the categories in Alyawarre and in the Kaytetye first person. The anomalous order, however, also occurs in Antekerrepenhe, where the ergative and dative case inflections normally precede the person suffix.

Turning now to reconstruction, we can match the kin possessor affixes in the different languages, on the basis of their similarity in form and meaning, and provide protoforms for them, as shown on Table 9-34. (The bracketed *u* in the reconstructed second person singular possessor conceals the fact that the Kaytetye and Arrernte forms are not exactly compatible historically. The pre-Kaytetye form would have been **(e)ngke* and the Proto-Arrernte **ungke*. Both presumably reflect an even earlier **yungke* < **nyunku;* Kaytetye would have lost the rounding on the vowel, while Arrernte retained it.) Although we can reconstruct the forms, we are left with the problem of their order. For first person singular we can safely reconstruct a suffix **-ye,* since only a suffix is indicated in the various dialects. For the other formatives, the disparity of position makes it impossible to reconstruct either suffixes or prefixes, since it is highly unlikely that any language had a change from suffixation to prefixation or vice versa. A better hypothesis is that the forms were originally separate words, which formerly could occur in variable order in a phrasal unit but became cliticised in different positions in each language. This hypothesis receives support from the fact that nonsingular pronominal possessors are expressed by a dative pronoun placed either before or after the possessed kinship noun, (although preceding position seems to be preferred at least in Kaytetye and Mparntwe Arrernte (Wilkins 1989). The free forms that gave rise to these affixes are likely to have been personal pronouns in the dative case both for this reason and because personal pronouns in a possessive

TABLE 9-34
Arandic kin possession markers

	'his/her'	'your'	'my'	'my'
Arrernte	-ikwe	-angkwe	-atye	(-ye)
Alyawarre	-ikwe	-ingkwe	-atye	-ye
Kaytetye	kwe-	ngke-		-ye
Proto-Arandic	*uke	*(u)ngke		*-ye

TABLE 9-35
Arandic kin possession markers compared to personal pronouns

	1Sg Pos	1Sg Pn	2Sg Pos	2Sg Pn	3Sg Pos	3Sg Pn
Kaytetye		atyenge	ngke-	ngkenge	kwe-	kwere
Arrernte	-atye	atyenge	-angkwe	ngkwenge	-ikwe	ikwere
proto-Arandic	*atye	*atyenge	*(u)ngke	*(u)ngkenge	*uke	*ukere

case are the typical diachronic source for person markers on nominals. Can such a development be supported with inner-Arandic evidence?

Table 9-35 sets out the Singular possessor affixes and the Dative forms of the corresponding personal pronouns. There it is possible to compare the possessor affixes with the corresponding personal pronouns in each language (as well as comparing each of these across languages). It can be seen that the possessor forms are identical (apart from a minor irregularity in the initial vowel of the second person singular) with the free dative pronouns in the same language except that they lack the final syllable of the latter, which is -nge in the first two persons and -re in the third person. This suggests that earlier both languages had both clitic and free dative singular pronoun forms (as a result of an earlier reinforcement of the free forms by an extra syllable), and that the kin possessors are reflexes of the clitic pronouns which became bound to the kin terms. The fact that in each language the kin possessors agree with the corresponding pronouns with respect to phonological details that differ between the languages (Kaytetye ngk versus Arrernte ngkw in the second person singular, Kaytetye kw versus Arrernte ikw in the third person singular) strongly suggests that the formation of kin possessor affixes was a language-particular (i.e. post-Proto-Arandic) development.

We are now in a position to tackle the problem of the variable order of case and possessor in Mparntwe Arrernte. If the possessor markers originated as bound pronouns, they would have attached originally to the outside of the inflected noun. Order (1) of Table 33 reflects this situation, as Wilkins (1989: 134 f) noted. Order (2), where Case follows Possessor, is a likely result of a reordering that effects a more iconic or diagrammatic coding of the semantic relations, as per Bybee's (1985) principle of relevance. Order (3) represents a compromise (of the type described by Haspelmath 1993) that both preserves some continuity with the older form and marks case in the appropriately external slot.

In summary, we have reconstructed a system where inflection of kin nouns for the person of possessor occurred only for the first person, by means of a suffix *-ye. Otherwise possession was marked by a pronoun in the dative case, which could occur on either side of the possessed noun (phrase). For singular possessors, short and clitic forms of the personal pronouns were available. These came to be fixed prenominally in Kaytetye and postnominally in Arrernte. They were reanalysed as affixes. As affixes they became subject to the ordering principle of relevance. In Arrernte, where they ended up in an antidiagrammatic order of suffixes, they were reordered to a position adjacent to the stem they modified.

This study illustrates the reconstruction both of the affixisation process and the reordering of morphemes within a word. It also provides an example of the diachronic explication of synchronic anomalies and of the simultaneous pursuit of comparative and internal reconstruction.

11.8 Arandic demonstratives and interrogatives

Certain pronominals in Alyawarre inflect in two different paradigms (the data is taken from Yallop 1977, chap. 9 with modernised spellings), as shown on Table 9-36. The two paradigms of 'this' are built on stems *nhe-* and *nhenhe* respectively. For historical reconstruction we need to decide which paradigm is archaic and which is innovative and explain how the new paradigm arose. If paradigm I is new, we need to explain the "elision" of *nhe*. If on the other hand paradigm II is the innovation, we need to account for the incorporation or absorption of *nhe* into the stem. Both paradigms are regular in the sense that they consist of normal nominal case forms added to an invariant stem. Notice that the paradigms share the same nominative/accusative case form *nhenhe*. In paradigm I it is analysed as stem *nhe-* followed by a suffix *-nhe*, whereas in paradigm II it must be interpreted as an stem *nhenhe* with zero suffix. This word form is thus ambiguous, and as such can easily have provided the locus for a reanalysis. If paradigm I is taken as the inherited inflectional system, we can see motivation for a reinterpretation of *nhe-nhe* as *nhenhe-Ø*. The general pattern in the language is for the nominative/accusative of nominals (except personal pronouns) to have zero inflection. Hence a reanalysis could be seen as analogical, extending and maximising the existing patterns (cf. Wurzel's (1984) system congruency). This reanalysis is also favoured by the diachronic tendency to replace marked coding of categories by unmarked coding (Mayerthaler 1981); the universally unmarked coding of nominative case is with a zero rather than an overt exponent. If we posit paradigm I as the earlier inflection, we can thus explain the creation of paradigm II by natural morphological processes. The opposite hypothesis, however, would require some explanation for the elision of the *nhe* suffix or syllable in all word forms except the nominative/accusative. No plausible explanation is available.

The paradigm of 'who' can be explained along the same lines as 'this'. Strehlow (1942–44: 98 f), based on research of the 1930s, gives the following paradigms for

TABLE 9-36
Alyawarre demonstratives and interrogatives

	'this' I	'this' II	'who' I	'who' II
NOM/ACC	nhenhe	nhenhe	ngwenhe	ngwenhe
ERG/LOC	nhele	nhenhele	ngwele	ngwenhele
DAT	nheke	nhenheke		
ALL	nhewarle	nhenhewarle		
ABL	nhetheye	nhenhetheye		
GEN				ngwenhekenhe

TABLE 9-37
Western arrernte interrogatives

	'who' I	'who' II	'what' I	'what' II
NOM	ngwenhe	ngwenhe	iwenhe	iwenhe
ACC	ngwenhe	ngwenhenhe	iwenhe	
ERG	ngwele		iwele	iwenhele
POSS	ngweke	ngwenheke	iweke	iwenheke
ABL		ngwenhenge		iwenhenge

(Western) Arrernte 'who' and 'what' (shown in Table 9-37 with modernised spellings). Although he refers to the words in paradigm I as "shortened" or "abbreviated" forms beside the "ordinary flexional forms" of paradigm II, it is clear that the paradigms labelled II are innovative and based on a reanalysis of the ambiguous nominative forms. Note that the human/name interrogative 'who' has an overt accusative suffix which is lacking in the 'what' form.

These examples illustrate internal reconstruction involving the deletion of morpheme boundaries where a morpheme is absorbed into a stem (cf. 4.5), which is the last step of the diachronic pathway mentioned in section 10.

NOTES

1. The internal structure of the Arandic subgroup of the Pama-Nyungan language family of Australia was described by Hale (1962) on the basis of cognate counts. His basic scheme is followed here, with terminology as follows:

Proto-Arandic
  Kaytetye
  Proto-Aranda
    Lower Aranda
    Proto-Arrernte
      Western Arrernte
      Eastern Arrernte
      Mparntwe Arrernte
      Aliterre
      Antekerrepenhe
      Alyawarre
      Anmatyerre

The main sources used are Strehlow (1942–4) for Western Arrernte and Aliterre, Wilkins (1989) for Mparntwe Arrernte, Yallop (1977) for Alyawarre, unpublished manuscripts (held in the Australian Institute of Aboriginal and Torres Strait Islander Studies, Canberra) by Gavan Breen for Antekerrepenhe, dictionaries in various stages of preparation by the Arandic Languages Dictionary Project (Institute for Aboriginal Development, Alice Springs) for Eastern Arrernte, and my own field notes for Kaytetye. Grateful acknowledgement is given for research support on Kaytetye from the Australian Institute of Aboriginal and Torres Strait Islander Studies and the Australian National University, and for comparative Arandic by the Australian Research Council. The preliminary reconstructions given here as examples of methodology will be elaborated within their Arandic and wider Australian linguistic context in work resulting from the research project on "Comparative vocabulary and grammar of the Arandic languages", which is currently being undertaken in collaboration with Gavan Breen.

REFERENCES

Alpher, B. (1990). Some Proto-Pama-Nyungan paradigms: a verb in the hand is worth two in the phylum. In G. N. O'Grady and D. T. Tryon, eds., *Studies in comparative Pama-Nyungan* 155–71. *Pacific Linguistics* C-111. Australian National University, Canberra.

Andersen, H. (1980). Morphological change: Towards a typology. In J. Fisiak, ed., *Historical Morphology* 1–50. Trends in Linguistics, Studies and Monographs, 17. Mouton, The Hague.

———. (1987). From auxiliary to desinence. In M. Harris and P. Ramat, eds., *Historical development of auxiliaries* 21–51. Trends in Linguistics, Studies and Monographs, no. 35. Mouton de Gruyter, Berlin.

Anderson, S.R. (1988). Morphological change. In F. J. Newmeyer, ed., *Linguistics: the Cambridge survey.* vol. 1, *Linguistic theory: Foundations* 324–62. Cambridge University Press, Cambridge.

———. (1988). Morphological theory. In F. J. Newmeyer, ed., *Linguistics: The Cambridge survey.* Vol. 1, *Linguistic theory: Foundations* 146–191. Cambridge University Press, Cambridge.

Anttila, R. (1989). *Historical and comparative linguistics.* 2nd rev. ed. Current Issues in Linguistic Theory, no. 6. John Benjamins, Amsterdam.

Arlotto, A. (1972). *Introduction to historical linguistics.* Houghton Mifflin, Boston.

Baldi, P., and W. R. Schmalstieg. (1990). Morphological change. In E. C. Polomé, ed., *Research guide on language change* 347–64. Trends in Linguistics, Studies and Monographs, no. 48. Mouton de Gruyter, Berlin.

Baudouin de Courtenay, J. (1895). *Versuch einer Theorie phonetischer Alternationen.* Trübner, Strassburg. Reprinted in English translation in Stankiewicz, E., ed. and trans. (1972). *A Baudouin de Courtenay anthology: The beginnings of structural linguistics.* Indiana University Press, Bloomington.

Bloomfield, L. (1935). *Language.* Allen and Unwin, London.

Bybee, J. L. (1985). *Morphology: A study of the relation between form and meaning.* Typological Studies in Language, no. 9. John Benjamins, Amsterdam.

Comrie, B. (1980a). Morphology and word order reconstruction: Problems and prospects. In J. Fisiak, ed., *Historical Morphology* 83–96. Trends in Linguistics, Studies and Monographs, 17. Mouton, The Hague.

———. (1980b). The order of case and possessive suffixes in Uralic languages: An approach to the comparative-historical problem. *Lingua Posnaniensis* 23: 81–6.

———. (1981). *The Languages of the Soviet Union.* Cambridge University Press, Cambridge.

———. (1985). Derivation, inflection, and semantic change in the development of the Chukchi verb paradigm. In J. Fisiak, ed., *Historical Semantics, Historical Word-Formation,* 85–95. Trends in Linguistics, Studies and Monographs, no. 29. Mouton, Berlin.

Dixon, R. M. W. (1980). *The languages of Australia.* Cambridge University Press, Cambridge.

Dressler, W. U. (1977). Morphologization of phonological processes (Are there distinct morphonological processes?). In A. Juilland, ed., *Linguistic Studies offered to Joseph Greenberg on the occasion of his sixtieth birthday,.* Vol. 2, *Phonology* 313–37. Anma Libri, Saratoga, Ca.

———. (1985). *Morphonology: The dynamics of derivation.* Karoma, Ann Arbor.

Dunkel, G. E. (1987). A typology of metanalysis in Indo-European. In C. Watkins, ed., *Studies in memory of Warren Cowgill (1929–1985)* 7–37. Walter de Gruyter, Berlin.

Ernout, A., and A. Meillet. (1985). Dictionnaire étymologique de la langue latine: histoire des mots. 4th ed. Klincksieck, Paris.

Ferguson, C. A. (1990). From esses to aitches: Identifying pathways of diachronic change. In W. Croft, K. Denning, and S. Kemmer, eds., *Studies in typology and diachrony: Papers presented to Joseph H. Greenberg on his 75th birthday,* 59–78. Typological Studies in Language, no. 20. John Benjamins, Amsterdam.

Greenberg, J. H. (1966). Some universals of language with particular reference to the order of meaningful elements. In J. H. Greenberg, ed., *Universals of language.* 2nd ed., 73–118. MIT Press, Cambridge, Mass.

———. (1969). Some methods of dynamic comparison in linguistics. In J. Puhvel, ed., *Substance and structure in language* 147–203. University of California Press, Berkeley and Los Angeles.

———. (1978). How does a language acquire gender markers? In J. H. Greenberg, ed., *Universals of human language.* Vol. 2, *Word Structure,* 47–82. Stanford University Press, Stanford.

Haas, M. R. (1969). *The prehistory of languages*. Mouton, The Hague.

Hale, K. L. (1962). Internal relationships in Arandic of Central Australia. In A. Capell, ed., *Some linguistic types in Australia* 171–83. Oceanic Linguistic Monographs, no. 7. University of Sydney, Sydney.

Hall, R. A., Jr. (1983). *Proto-Romance morphology*. John Benjamins, Amsterdam.

Haspelmath, M. (1993). The diachronic externalization of inflecton. *Linguistics* 31: 279–309.

Heath, J. (1978). *Linguistic diffusion in Arnhem Land*. Australian Institute of Aboriginal Studies, Canberra.

Heath, J., F. Merlan, and A. Rumsey, eds. (1982). *The languages of kinship in Aboriginal Australia*. Oceania Linguistic Monographs, no. 24. University of Sydney, Sydney.

Heine, B. and M. Reh. (1984). *Grammaticalization and reanalysis in African languages*. Buske, Hamburg.

Hetzron, R. (1976). Two principles of genetic reconstruction. *Lingua* 38: 89–108.

Hock, H. H. (1991). *Principles of historical linguistics*. 2nd ed. Trends in Linguistics, Studies and Monographs, no. 34. Mouton de Gruyter, Berlin.

Hoenigswald, H. M. (1991). Morphemic change, typology, and uniformitarianism: a study in reconstruction. In W. P. Lehmann and H-J. J. Hewitt, eds., *Language typology 1988: Typological models in reconstruction* 17–26. John Benjamins, Amsterdam.

Hooper, J. B. (1976). *An introduction to natural generative phonology*. Academic Press, New York.

Hopper, P. J. (1990). Where do words come from? In W. Croft, K. Denning, and S. Kemmer, eds., *Studies in typology and diachrony: Papers presented to Joseph H. Greenberg on his 75th birthday* 153–60. Typological Studies in Language, no. 20. John Benjamins, Amsterdam / Philadelphia.

Hopper, P. J., and E. C. Traugott. (1993). *Grammaticalization*. Cambridge University Press, Cambridge.

Hudson, J. (1978). *The core of Walmatjari grammar*. Australian Institute of Aboriginal Studies, Canberra.

Jeffers, R. J. and Lehiste, I. (1979). *Principles and methods for historical linguistics*. MIT Press, Cambridge, Mass.

Keller, R.E. (1978). *The German language*. Faber and Faber, London.

Klausenburger, J. (1979). *Morphologization: Studies in Latin and Romance morphophonology*. Niemeyer, Tübingen.

Koch, H. (1973). Indo-European denominative verbs in -nu. PhD. diss., Harvard University. Published by University Microfilms, Ann Arbor, Michigan, 1979.

———. (1995). The creation of morphological zeroes. In G. Booij and J. van Marle, eds., *Yearbook of Morphology 1994*, 31–71. Kluwer, Dordrecht.

Kruszewski, M. (1881). *Über die Lautabwechslung*. Universitätsdruckerei, Kazan.

Lehmann, W. P. (1992). *Historical linguistics: an introduction*. 3rd ed. Routledge, London and New York.

Lehmann, W. P., and Y. Malkiel, eds., (1968). *Directions for historical linguistics: a symposium*. University of Texas Press, Austin.

Maiden, M. (1992). Irregularity as a determinant of morphological change. *Journal of Linguistics* 28: 285–312.

Malkiel, Y. (1968). The inflectional paradigm as an occasional determinant of sound change. In Lehmann and Malkiel, 21–64.

Mańczak, W. (1957–58). Tendances générales des changements analogiques. *Lingua* 7: 198–325; 387–420.

Matthews, P. H. (1972). *Inflectional morphology: A theoretical study based on aspects of Latin verb conjugation*. Cambridge University Press, Cambridge.

———. (1991). *Morphology*. 2nd ed. Cambridge University Press, Cambridge.

Mayerthaler, W. (1981). *Morphologische Natürlichkeit*. Linguistische Forschungen, 28. Akademischer Verlag Athenaion, Wiesbaden. English translation by J. Seidler (1988). *Morphological Naturalness*. Karoma, Ann Arbor.

Meillet, A. (1912). L'évolution des formes grammaticales. *Scientia (Rivista di scienza)* 12 (26) 6ff. Reprint in *Linguistique historique et linguistique générale* [1921] 130–48. Champion, Paris.

Meiser, G. (1992). Syncretism in Indo-European languages—Motives, process and results. *Transactions of the Philological Society* 90(2):187–218.

Palmer, L. R. (1954). *The Latin language*. Faber and Faber, London.

Panagl, O. (1987). Productivity and diachronic change in morphology. In W. U. Dressler et al., *Leitmotifs in Natural Morphology*, 127–51. Studies in Language Companion Series, no. 10. John Benjamins, Amsterdam.

Ramat, P. (1987). *Linguistic typology*. Mouton de Gruyter, Berlin.

Schindler, J. (1974). Fragen zum paradigmatischen Ausgleich. *Die Sprache* 20: 1–9.

Strehlow, T. G. H. (1942–44) *Aranda phonetics and grammar* Oceania Monographs, no. 7. Australian National Research Council, Sydney.

Thomason, S. G. (1980). Morphological instability, with and without language contact. In J. Fisiak, ed., *Historical morphology* 359–72. Trends in Linguistics, Studies and Monographs, no. 17. Mouton, The Hague.

Tiersma, P. M. (1982). Local and general markedness. *Language* 58: 832–49.

Traugott, E. C. and B. Heine, eds., (1991). *Approaches to grammaticaliztion.* 2 vols. John Benjamins, Amsterdam.

Ultan, R. (1978). On the development of the definite article. In H. Seiler, ed., *Language universals: Papers from the conference held at Gummersbach/Cologne, Germany, October 3–8, 1976* 249–65. Tübinger Beiträge zur Linguistik, no. 111. Gunter Narr, Tübingen.

Vennemann, T. (1972). Rule Inversion. *Lingua* 29: 209–42.

———. (1974). Restructuring. *Lingua* 33: 137–56.

Watkins, C., ed (1985). 1985. *The American Heritage Dictionary of Indo-European roots.* Rev. ed. Houghton Mifflin, Boston.

Wilkins, D. (1989). *Mparntwe Arrernte: Studies in the structure and semantics of grammar.* PhD diss. Australian National University, Canberra.

Wurzel, W. U. (1980). Ways of morphologizing phonological rules. In J. Fisiak, ed., *Historical morphology* 443–62. Trends in Linguistics, Studies and Monographs, no. 17. Mouton, The Hague.

———. (1981). Problems in morphonology. In W. U. Dressler, O. E. Pfeiffer, and J. R. Rennison, eds., *Phonologica 1980: Akten der Vierten Internationalen Phonologie-Tagung, Wien, 29. Juni–2. Juli 1980* 413–34. Innsbrücker Beiträge zur Sprachwissenschaft, no. 36. Institut für Sprachwissenschaft der Universität Innsbruck, Innsbruck.

———. (1984). *Flexionsmorphologie und Natürlichkeit: Ein Beitrag zur morphologischen Theoriebildung.* Studia Grammatica, no. 21. Akademie-Verlag, Berlin. English translation by M. Schentke. (1989). *Inflectional morphology and naturalness.* Studies in Natural Language and Linguistic Theory no. 9. Kluwer, Dordrecht.

Yallop, C. (1977). *Alyawarra: An Aboriginal language of Central Australia.* Australian Institute of Aboriginal Studies, Canberra.

10 Natural Tendencies of Semantic Change and the Search for Cognates[1]

DAVID P. WILKINS

> In general, the criteria of formal reconstruction can be strict because they stem from precise rules that cannot be set aside unless one is in a position to substitute more exact rules for them. The whole apparatus of phonetics and morphology enters in to sustain or refute these endeavours. But when it is a matter of meaning, one has as a guide only a certain probability based on 'common sense, on the personal evaluation of the linguist, and on the parallels that he can cite. The problem is always, at all levels of analysis, within just one language or at different stages of a comparative reconstruction, to determine if and how two morphemes which are formally identical or similar can be shown to coincide in meaning. (Benveniste 1971: 249)

1 INTRODUCTION

The first and most fundamental step in comparative reconstruction is the identification of tentative cognates, and the first tool which tends to be employed in the search for cognates is a Swadesh-type *basic vocabulary list* of between fifty and two hundred items. In employing such lists it is common to examine the forms which the languages under comparison show for a particular gloss and, armed with a knowledge of what are plausible phonetic and phonological changes, determine which items within the set are formally similar. During this process, one may notice, or know of, a form which is phonologically similar to one of the forms under inspection, but which has a different meaning. When this occurs, one is faced with the problem of deciding whether or not these formally similar items are also semantically similar and, thus, whether or not they should be considered possible cognates. Swadesh (1972: 39) admits that '[t]he problems of cognate identification are, of course complicated by semantic change, which . . . is extremely frequent', and it is therefore 'a commonplace rule of comparative linguistics that meanings of cognate forms need not be identical'.

But, as Benveniste notes in the epigraph, the process for deciding semantic similarity has not been governed by the same methodological rigor as that which governs the identification of phonetic and morphological similarity. How can we be sure that two distinct meanings are related?

This chapter is a move towards answering the preceding question. Its primary purpose is to demonstrate that there are natural tendencies of semantic change involving core vocabulary and to show how these natural tendencies can be utilised at the outset of comparative research to search for, as well as establish, cognates. In section 2, a brief historical sketch of thinking in diachronic semantics is given in order to provide background to the problem of establishing semantic relatedness and identifying cognates. An overview of what this chapter takes semantic change to be is given in section 3. Section 4 discusses natural tendencies of semantic change discovered within the semantic domain 'parts of a person', and focuses in particular on a unidirectional change involving parts and wholes. In section 5, some examples involving Australian Aboriginal languages are given to demonstrate how a knowledge of the natural tendencies of semantic change within the semantic domain 'parts of a person' can be used to identify and establish cognates. Conclusions are provided in section 6.

2 BACKGROUND TO THE PROBLEM

Blust (1988: 25) has observed that, '[a]s linguists of all theoretical persuasions have long recognized, the demonstration of semantic relatedness poses far greater problems than the demonstration of phonological relatedness between forms.' There has been some debate, however, over what the source of these difficulties is. Some linguists believe that the problem is inherent to the nature of semantics, semantic relations, and semantic change. Hock (1986: 308), for instance, claims that it is a "fact that in most cases, semantic change is 'fuzzy', highly irregular, and extremely difficult to predict" and sees this as the reason for why "there seems to be no natural constraints on the directions and results of semantic change." Other linguists, such as Ullmann (1963) and Arlotto (1972), have claimed that the problem is not intractable and the stumbling block rests in our understanding of, and our approach to, meaning and meaning change, not in the nature of meaning itself. As Arlotto (1972:165) points out: 'Studies in semantic change so far have not resulted in the formulation of abstract models or even in the reasoned educated guesswork that pervades the study of phonological, morphological, and syntactic change. One reason for this is quite obvious, the semantic models of general or synchronic linguistics are themselves quite limited and not applicable to all cases.'

Starting with Michel Bréal's classic work *Semantics: Studies in the science of meaning* (1900), the tradition in diachronic semantics has been to propose taxonomic classifications of semantic changes and then to set about placing such changes into their proper class. Stern's (1931) *Meaning and change of meaning* is a work in this tradition, as is Ullmann's (1951) *The principles of semantics*. A more recent, cognitively oriented, 'reclassification' is that of Geeraerts (1983), who recognises that 'classifying semantic changes isn't the whole point', but also notes classification "has always been the epitome of diachronic semantics" (217). The obligatory chapter on semantic change in textbooks on comparative and historical linguistics trots out such classifications and laments that, unlike sound change, 'it has not been possible to formulate truly general laws of semantic change' (Anttila 1972: 147). As far as the comparative method is concerned, this is the crux of the problem; the ability to classify a sound change as an assimilation, dissimilation, or metathesis is not what helps in identifying correspondences and reconstructing forms; it is the knowledge of what constitutes crosslinguistically typical and atypical associations of classes of sounds and what constitute crosslinguistically natural, sporadic, and unnatural pathways of change under given environmental conditions. Merely classifying semantic changes is not sufficient for the purposes of comparative reconstruction: We must identify crosslinguistically regular tendencies of semantic association, where they exist, and then use these natural tendencies to justify and/or to search for plausible cognates.

Over the past twenty-odd years, the rise of functional approaches to linguistics, the birth of cognitive semantics, the expansion of the Greenbergian-style approach to linguistic universals, and the increased interest in the mechanisms and pathways of grammaticalization have all, in their own way, lead to an increased theoretical interest in diachronic semantics. These trends have lead to a view that, instead of being wild, chaotic, and unpredictable, semantic change is in many cases regular and is often predictable and that natural tendencies of semantic change arise out of the universality of certain cognitive processes and/or out of universal traits to be found in the production and interpretation of fully contextualised natural discourse. Amongst the researchers who are currently working to establish and support such a view in the field of diachronic semantics are Traugott (1985a, 1985b, 1986a, 1986b, 1988, 1989), Traugott and Dasher (1987), Traugott and Heine (1991), Traugott and König (1991), Sweetser (1982, 1987, 1990), Nikiforidau and Sweetser (1989), Bybee (1985, 1988, 1990), Bybee and Pagliuca (1985), Bybee et al. (1991), Heine (1992), Heine et al (1991), Geeraerts (1983, 1985, 1986), Evans (1992), and Wilkins (1981, 1989b, 1991). Berlin and Kay's (1969) pioneering work on colour terms, along with follow up work such as Kay (1975) and MacLaury (1991), destroyed the myth that semantic mapping in languages is totally arbitrary, and can be seen as the first true step towards rooting the diachronic development of particular semantic fields in facts about neurophysiology and cognition. Williams' (1976) paper entitled "Synaesthetic adjectives in English: A possible law of semantic change" is also notable as an early paper that uses crosslinguistic data pertaining to a single semantic domain to establish regularities of semantic shift, both unidirectional and reciprocal, and which suggests that the explanation of these changes might be found in brain organization. Lehrer (1978, 1985), who provided an alternative analysis for Williams' data, has worked to apply semantic field theory to diachronic semantics and has been a strong advocate of the view that our knowledge of the principles of semantic change can be greatly enhanced by 'looking, not at the whole lexicon, but at words which belong to a single semantic field' (1985: 283).

Due in part to the privilege that the field of linguistics in general accords to the study of morphosyntactic phenomena, as well as to the fact that the unidirectional tendency for concrete notions to give rise to more abstract notions is well known and relatively easy to study, most of the recent research into semantic change has focused on the development of morphemes which refer to abstract (i.e. nonconcrete) notions. For example, Sweetser (1990, 1982) examines the development of epistemic senses from root senses of English modal verbs, Bybee (1990) investigates the semantic development of past tense modals in English, Traugott (1985) undertakes a crosslinguistic examination of the development of conditional markers, and Svorou (1988, 1986) and Heine et al. (1991) discuss the natural tendency of nominal sources referring to body parts and environmental landmarks to give rise to locative expressions. This intensive research into grammaticalization and the development of abstract notions has certainly been very fruitful, and will be of great use in the advanced stages of comparative historical reconstruction, but it has little to contribute to our knowledge of the initial stages of cognate collection and comparison. Indeed, with the exception of the work of Matisoff (1978) and Traugott, little concern has been shown for how the findings of research into semantic change can be utilised in internal and comparative reconstruction. Furthermore, very few studies have been undertaken to show the natural tendencies of semantic change which give rise to terms that label (core) concrete notions such as body parts. It is these gaps in the literature which this chapter, along with works such as Evans (1992), will hopefully help to fill.

With respect to comparative-historical reconstruction, it is important to emphasise that, in the case of language families for which reconstruction is quite advanced, researchers have certainly attended to issues of semantic change. Indeed, part of the traditional skills of etymologists has been to establish semantic associations and paths of change by identifying parallel changes and by using their intimate knowledge of the cultural and linguistic facts of the language family, along with their knowledge of prior reconstructions in the family, to guide them in establishing semantic connections. It is this prior, family-specific, research that now enables researchers to undertake cross-family comparisons of changes to see whether any universal tendencies of semantic change emerge. One of the central claims of this chapter is that we no longer need to wait until more advanced stages of reconstruction before considering issues of semantics. Instead, it is currently possible to utilise, and build upon, traditional knowledge and insights, and thereby to identify universal patterns of semantic association and change which can be used in the earliest stages of comparative research to help search for tentative cognates.

3 SEMANTIC CHANGE DEFINED

For the purposes of this chapter I will be concerned with discussing semantic change only as it affects lexemes. It is not uncommon to find the terms 'lexical change' and 'semantic change' used interchangeably (e.g. Jeffers and Lehiste 1979; Brown 1979), however, it is important to realise that, within the present discussion, semantic change is to be considered a subtype of lexical change. Mel'čuk (1976: 59) has expanded upon the Saussurean bipartite notion of a linguistic sign by claiming that a lexical item is an 'ordered triple' consisting of *significant*, *signifié*, and 'information about combinatorial properties of the sign, which in their totality may be spoken of as syntactics'. Following this view, lexical change is to be regarded as a change which affects any of these three aspects of the sign, either individually or in combination. That is, change in form, change in meaning, and/or change in combinatorial properties constitute a lexical change. As an idealisation, a true semantic change is one in which only the meaning of a lexeme changes while other aspects of the item remain constant. Significantly, certain changes which would have been regarded by Stern and Ullmann as semantic changes are ruled out by the present position. For example, the reductions of the collocations 'private soldier' to 'private' and 'commercial advertisement' to 'commercial', are here considered to be simple form changes akin to the reduction of 'telephone' to 'phone'. In each of these three cases an item with one meaning has been shortened in form, but the resultant form retains that same meaning. Of course, there is the mirage of semantic change in the case of 'private' and 'commercial' because the number of meanings associated with these forms is increased by virtue of the nature of the form reduction. However, this appearance is illusory, since the number of meanings in the original system have not altered, only the forms used to convey those meanings (i.e. the meaning originally associated with the fixed phrase 'commercial advertisement' is now associated with the lexical form 'commercial' because of form reduction, not semantic change, although the result is that an existing lexical form is now associated with two categorially distinct meanings: its original adjectival meaning and a semantically related nominal meaning that had previously been coded by a distinct, but related, form).

It has been common to talk about semantic change as though it involved an actual mutation of meaning from one time to the next. Jeffers and Lehiste (1979: 62) define semantic change as 'a change in the set of contexts in which a given word might occur', and since their conception of meaning is 'the set of contexts in which a word occurs', this definition of change implies that the original meaning (M_1) automatically shifts to (M_2). Similarly, Matisoff (1978: 173), who allows for a notion of semantic vagueness as a type of intermediate step in semantic change, defines a semantic shift as follows: 'An etymon E has **shifted** in meaning through time if at one stage in the language's history, S_1, it used to mean "M_1 but not M_2", while at a later stage in the language's history, S_2, it came to mean "M_2 but not M_1'. This conception of semantic change may be diagrammed as in Figure 10-1.

The problem with talking about semantic change in this way is that it suggests that at no time do M_1 and M_2 coexist, polysemously attached to the one form. This is a conception which still appears to be tied to the Neogrammarian view of the imperceptability of linguistic change. If, however, we accept that, in gross terms, semantic change operates like other types of linguistic change then we expect it to manifest the type of socially determined variation manifested by sound change, morphological change, and syntactic change. Jakobson (1973: 22–23) states: 'The start and finish of any mutational process coexist in the synchrony and belong to two different subcodes of one and the same language. Hence no changes can be understood or interpreted without reference to the system which undergoes them and to their function within the system. . . .'

In a similar vein, Weinreich, Labov, and Herzog (1968: 188) observe that 'not all variability and heterogeneity in language structure involves change, but all change

Time (T)	:	T1	T2
Form (F)	:	F1	F1
Meaning (M)	:	M1 $\rightarrow$	M2

Figure 10-1. The "immediate mutation" view of semantic change

involves variability and heterogeneity', and further that 'linguistic change is transmitted within the community as a whole; it is not confined to discrete steps within the
family. Whatever discontinuities are found in linguistic change are the products of
specific discontinuities within the community rather than inevitable products of the
generation gap between parent and child.'

Like any linguistic change, a semantic change is not acquired simultaneously by
all members of a speech community. An innovation enters into a language and spreads
through the speech community along socially determined lines. The original meaning of a form is not immediately displaced by the innovated meaning, but the two coexist for some time. Within this model, it is assumed that the two meanings share significant semantic features and that for a new meaning of a form to spread within the
community (without the perception that it constitutes a new lexeme) there must not
be a radical departure from the original meaning of the form. That is to say, change
within the linguistic system of a single speech community is presumed to be a feature-
by-feature change with the original linguistic system exercising a conservative influence on the type of innovation that can occur. Features are here taken to be the set of
knowledge structures and propositional structures which constitute what speakers
identify as the conventional conceptualization encoded through the use of a lexeme.
This alternative view of semantic change can be represented as in Figure 10-2. The
actual steps by which a semantic change proceeds through the speech community can
be idealised as in Figure 10-3.

The conception of semantic change which is represented in Figures 10-2 and 10-
3 is the view that is taken in this chapter. Semantic change is not a change in meanings per se, but the addition of a meaning to the semantic system or the loss of a meaning from the semantic system while the form remains constant. It is important to
realise that all semantic changes within a speech community involve polysemy at
their beginning point or at their endpoint. Under this view, what has typically been
characterised as a single semantic change (cf. Figure 10-1) is in fact two semantic
changes; the first semantic change resulting in polysemy through the addition of a
meaning to the system and the second semantic change involving the eradication of
polysemy through the loss of a meaning from the system. Synchronic polysemy becomes crucial in the investigation of semantic changes because it acts as a proof of
the plausibility that two meanings are semantically related and that one meaning
could give rise to the other.[2] As Evans (1992) notes with respect to the approach to
semantic change that he and I have been developing together:

> In seeking to uncover the synchronic linguistic manifestations of culturally unfamiliar
> conceptualizations, we draw heavily on the study of synchronic polysemy: cultural 'ex-
> planations' are only appropriate, or necessary, when the proposed semantic change has
> been demonstrated from purely linguistic evidence.

Time (T)	:	T1	T2	T3
Form (F)	:	F1	F1	F1
Meaning (M)	:	M1 $\rightarrow$	M1 & M2 $\rightarrow$	M2
Features	:	p,q,r	p,q,r q,r,s	q,r,s

Figure 10-2. The "polysemous" view of semantic change

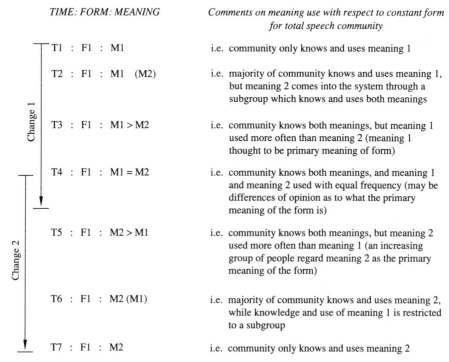

TIME: FORM: MEANING   *Comments on meaning use with respect to constant form for total speech community*

T1 : F1 : M1   i.e. community only knows and uses meaning 1

T2 : F1 : M1 (M2)   i.e. majority of community knows and uses meaning 1, but meaning 2 comes into the system through a subgroup which knows and uses both meanings

T3 : F1 : M1 > M2   i.e. community knows both meanings, but meaning 1 used more often than meaning 2 (meaning 1 thought to be primary meaning of form)

T4 : F1 : M1 = M2   i.e. community knows both meanings, and meaning 1 and meaning 2 used with equal frequency (may be differences of opinion as to what the primary meaning of the form is)

T5 : F1 : M2 > M1   i.e. community knows both meanings, but meaning 2 used more often than meaning 1 (an increasing group of people regard meaning 2 as the primary meaning of the form)

T6 : F1 : M2 (M1)   i.e. majority of community knows and uses meaning 2, while knowledge and use of meaning 1 is restricted to a subgroup

T7 : F1 : M2   i.e. community only knows and uses meaning 2

Change 1 / Change 2

Figure 10-3. Idealization of steps by which, in the "polysemous view" of semantic change, semantic changes proceed with respect to a complete speech community.

Our basic premise is, in other words, that putative semantic changes are the *explicatum* and attested synchronic polysemy are the *explicans*. Given a hypothesized semantic change from A to Z, our problem is to find a link of attested synchronic polysemies that would form a chain connecting A and Z. Since these chains may involve a large number of links (sometimes around a dozen), it is not usually possible to find them all in the language under study, so evidence from other related languages or semiotic systems must be brought in.

Some qualifications must be made with respect to the use and identification of polysemies. Firstly, two subtypes of polysemy are consistent with the model presented above. The first subtype we may label 'societal polysemy'; this is a situation in which distinct subgroups of the same larger speech community each have their own meaning for a particular form and neither group uses or recognises the other meaning. The second subtype is the traditional concept of polysemy in which individuals recognise that a lexeme has more than one related meaning. It is theoretically possible for a lexeme to manifest both types of polysemy, as for instance when an older age group and a younger age group maintain distinct meanings for the same form while an intermediate age group understands and uses both meanings. The second qualification is the acknowledgment that not all cases of synchronic polysemy arise from semantic change, as for example the cases of 'private' and 'commercial' demonstrate.

As a final note, it is worth observing that the notion of semantic change that has been defined in this section does not extend to cover meaning changes that occur in the process of one language borrowing a lexeme from another language. While meaning changes in borrowing can parallel semantic shifts that occur in the history of a particular language, it is also possible for there to be radical departures. Key to the current model of semantic change is the notion that the speech community exercises a conservative influence over the nature and type of semantic change a lexeme can undergo, because members of the community must be able to reconcile (cognitively) the association of both the older meaning and the innovated meaning with the same form. With semantic shifts during borrowing there is no intermediate stage of polysemy, and there need be no conservative influence over the nature, degree, and type of shift a lexeme undergoes.

4 NATURAL TENDENCIES OF SEMANTIC CHANGE IN THE SEMANTIC FIELD 'PARTS OF A PERSON'

Wilkins (1981) presents a crosslinguistic investigation of the semantic origins of terms for 'parts of a person', and the present section discusses some of the findings of that study. The notion 'parts of a person', or 'parts of a human being', is preferred over the more common 'body parts' because investigation revealed that 'body' is in fact a diachronically unstable term which is often found to be labelled by the same term as the term for 'skin', 'trunk', or 'person', or is not labelled at all. In Kâte (Papuan; Flierl and Strauss 1977), for instance, the word *sahac* has a primary meaning 'skin' and a secondary usage for 'body'. Lewis (1974: 52) notes for Gnau (Papuan) that 'there is no single word corresponding to the English 'body' for the whole'. Instead a lexeme *matil* meaning 'human', which must be distinguished for sex in its singular form, is used where the material aspect of a human being is to be indicated. Lewis makes it clear that there is no polysemy involved here, it is 'human being', not 'body', which is referred to when *matil* is used.[3] 'Person' ('human being'), as it turns out, is a better candidate for the unique beginner in this domain since it, unlike 'body', appears to be a universally named notion, and terms used to label this notion are less likely to polysemously cover other notions within the same domain. With 'person' as the unique beginner, notions like 'spirit', 'soul', and 'mind' enter into this partonomy along with the physical aspects of a person.[4] This distinction is made explicitly in Ponapean where *pali-war*, the word for 'body', literally means 'vessel side' and is opposed to *pali-ngen* meaning 'spirit side'.

The original study searched for the various semantic sources that can be shown to give rise to the following forty-one notions:

person, soul, corpse, body, belly, chest, breast, head, face, eye, ear, nose, mouth, lip, tooth, jaw, cheek, chin, leg, foot, toe, toenail, thigh, knee, arm, hand, finger, fingernail, elbow, penis, testicle, skin, bone, skull, brain, intestines, heart, liver, kidney, lungs, blood

Four language families for which there are good sources of etymological and/or comparative historical data were chosen for initial investigation. These were Dravidian, Bantu, Indo-European, and Tibeto-Burman, and the main sources were Burrow and Emeneau's (1961) *Dravidian etymological dictionary*[5], Guthrie's (1967–70) multi-volume *Comparative Bantu*, Buck's (1949) *Dictionary of selected synonyms in the principal Indo-European languages*, and Benedict's (1972) *Sino-Tibetan: A conspectus* augmented by Matisoff's (1978) *Variational semantics in Tibeto-Burman*. The examination of sources for these families resulted in 225 distinct semantic changes, each change having one of the the forty-one person-part notions listed above as the endpoint of the change. A change had to be indisputable to be recorded; that is to say, changes or associations which were regarded by an author as speculative or questionable were not recorded, nor were changes for which there was insufficient exemplification. Only 61 of these 225 changes are attested in two or more languages families, while the remaining 164 changes were attested in only one of the four families. For example, 1 of the 225 changes that is attested for all four families is the change 'to flay' → 'skin'(noun)[6], while the change 'unripe fruit' → 'kidney' is found in only one family (Dravidian).

To increase the language base, sources for Austronesian (especially Polynesian), Papuan, and Native American Indian languages were checked to see if there was any evidence of these 225 changes, or similar changes, having occurred, and any such parallel evidence was recorded. As the aim of the investigation was to try to find crosslinguistic tendencies of change, only one example of a particular change was recorded and counted for each family; no attempt was made to find out how common a change was within a particular family, since frequency could be a property of genetics or contact. It was assumed that if three language families showed the same change, or the same type of change, then the change was to be regarded as a crosslinguistically natural change. While most of the individual changes which were collected are attested in only one family, many of these changes in fact show parallels in other language families, and taken together these parallel changes also constitute natural tendencies of change. For example, the five individual family-specific changes of 'nest' → 'belly' (Dravidian), 'cave' → 'belly' (Tibeto-Burman), 'hollow' → 'belly' (Indo-European), 'bag' → 'belly' (Bantu), 'basket' → 'belly' (Papuan) are all taken to be parallel changes which constitute a single natural tendency of change which can be stated roughly as follows: It is a natural tendency for a term for something perceived as having a 'hemispherical, container-like' shape to take on the meaning 'belly' (by virtue of metaphorical association).

Approximately 70% of the recorded changes patterned into crosslinguistic natural tendencies. Of the remaining 30%, several were clearly culture-specific changes. For example, the New Greek word for liver *sukôti* derives from the notion of 'fig' (Late Greek *sukon*) through the notion of 'the liver of animals fed on dried figs' (*êpas sukôton*). Other changes may yet prove to be crosslinguistically natural. Three changes attested only in Dravidian languages—'foot ring' → 'foot', 'earring' → 'ear', 'pubic tassel' → 'penis'—suggest that this family may have a regular pattern of association whereby a term for an ornamental piece worn on/over a specific part of the body shifts, by metonymy, to refer to the associated body part. The reverse change, the use of body part terms to label items, or parts of items, that are worn on the body, is crosslinguistically well attested, and it may turn out that the Dravidian changes pattern into a common bidirectional change in which one direction of change ('body part'

→ 'item worn on/over body part') is more common than the reverse ('item worn on/over body part' → 'body part').

Of the natural tendencies, we may distinguish between those that are specific to a particular person-part and those that are generalised to account for changes involving a number of different person-parts. Of the natural tendencies that are specific to a certain person-part we have already encountered two types, one in which the actual source notion is consistent across language families, as was the case of 'to flay' → 'skin (noun)', and the other in which there are parallel languages or family-specific source notions which give rise to the person-part term, and one must extract the common features shared by these source notions in order to state the tendency, as in the case of the changes to 'belly' discussed above. Another example of this last type is provided by the changes which give rise to 'testicle'. In Indo-European we find the Lithuanian form for 'testicle', *pautas*, originally meant 'egg'; Danish and Swedish *sten*, also meaning 'testicle', is originally from the general Germanic word for 'stone'; the Dutch words for 'testicle' are *zaadbal* and *teelbal* which mean 'seed ball' and 'beget ball', respectively; and common nonmedical English terms for 'testicles' are 'nuts' and 'balls'. Similarly, in Dravidian, a low-level reconstruction for 'egg' (*muṭṭai*), based on seven languages, is realised in Koḍagu with a reflex meaning both 'egg' and 'testicle', and a reconstructed form for 'nut' or 'seed' (*kaṭṭo*) shows up in Kota as *keṭ* with the meaning 'testicle'. Proto-Polynesian *fua* 'fruit' has the reflex *hua*, meaning 'testicle', in the language of Easter Island, and in the Papuan language Yagaria the form for 'testicle' is *aga'mo' laga,* which literally means 'scrotum fruit'. Finally, in the Native American language Delaware the word for 'potato', *hopəmis(ak)*, has also come to refer to 'testicle' (Miller 1977: 142). Thus, it appears that it is a natural tendency for a term originally referring to something smallish (that is, that can be held in one hand) and roundish (ovoid to spherical), and preferably naturally occurring (that is, found in the natural environment rather than man-made) to take on the meaning 'testicle'. However, the actual source notion may vary from language to language and family to family, although 'egg', 'seed', and 'fruit', all of which are involved in nonhuman procreation, are the most common crosslinguistical sources (see also Brown 1989). In Wilkins (1981), I discuss twenty-eight natural tendencies which are specific to particular person-part notions; for twelve of these tendencies the source notions are constant across families, and for the other sixteen there are conceptually related, but crosslinguistically divergent, sources.

There are five natural tendencies, which have been formulated, exemplified, and discussed in detail in Wilkins (1981), that are generalised statements covering changes involving many different person-parts. Those can be roughly formulated as follows:

i. It is a natural tendency for a term for a visible person-part to shift to refer to the visible whole of which it is a part, but the reverse change is not natural (e.g. 'navel' → 'belly' → 'trunk' → 'body' → 'person').

ii. It is natural tendency for a person-part term to shift to refer to a spatially contiguous person part within the same whole (e.g. 'belly' ⇔ 'chest'; 'skull' ⇔ 'brain').

iii. Where the waist provides a midline, it is a natural tendency for terms referring to parts of the upper body to shift to refer to parts of the lower body and vice versa (e.g. 'elbow' ⇔ 'knee'; 'uvula' → 'clitoris'; 'anus' → 'mouth').

iv. It is a natural tendency for the term for an animal part to shift to refer to a person part (e.g. 'snout' → 'nose'; 'beak' → 'face').

v. It is a natural tendency for a term for a verbal action involving the use of a particular person part to shift to refer to that person part (e.g. 'walk' → 'leg'; 'hold' → 'hand').

Of these tendencies only the first is a purely unidirectional change, and it is discussed in more detail below in section 4.1. It is worth noting that these five tendencies account for approximately 50% of the attested changes.

To facilitate discussion and analysis, each change was classified using two intersecting parameters. Following Matisoff (1978: 176–79), changes are classified according to whether the two meanings involved belong to the same semantic field, **intrafield** changes, or whether they belong to different semantic fields, **interfield** changes.[7] Changes are also classified according to whether the meanings are associated by virtue of metonymy (conceptual or physical) or by virtue of metaphor.[8] The four general classes of change which this yields are **intrafield metonymic changes** such as 'finger' → 'hand', or 'chest' ⇔ 'heart'; **intrafield metaphoric changes** such as 'cheeks' → 'buttocks'; **interfield metonymic changes** such as 'to slap' → 'palm (of hand)', or 'earring' → 'ear'; and **interfield metaphoric changes** such as 'hoof' → 'foot', or 'boiled rice' → 'brain'.

It was found that, in general, the most common source for a person-part notion was to be found within the semantic field of person parts itself. In other words, due largely to the high number of intrafield metonymic changes, intrafield changes were more common than interfield changes. However, it is to be noted that for particular items like 'eye', 'testicle', and 'penis' the most likely sources are to be found outside the field of person parts. It was also found that metonymic changes gave rise to person-part terms much more commonly than did metaphorical changes. However, once again, specific items like 'skull' and 'testicle' run counter to this trend. The four classes of change may be ranked hierarchically, as in Figure 10-4, from the most common type of change which gives rise to a person-part notion to the least common type of change giving rise to a person-part notion. Not surprisingly, metonymic changes are more likely to be intrafield rather than interfield, while metaphoric changes are more likely to be interfield than intrafield.

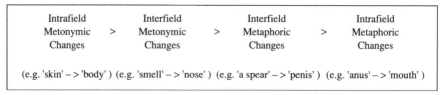

Intrafield Metonymic Changes		Interfield Metonymic Changes		Interfield Metaphoric Changes		Intrafield Metaphoric Changes
	>		>		>	
(e.g. 'skin' – > 'body')		(e.g. 'smell' – > 'nose')		(e.g. 'a spear' – > 'penis')		(e.g. 'anus' – > 'mouth')

Figure 10-4. Hierarchical (from most to least frequent) representation of relative degree to which different classes of change give rise to terms for notions within the semantic field "parts of a person."

4.1   A Unidirectional Law of Synecdochic Change

Synecdoche is the traditional term used to classify changes involving parts and wholes (i.e. part > whole; whole > part), and in this section I examine in more depth the natural tendency which constrains the directionality of synecdoche in the semantic domain 'parts of a person'. We may restate the generalised constraint that is proposed here as follows:

> In the semantic domain 'parts of a person', it is a natural tendency for a term referring to a visible part to come to refer to the visible whole of which it is an immediate, and a spatially and/or functionally integral, part. The converse change is not natural; the term for a visible whole **does not** shift to refer to one of its visible parts. (i.e. visible part > visible whole; visible whole ≯ visible part)

The particular intrafield metonymic changes from which this constraint was extracted are shown in Figure 10-5. Each change is labelled with the language family or families in which the change has been found (B = Bantu; Dr = Dravidian; IE = Indo-European; TB = Tibeto-Burman; AN = Austronesian).

As Figure 10-5 demonstrates, there are four distinct continua evidenced by these changes; one which ends at 'leg', one which ends at 'arm', one which ends at 'head', and one which ends at 'person', the unique beginner for the semantic field under consideration. Significantly, terms for 'leg', 'arm', and 'head' do not shift to refer to any notion, such as 'body' or 'person', that might, pretheoretically, be considered partonomically superordinate. In the data examined, the only terms for parts of the body that actually shift to refer to the notion 'body' itself are 'trunk', 'skin' and 'skeleton'.

The clearest examples of the change of visible part to visible whole are those which show the same historical form shifting more than once along a continuum. For Proto-Bantu, Guthrie reconstructs *-yádá 'fingernail'. In fifty-three modern languages 'fingernail' is the meaning of the reflexes of this protoform (e.g. Herero *on-yara* [class 9/10] and Ndandi *eky/ala* [class 7/8]); in fifteen languages the meaning is 'finger' (e.g. Nyoro *eky/ara* [class 7/8] and Kamba *n/zaa* [class 10]) and in 3 the meaning is 'hand' (eg. Ndau *nyara* [class 9/10]). In Gekoyo the root *-ara* is polysemous and takes the class 11/10 prefix *ro-* to give 'fingernail' and the class 7/8 prefix *ke-* to give 'finger'.[9] The shift of 'hand' → 'arm' is not attested in Bantu mainly because 'hand' and 'arm' are usually referred to by the same term.

The shift of 'fingernail' → 'finger' → 'hand' is also attested in the Austronesian family. Proto-Austronesian *kuku 'nail, claw' gives rise to Malay *kuku* 'nail' and Proto-Ambonese *gugu 'finger', while Grace's (1969) Proto-Oceanic reconstruction for both 'finger' and 'hand' is also *kuku. The shift of 'hand' → 'arm' is also attested in Austronesian where Proto-Austronesian *lima 'five, hand' is realised in Palauan as *ʔim* 'hand, arm and hand'.

The shifts towards 'arm' are paralleled by shifts towards 'leg'. The Proto-Indo-European reconstruction *(o)nogh 'nail, claw' gives rise to German *Nagel* 'fingernail or toenail' (and English *nail*), and the common Slavic word for 'foot', *noga*, also arises from a reflex of this protoform through a Balto-Slavic form which retained the original meaning. Lithuanian *nagas* preserves the original meaning of 'nail on finger

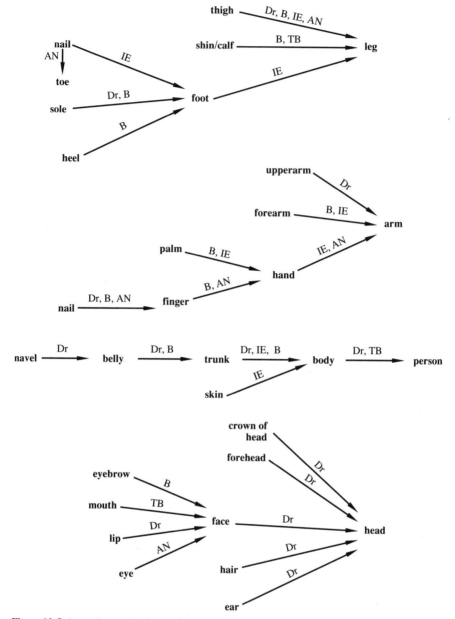

Figure 10-5. Attested semantic changes involving visible parts and visible wholes

or toe, claw', while Polish *noga* shows a shift of the term to refer to both 'foot' and 'leg', as has happened in most Slavic languages. Old Church Slavic shows *noga* 'foot' next to *nogŭtĭ* 'nail', while the form for 'leg' is *golěnĭ*.

Along the continuum of shifts which ends with the superordinate notion 'person', we find that the notion that is immediately subordinate to 'person' is 'body', the visible, concrete aspect of a person. In Dravidian, eight languages (Malayalam, Kota, Telugu, Tulu, Toda, Kannaḍa, Koḍagu, and Tamil) reflect a form meaning 'body' which is reconstructed as *may. In two of these languages, Malayalam (mai) and Tulu (mai), this form has become polysemous, referring to both 'body' and 'person'. Still in Dravidian, *utal/otal 'belly' is realised as udalu 'belly, stomach' in Tulu, oṛi 'belly, trunk' in Kota, utal 'trunk, body' in Malayalam, and oḍalu 'body' in Telugu. This clearly reflects a shift of 'belly' → 'trunk' → 'body' with all the expected intermediate polysemies.

The continuum with 'head' as its end point is the most questionable of the continua since five of the six intrafield shifts to 'head' are attested in a single family, Dravidian, and none of the changes involved in the continuum is found in more than one family, although Malcolm Ross (personal communication) reports that the shift of 'forehead' → 'head' also occurs in Oceanic Austronesian. However, given the parallel nature of the particular changes, given that the principle of 'visible part' → 'visible whole' is well established by the other continua, and given that there is no evidence to the contrary, the continuum involving 'head' will be considered as a further manifestation of the general tendency under discussion. Nevertheless it is acknowledged that further data are required to establish this continuum more firmly (see discussion of data in Tables 10-6 to 10-14 in section 5).

It is important to emphasise the fact that languages can differ regarding what is to be considered the immediately superordinate whole of a particular visible person part; not all languages manifest exactly the same number of partonomic divisions within these continua. Thus, if 'finger' is a named part, it is not entailed that 'hand' also be named, it is only entailed that some part which in real terms contains the hand is labelled. Thus, in Chirah-mbaw, a language of the Camerouns, posiy-mbo 'fingers' is immediately possessed by mbo 'arm including hand', and there is no term for 'hand' (i.e. mbo is not polysemous; Brown 1976: 408). Under such conditions it seems clear that a change of 'finger' → 'arm' is possible if there is no labelling of a part which is at a level in the partonomy intermediate between these notions. This may provide an explanation for why 'toe' is missing from the Slavic shift of 'nail' → 'foot' discussed above.

That there are four distinct chains of principled, unidirectional synecdochic change which emerge from the data is a fact which inivites speculative explanations. It is tempting, for instance, to suggest that 'head', 'arm', and 'leg' are viewed as self-contained wholes, peripheral to the main part of the body itself, but still connected to it. If we wish to consider the 'head', 'arm', and 'leg' as parts of the body, or parts of a person, then it would appear to be a conceptually different notion of part-of than that evidenced by such changes as 'thigh' → 'leg', 'hand' → 'arm', 'forehead' → 'head' and 'trunk (of body)' → 'body (as a whole)'. In trying to further explain the discontinuities, one could venture that, in terms of shape, spatial relations and primary functions, the four continua under discussion are clearly perceptually and conceptually distinct. The head's salient position at the top of the body is supported by a common bidirectional change of 'top' ⟺ 'head' (attested in Dravidian, Bantu, Indo-European, and Austronesian), and its rounded, containing shape is reflected in such changes as 'gourd' → 'head' and 'bowl' → 'head'. Functionally, the head is the seat of the organs of seeing, hearing, smelling, and taste. The legs, by contrast, are long, paired extensions at the lower part of the body used for support and locomotion. Attested changes such as 'stem, stalk' → 'leg', 'base of tree' → 'leg', 'stand' → 'leg', and 'walk' → 'leg' reveal these important aspects of the conception of 'leg'. The notion of the arms as long, paired extensions from each side of the body drives changes such as 'side of body' → 'arm', and we can observe that functionally the 'arms' are for reaching, holding, throwing, and gesturing. Finally, the head, legs, and arms are attached to the large central trunk, which is the main mass of the body and contains the primary internal organs governing respiration, circulation, digestion, and reproduction. Each of the four continua of synecdochic changes, then, could be taken to represent distinct spatial and functional complexes which are each perceived as having a conceptual unity of their own, and the subparts within each continuum may be seen as entities which are significantly integral to the perceived nature, shape, and/or uses of each of the four main wholes. However, while these hypothesised cognitive-functional explanations may be plausible, and do suggest avenues for further investigation, it must be admitted that the question of why the linguistic data here pattern into four distinct continua, each internally manifesting the same governed rule of semantic association, is still in need of a conclusive and demonstrable answer.

The natural tendency of synecdochic change which has been stated here is constrained to visible person parts and visible wholes because nonvisible internal parts do not appear to pattern in the same way. For example, the skull is often considered to be a part of the head, but the changes involving 'head' and 'skull' are not unidirectional, but, instead, are bidirectional (i.e. 'skull' ⇔ 'head'). Similarly, the changes 'leg' → 'bone' and 'bone' → 'leg' are also attested. The bidirectional changes of 'internal (nonvisible) part' and 'external (visible) whole' may arise because this 'part-of' relation is in fact more of a 'container-contained' relationship involving entities made of different stuff than it is a gestalt perception of a whole which can be visually resolved into parts whose dividing boundaries are not clearly fixed.

The polysemous stage which is said to be a part of all semantic changes (cf. section 3) has been noted for many of the changes discussed above. Interestingly, a number of the polysemies involving parts and wholes in the person-part domain are extremely stable and crosslinguistically widespread. Brown and Witkowski (1983) observe that approximately one-half of the languages of the world have a single term to cover the notions 'eye' and 'face'. On the basis of an investigation of 109 genetically and areally distinct languages, Witkowski and Brown (1985: 198) have noted that "50 have hand/arm polysemy, a frequency of about 46 per cent on a worldwide basis" and they also observe that 42 languages "have foot/leg polysemy, a frequency of about 39% on a worldwide basis" (1985: 202). In line with the findings of Wilkins (1981) reported earlier in this chapter, Witkowski and Brown (1985: 203) go on to observe '. . . hand/arm polysemy will typically develop through expansion of 'hand' to encompass arm. Similarly, foot/leg polysemy will develop through expansion of 'foot' to include leg. Expansion in the opposite direction . . . is not common'.

However, their proposed explanation of these facts is not supported by the study under discussion. They suggest that "unmarked terms for highly salient referents often expand to include less salient referents", and they regard 'hand' and 'foot' as high salience referents while 'arm' and 'leg' are of relatively less referential salience. As they put it,

'Evidence cited here lends support to the hypothesis that development of limb polysemy involves expansion of an unmarked term for hand to arm and an unmarked term for foot to leg rather than the reverse direction. For the limb domain, then unmarked terms for high salience referents often expand referentially by absorbing low salience referents'.

Relative referential salience is one of those notions which is extraordinarily difficult to characterise, and we must take care not to use semantic changes as our only evidence of relative salience if we are also going to use this as our explanation of those same changes. By looking at only two changes in isolation from other synecdochic changes within the domain of person parts, Witkowski and Brown have glimpsed only a small part of a very complex picture. It does not seem plausible to say that 'nail' is the most salient referent in the chain of changes which, in the limb domain, leads to 'arm' and 'leg' (i.e. 'nail' → 'finger' → 'hand' → 'arm', and 'nail' → 'foot' → 'leg'), but this would seem to be the logical outcome of the extension of their analysis to the new data. Moreover, there is no evidence of the distinctiveness, or privileged status, of the expansions of 'hand' → 'arm' and 'foot' → 'leg': they appear to pattern like the other changes. In parallel with 'foot' → 'leg', we also have 'thigh' → 'leg' and 'shin/calf' → 'leg'. In other words, terms for each of the three contiguous segments of which the leg is composed may all shift to refer to the whole leg as well. Does this mean that each of 'thigh', 'foot', and 'shin/calf' are all relatively more salient than 'leg'? If so, in what sense are they more salient? Perhaps the stability and crosslinguistic distribution of particular polysemies may be an indicator of certain significant relationships, but it should be noted that 'finger' and 'hand' are also very commonly labelled by the one term, and there is no independent evidence to suggest that 'finger' is a more salient referent than 'hand'.

Of course, such a consistent unidirectional pattern of change does cry out for explanation. I originally suggested (Wilkins 1981: 99) that the rationale behind this unidirectional tendency of semantic change might be as follows: The notion 'part', by definition, entails some idea of a 'whole', but a 'whole' does not entail a notion of a 'part'. Thus, a language could just have a term for 'arm' with no terms for parts of the arm. However, a term for 'finger' would logically imply the labelling of at least one other part, superordinate to finger, along the 'arm' continuum. This being so, changes along part-of relations would be naturally unidirectional. The problem with the phrasing of the rationale as given here is that it should apply to all part-whole relations, but I have already noted that, even within the domain of person-parts, not all relations which could be construed as part-whole relations are constrained by this natural tendency of change. Notions such as 'arm', 'head', and 'leg' do not shift to their supposed superordinate whole, 'body', and 'internal nonvisible parts' and 'external visible wholes' manifest the possibility of bidirectional shifting. I have suggested in the foregoing discussion that differing perceptual, functional, spatial, and material distinctions may in fact contribute to different kinds of part-of relation.[10] As Iris, Litowitz, and Evens (1988: 284–5) observe:

All part-whole schemata are derived originally from physical knowledge of the world. For this reason, discreteness, formedness, attachment, spatial inclusion, and questions of alienable vs. inalienable possession are all implicated. . . . Obviously very basic topological issues are implicated; some objects are perceived as cavitied (closed, potential containers, e.g., the body contains the heart) while others are perceived as biplanar or open (e.g., arms have hands). . . . *Part-whole is, then, not one relation, or even two, but a whole family of relations.* [emphasis mine]

The trick, then, is to characterise the particular part-of relation which drives this particular unidirectional shift.

In her lexical semantic study of body-part terminology in Hebrew, Petruck (1986) has demonstrated the usefulness of the Fillmorean notion of 'frame' in the description of this domain. Similarly, Nikiforidou and Sweetser (1989: 26) appeal to the notion of 'frame' in the following reanalysis of the proposal found in Wilkins (1981):

> Wilkins suggests that part-for-whole is more common than whole-for-part because a part implies the existence of some whole of which it is a part, while a whole need not have parts. Of course, it is not some real, extant whole which is implied by a part, but some CONCEPT of a whole which frames our understanding of the part. Thus an object can be 'part' of some particular variety of car, even if it was never used in the assembly of any whole car, or even if no such cars ever made it to the assembly line. Given this idea of the whole as a FRAME for the part (an idea strongly supported for body part terms by work of Petruck, 1986) we might extend metonymy to include other kinds of framing.

It is important to realise, however, that as Petruck (1986) demonstrates nicely, the 'Body Frame' is unique by virtue of the varied modes of personal and interpersonal experiential access to our concepts within this frame. Thus, the notion of the 'whole as a frame for the part' may be construed in a radically different way in the 'Body Frame' than it is in the 'Car Frame'. For one thing, there is a difference between whether the whole is prior and the parts are distinguished as a later step, or whether the parts are prior and come together to construct the whole. In their discussion of functioning units in a whole Iris, Litowitz, and Evens (1988) observe:

> . . . parts may exist prior to their inclusion in the whole, as in the parts of a bicycle. In fact, the whole is built up out of the logical and systematic assemblage of its parts. However, this is not true in all instances, since the organs of the body . . . derive their meaning from their inclusion in the whole and function solely with reference to it . . . (272)
>
> Paraphrases can also capture the differences between part-whole relations where the whole precedes the part. For example, a face contains eyes, nose, and mouth, but we do not say that a bicycle contains a wheel, or a wheel contains a spoke. In contrast, a bicycle consists of wheels, pedals, etc. (285)

From the point of view of the tendency under discussion, the facts that (i) a visible person part is difficult to view independently of its contiguous parts (that is, there is visual topological continuity from one externally visible body part to the next); (ii) there is nonseparability and inalienability of person parts; (iii) there is functional integration of parts within the same continua; (iv) there is continuity of sensation within and across continua, and (v) wholes precede (that is, are conceptually prior to) parts in the domain of person-parts, may all be hypothesised as working in tandem to give rise to the particular notion of part of that drives this particular unidirectional tendency of change. As Newmeyer (personal communication) points out, had the unidirectional tendency operated in the opposite direction (that is, from visible whole to visible part), a largely identical set of cognitive-functional features as is listed here could be proposed to explain the foundations of the change. Thus, the unidirectionality which is a fact of the linguistic data has yet to be connected to a known nonlinguistic cognitive mechanism which provides a plausible explanation for its existence.

As a brief digression, it is worth mentioning in this context an insightful discussion of metonymy by Traugott (1988) who expands on a Peircean notion as treated by Anttila (1972). Traugott notes that metonymy can be viewed as an indexical process: An idea or entity may be used to point to, or indicate, a contiguous idea or entity. Where parts and wholes are concerned, as long as the parts are perceptually and/or conceptually available, they may be used to call up the whole of which they are an integral and immediate part. A whole, on the other hand, cannot always be relied upon to uniquely index a particular part. Traugott points out that the unidirectional change involving body parts parallels a synecdochic change in which conversational implicatures are conventionalized and informativeness is strengthened. One could propose that such parallelism between quite divergent concrete and abstract domains might be due to a deep cognitive mechanism which governs the discrimination and conception of 'parts' and 'wholes' of all kinds and determines the nature of our understanding of part-whole relations, including any indexical aspects of the relation. In pursuing this line of reasoning it would be necessary to identify the cognitive constraints on indices and the indexical relation, as well as coming to grips with the more particular problem of what kinds of parts can be used to index wholes, and discovering what semantic and pragmatic features, if any, are shared by the various part-whole relations in which parts can index wholes, but wholes cannot index parts.

Returning to the main topic, implicit in the presentation and discussion of the data upon which the unidirectional constraint on synecdochic change is founded is the fact that no clear examples of changes in the reverse direction have been found. While this is true, it should be noted that this constraint is presented as a tendency rather than a law, since it is easy to construct hypothetical situations in which the reverse change could possibly happen. Although they do not give any examples, Witkowski and Brown (1985: 203) claim, in their discussion of the expansion of terms for 'hand' and 'foot' to include 'arm' and 'leg' respectively, that expansion in the opposite direction is not unknown, but is uncommon. They state that most cases of change in the opposite direction involve euphemism or use of figurative language. Petruck (1986: 141, 174) suggests that *zro'a* was originally the Biblical Hebrew word for 'arm' and it has come to refer to the 'upper arm' in Modern Hebrew. If this is the case, then this would certainly constitute a change which runs counter to the tendency as stated. However, Petruck is also careful to note that it is not possible to determine with certainty whether or not the form also applied to the 'upper arm' in Biblical Hebrew, and in Modern Hebrew *zro'a* may still refer to 'arm' in archaic usage.

In this extended discussion of natural tendencies of semantic change in the domain of person parts, and in particular in the discussion of the unidirectional change of 'visible part' → 'visible whole', I have tried to address explicitly the question of how we can know that two meanings are related in this restricted domain of concrete vocabulary. Moreover, I have tried to indicate the kind of elements that would be needed in an abstract theoretical model that seeks to explain natural tendencies of change and attempts to provide a precise formulation of rules of semantic association and semantic development. The existence of natural tendencies of semantic change in the semantic field 'parts of a person' adds to the growing body of facts which demonstrate the nonarbitrary nature of semantic change. As is demonstrated in the following section, a knowledge of these natural tendencies of change provides a powerful predictive tool for the discovery and establishment of cognates.

4.2   Using Natural Tendencies of Semantic Change in the Search for Cognates: Some Australian Examples

Ullman (1963: 248), anticipating the existence of natural tendencies of semantic change such as those discussed in section 4, noted that they could help the etymologist and comparativist in two ways. 'First it would tell him what kind of changes to expect, and whether a particular change suggested by his data would be common or infrequent, normal or exceptional. Second, it would enable him to choose between alternative explanations'. In this section, it is demonstrated how, armed with a knowledge of the natural tendencies of semantic change in a given semantic domain, one can, from the very beginning of comparative-historical research, profitably search for cognates from the meaning side. Once semantically divergent cognates are established, it is possible to anticipate the original meaning of the cognate form in those cases where the shifts involved are known to operate unidirectionally. Of course, the best way to demonstrate the universality, usefulness, and predictive power of the natural tendencies discussed above is to apply them to the search for cognates within a language family which did not contribute to their original discovery and formulation. To this end, only Australian examples will be discussed here. The forty-five word lists in the *Sourcebook for Central Australian languages* (Menning and Nash, 1981), supplemented by two comparative word lists for the Arandic group of Central Australia (Hale 1962 , n.d.) provide the main database,[11] and one of the aims of the current demonstration is to show that a large amount of important etymological and historical information can be garnered by looking at traditionally organised word lists in a new way.

4.3   A Semantically Organised Word List for Comparative Research

Matisoff (1978: 133), in discussing his "CALMSEA lexicostatistical list" (Culturally And Linguistically Meaningful for SouthEast Asia), observed that '. . . even if we have no great faith in glottochronology on methodological grounds, it might at least be worthwhile to try and improve the basic wordlists that are commonly used in these studies, the so-called "Swadesh lists"'. One way to improve such basic word lists would be to organise them such that words for notions that are commonly associated through natural semantic shifts lie near one another in the list. Indeed, the list should indicate the typical directionality of shifts so that the researcher will be able both to trace along a network of notions in trying to identify cognates, and to anticipate the source notion for a certain form. Based on the study discussed in section 4, I have devised a preliminary seventy-five-item word list centred on the most commonly at-

Figure 10-6

tested semantic changes within the domain of person-parts. The list is given in Table 10-1, and the following conventions are used: notions are numbered on their first appearance in the list, but when a notion participates in more than one change it may be necessary to repeat the notion, in which case further occurrences are unnumbered. A bracketed number after these repeated occurrences cross-references the notion to its first appearance. A box around a series of notions means that those notions operate in a parallel way. Where an arrow points to a box (without entering the box), it means that any of the items in the box may be the possible endpoint of a particular shift. In the case of a bracket and an arrow coming from a box, it means that any of the notions in the box is the possible source of a particular shift. When an arrow breaks into the side of a box, only the particular item in the box that the arrow goes to or from is implicated in a given shift. Unidirectional and bidirectional shifts are indicated in the conventional manner. Thus the chain of shifts diagrammed in Figure 10-6 would be interpreted to mean that a term for notion 'A' commonly shifts unidirectionally to cover notion 'B', terms for notions 'B', 'C', and 'D' are all attested as having shifted unidirectionally to cover notion 'F', and there is a common bidirectional shift between terms for notions 'C' and 'D'. The Australian data in the examples discussed below will be organised around sections from this new type of word list.

4.4 In Search of the Origins of Arandic 'hand'

In the first example, an attempt is made to resolve a problem surrounding the common Arandic word for 'finger' and 'hand'. This word, which can be reconstructed as *iltye* 'hand, finger', shows no cognates with forms for 'hand' in other Australian languages.[12] On the basis of the knowledge that a term for 'fingernail' commonly shifts to refer to 'finger' and terms for 'finger' or 'palm' often shift to 'hand' we can propose to search our word lists for these items. Here we are limited by the word lists used (that is, those in Menning and Nash 1981) to just two entries 'fingernail' and 'hand', with a note in the introduction of the source that 'hand' usually also refers to 'finger'.[13] Table 10-2 gives the full set of forms for these two entries in four subgroups of the Pama-Nyungan family of Australian Languages (Arandic, Ngarrka, Western Desert, and Ngumpin).

The Arandic group is known to have undergone extensive sound changes, including the loss of initial consonants and the neutralization of all final vowels to schwa. Thus, we would expect to be looking for cognates which in other Pama-Nyungan languages have an initial consonant and a final vowel other than schwa. A casual examination of the forms given in Table 10-2 reveals that the Ngarrka, Western Desert, and Ngumpin subgroups all have languages with words for 'fingernail' that are plausible cognates with Arandic *iltye* 'hand, finger'. Our confidence in this association must be tempered slightly by the fact that no language manifests the stage of intermediate polysemy that would be predicted. However, it appears that a reconstructable form *miltyarn* reduced in the Western Desert languages to *miltyi* and with loss of the ini-

TABLE 10-1

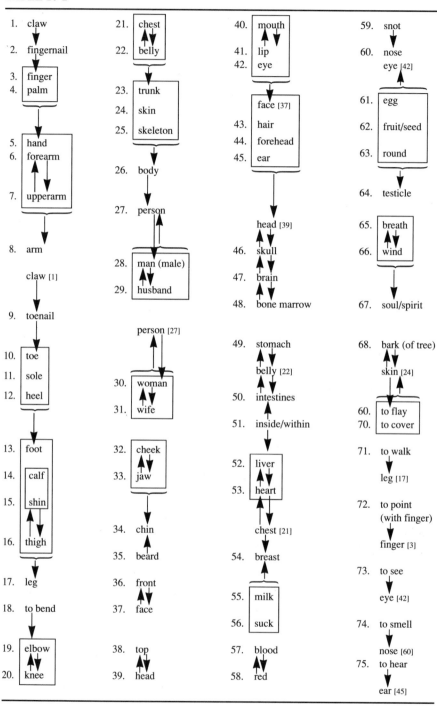

1. claw
2. fingernail
3. finger
4. palm
5. hand
6. forearm
7. upperarm
8. arm
    claw [1]
9. toenail
10. toe
11. sole
12. heel
13. foot
14. calf
15. shin
16. thigh
17. leg
18. to bend
19. elbow
20. knee

21. chest
22. belly
23. trunk
24. skin
25. skeleton
26. body
27. person
    person [27]
28. man (male)
29. husband
30. woman
31. wife
32. cheek
33. jaw
34. chin
35. beard
36. front
37. face
38. top
39. head

40. mouth
41. lip
42. eye
    face [37]
43. hair
44. forehead
45. ear
    head [39]
46. skull
47. brain
48. bone marrow
49. stomach
    belly [22]
50. intestines
51. inside/within
52. liver
53. heart
    chest [21]
54. breast
55. milk
56. suck
57. blood
58. red

59. snot
60. nose
    eye [42]
61. egg
62. fruit/seed
63. round
64. testicle
65. breath
66. wind
67. soul/spirit
68. bark (of tree)
    skin [24]
60. to flay
70. to cover
71. to walk
    leg [17]
72. to point
    (with finger)
    finger [3]
73. to see
    eye [42]
74. to smell
    nose [60]
75. to hear
    ear [45]

TABLE 10-2

Group	Language	'fingernail'	→	('finger'/)'hand'
ARANDIC	E. Aranda	tywepmwere		**iltye**
	W. Aranda	tjipmarra		**iltya**
	L. Aranda	irlkilthele		**iltye**
	Anmajirra	jupmara		**ilja**
	Alyawarra	ingkilthelh		**eltye**, etep
	Antekerrepenh	ingkalthel		**iltye**
	Kaytej	ngkelthel		**elja**
NGARRKA	Warlpiri	**miljarnpa, yiljirli**		rdaka
	Warlmanpa	lippi		taka
	Ngari	**miljarn**		marumpu
WESTERN DESERT	Pitjantjatjara	**miltji**		mara, manyirka
	Kukatja	milpinpa		marumpu
	Yankunytjatjara	**milytji**		mara
	Ngaanyatjarra	**miltji**		mara
NGUMPIN	Mudbura	**milyarna**		wartun, nungkuru
	Gurindji	lipi		wartan
	Jaru	**miljan**		marla
	Nyininy	**milyjarn**		pingka
	Malngin	**mujin**		marla
	Ngarinman	lipi		malamurri, marla,wartan
	Walmatjari	**miljarn**		taka, kurrapa, ngarrpi

tial consonant and neutralization of final vowel, the Arandic form was born. Note that Warlpiri shows two apparently related forms *miljarnpa* and *yiljirli*. It is a very real possibility, given the contact between Arandic and Warlpiri, as well as the fact that Warlpiri tends to add a 'y' to vowel initial borrowings, that *yiljirli* results from a borrowing of the Arandic form.

But what was the meaning of the original form? Is Arandic semantically conservative or innovative? Given that the association under discussion would follow the natural unidirectional tendency of 'visible part' → 'visible whole', the logical conclusion is that the original meaning of the form was 'fingernail' (or perhaps just 'nail' and/or 'claw'). This means that the languages of the Arandic subgroup can be identified by the shared semantic innovation of 'fingernail' to 'hand, finger'.[14] This fact provides some support to Matisoff's (1978: 231–2) statement: 'The shifting patterns of semantic association within a language or a language-family are at least as interesting as phonological changes through time, and may prove to be equally criterial for establishing degrees of genetic relationship'.

4.5 Tracing the Chain 'skin' → 'body' → 'person'⇔ 'man (male)' in the Western Desert Languages

For the next two examples we will use the unidirectional chain of shifts 'skin' → 'body' → 'person' to search for cognates. In the first case this chain will be augmented

by the bidirectional shift 'person' ⇔ 'man (male)', and in the second case this will
be augmented by the bidirectional shift 'person' ⇔ 'woman'. Note that these chains
of semantic changes show that the notion 'person' is at the head of two distinct semantic fields, the person-part partonomy and the taxonomy of human classification.
Examine Table 10-3, which involves forms from the Western Desert group.

Clearly the most striking aspect of the comparative set given above is that four of
the five languages show an obviously similar form, *pantu ~puntu*, but each of the four
languages has a distinct meaning range for the form—Yankunytjatjara *pantu* 'skin',
Pitjantjatjara *puntu* 'body', Kukatja *puntu* 'body, man', Pintupi *puntu* 'man'. By
virtue of the fact that we used natural tendencies of meaning association to search for
such cognate forms, we can be confident that the forms are semantically similar, but
what meaning do we reconstruct for the original form? Once again the unidirectionality of the natural tendency 'visible part' → 'visible whole' suggests to us that the
original meaning of the form, which for now I will reconstruct as **pVntu,* is 'skin'.
Fortunately, there is evidence both internal and external which corroborates this conclusion. By sheer weight of numbers (four out of five languages), the obvious reconstruction for 'man (male)' is **wati*. Similarly, **(y)arnangu* seems the obvious
favourite for reconstruction as the Proto-Western Desert form for both 'body' and
'person'; as for any language, we would presume that polysemy was a fact of life in
protolanguages. The only notion for which there is no clear favourite is 'skin', and
given that *pantu ~ puntu* seems to reflect a local word which we would want to reconstruct for Proto–Western Desert, the only notion left to connect it with is 'skin'.
If we look outside this group, the only obvious candidate for cognacy with *pantu ~
puntu* is Warlpiri *pinti* which is glossed as both 'skin' and 'bark' (cf. Table 10-4). If
the Warlpiri form is indeed cognate, then we have extended the chain of associations
here from 'bark' to 'man' and shown that if we were confronted with similar forms,
one meaning 'bark' and one meaning 'man', we could not dismiss them as noncognate until we have failed at the attempt to establish the common intermediate links
that are known to bridge the two notions. Note that the claimed shift of 'person' to
'man' in this data is given strength by the attested polysemy in Kukatja. Furthermore,
four of the five languages have a form that is polysemous for 'body' and 'person', a
fact which at least provides a parallel for the claimed shift of *puntu* 'body' to *puntu*
'person'. There is no evidence in the word lists themselves that would support the polysemy of 'skin' and 'body' hypothesised as a necessary stage in this chain of shifts.

TABLE 10-3

Group	Language	'skin' →	'body' →	'person' ⇔	'man'
WESTERN	Yankunytjatjara	**pantu**	aṉangu	aṉangu	wati
DESERT	Pitjantjatjara	miri, pi	**puntu** aṉangu	aṉangu	wati
	Kukatja	tyartinypa	yanangu	**puntu**	**puntu**
	Pintupi	minyarra, pangki	yaṉangu	yaṉangu	**puntu,** wati, matu
	Ngaanyatjarra	minyarra, miri	yarnangu	yarnangu	wati

However, Goddard (1987: 99) indicates that a secondary meaning of Yankunytjatjara *pantu* is, in fact, 'body'.

4.6 Using the Chain 'skin' → 'body' → 'person'⇔ 'woman' to Sort Out Lexical Mysteries in the Arandic Subgroup

The data for the next demonstration is provided in Table 10-4. The focus is on data from the Arandic group, with other relevant data provided from some of the languages in the Ngarrka, Western Desert, and Ngumpin Groups. The data in Table 10-4 is not as easily interpreted as that in Table 10-3 was. However, the following facts are clear. All seven languages of the Arandic group have a form *(a)relh(e) ~ (a)rilh(e)*, and for three of these languages (Antekerrepenh, W. Aranda, and L. Aranda) this form means 'person', for another three of these languages (Kaytej, E. Aranda, and Alyawarra) this form means 'woman', and one language (Anmajirra) attests the polysemy of 'woman' and 'person' that would be expected to occur in a shift from one notion to the other. Given the bidirectionality of the shift between 'person' and 'woman' we cannot suggest a priori which meaning is original. However, since there is another strong candidate for reconstruction as 'woman' (evidenced by L. Aranda *arrkutja*, W. Aranda *arrkutja*, Antekerrepenh *arrkwety*, and Alyawarra *errkwely* next to Warlpiri *mardukuja*), and since, as discussed later, it appears that in Eastern Aranda and Kaytej a borrowed form which was taken in for 'body' expanded to cover 'person' as well, I propose that there was a Proto-Arandic form **arelhe* which originally meant 'person' and which narrowed to 'woman' in four of the languages (three of these languages taking on a new form for 'person' and one retaining the intermediate polysemous stage of 'person, woman').

TABLE 10-4

Group	Language	'skin' →	'body' →	'person' ⇔	'woman'
NGARRKA	Warlpiri	pinti ('bark' also) pangki	palka	yapa	mardukuja, karnta, ngama
	Ngari	**jarrja**	—	ngantany	karntarr
NGUMPIN	Walmatjari	**jarrja,** partu, parntapi	karrkin	piyirn	marnin
WESTERN DESERT	Kukatja	**tyartinypa,** **tya(r)tin**	yarnangu	puntu	tutju
ARANDIC	Kaytej	perr	**eyterretye,** arlke	**eyterretye**	*arelh*
	E. Aranda	yenpe	**tyerrtye**	**tyerrtye**	*arelhe*
	Alyawarra	yenp, erriny	arlke	artwe errpurl	*arelh,* errkwely
	Anmajirra	ayinpa	kururna	*arilh*	*arilh*
	Antekerrepenh	yenp	alke	*arelh*	arrkwety
	W. Aranda	yinpa	mpurrka	*rilhe*	arrkutja
	L. Aranda	puulhe	mperra	*relhe*	arrkutja

Also clear from Table 10-4 is the fact that Kaytej and Eastern Aranda have apparently cognate forms, *eyterretye* and *tyerrtye*, respectively, which are polysemous for 'body' and 'person'. No other Arandic language shows these forms, and a search for related forms outside this group, which takes into account the fact that 'skin' commonly shifts to 'body', reveals that three languages in three different groups[15] have plausibly related forms meaning 'skin': Ngari **jarrja**, Walmatjari **jarrja** and Kukatja **tyartinypa, tya(r)tin**. As mentioned above, we expect Arandic forms to show initial consonant loss in comparison to forms from other Pama-Nyungan languages. However, the fact that both the Arandic and the non-Arandic forms reflect a lamino-palatal stop as the first consonant strongly suggests a borrowing relation. While the borrowing could go either way, it seems more likely that the forms in Kaytej and E. Aranda have been borrowed, because this restricts the borrowing to one group. Thus, it is hypothesised that a form *jarrja* meaning 'skin' was borrowed into Kaytej and E. Aranda to refer to 'body'. In tandem with the shift of 'person' to 'woman' in these two languages, it is suggested that this borrowed form for 'body' expanded to refer to 'person'.[16] We do not expect intermediate polysemies in semantic shifts during borrowing, so the lack of any 'skin'/'body' polysemy here is not a problem. What is strange about this account is the parallelism between Kaytej and E. Aranda, because they belong to distinct subfamilies of the Arandic group (Hale 1962, Wilkins 1989a) and there is no account of regular contact between them.

As a final note to the discussion of Table 10-4, it is worth pointing out that Kaytej *arlke*, Antekerrepenh *alke*, and Alyawarra *arlke*, which all mean 'body', appear to reflect a widespread form for 'flesh' and 'body'. In the Ngarrka group the Warlpiri form for 'body' is *palka*, and in the Karnic group (*not* shown in Table 10-4) we find Diyari *parlku* 'body', Yandruwandha *parlaka* 'body', Arabana *palku* 'flesh, body', and Wangkanguru *palku* 'flesh, body'. Note also that W. Aranda *mpurrka* 'body' and L. Arrernte *mperrke* 'body' correspond to Mparntwe Arrernte *mpwerrke*, which covers the following semantic range: 'whole', 'complete', 'fat', 'healthy', 'full', 'body' (Wilkins 1989a: 5 84).

4.7   Searching for Cognates with the Chain 'liver' ⇔ 'heart' ⇔ 'chest'

For the fourth investigation, the set of bidirectional changes 'liver' ⇔ 'heart' ⇔ 'chest' will be used to identify possible cognates. Table 10-5 organises data from the Karnic, Ngarrka, and Arandic groups around this chain of changes. Starting with the forms in the Karnic group, we find once again that the reorganization of basic word list data according to common semantic changes brings to the fore a number of plausibly related forms. Firstly, *ngarangara* 'heart' in Arabana, Wangkanguru, and Diyari, clearly corresponds to Yandruwandha *ngarangara* 'liver'. Although there is a common bidirectional shift between terms for 'heart' and 'liver', it is safe to presume in this case that the change was from 'heart' to 'liver'. This direction of shift is chosen because all Karnic languages, including Yandruwandha, show a clearly related form for 'liver' (**kaLu*) and because it is crosslinguistically common for the term for 'heart', but not 'liver', to be a reduplicated form. Secondly, the Arabana and Wangkanguru form for 'chest', *ngararra*, is so similar to the 'heart' form in those languages that we might posit, as an initial hypothesis, that the form meaning 'heart' (*ngarangara*) is derived from the form meaning 'chest' through reduplication. Moreover, the relation be-

TABLE 10-5

Group	Language	'liver' ⇔	'heart' ⇔	'chest'
KARNIC	Arabana	kadlu	**ngarangara**	**ngararra**
	Wangkanguru	kalyu	**ngarangara**	**ngararra**
	Diyari	kalhu	**ngarangara**	*murnampidi*
	Yandruwandha	**ngarangara**, kalu	tupurru, *marnu*	*murnathitha*
	Pitta Pitta	kalu	*marnu*	*murna*
ARANDIC	Alyawarra	alem	*rtakurt*	anelty
	Anmajirra	alima	*rtukurta*	arnarnka
	E. Aranda	aleme	*ewrtakwerte*	**arerre**, inwenge
	W. Aranda	lima	*tukurta*	inarnka
	L. Aranda	aleme	*urtakerte*	inenge, annge
NGARRKA	Warlpiri	nyilima, yilima	kurturdurru, martulyka	*rdukurduku*, mangarli
	Ngari	mirliki	turlpu	*tukurtuku*
	Warlmanpa	japarrka	marnturlka	mangarli

tween the notions 'heart' and 'chest' in this group is strengthened by the very strong similarity in form between *marnu* 'heart' (Yandruwandha, Pitta Pitta) and *murna* (Pitta Pitta), *murnathitha* (Yandruwandha), and *murnampidi* (Diyari) 'chest'.

The Arandic and Ngarrka groups show no evidence of shifts associating 'liver' and 'heart', but we would want to suggest a relationship between the Arandic forms for 'heart' (*rtakurt, rtukurta, ewrtakwerte, tukurta, urtakerte*) and the Warlpiri and Ngari forms for 'chest' (*rdukurduku* and *tukurtuku*, respectively). Once again, the fact that forms for 'heart' tend to be reduplicated and, as in this case, are likely to be onomatopoeic suggests that the forms meaning 'chest' in the Ngarrka group originally arise from a form (**rtukurtuku*) meaning 'heart'. Although the Arandic forms for 'heart' have lost the last syllable in relation to the Ngarrka forms, we would also have expected a loss of the initial consonant as well. Note that O'Grady (1987: 526) gives **tUku* as a Proto–Nuclear-Pama-Nyungan reconstruction for 'heart'.

Some final miscellaneous observations concerning data in Table 10-5 are in order. First, note that E. Aranda *arrere* 'chest' is almost certainly related, perhaps only by borrowing, to the Arabana and Wangkanguru form *ngararra* 'chest'. Secondly, there is a natural tendency for terms for major internal organs, especially adjacent ones, to trade referents, as in the case of 'liver' ⇔ 'heart'. This being so, it is worth pointing out that Warlmanpa (Ngarrka) *japarrka* 'liver' (listed in Table 10-5), as well as Mudbura (Ngumpin) *japarrka* 'liver', are likely to be related to forms for 'kidney' in Arandic languages (E. Aranda *arteperrke*, Kaytej *erteperrke*, Anmajirra *itiperrke*).

4.8 Looking Further Afield for Tentative Cognates with the Changes 'hair' → 'head' and 'forehead' → 'head'

In section 4.1 it was noted that, of all the changes that were used to substantiate the natural unidirectional tendency of 'visible part' → 'visible whole', the changes in the continuum ending at 'head' were the least represented. Still, in accordance with the natural tendency, part-whole changes giving rise to 'face' and 'head' have been incorporated into the newly devised comparative list given in Table 10-1. In this fifth and final exploration, the validity of incorporating these changes will be tested, at least in part, through attempting to use the changes of 'hair' → 'head' and 'forehead' → 'head' to gather possible cognates.

In the four previous explorations the data examined was restricted to those languages of the Pama-Nyungan subgroup of Australian languages found in central Australia. A second aim of this final exploration is to expand the focus of investigation such that it includes data from non-Pama-Nyungan languages in the central Australian region. In the Australianist context there has been a problem in proving a genetic link between Pama-Nyungan and non-Pama-Nyungan languages due to a lack of sufficient cognates. It is possible that if one is able to account for semantic shifts, then one could gather a larger cognate base for a determination of the nature of the relationship between non-Pama-Nyungan languages and languages of the Pama-Nyungan family. The data for this exploration is given in Table 10-6. The three Pama-Nyungan groups are Western Desert, Ngumpin, and Wakayic, and the two non-Pama-Nyungan groups are Jingiluan and Karawan.[17] The languages and language families have been organised according to their geographical proximity to one another, which explains why the Pama-Nyungan groups occur on either side of the non-Pama-Nyungan languages in the data of Table 10-6. As there is too much data to discuss all at once I will discuss subsets of the data.

A first step in establishing that shifts involving the notions 'hair', 'head', and 'forehead' are natural in the Australian context would be to identify any existing polysemies which connect these notions. Table 10-7 shows that, in the data under consideration, three different groups (two Pama-Nyungan [three languages] and one Non-Pama-Nyungan [one language]) manifest five cases of polysemy. There are three examples of polysemy between 'hair' and 'head' (Nyininy *langka*, Wampaya *tamangka*, Wakaya *kula*) and two examples of polysemy between 'forehead' and 'head' (Ngarinman *ngalaka* and Wakaya *rlayi*). There are no examples of a polysemy between 'hair' and 'forehead'. These polysemies, therefore, establish the likelihood of shifts between 'hair' and 'head', and 'forehead' and 'head', but do not give any clues to directionality.

Further evidence of the naturalness of these associations is the fact that a single group may show the same associations repeated across a number of different languages in the group. These associations need not only be identified by polysemies, but may also be identified by the fact that one language has a particular form for one notion, and another language in the same group has an essentially identical form for a different, but related, notion. Witness the interlocking relationships of associated forms and associated meanings which are demonstrated for the Ngumpin group in Table 10-8. Note that there are two distinct associations in the group which establish a link between 'hair' and 'head', and there are also two distinct associations which establish a link between 'forehead' and 'head'.

In Table 10-9, we turn to the initial gathering of possible cognates. There we find what appears to be a widespread form, which for now we can represent as *kula*, that is represented in the two non-Pama-Nyungan groups (five languages) and in two of the Pama-Nyungan groups (three languages). This form, or its derivatives, span all three notions, 'hair', head', and 'forehead'. Inspection of Table 10-9 reveals that there

TABLE 10-6

Group	Language	'hair' →	'head' ←	'forehead'
WESTERN DESERT	Yankunytjatjara	mangka	kata	ngalya
	Pitjantjatjara	mangka	kata	ngalya
	Ngaanyatjara	mangka	kata	ngalya
	Pintupi	mangka, yurru	kata, ngamanypa	ngalya
	Kukatja	mangka, ngangi	kata	nalya, nala
NGUMPIN	Nyininy	langka, wirrkil	langka	—
	Jaru	wirrkil	langka	—
	Walmatjari (a)	wirrkil, ral	jurlu, wangkalman	janginy
	Walmatjari (b)	ral	wirrkil	nanyin
	Malngin	kiwan	walu	lungan
	Ngarinman	ka(r)tpi, yamparra	ngalaka	ngalaka, kulaka
	Pilinara	katpi	warlu	tiwa
	Gurindji	kartpi	ngarlaka	ngamany
	Mudbura	winjarlma	walu, kurlaka	wituru
JINGILUAN	Jingilu	malipanya	tamangka	wirturru, kuya
	Wampaya	tamangka	tamangka, kula	wara
	Kutanji	nyung(k)a	kula	wara
	Ngarnji	nyirra	tamangka	warra
KARAWAN	Karawa	nyungka	kulaji	wali
	Wanyi	nyungka	kuyi, kuwi	wali ('face' also)
WAKAYIC	Wakaya	kula	kula, rlayi	rlayi
	Warluwara	walangantha	mirti	kurukuru

is no evidence of unidirectional changes of 'hair' → 'head' or 'forehead' → 'head'. Indeed, both the fact that the majority of items in this set are glossed as 'head' and the fact that in each group which attests this form one or more languages use the form to refer to 'head' strongly suggest that *kula* originally meant 'head'. If all of these items are truly related genetically, rather than being related through borrowing or chance

TABLE 10-7

Group	Language	'hair' →	'head' ←	'forehead'
NGUMPIN	Nyininy	langka	langka	
	Ngarinman		ngalaka	ngalaka
JINGILUAN	Wampaya	tamangka	tamangka	
WAKAYIC	Wakaya	kula	kula, rlayi	rlayi

TABLE 10-8

Group	Language	'hair'	→	'head'	←	'forehead'
NGUMPIN	Nyininy	langka, wirrkil		langka		
	Jaru	wirrkil		langka		
	Walmatjari (a)	wirrkil				
	Walmatjari (b)			wirrkil		
	Ngarinman			ngalaka		ngalaka, kulaka
	Gurindji			ngarlaka		
	Mudbura			kurlaka		

resemblance, then this would be evidence against the proposed directionality of changes.

Another set which suggests relations between Pama-Nyungan and non-Pama-Nyungan languages is shown in Table 10-10. Here we find the regular Western Desert form for 'hair', *mangka*, associated with the most common Jingiluan form for 'head' *tamangka*. The Wampaya form shows *tamangka* to be polysemous between 'hair' and 'head', which in the context of the Western Desert data might be taken as evidence for the directionality of a shift from 'hair' to 'head'. This, however, is a very weak argument, and the best that can be said is that there is no clear evidence of directionality. The data of Table 10-10 was set up on the basis of conservative phonological criteria; if those criteria were relaxed somewhat, this comparative set could be increased by the addition of Nyininy *langka* 'hair, head', Jaru *langka* 'head', and Walmatjari (a) *wangkalman* 'head'.

Another possible association between 'hair' and 'head' that would be worth investigating further is given in Table 10-11. This set demonstrates that the common Western Desert form for 'head', *kata*, could possibly be cognate with a form *ka(r)tpi*

TABLE 10-9

Group	Language	'hair'	→	'head'	←	'forehead'
NGUMPIN	Ngarinman					kulaka
	Mudbura			kurlaka		
JINGILUAN	Jingilu					kuya
	Wampaya			kula		
	Kutanji			kula		
KARAWAN	Karawa			kulaji		
	Wanyi			kuyi, kuwi		
WAKAYIC	Wakaya	kula		kula		

TABLE 10-10

Group	Language	'hair'	→	'head'	←	'forehead'
WESTERN	Yankunytjatjara	mangka				
DESERT	Pitjantjatjara	mangka				
	Ngaanyatjara	mangka				
	Pintupi	mangka				
	Kukatja	mangka				
JINGILUAN	Jingilu			tamangka		
	Wampaya		tamangka	tamangka		
	Ngarnji			tamangka		

'hair' found in three Ngumpin languages, Ngarinman, Pilinara, and Gurindji. Note, however, that the association of forms is not confirmed by an intermediate polysemy.

Table 10-12 and 10-13 both reveal correspondences of 'forehead' and 'head' in the Western Desert and Ngumpin groups. In Table 10-12, the common Western Desert form for 'forehead', *ngalya*, corresponds to Ngarinman *ngalaka* 'forehead, head' and Gurindji *ngarlaka* 'head'. O'Grady (1979:128) uses Nyangumarda *ngalyi* 'neck', Yulbaridja *ngalya* 'face', Warlpiri *ngalya* 'forehead', and Pitta Pitta *ngalya* 'cheek' as evidence for the reconstruction of a Proto–Nuclear-Pama-Nyungan form, **ŋAlja*, which he does not gloss. We may add the Western Desert and Ngumpin forms in Table 10-12 to O'Grady's etymological set and note that the vast majority of forms refer to parts of the head, rather than the head itself. This suggests that the Ngumpin forms for 'head' arise out of the regular shift of 'visible part' → 'visible whole'. O'Grady also points out that reflexes of his reconstruction show up in derived forms for entities, such as cliffs and sandhills, which have a vertical face. In Australia, 'forehead' or 'brow', but not 'face' as O'Grady suggests, seems to be commonly associated by virtue of metaphorical extension to such naturally occurring entities with a sheer or steep vertical slope. On these grounds I would tentatively propose that at least one of the meanings of O'Grady's **ŋAlja* is 'forehead'. The natural tendency of a term for a part to shift to refer to the adjacent part within the domain of the same whole, and the natural tendency 'visible part' → 'visible whole' would explain all of the metonymic extensions from this one meaning to other 'head-part' notions. For Table

TABLE 10-11

Group	Language	'hair'	→	'head'	←	'forehead'
WESTERN	Yankunytjatjara			kata		
DESERT	Pitjantjatjara			kata		
	Ngaanyatjara			kata		
	Pintupi			kata		
	Kukatja			kata		
NGUMPIN	Ngarinman	ka(r)tpi				
	Pilinara	katpi				
	Gurindji	kartpi				

TABLE 10-12

Group	Language	'hair'	→	'head'	←	'forehead'
WESTERN DESERT	Yankunytjatjara					ngalya
	Pitjantjatjara					ngalya
	Ngaanyatjara					ngalya
	Pintupi					ngalya
	Kukatja					nalya, nala
NGUMPIN	Ngarinman			ngalaka		ngalaka
	Gurindji			ngarlaka		

10-13 the only relevant observation is the fact that this time a Ngumpin language, Gurindji, has a form for 'forehead', *ngamany*, which closely corresponds to a form for 'head', *ngamanypa*, in a Western Desert language, Pintupi.

Perhaps the most speculative group of possibly cognate forms referring to 'hair', 'head', and 'forehead' is presented in Table 10-14. Here two Pama-Nyungan groups (Ngumpin [three languages] and Wakayic [one language]) and one non-Pama-Nyungan group (Karawan [two languages]) appear to reflect the recurrence of a form which we can represent as *walV*. The problem is that each group shows a different final vowel and a different meaning for the supposedly correspondent forms. In the relevant Ngumpin languages *wa(r)lu* refers to 'head', in Karawan *wali* refers to 'forehead' and 'face', and in Wakayic *wala* is the initial part of a form, *walangantha*, referring to 'hair'. The plausibility of the grouping, however, is buoyed up by all the previous parallel examples which we have cited, and since we are only concerned here with the initial selection of possible and plausible cognate forms, this set deserves further investigation before being dismissed.

Once again, if the criteria for phonological similarity were to be relaxed slightly, the following Jingiluan (non-Pama-Nyungan) forms for 'forehead' could be added to the set in Table 10-14: Ngarnji *warra* and Wampaya and Kutanji *wara*. With respect to these Jingiluan forms, note that O'Grady (1979: 127–28) has reconstructed a Proto–Nuclear-Pama-Nyungan form **waara* which he suggests originally referred to 'face'. As we have seen previously, the association of 'forehead' and 'face' is not uncommon, and this strongly suggests a connection between the non-Pama-Nyungan Jingiluan forms and this Pama-Nyungan reconstruction.

Through this final exploration I have tried to give a sense of the very rich body of correspondent forms that a simple chain of universal semantic associations is able to reveal. While the proposed unidirectional changes of 'hair' → 'head' and 'forehead'

TABLE 10-13

Group	Language	'hair'	→	'head'	←	'forehead'
WESTERN DESERT	Pintupi			ngamanypa		
NGUMPIN	Gurindji					ngamany

TABLE 10-14

Group	Language	'hair'	→	'head'	←	'forehead'
NGUMPIN	Malngin			walu		
	Pilinara			warlu		
	Mudbura			walu		
KARAWAN	Karawa					wali
	Wanyi					wali (face also)
WAKAYIC	Warluwara	walangantha				

→ 'head' were neither fully supported nor totally disconfirmed, the naturalness of shifts involving these notions seems incontestable. Moreover, it has been shown that by taking into account semantic shifts, and by using them to gather plausible cognates, we can substantially increase the initial tentative cognate base for languages and groups for which there were previously meagre and questionable cognate sets. In particular, several hypothesised connections given here concerning forms in non-Pama-Nyungan languages and forms in Pama-Nyungan languages deserve to be explored further.

4.9 What About Culture-Specific and Family-Specific Tendencies of Change?

I have consciously avoided extending the discussion in this section to culture-specific and family-specific tendencies of change. If, as much of the work in Cognitive Semantics and Cognitive Linguistics suggests, our understanding and perception of our own personal sphere, especially our own body, provides the basic framework for much of the conceptualisation and expression of the cultural and intellectual world beyond ourselves, then we must first consolidate our understanding of the relations within the personal sphere so that we can, with a minimum of speculation, anchor any further extensions to it. For instance, Von Brandenstein (1982: 7) has pointed out that

> . . . in the Aboriginal conception the relevant category of totemic classification is to be sought in the sphere of human physique and character. Classifying divisions would differ for the shape of the body, consistency of the flesh, colour of the skin, shape of the head, dimensions of the face or forehead, growth and texture of the hair, look of the eyes, voice, taste, scent, and the state of the liver as the seat of temperament.

He observes (Von Brandenstein 1982: 6) that a linguistic correlate of this conceptualisation is the fact that the general term for totem or social division in different Australian languages often also refers to one of the many 'person-part' notions we have discussed in this section, such as 'body', 'skin', 'head', 'forehead', 'face', 'hair', 'eyes', 'flesh', or 'liver'. However, I would contend that we should not weave this culture-specific extension into the comparative-historical picture until we understand the more universal associations upon which it is overlaid. Certainly I would agree that family-specific extensions of the semantic change-based word list given in Table 10-1 can, and should, be formulated, and the work of O'Grady (1979), Evans (1992), and Wilkins (1989b) moves us in that direction for the Australian context.

4.10   Semantic Change and Genetic Classification

Dixon (1980: 260–65), in discussing attempts at the genetic classification of Australian languages, notes the unsatisfactory nature of lexicostatistic studies, but also observes (264) that the lexicostatistic classifications are "the ONLY attempt at subgrouping which is readily available". He goes on to state:

> In fact, present knowledge of the relationships between Australian languages is not sufficient to justify any sort of fully articulated 'family tree' model. Further work on the historical development of Australian languages is urgently needed, to discover whether our present low-level subgroups can be linked together to form larger genetic groupings, and to investigate how genetic factors interrelate with areal traits.

The discussion throughout this section has been an attempt to help further the investigation of the historical development of Australian languages, through the application of a slight revision to the initial stages of the established methodology of comparative linguistics (i.e. cognate identification). However, while most linguists would agree that lexicostatistics is only good for initial hypothesis formation concerning the possible genetic relatedness of the languages under investigation and does not prove such genetic relationships, it is also true that in the Australian context the only information that exists for some languages is word lists. Thus, anything that might improve our use and interpretation of word lists for the purposes of genetic classification would be valuable.

Matisoff (1978: 101) rightly observes that the lexicostatistician's disregard of semantically skewed cognates causes them "to lose a great deal of vital information that might enable him to make his judgments of degree of relationship much more subtle and refined." For example, in examining Hale's (1962) lexicostatistic subgrouping of the Arandic languages, based on a one-hundred-word list, I have found that at least five of the thirty-five items from the person-part domain of Kaytej which were scored as noncognate with forms in one or more other Arandic language are in fact semantically shifted, although Hale makes no mention of this. Thus, Kaytej *urle* (*erlwe*) 'eye' is a semantically shifted reflection of the common Arandic word for 'forehead' (*urle*); Kaytej *pwer* 'vagina' corresponds to *pwere ~ pare* 'penis, tail' in five of the Arandic varieties Hale examines; the form *alem*, which is the Kaytej entry for both 'liver' and 'stomach, belly', is scored as noncognate with all other Arandic forms for 'stomach, belly'(*(a)tnerte*), but the fact is that the word for 'liver' reflected in all Arandic varieties (*aleme*) has expanded its range of application in Kaytej and displaced the original 'belly, stomach' form; in the discussion of Table 10-4, I noted that Kaytej *arilh* 'woman' was a semantically shifted reflex of a form that originally meant 'person'; and finally, the Kaytej form for 'heart', *anajanaj*, which is not cognate with any other Arandic form meaning 'heart', is derived, on the basis of a metaphorical association of shape, from a reduplication of *anatye* the common Arandic word for 'yam'. Taking such changes into account could substantially alter the lexicostatistic counts.

Matisoff (1978: 104–5) advocates a graduated system of scoring vocabulary correspondences on a scale from 0 (lowest) to 10 (highest) in which scores are assigned both on the degree of phonological divergence and the degree of semantic divergence. He notes (1978:105) that such a proposal is complicated by the fact that 'we do not have principled ways of measuring degrees of semantic divergence'. I would suggest that our knowledge of what constitutes crosslinguistically natural tendencies of semantic change, along with a coding of distances between notions along a common pathway of change, might help in devising a principled measure of degree of semantic divergence. For instance, phonologically similar forms for 'lip' and 'bone marrow' might receive a semantic distance score of 6 because it would normally take 6 natural semantic shifts to bridge these notions: 'lip' → 'mouth' → 'face' → head' → 'skull' → 'brain' → 'bone marrow'. The distance here might be weighted even more heavily due to the fact that the strictly unidirectional changes of 'mouth' → 'face' → 'head' mean that 'lip' and 'bone marrow' are not equally plausible starting points for the association; 'lip' had to be the starting point. So, while 'lip' and 'bone marrow' are semantically very divergent, they are not so divergent that phonologically similar forms for these two notions can be summarily dismissed as unrelated.

A metric for weighting semantic divergence has yet to be formulated, but the purpose of this excursus has been to suggest that the lexicostatistical approach could be refined to more precisely gauge possible genetic affiliation for those cases where the only information we have for a language is word lists, and our knowledge of natural tendencies of semantic change would be crucial in that refinement. Such a metric would also need to take into account the commonality (or frequency) of each change that forms a link in a chain, an issue which has not been touched on in the present study (that is, in the present treatment all shifts are treated equally, but it is clear that some natural changes are more common than others).

4.11 Summary of Main Points

In this section, five examples were adduced to demonstrate the efficacy of using natural tendencies of semantic change in searching for, and establishing, cognates. In discussing those examples it has been shown that an understanding of natural tendencies of semantic change and a knowledge of the directions in which they operate, can be used to (i) direct researchers in their initial search for tentative cognate forms, (ii) establish the original meaning of a reconstructed form, (iii) help establish genetic affiliation, (iv) establish chains of cognacy in which the ends may be semantically very divergent, but where each link is a common association, (v) help explore borrowing and contact relations, (vi) both construct and expand substantial etymological sets, (vii) increase the cognate base for groups and languages which had previously had a dearth of cognate sets, and (viii) generate a wealth of hypotheses to be followed up by further comparative-historical investigations. The use of Australian data in these examples has not only helped to contribute to the growing body of research concerning genetic affiliations and comparative reconstruction of Australian languages, it has also helped to reinforce the proposed naturalness (i.e. universality) of the tendencies of semantic change which were established on the basis of other language families.

5 CONCLUSION

The purpose of the current volume is to review and, where necessary, revise the assumptions and methodology of the comparative method of historical reconstruction. This chapter has attempted to contribute to this end by:

i. demonstrating that there are natural tendencies of semantic change which give rise to core vocabulary, or to be more precise, demonstrating that there are crosslinguistically natural semantic shifts which give rise to terms in the semantic domain 'parts of a person' (cf. section 4);

ii. developing a seventy-five item comparative word list (cf. Table 10-1) which is based on regular semantic changes in the 'person-part' domain and which shows explicitly the most commonly attested chains of related changes in this domain and the typical directionality of each change; and

iii. showing how natural tendencies of semantic change can be used in the initial steps of the comparative method (that is, searching for, identifying, and establishing cognates (cf. section 5).

One of the practical outcomes of this last demonstration is a large body of fully discussed comparative sets for central Australian languages which, among other significant results, has helped to establish and extend a number of etymological sets for that region.

Traugott (1985b) has rightly argued that there is both a sociohistorical and a cognitive dimension to semantic change. In section 3, a model of semantic change was presented which explicitly acknowledges that the mechanism by which changes enter into the language and catch hold in the system is a socially driven historical process. A keystone of this model is the fact that every natural semantic change, by virtue of the nature of communities and the conservative influence they have on what are plausibly related meanings, requires polysemy at its end point or at its beginning point. In establishing that two phonologically similar, but semantically divergent, forms are cognate, the identification of a third similar form which is polysemous for the two notions involved is taken as evidence for the relatedness of the first two forms.

The cognitive dimension comes in when one is trying to explain why two or more notions tend to be naturally associated with one another through parallel semantic changes in a number of genetically and areally distinct language families. An underlying assumption throughout this chapter has been that crosslinguistically natural tendencies of semantic change arise out of universally shared perceptual and cognitive mechanisms which regularly trigger the same kind of association independent of language or culture. As noted in section 4, these crosslinguistically natural tendencies of change can have a culture-specific manifestation, suggesting that while the underlying basic conceptual/perceptual features which are involved in the change may be cognitively universal, the way they often surface is through language-specific and culture-specific concepts (or conceptual clusters) which are associated with particular linguistic forms. In section 4.1 in particular, I discussed at length the kind of cognitive factors that might provide the underpinnings for the unidirectional tendency of a term referring to a visible person-part to shift to refer to the visible whole of which it is an immediate, and a spatially and/or functionally integral, part. We are, however, a long way from fully establishing such putative links between language change and cognition.

In section 2, I briefly discussed some perspectives on the history of studies in semantic change, and outlined some of the current thinking in this field. Although interest in semantic change has blossomed in recent years, and much valuable work has been done, there are three unfortunate trends which this chapter has tried to counteract. First, interest in grammatical change has placed a concentrated focus on the development of abstract notions at the expense of the study of concrete notions. As demonstrated here, even basic vocabulary items have their semantic origins, and we will not fully understand the mechanisms of semantic change until we understand how both concrete and abstract notions develop. Second, this interest in the development of abstract notions has lead to a belief that metaphor is a more important factor in semantic change than metonymy. Traugott (1988: 407) observes that "[m]etaphoric processes have recently been considered to be major, indeed *the* major, factors in semantic change", and goes on to note (1988: 411) that metonymy "has not been assigned the overall significance that metaphor has." The facts discussed in sections 4–5 of this chapter suggest that metaphor and metonymy may be employed to different degrees in semantic change, depending on the particular semantic domain under inspection and the particular items involved. As far as the origin of 'person-part' terms is concerned, metonymy plays a significantly more important role than metaphor does. Finally, with a few notable exceptions, there has been little attempt in most of the recent theoretical research to show how the methods and findings are directly relevant to issues and concerns in comparative-historical reconstruction. The main focus of this chapter has been to demonstrate that the discovery of natural tendencies of semantic change allows us to make a substantial revision to the comparative-historical method. This revision is a step towards the systematisation of traditional insights and methods of semantic exploration in the comparative-historical domain, especially in the domain of etymology, and it clearly builds on the results of the family-specific employment of such traditional methods. It is the sound etymological work that already exists for particular language families which has enabled a more advanced conception of semantic relatedness to be brought into the preliminary stages of comparative research.

There is no longer any excuse for teaching students of comparative historical linguistics that there are no laws of semantic change and that there is no rigorous way of using semantic change to establish cognates and genetic unity. Within the semantic domain of 'person-parts', which forms a large part of the conservative core vocabulary proposed by Swadesh, there are consistencies of semantic change which allow the comparativist to replace intuitive judgements concerning the relatedness of meanings with empirically based statements as to what is, and what is not, a plausible semantic association. The final passage from Meillet provides a fitting complement to Benveniste's opening quotation. It is hoped that this chapter helps to provide the methodological rigour in the semantic aspects of reconstruction that Benveniste and Meillet sought and demanded.

> The agreement in meaning should be as exact and precise as the agreement in phonological form (according to rules of correspondence). This does not mean that meanings should coincide more than phonological elements; only the differences in the meanings, if there are any, should be explained not by vague and general possibilities, but by special circumstances (1967: 52).

NOTES

1. Many of the ideas in this chapter have been clarified and/or developed in collaboration with Nick Evans. Although initially skeptical, R.M.W. Dixon provided invaluable encouragement and supervision for the original research which is reported on in section 4 of this chapter. I would also like to thank Cynthia Allen, Balthasar Bickel, Dan Devitt, Matthew Dryer, Patricia Fox, Karin Michelson, David Nash, Fritz Newmeyer, Robert D. Van Valin Jr. and Barbara Villanova for their advice and suggestions concerning various aspects of this paper. Mark Durie and Malcolm Ross are especially to be thanked for their valuable editorial insights and their patience. I would also like to thank the Cognitive Anthropology Research Group of the Max-Planck-Institute for Psycholinguistics in Nijmegen for providing the atmosphere and resources which enabled me to make the final revisions of the chapter.

2. Other researchers who have recognised the importance of polysemy in the investigation of semantic change and in the application of the methods of historical reconstruction are Brown and Witkowski (1983), Brown (1989) and Traugott (1986b). Traugott (1986b: 539), for instance, shows that 'admitting polysemy in semantic theory has the added methodological advantage of allowing us to do extensive internal semantic reconstruction'.

3. Foley (personal communication) observes that in Yimas, another Papuan language, there is also no word for 'body'. These facts run contrary to Brown's (1976: 404, 420) and Andersen's (1978: 352) claim that the body is labelled in all body-part partonomies.

4. Note also that it has been commonly observed that many languages treat notions like 'name', 'shadow', and 'tracks' as they do body parts; this tends to make more sense when we realise that a notion like 'name' is not being treated analogically or metaphorically like a body-part, but that it is being treated in the same way as all other parts which are seen to constitute the unity of a socially placed human being.

5. Matisoff (1990: 111) observes that '[a]lthough this great work [ie. the *DED*] contains almost 6000 cognate sets, it does not offer any reconstructions either—but this is simply because, after many decades of toil, the authors felt they had not yet resolved all the problems of the vowels.' He goes on to note 'the sets of forms presented are truly cognate, and any irregularities are at least identified and possible explanations are suggested.' With such good data, I was able to reconstruct obvious semantic changes, but it must be made clear that many of the posited reconstructions for Dravidian are my own, based on Burrow and Emeneau's work along with other works such as Zvelebil (1970).

6. It is important to remember that, in keeping with the discussion in section 3, a change represented as X → Y is to be interpreted as X → [X & Y] → Y (or, more precisely, X → [X & Y] and then [X & Y]→ Y), with the intermediate polysemy.

7. Matisoff in fact deals with the classification of semantic associations rather than semantic changes, but the principles remain the same, especially given the fact that the cognitive association of semantic notions smooths the path for semantic change, and the results of semantic change (polysemy) are proof of semantic association. Also note that while Matisoff (1978: 176) talks of "**extra-**, **inter-**, or **trans-field association**" he opts for the term 'trans-field' while I opt for the term 'interfield'.

8. In principle metaphoric association and metonymic association are not mutually exclusive. For instance, the Australian English use of the terms 'neck' or 'arm' to refer to the collar or sleeve of a shirt may be driven by both metonomy and metaphor: when wearing a shirt the 'neck' of the shirt is physically contiguous to the neck of the body and the 'arm' is physically contiguous to the actual arm, thus there is a metonymic association, but off the body the 'arm' of a shirt and the 'neck' of a shirt are similar to the human body both in terms of spatial arrangement with respect to other parts and gross shape, and thus there

is a metaphoric association. However, for the purposes of the study under discussion, changes were classified as one or the other, and in practice there was no problem in designating a particular change as being a case of 'metaphor' or 'metonymy'.

9. Guthrie notes that '[t]he implied mutation of meaning 'fingernail' → 'finger' was apparently correlated with a shift of class to classes 7/8'. Note also that six languages have reflexes which gloss as 'thumb'.

10. Goddard (1988 and 1989) makes similar observations and concludes that 'part of' is not a satisfactory primitive term for use in typological semantics. He argues that in discussing the realm of the personal (including the body), 'whole' or 'all of' are better primitive expressions.

11. The spelling of Central Australian language names and the orthographic conventions for each of these languages follows that of Menning and Nash (1981). So, for instance, although Kaytetye and Arrernte are currently the favoured representation of the languages which are here written as Kaytej and Aranda, I have decided not to alter the original conventions of my main data source.

12. As Capell (1956) noted, the Common Australian form for 'hand' is *mara ~ mala*. Reflexes of this form can be found in Table 10-2 in the Ngumpin and Western Desert groups.

13. As an interesting demonstration of this last fact, note that the Nyininy entry for 'hand' in Table 10-2 is *pingka*, a borrowing of English 'finger' which now covers both 'finger' and 'hand'. In a parallel fashion, the Roper Kriol form '(h)an(d)' has come to designate both 'hand' and 'arm'.

14. Further information about Arandic allows the following observations to be made. The forms for 'fingernail' in Alyawarra (*ingkilthelh*), Antekerrepenh (*ingkalthel*), and Kaytej (*ngkelthel*) appear to be a compounding of the basic Arandic form for 'foot' (**ingke*) with the form *'ilthele'*. Given that lamino-dentals (in this case 'lth') commonly correspond to lamino-palatals (in this case 'lty'), it is probably the case that *'ilthele'* and *iltye* derive from the same historical source, but the element in the compound did not shift semantically (that is, it remained as 'nail'). Thus these forms for 'fingernail' probably derive from a form that originally meant 'toenail' (foot-nail), and if this is the case it would suggest that the form that gave rise to *iltye* probably meant just 'nail', prototypically interpreted as 'fingernail'. This evidence would suggest that the primary sound changes which shaped the form, initial loss, and final vowel neutralization, took place before the shift of meaning.

15. Although the three languages belong to different groups, they are geographically very close to one another.

16. What is being suggested here is a type of semantic drag chain. Lehrer (1985) has argued that, by virtue of the conceptual integrity of semantic fields, a shift in one notion in a field is likely to drag other items in the same domain into parallel shifts.

17. Blake (1988) has argued that the Karawan group is in fact closer to the Pama-Nyungan family than other non-Pama-Nyungan groups. He notes that Karawan pronouns are neither clearly northern nor clearly Pama-Nyungan and he notes that Karawan case paradigms look non-Pama-Nyungan, but proto–case markers which are commonly reflected in the Pama-Nyungan languages show up as minor allomorphs and with shifted functions. For present purposes the grouping of Jingiluan and Karawan together as non-Pama-Nyungan simply means that neither group clearly belongs to the Pama-Nyungan family; it does not suggest a close genetic relationship between Jingiluan and Karawan.

REFERENCES

Andersen, E. S. (1978). Lexical universals of body-part terminology. In J. Greenberg, ed., *Universals of human language*. Vol. 3, *Word structure* 335–68. Stanford University Press, Stanford.

Anttila, R. (1972). *An introduction to historical and comparative linguistics*. Macmillan, New York.

Arlotto, A. (1972). *Introduction to historical linguistics*. Houghton Mifflin, Boston.

Benedict, P. K. (1972). *Sino-Tibetan: A conspectus*. Cambridge University Press, Cambridge.

Benveniste, E. (1971). Trans. M. E. Meek. *Problems in general linguistics*. University of Miami Press, Coral Gables, Fla. (Esp. 249–64: Semantic problems in reconstruction; first published in French in *Word* 10: 251–64 [1954]).

Berlin, B., and P. Kay. (1969). *Basic color terms: their universality and evolution*. University of California Press, Berkeley and Los Angeles.

Blake, B. J. (1988). Redefining Pama-Nyungan: towards the prehistory of Australian languages. *Aboriginal Linguistics* 1: 1–90.

Blust, R. (1988). *Austronesian root theory: An essay on the limits of morphology.* John Benjamins, Amsterdam.

Brandenstein, C. G. von (1982). *Names and substance of the Australian subsection system.* University of Chicago Press, Chicago.

Bréal, M. (1900). *Semantics: Studies in the science of meaning.* Trans. H. Cust. Heinemann, London. First published in 1897 as *Essai de sémantique.* Hachette, Paris.

Brown, C. H. (1976). General principles of human anatomical partonomy and speculations on the growth of partonomic nomenclature. *American Anthropologist* 3: 400–24.

Brown, C. H. (1979). A theory of lexical change (with examples form folk biology, human anotomical partonomy and other domains). *Anthropological Linguistics* 21: 257–76.

———. (1989). Universal constraints on polysemy and overt marking. *Quaderni di Semantica* 10: 33–50.

Brown, C. H., and Stanley R. Witkowski. (1983). Polysemy, lexical change, and cultural importance. *Man* 18: 72–89.

Buck, C. D. (1949). *A dictionary of selected synonyms in the principal Indo-European languages: A contribution to the history of ideas.* University of Chicago Press, Chicago.

Burrow, T., and M. B. Emeneau. (1961). *Dravidian etymological dictionary.* Rev. ed. Oxford University Press, London.

Bybee, J. (1985). *Morphology: A study of the relation between meaning and form.* John Benjamins, Amsterdam.

———. (1988). Semantic substance vs. contrast in the development of grammatical meaning. *Proceedings of the Fourteenth Annual Meeting of the Berkeley Linguistics Society* 247–64.

———. (1990). The semantic development of past tense modals in English. In W. Wölck, B. Brown, and D. Devitt, eds., *Buffalo Working Papers in Linguistics* 13–30. SUNY, Buffalo, N.Y.

Bybee, J., and W. Pagliuca. (1985). Cross-linguistic comparison and the development of grammatical meaning. In J. Fisiak, ed., *Historical semantics and historical word-formation* 60–83. Mouton de Gruyter, Berlin.

Bybee, J., W. Pagliuca, and R. Perkins. (1991). Back to the future. In E. C. Traugott and B. Heine, eds., *Approaches to grammaticalization.* Vol 2, 17–58. John Benjamins, Amsterdam.

Capell, A. (1956). *A new approach to Australian linguistics.* Oceania Linguistic Monographs, no. 1. University of Sydney, Sydney.

Dahl, O. C. (1976). *Proto-Austronesian.* 2nd rev. ed. Curzon Press, London.

Dixon, R. M. W. (1980). *The languages of Australia.* Cambridge University Press, Cambridge.

Evans, N. (1992). Multiple semiotic systems, hyperpolysemy, and the reconstruction of semantic change in Australian languages. In G. Kellermann and M. Morrissey, eds., *Diachrony within Synchrony* 475–508. Peter Lang, Bern.

Flierl, W., and H. Strauss, eds. (1977). *Kâte dictionary. Pacific Linguistics* C41. Pacific Linguistics, Canberra.

Geeraerts, D. (1983). Reclassifying semantic change. *Quaderni di Semantica* 4: 217–40.

———. (1985). Cognitive restrictions on the structure of semantic change. In J. Fisiak, ed., *Historical semantics and historical word-formation* 127–53. Mouton de Gruyter, Berlin.

———. (1986). Functional explanations in diachronic semantics. In A. Bossuyt, ed., *Functional explanations in linguistics. Belgian Journal of Linguistics* 1: 67–93.

Goddard, Cliff. (1987). *A basic Pitjantjatjara/Yankunytjatjara to English dictionary.* Institute for Aboriginal Development, Alice Springs.

———. [1988]. A 'hand' is not a 'body-part'. Paper presented in the 'Body Parts in Grammar' workshop at the Australian Linguistics Society Conference, Armidale.

———. 1989. Issues in natural semantic metalanguage. *Quaderni di Semantica* 10: 51–64.

Guthrie, M. (1967–70). *Comparative Bantu.* 4 vols. Gregg International Publishers, Farnborough.

Hale, K. (1962). Internal relationships in Arandic of Central Australia. In A. Capell, ed. *Some linguistic types in Australia* 171–83. Oceania Linguistic Monographs, no. 7, University of Sydney, Sydney.

———. (n.d.) *Arandic word list.* MS.

Heine, B. (1992). Grammaticalization chains. *Studies in Language* 16: 335–68.

Heine, B., U. Claudi, and F. Hünnemeyer. (1991). *Grammaticalization: A conceptual framework.* University of Chicago Press, Chicago.

Hock, H. H. (1986). *Principles of historical linguistics.* Mouton de Gruyter, Berlin.

Iris, M., B. Litowitz, and M. W. Evens. (1988). Problems of the part-whole relation. In M.W. Evens, ed., *Relational models of the lexicon* 261–88. Cambridge University Press, Cambridge.

Jakobson, R. (1973). *Main trends in the science of language.* George Allen & Unwin, London.

Jeffers, R. J., and I. Lehiste. (1979). *Principles and methods for historical linguistics.* MIT Press, Cambridge, Massachusetts.

Kay, P. (1975). Synchronic variability and diachronic change in basic color terms. *Language in Society* 4: 257–70.

Lehrer, A. (1978). Structure of the lexicon and transfer of meaning. *Lingua* 45: 95–123.

———. (1985). The influence of semantic fields on semantic change. In J. Fisiak, ed., *Historical semantics and historical word-formation* 283–96. Mouton de Gruyter, Berlin.

Lewis, G. (1974). Gnau anatomy and vocabulary for illness. *Oceania* 45: 50–78.

MacLaury, R. E. (1991). Social and cognitive motivations of change: Measuring variability in color semantics. *Language* 67: 34–62.

Matisoff, J. A. (1978). *Variational semantics in Tibeto-Burman: The 'organic' approach to linguistic comparison.* Institute for the Study of Human Issues, Philadelphia.

———. (1990). On Megalocomparison *Language* 66:106–20.

Mel'čuk, I. A. (1976). *Das Wort: Zwischen Inhalt und Ausdruck.* Wilhelm Fink Verlag, München.

Menning, K., and D. Nash. (1981). *Sourcebook for Central Australian languages* [Pilot edition]. Institute for Aboriginal Development, Alice Springs.

Miller, J. (1977). Delaware anatomy with linguistic, social and medical aspects. *Anthropological Linguistics* 19.4: 144–66.

Nikiforidou, K., and E. Sweetser. (1989). *Diachronic regularity and irregularity: Structural parallels between semantic and phonological change.* Berkeley Cognitive Science Report, no. 60. University of California, Berkeley.

O'Grady, G. N. (1979). Preliminaries to a Proto–Nuclear Pama-Nyungan stem list. In S. Wurm, ed., *Australian Linguistic Studies.* Pacific Linguistics C54, 107–39. *Pacific Linguistics,* Canberra.

———. (1987). The origin of monosyllabic roots in Eastern Pama-Nyungan. In D. C. Laycock and W. Winter, eds., *A world of language: Papers presented to Professor S.A. Wurm on his 65th birthday* 517–29. *Pacific Linguistics* C100. Pacific Linguistics, Canberra.

Petruck, M. (1986). Body part terminology in Hebrew: A study in lexical semantics. PhD diss. University of California, Berkeley.

Stern, Gustaf. ([1931] 1968). *Meaning and change of meaning,.* Indiana University Press, Bloomington. First published by Elanders Boktryckeri Aktiebolag, Gothenberg.

Svorou, S. (1986). On the evolutionary paths of locative expressions. *Proceedings of the Twelfth Annual Meeting of the Berkeley Linguistics Society* 515–27.

———. (1988). The experiential basis of the grammar of space: Evidence from the languages of the world. PhD diss. State University of New York at Buffalo, N.Y.

Swadesh, M. (1972). *The origin and diversification of language.* Routledge & Kegan Paul, London.

Sweetser, E. (1982). Root and epistemic modals: Causality in two worlds. *Proceedings of the Eighth Annual Meeting of the Berkeley Linguistics Society* 484–507.

———. (1987). Metaphorical models of thought and speech: A comparison of historical directions and metaphorical mappings in two domains. *Proceedings of the Thirteenth Annual Meeting of the Berkeley Linguistics Society* 446–59.

———. (1990). *From etymology to pragmatics: The mind-as-body metaphor in semantic structure and semantic change.* Cambridge University Press, Cambridge.

Traugott, E. C. (1985a). Conditional markers. In J. Haiman, ed., *Iconicity in syntax* 289–307. John Benjamins, Amsterdam.

———. (1985b). On regularity in semantic change, *Journal of Literary Semantics* 14: 155–73

———. (1986a). On the origins of 'and' and 'but' connectives in English. *Studies in Language* 10: 137–50.

———. (1986b). From polysemy to internal semantic reconstruction. *Proceedings of the Twelfth Annual Meeting of the Berkeley Linguistics Society* 539–50.

————. (1988). Pragmatic strengthening and grammaticalization. *Proceedings of the Fourteenth Annual Meeting of the Berkeley Linguistics Society* 406–16.

————. (1989). On the rise of epistemic meanings in English: An example of subjectification in semantic change *Language* 65: 31–55.

Traugott, E. C., and R. Dasher. (1987). On the historical relation between mental and speech act verbs in English and Japanese. In A. G. Ramat et al., eds., *Papers from the Seventh International Conference on Historical Linguistics* 561–73. John Benjamins, Amsterdam.

Traugott, E. C., and B. Heine. (1991). Introduction. In E. C. Traugott and B. Heine, eds., *Approaches to grammaticalization*. (2 vols. Vol. 1, 1–14. John Benjamins, Amsterdam.

Traugott, E. C., and E. König. (1991). The semantics-pragmatics of grammaticalization revisited. In E. C. Traugott and B. Heine, eds., *Approaches to grammaticalization*. Vol. 1, 189–218. John Benjamins, Amsterdam.

Ullmann, S. (1951). *The principles of semantics*. Jackson, Glasgow.

————. (1963). Semantic universals. In J. Greenberg, ed., *Universals of language* 172–207. MIT Press, Cambridge.

Walsh, D. S., and B. Biggs. (1966). *Proto-Polynesian word list 1*. Te Reo Monographs, no. 1. Linguistics Society of New Zealand, Auckland.

Weinreich, U., W. Labov, and M. I. Herzog. (1968). Empirical foundations for a theory of language change. In W. Lehmann and Y. Malkiel, eds., *Directions for historical linguistics* 95–188. University of Texas Press, Austin.

Wilkins, D. (1981). *Towards a theory of semantic change*. Honours thesis. Australian National University Canberra.

————. (1989a). Mparntwe Arrernte: Studies in the structure and semantics of grammar. PhD diss. Australian National University, Canberra.

————. (1989b) Travels in Australian Aboriginal semantic space. Invited paper read to Berkeley Linguistics Department.

————. (1991). The semantics, pragmatics and diachronic development of 'associated motion' in Mparntwe Arrernte. In D. Devitt et al., eds. *Buffalo Papers in Linguistics* 207–57. State University of New York at Buffalo, N.Y.

Williams, J. M. (1976). Synaesthetic adjectives: a possible law of semantic change. *Language* 53: 461–78.

Witkowski, S. R., and C. H. Brown. (1985). Climate, clothing and body-part nomenclature. *Ethnology* 24: 197–214.

Zvelebil, K. (1970). *Comparative Dravidian phonology*. Mouton, The Hague.

Contributors

Robert Blust, University of Hawaii at Manoa, United States
Lyle Campbell, University of Canterbury, New Zealand
Mark Durie, University of Melbourne, Australia
George Grace, University of Hawaii at Manoa, United States
Harold Koch, Australian National University, Australia
John Newman, Massey University, New Zealand
Johanna Nichols, University of California, Berkeley, United States
Malcolm Ross, Australian National University, Australia
David Wilkins, Max-Planck Institute of Psycholinguistics, The Netherlands

Subject Index

Abductive change, 33 n.22. *See also* Hypocorrection
"Aberrant" languages, 158–60, 168, 175
Ablaut, 32 n.5, 53–54, 59
Absorption. *See* Morphological change
Adjectival concord, 68 n.13
Adpositional phrases, 186, 188–95, 201, 202
Adstrate, 213 n.40
Affective symbolism, 72–77, 86, 86 n.4, 112. *See also* Sound symbolism
Affixization. *See* Morphological change
Affix replacement, 234–35
Agriculture, 10
Allomorphic change. *See* Morphological change
Analogy, 13–14, 91, 112, 137, 197
    analogical extension, 220
    analogical leveling, 118, 219
    analogical reading (of characters), 99–101
    sources of, 227
    spurious appeal to, 117, 124, 131
Anthropology, 14
Arbitrariness, 5
Archaic forms, use of, in reconstruction, 92–97, 219–20
Archaic heterogeneity, 219
Archeology, 5, 65
Areal features, 72, 80, 86, 169, 184–202
Articulation, 27
    articulatory gesture, 151–52, 155 nn.21,22
    articulatory target, 151–52
Assimilation, 137, 152
Attitudes, speaker, 21, 181–84
Attributive adjectives, 186, 197, 202
Avoidance of merger, 129

Backformation, 239. *See also* Morphological change
Basic word order, 186, 188, 201–2
Bewegungsgefühl. *See* Articulation: articulatory gesture
Bilateral comparison, 59–60

Bilingualism, 11, 13, 29. *See also* Multilingualism
Biology, 65, 136
Body parts, 271–300
Borrowing. *See* Language contact
"Bottom-up" approach to reconstruction, 160, 163–67
Breathy voice, 73

Case forms, preferred, as explanation of sound change, 132 n.16
Ceremonial interaction, 174
Chains of changes, 20
Characters, Chinese, 92–97, 99–101, 109
Clause linkage, 186–88, 194, 202
Cliticization. *See* Morphological change
Cognacy, 7, 9, 220. *See also* Semantic similarity
    and assumed relatedness of languages, 41
    irregular cognate sets, 12, 160–67
    partial resemblance, 63
    and semantic similarity, 57, 298–99
    and sound correspondences, 10–12, 56–59, 63
    statistical probability of, 14, 49–56
Cognition, 13, 16, 72–77, 271–82, 299
Cognitive semantics, 266
Comparative method, 6–7, 48–60, 160–67, 220–22
    "failure" of, 28–31, 157–79
    problems in application of, 60–64
Conditioned sound change, 142, 144–45, 167
"Consonant grade" in Oceanic languages, 144
Constraints on innovation, 17–20, 149–51, 247–48, 270–81
Contact-induced change, 180–213
Cosignals of grammatical categories, 233
Counterfeeding, 106
Cranberry morphs, 243
Creole studies, 209

Culture contact, 210
Culture history of Slavic family, 42

Decay, 9, 10
Deductive change, 33 n.22. *See also*
    Hypocorrection
Degradation. *See* Decay
Degrammaticalization, 241–42. *See also*
    Morphological change
Demorphologization, 244. *See also*
    Morphological change
Denasalization, 143
Diachronic trajectories, 247
Diagrammaticity. *See* Iconicity
Dialect mixture, 26, 91
Dialectology, 110 n.6
Diffusion, 171, 175
Diversification, 41
Doublets, 148–49, 154 n.13

Economy of rules, 143, 221–22, 225

Edda, 132 n.12
Emblematic languages, 28–31, 174, 181–83,
    204–5, 210
Endocentricity, 34 n.24. *See also*
    Esoterogeny
Entrenchments, 203
Esoterogeny, 21–22, 34 n.24, 183–84,
    192–211
Ethnicity, 42–43
Ethnology, 5
Evidence, 7–10, 44, 48, 60–64
    adequacy of, 41
    in closed sets vs. samples, 61–62
    diagnostic of language family, 59
    grammatical, 44
    in isolating languages, 63–64
    lexical, 44–45, 47, 50, 63
        systematically structured, 54–56
    in morphological paradigms, 44–48,
        50–52
    spurious individual identifying, 62–63
    statistical thresholds for, 49–55, 65–67
Evolution, 136
Exceptions to rules, "extraordinary" and
    "ordinary," 99
"Exemplary" languages, 158–60
Exocentricity, 34 n.24. *See also* Exoterogeny
Exoterogeny, 21–22, 34 n.24, 183–84

"Exotic" languages. *See* Unwritten
    languages
Explanation, 15–16, 33 n.15, 132 n.16, 299
Expressive symbolism. *See* Affective
    symbolism

Facultative nasal, 139–44
Feeding, 106
Form reduction, 268
Formulaism, 12–13, 33 n.11
Fortition, 19
Frequency of sound changes, 121–31
Functionalism, 14, 266
Functional load of phonemic contrast, 130
Functional shift, 9

Gaps in linguistic subsystems, 19
Gender, 51–52, 61–62
Gender symbolism, 61
Genetically diverse language areas, 181–211
Genetic diversity of languages, 65
Geology, 136
Glottochronology, 5
GoldVarb 2, 120–21
Gradualness of sound change, 24, 131
Grammatical correspondences, 40, 47
Grammaticalization, 5, 206, 240, 266. *See
    also* Morphological change
    and diachronic trajectories, 247
Grammatical reconstruction, 39–71. *See also*
    Morphological reconstruction
Grassmann's Law, 136
Great Vowel Shift, 19
Grimm's Law, 135–136
"Growth" of language family, 59–60

Haplology, 112
Homophony, 13, 20, 72, 77–78, 164
    and taboo associations, 92, 101–4
    Hrafnkels Saga, 118
Hypercorrection, 33 n.23
Hypocorrection, 19, 33 n.23, 149–51

Iconicity, 235–36, 239, 244, 251, 258
Identity
    acts of, 21
    social, 22, 181–84
Ideophones. *See* Sound symbolism
Idioms, 183
Implicature, conversational, 281

Independent parallel innovation, 6
Individual-identifying criterion, 8–9, 13,
    41–64, 183, 199. *See also* Evidence
"In group" codes. *See* Esoterogeny
"Intergroup" codes. *See* Exoterogeny
Internal classification of language family,
    56–59, 64
Internal reconstruction, 225, 230, 249,
    259–60
Interruptions of communication within
    speech comunity, 170
Intrusive languages, 181
Isolating languages, 63–64, 248

Laboratory phonology, 18
Language boundaries, 157
Language change
    as "decay," 85
    as "progress," 85
Language contact, 4, 137, 180–213. *See also*
    Multilingualism
    and changes to phoneme systems, 11
    and culture contact, 210
    and etymological dictionaries, 7
    and facultative nasals in Austronesian,
        142–43
    intense, 166, 168
    and morphological change, 13
    and mutilingualism, 29
    and rate of lexical retention, 9
    relative importance vs. relatedness,
        178 n.9
    and time-depth of comparative method, 10
Language and community, noncoincidence
    of, 170–72
Language death, 11, 72, 80–81, 86, 210
Language as organism, 14, 23
Language-oriented framework for
    comparative method, 31
Language-shift, 29, 182–83, 184, 185. *See*
    also Language contact
Laryngeals, 59, 73
Lautbild. See Articulation: articulatory
    target
Lexical change, 267
Lexical correspondences, 47, 64
Lexical diffusion, 23–28, 31, 34 n.25, 91, 107
    and lexical phonology, 34 n.28
Lexical innovation, 7, 9
Lexical reconstruction, 64

Lexical sets in reconstruction, 8, 61–62,
    63–64
Lexicostatistics, 4–5, 8
Linga franca, 181, 211 n.4. *See also*
    Exoterogeny
Location, expression of, 189–90
Locus of diachronic process, 15, 157,
    172–75
Logistic regression. *See* Variable rules
Long-range comparison, 8–9, 33 n.10. *See*
    also Multilateral comparison

Macrofamilies, 9, 39. *See also* Multilateral
    comparison
Marriage, 174
Mass comparison. *See* Multilateral
    comparison
Memory-picture. *See* Articulation:
    articulatory target
Metaphor, 299, 300 n.8
    interfield metaphoric change, 274
    intrafield metaphoric change, 274
Metathesis, 112, 137, 152, 178 n.3
Metatypy, 13, 34 n.33, 182–211
Metonymy, 272–73, 280–81, 299, 300 n.8
    interfield metonymic change, 274
    intrafield metonymic change, 274
Monolingualism, 171
Morpheme boundaries, change in. *See*
    Morphological change
Morpheme doubling. *See* Morphological
    change
Morphological change, 7, 12, 220–48
    allomorphic change, 224–37, 248
        conditioning of allomorphy, 224,
            227–29
        development of allomorphy, 224–27
        loss of allomorphy, 224, 229–31, 250
        redistribution of allomorphs, 224,
            231–37
        rule inversion, 224, 227
    change in boundary placement, 237–240,
        248
        creation of morpheme boundary,
            238–39
        loss of morpheme boundary, 237–238,
            259–60
        shift of boundary, 239–40
    change in morphosyntactic status of
        morpheme, 242–44, 248

Morphological change (*continued*)
  absorption, 244
  affixization, 243, 247
  cliticization, 242–43, 247
  phrasal becomes affixal, 243–44
  and language contact, 13
  morpheme doubling, 246
  morph replacement, 224
  paradigm leveling, 229–33
  paradigm split, 229, 231
  reordering of morphemes, 224–46, 258–59
  unidirectionality in, 247–48
Morphologically conditioned sound change,
    11, 13, 78–80, 113
Morphological paradigms, 8, 9, 45, 220–48
Morphological reconstruction, 4, 41,
    218–23, 248–60. *See also*
    Grammatical reconstruction
  vs. etymology, 223
  methodology for, 220–21
  vs. phonological reconstruction, 222–23
  vs. semantic reconstruction, 223
  vs. syntactic reconstruction, 223
Morphologization of phonological rules,
    228–29
Morphology, fossilized, 137, 142
Morphosemantic transparency, 236
Morphosyntactic innovation, 7, 13,
    182–211, 224–40
Morphosyntactic status, change in. *See*
    Morphological change
Morphotactics, 222
Morphotactic transparency, 236
Motivation for linguistic change, 16, 20–23.
    See also Articulation; Cognition;
    Homophony; Prestige; Social
    identity
Motor sensation. *See* Articulation:
    articulatory gesture
Multidimensional paradigmaticity, 46, 48,
    52, 64, 68 n.13
Multilateral comparison, 5, 8–9, 40, 60
Multilingualism, 171–75, 181, 182–211, 245
Multiple disjunct probablity, 65–67
Murmur. *See* Breathy voice

Nasals, 55
Natural selection, 14, 33 n.13
Neogrammarian hypothesis, 3–4, 13–18,
    24–25, 135–37, 268

"Normally transmitted" languages, 208
"Nuclear" zones, 181

Occam's razor. *See* Economy of rules
Onomatopoeia, 11, 13, 72, 73–77, 86.

Paradigmatically structured morphemes,
    54–56, 63–64. *See also*
    Multidimensional paradigmaticity
  case endings, 54
  deictic roots, 54
  kin terms, 54
  personal pronouns, 54–56
Paradigm shift, 13–31
Parts of a person, 271–300
Part-whole relationships, 275–82
Perception of sounds, 27, 149–51
Perceptually motivated sound change, 152
Philology
  Chinese, 92–97, 109, 110 nn.2,4
  Germanic, 115, 131 nn.3,6
Phoneme inventories, large, 164
Phonetic theory and comparative
    linguistics, 150–52
Phonetic universals, 151–52
Phonological change
  phonemic overlap, 131
  phonemic split, 164, 168
  restructuring of phonological systems,
    131 n.1
Phonological correspondences, 7, 9–10, 40,
    56–59
  and cognate sets, 10–12, 56–59
  partial, 63, 182
Phonological reconstruction, 7, 40, 160–67,
    220–23
  and phonotactics, 221
Phonological theory, 18, 27, 33 nn.19,20,
    34 n.28
Phrasal lexemes, 191. *See also* Speech
    formulae
Physiology, 18
Polysemy, 269–71, 300 n.7
  individual, 270, 298
  societal, 270, 298
Possession, 186, 188, 192, 196, 200, 202,
    212 n.24
Post-lexical rules, 33 n.20, 34 n.28
Potential duration of voicing, 149–50
Prenasalization, medial, 137, 139–45

Prestige, 21
Probability, 65–67
    probabilistic phonetic conditioning,
        25–26, 31, 120–31
    sequential, 65–67
    simultaneous, 65, 67
Pronouns, 54–56, 69 n.15, 186–94, 201–2

Qièyùn, 92–94, 96–97

Realism, 12–13
Reality, linguistic construction of, 203–5
Reanalysis, 117, 237–40, 247
Reconstruction, 12–13. *See also* Grammatical
        reconstruction; Lexical reconstruction;
        Morphological reconstruction;
        Phonological reconstruction
"Recurrence" in sound change, 153
Regrammaticalization, 240–41. *See also*
        Morphological change
Referential salience, 279
Regularity, 6, 13, 23–28, 29, 31–32, 47
    universal exceptions to, 152
Relatedness, 41, 47
    transparency of, 45
"Relevance" in morpheme ordering, 244–46,
        258
Relic forms, 226–27
Reordering of morphemes. *See*
        Morphological change
Residual zones, 181, 184–211
Ruki, 86 n.6
Rule interaction, 92, 104–9
Rule ordering, 105

Semantic change, 7, 10, 13, 40, 182, 240–42,
        264–304. *See also* Grammaticalization
    bidirectional, 277–300
    definition of, 267–71
    natural tendencies of, 264, 271–300
    semantic drag change, 288, 301 n.16
    semantic restructuring, 206
    taxonomic classification of, 265–66
    unidirectional, 275–300
Semantic similarity, 57, 264–301. *See also*
        Cognacy
Signs, linguistic, 5, 222
Social identity, 16, 21, 22, 29, 181–84. *See*
        also Esoterogeny; Exoterogeny;
        Speech community

Sociology, 14
Sound change
    in progress, 131, 145, 170–72
    regular. *See* Neogrammarian hypothesis
    sporadic, 11, 139–44, 145–53
Sound symbolism, 11, 13, 72–74, 86. *See*
        also Affective symbolism
Speaker innovation, 15, 269–71
Speaker-oriented framework, 31
Speakers, 14, 16, 23–28
Speech community, 16–17, 170–75. *See also*
        Social identity
    linguistically defined, 170, 173–74
    local comúnities nested in larger
        communities, 172–74
Speech formulae, 203–6, 213 n.33
Speech physiology, 13, 152
Speech processing, 13, 149–51
Sprachbund, 28, 169–75, 178 nn.4,8
    and *Sprachfamilie,* 169–75
Spread of innovation, 24. *See also* Language
        contact
"Spread" zone, 181
Stepwise regression, 121
"Strong" inflections, 131 n.6
Structuralism, 14, 18, 78
Structural paradigmaticity, 64
Substrate, 213 n.40
Superstrate, 213 n.40
Suppletion, 50, 197
Swadesh vocabulary lists, 264, 282–84, 299
Syncope, 63
Syncretism, 220, 241
Synecdoche, 275–82
    bidirectional synecdochic change, 278,
        279
    unidirectional synecdochic change,
        275–82
Syntactics of linguistic signs, 267
System congruency, 235–36, 252–53, 259

Taboo avoidance, 11, 92, 101–4, 109, 202
Tense/aspect/mood, 186, 187, 196–97, 200
"Test" languages, 140
Test-Sprachen. See "Test" languages
Time-depth, 9, 10, 39
Tone Sandhi, 248
"Top-down" approach to reconstruction,
        160–63
Trade Networks, 174

"Transitional" zones, 180
Type-identifying evidence, 48. *See also* Typology
Typology, 5, 12–13, 221, 223. *See also* Type-identifying evidence

Umlaut, 112–34, 229
Unwritten languages, 72, 81–86

Variable rules, 25, 113, 120–31
Velar voicing, instability of, 146–48

Verner's Law, 136
Voice onset time, 149–50
Voicing crossover, 137, 145–53, 154 n.13, 155 n.20

Warfare, 174
"Weak" inflections, 131 n.6
Word formation, 242
Written languages, 81, 83–85, 92
Zìbiǎo, 102
Zìhuì, 97, 101–3, 107

Language Index

African languages, 32 n.7
Afrikaans, 6
Afro-Asiatic family, 10, 30, 61, 64, 138
Albanian, 59, 60, 205, 213 n.33
Algonkian family, 45, 62–63, 83, 138
Aliterre, 252–53
Altaic languages, 13, 209
Alyawarra. *See* Alyawarre
Alyawarre, 250–57, 259, 285, 287, 288, 289, 301 n.14
Ambonese subgroup, 275
Amerind languages, 8, 32 n.7, 39, 52, 54, 58, 69 n.15
Anêm, 205–6, 212 n.32, 213 n.34
Anindhilyagwa, 32 n.6
Anmajirra, 285, 287, 289
Antekerrepenhe, 257, 285, 287, 288, 301 n.14
Arabana, 288, 289
Arabic, 220, 226
Aranda. *See* Arrernte
Arandic subgroup, 81, 83, 218, 242–43, 250–60, 282–83, 285, 287–89, 296, 301 n.14
Aranta. *See* Arrernte
Arapaho, 63
Arawakan subgroup, 138
Are, 212 n.24
Are-Taupota subgroup, 193, 207
Arifama, 194, 195, 197
Armenian, 48, 59, 241
Aromanian, 213 n.33
Arrernte (Aranda), 30, 83, 235, 241, 242, 243, 244, 250–59, 260, 301 n.11
   Eastern Arrernte, 250–56, 260, 285, 287–89
   Lower Aranda, 254–56, 260, 285, 287–89
   Mparntwe Arrernte, 256–58, 260, 288
   Western Arrernte, 241, 250–56, 260, 285, 287–89
Arvanitic, 205
Asiatic Eskimo, 213 n.39

Athabaskan family, 82
Athapaskan-Eyak, 245
Australian languages, 10, 39, 83, 282–98
Austroasiatic family, 63, 138
Austronesian family, 4, 9, 10–11, 27, 137–55, 157–79, 180–217, 272–79
   western languages of, 4
Austro-Tai languages, 62
Awiya, 155 n.19

Balinese, 144, 204
Balto-Slavic subgroup, 44, 59, 68 n.1, 275
Bantu family, 45, 138, 213 n.39, 272–79
Bario Kelabit, 147
Baruga, 194, 195, 196, 212 n.25
Bel subgroup, 24, 187–92, 207
Bilinara, 249
Binandele. *See* Binandere subgroup
Binandere subgroup, 194, 198–99, 202
Bontok, 143
Bulgarian, 48, 210, 213 n.33
Buru, 203

Cakchiquel, 75
Cantonese, 11, 91–110
Cebuano Bisayan, 146
Celtic subgroup, 45, 59
Central Algonkian subgroup, 83–84, 136
Chadic subgroup, 138
Chángshā, 94, 95, 96, 107
Cháozhōu, 94, 95, 96, 107
Cheyenne, 62
Chinese, 4, 11, 63, 91–110
Chirah-mbaw, 277
Chiwere-Winnebago, 73
Choctaw, 63
Chol, 74, 75
Cholan subgroup, 74–76, 77, 86 n.2
Cholan-Tzotzilan subgroup, 74–76
Chukchi, 246
Classical Armenian, 231
Colonial Tzotzil, 74

Common Slavic, 42
Cree, 62, 84
Creek, 63

Dagan families, 192
Dakota, 73
Danish, 6, 22, 273
Delaware, 273
Dhegiha (Osage), 73
Diyari, 243, 288, 289
Dravidian family, 53, 80, 87 n.6, 138, 205,
    271–79
Dutch, 6, 22, 150, 204, 273

English, 6, 73, 77, 149–50, 172, 173, 203.
    209, 210, 211 n.4, 213 n.39, 219,
    229, 231, 236, 237, 239, 240, 243,
    246, 255, 273, 275
  Belfast, 170–71
  Martha's Vineyard, 170–71
  New York City, 170–71
  Philadelphia, 24–25
Estonian, 79
Ethiopic subgroup, 220, 226
Eurasiatic languages, 58
Ewe, 48

Fijian, 138, 140
Finnish, 73
Finno-Ugric family, 219
Fox, 62, 84
French, 48, 77, 204, 209, 210, 219, 243
Friesian, 6
Futunan, 138
Fúzhōu, 94, 95, 96, 107

Gedaged, 188, 190, 197, 199, 202
Gekoyo, 275
Georgian, 245
German, 6, 22, 23, 77, 78, 90–91,
    110 n.1, 204, 229, 230, 233, 236,
    239, 240, 275
Germanic subgroup, 4, 6, 25–27, 45, 90–91,
    112–34, 180, 230
  Northwest Germanic subgroup, 114, 123
Gnau, 271
Gothic, 6, 59, 113, 114, 115, 118, 126
Grand Couli, 160–61, 163–69, 172–77,
    178 n.2
Greater Lowland Mayan subgroup, 75

Greek, 6, 46, 59, 127, 174, 205, 213 n.33,
    230, 231, 232, 272
Gurindji, 285, 291, 292, 293, 294

Hebrew, 280, 281
Herero, 275
Hiri Motu, 211 n.4
Hitchiti, 63
Hittite, 59, 237, 238
Hmong-Mien family, 62
Hokan family, 138
Huastec, 75, 86 n.2
Hungarian, 246

Iban, 144, 147, 148
Icelandic, 6
Ilokano, 143, 147
Indo-Aryan family, 80, 87 n.6
Indo-European family, 4, 6, 9–10, 30–32, 32
    n.5, 33 n.8, 39–71, 80, 82, 91,
    113–14, 116, 127, 132 n.13, 133
    n.33, 135, 180–81, 231, 234–35, 239,
    272–79
Indonesian, 211 n.4. *See also* Malay
Indo-Pacific languages, 39
Iranian, 86 n.6
Italian, 226
Itza, 75

Jacaltec, 75
Japanese, 104, 110 n.3, 209, 210
Jaru, 285, 291, 292
Javanese, 138, 139, 140–48, 153,
    154 nn.13,16, 158
Jingilu, 291, 292, 293
Jingiluan subgroup, 290–95, 301 n.17
Jumaytepeque Xinca, 81

Kadazan, 147
Kalam, 203
Kamba, 275
Kanjobal, 75
Kannaḍa, 205, 277
Kapampangan, 147
Karawa, 291, 292, 295
Karawan subgroup, 290–95, 301 n.17
Karnic subgroup, 243, 288–89
Karo Batak, 142, 147
Kartvelian, 52–53, 69 n.14
Kâte, 271

Kayan, 146
Kaytej. *See* Kaytetye
Kaytetye, 225, 228, 241, 242, 243, 244,
    250–52, 254–59, 285, 287, 288, 289,
    296, 301 nn.11,14
Kekchí, 75, 79
Khoisan family, 213 n.39
Kickapoo, 62
Kil'din Lappish, 245
Kiwai subgroup, 201
Klamath, 155 n.19
Koasati, 63
Koḍagu, 273, 277
Koiari, 204
Koiarian languages, 192
Korafe, 195, 196, 198, 204
Korean, 110 n.3
Kormatiki Arabic, 213 n.41
Kota, 273, 277
Kukatja, 285, 286, 287, 288, 291, 293, 294
Kutanji, 291, 292, 294
Kwa, 63

Lak, 155 n.19
Latin, 46, 59, 77, 85, 174, 210, 226–27, 230,
    231, 232, 234, 235, 243, 246
Lewo, 204
Lithuanian, 273, 275
Lundu, 147
Lusi, 205–6, 212 n.32

Ma'a, 213 n.41
Macro-Awakan family, 138
Maisin, 22, 29, 185, 186, 192–202, 207,
    208, 209, 210, 212 nn.16,24,26
Malagasy, 138, 140–48, 154 n.13
Malay, 138, 139, 140–48, 153, 154 n.11, 275
Malayalam, 277
Malayo-Polynesian subgroup, 184, 211 n.7
Malngin, 285, 291, 295
Maloh, 144
Mam, 75, 86 n.2
Mandan, 72–73
Mandarin, 107
Mansaka, 146
Maranao, 147
Marathi, 205
Maru, 22
Mayan family, 4, 74–77, 86 n.2, 138
Méixiàn, 94, 95, 96, 107

Menomini, 62, 84
Miami, 62
Middle Chinese, 11, 91–110
Middle English, 26, 78, 209
Middle High German, 91, 233
Middle Russian, 236
Miri, 147
Mongolian family, 209
Mudbura, 249, 285, 289, 291, 292, 295
Muskogean, 63, 219

Nánchāng, 94, 95, 96, 107
Native-American languages, 272–79
Ndandi, 275
Ndau, 275
New Caledonia subgroup, 4, 28–31, 34 n.31,
    157–79
Ngaanyatjarra, 285, 286, 291, 293, 294
Ngaju Dayak, 138, 140–48, 153,
    154 nn.10,13
Ngandi, 32 n.6
Ngari, 285, 287, 288, 289
Ngarinman, 285, 291, 292, 293, 294
Ngarnji, 291, 293, 294
Ngarrka subgroup, 283, 285, 287–89
Ngero subgroup, 213 n.36
Ngumpin subgroup, 248, 283, 285, 287–95,
    301 n.12
Nguni subgroup, 213 n.39
Niger-Congo family, 63, 138
Nilotic family, 138
Non-Pama-Nyungan Australian languages,
    290–95
Norse, East, 117, 132 n.12
North New Guinea subgroup, 185, 187–92
Norwegian, 6, 204
Nostratic languages, 9, 39, 52–54
Nyangumarda, 293
Nyininy, 285, 290, 291, 292, 301 n.13
Nyoro, 275

Oceanic subgroup, 24, 139–40, 144, 157–79,
    180–217, 275, 277
    Western Oceanic subgroup, 185–217
Ojibwa, 62, 84
Old Church Slavic, 57, 58, 276
Old English, 114–33, 230
Old Frisian, 126
Old High German, 26, 90–91, 114–33, 241
Old Icelandic, 114–133

Old Norse, 117, 132 n.12, 230, 231, 233
Old Persian, 59
Old Saxon, 126
Ömie, 195
Osage. *See* Dhegiha

Palauan, 275
Pama-Nyungan family, 4, 33 n.9, 83, 248, 283–98
Papua New Guinea Austronesian languages, 4, 31, 180–217
Papuan languages, 4, 10, 181–217, 272–79
Papuan Tip subgroup, 185, 189, 192–202
Passamaquoddy, 63
Peking Chinese, 94, 95, 96, 101, 105, 107
Penobscot, 63
Pilinara, 291, 293, 295
Pintupi, 286, 291, 293, 294
Pitjantjatjara, 285, 286, 291, 293, 294
Pitta Pitta, 289, 293
Plains Cree, 84
Pokom subgroup, 76
Pokomchi, 75, 86 n.2
Polish, 21, 243, 276
Polynesian subgroup, 45, 139, 272, 273
Ponapean, 271
Proto-. *See under subgroup or family entry*
Provençal, 22

Quiche, 75, 77

Rhaeto-Romance, 22
Ritharngu, 32 n.6
Romance subgroup, 23, 83, 85, 180
Roper Kriol, 301 n.13
Rotuman, 161, 178 n.3
Rumanian, 210
Runic Norse, 126, 131 n.5
Russian, 58, 204, 235, 236

Sa'a, 138, 140
Samoan, 27, 138
Sangir, 147
Sanskrit, 6, 46, 59, 85, 86 n.6, 139, 144, 148, 231, 239
Semitic family, 138
Serbocroatian, 213 n.33
Shuāngfēng, 94, 95, 96, 107
Sino-Caucasian languages, 9
Sino-Tibetan family, 63, 138

Siouan family, 138
Slavic subgroup, 4, 39–71, 83, 86 n.6, 235, 275–77
Sogdian, 241
Sotho-Tswana subgroup, 213 n.39
Spanish, 74, 226, 246
    Latin-American Spanish, 73
Sūzhōu, 94, 95, 96, 107
Swampy Cree, 84
Swedish, 6, 273

Tagalog, 138, 139, 140–48, 153, 154 nn.8,13,15,16,17, 158, 213 n.39
Tai family, 62, 63
Takia, 185, 186, 187–92, 202, 204, 205, 206, 207, 208, 209, 210, 211 nn.12,13
Taman, 154 n.8
Tamil, 277
Tapuh, 147
Tawala, 189
Teco, 86 n.2
Telugu, 277
Thai, 150
Tibeto-Burman subgroup, 272–79
Tiruray, 147
Tlingit, 30–31, 155 n.19, 245
Toba Batak, 138, 139, 140–48, 153, 154 nn.7,8,13, 158
Toda, 277
Tojolabal, 75
Tokelauan, 204
Tokharian, 47, 59
Tok Pisin, 202, 211 nn.4,6
Tongan, 138
Torau, 213 n.36
Trans-New Guinea Phylum, 13, 185, 186–217
Tubetube, 212 n.22
Tulu, 277
Tungusic family, 53, 209
Turkic family, 58, 209, 245
Tzeltal, 75, 86 n.2
Tzotzil, 75, 86 n.2

Ubir, 212 n.24
Ugric subgroup, 245
Uralic family, 9, 30, 33 n.8, 39, 53, 54, 245
Urdu, 205

Vietnamese, 63, 110 n.3

Wakaya, 290, 291, 292
Wakayic subgroup, 290–95
Walmajarri, 248–50, 285, 287, 288, 291, 292
Walmatjari. *See* Walmajarri
Wampaya, 290, 291, 292, 293, 294
Wangkangurru, 241, 288, 289
Wanyi, 291, 292, 295
Warlmanpa, 285, 289
Warlpiri, 228, 250, 285, 286, 287, 288, 289, 293
Warluwarra, 291, 295
Waskia, 188–92, 205, 206, 207, 208
Wedau, 189, 212 n.24
Wēnzhōu, 94, 95, 96, 107
Western Bukidnon Manobo, 144, 146
Western Desert subgroup, 283, 285–94, 301 n.12

West Uvean, 213 n.39
Wú dialects, 94, 104

Xãrãcɨ̈, 160–69, 172–77
Xiàmén, 94, 95, 96, 107

Yagaria, 273
Yamalele, 194, 195, 196
Yandruwandha, 288, 289
Yankunytjatjara, 285, 286, 287, 291, 293, 294
Yareba, 195, 199
Yareban subgroup, 192
Yimas, 300 n.3
Yucatecan subgroup, 75, 86 n.2
Yulbaridja, 293
Yuman subgroup, 138

Name Index

Abramson, A. S., 149, 150
Adelaar, K. A., 142
Alexandre, P., 213 n.39
Alpher, B., 250
Andersen, H., 21–22, 33 n.22, 82, 224, 235, 236, 243
Anderson, E. S. 300 n.3
Antilla, R., 12, 33 n.11, 77, 79, 218, 219, 231, 240, 243, 266, 280
Antonsen, E., 114
Appel, R., 209
Arlotto, 219, 265
Austerlitz, R., 33 n.10

Bach, A., 77
Bailey, C.-J. N., 209
Baldi, P., 18, 81, 83
Ball, J. D., 103
Baudoin de Courtenay, J., 228
Beeler, M. S., 114
Bellwood, P., 10
Bender, B., 58
Benedict, P.K. 62, 272
Benediktsson, H., 114
Benveniste, E., 264, 265, 300
Berlin, B., 266
Besnier, N., 178 n.3
Blake, B., 301 n.17
Bloch, B., 136
Bloomfield, L., 33 n.11, 82, 83–84, 136, 219
Blust, R., 4, 9, 11, 13, 18, 19, 27, 32, 142, 153 n.1, 154 nn.4,5, 211 nn.7,8, 265
Boas, F., 14, 207
Boretzky, N., 30, 81, 83
Brandenstein, C. G. Von, 295
Braune, W., 90, 127, 128, 132 n.11
Bréal, M., 265
Brown, C. H., 267, 273, 277, 278–79, 281, 300 nn.2,3
Brugmann, K., 3, 85, 135–36, 153 nn.1,2, 209
Buck, C. D., 59, 272
Burchfield, R., 93

Burling, R., 22
Burrow, T., 80, 138, 272
Bybee, J., 231, 235, 245–46, 258, 266–67
Bynon, T., 14

Campbell, L., 4, 11, 13, 20, 32, 40, 73, 76, 77, 79–80, 81, 112, 138
Cann, R. L., 39
Capell, A., 185, 192, 199, 201–2, 209, 212 n.26, 301 n.12
Cavalli-Sforza, L. L., 39
Cedergren, H., 120
Cercignani, F., 114, 117, 118, 126–27, 129
Chen, M. Y., 91, 92, 93, 105, 108, 110 n.4
Cheng, C.-C., 23, 97
Chrétien, C. D., 139, 140
Christy, C., 85
Cohen, M., 33 n.13, 82
Churchward, C. M., 178 n.3
Coetsem, F. van, 119
Comrie, B., 5, 8, 34 n.33, 245–46
Condax, I., 154 n.18
Cook, E. D., 81
Cowles, R. T., 103
Croft, W., 5
Cross, S. H., 42

Dahl, O., 153 n.1, 211 n.7
Darwin, C., 136
Dasher, R., 260
Delbrück, B., 85, 153 n.1
Dempwolff, O., 138, 139–43, 145–49, 153, 154 nn.6,10,11,12,14,15,16, 158–59, 184–85, 199, 211 nn.7,8,9
Dixon, R. M. W., 83, 249
Dobrovský, J., 43, 45
Dogopol'skij, A. B., 58
Donegan, P. J., 18, 19
Dressler, W. U., 81, 228–29, 235, 251
Dunkel, G. E., 239
Durie, M., 4, 12, 14, 18, 25–27, 32
Durkheim, E., 14

Dutton, T., 199, 212 n.16
Dyen, I., 5, 136–37, 138, 140, 148, 154 n.6, 178 nn.1,5

Eckert, P., 20
Eggers, H., 127, 128, 132 n.11
Emenau, M. B., 138, 272
Ernout, A., 230
Evans, N., 266–67, 269, 296
Evens, M. W., 279–80

Farr, C., 202
Farr, J., 202
Fasold, R., 120
Ferguson, C. A., 18
Fillmore, C., 280
Flierl, W., 271
Flom, G. T., 128
Foley, J., 18, 20
Foley, W. A., 13, 181, 187, 211 n.11, 300 n.3
Fortunatov, F. F., 44

Geeraerts, D., 265, 266
Geraghty, P., 144
Gillieron, J., 77, 136
Goddard, C., 287, 301 n.10
Goddard, I., 138
Gonda, J., 144
Gordon, E. V., 118
Gould, S. J., 39
Grace, G. W., 4, 7, 12–13, 16–17, 28–29, 30–31, 32, 160–63, 168–69, 178 nn.4,8, 181, 203, 211 n.8, 212 nn.27,31, 275
Grassmann, H., 135–36
Greenberg, J. H., 5, 8, 32 n.7, 40, 54, 55, 57, 58, 60, 69 n.15, 235, 266
Grimm, J., 135
Gumperz, J. J., 205, 210
Guthrie, M., 272, 275, 301 n.10

Haas, M. R., 62, 83, 219
Hale, K., 83, 282, 288, 296
Hall, R. A., Jr., 219
Hardeland, A., 154 n.10
Harris, R., 203
Harris, W., 22, 34 n.28
Hashimoto, M. J., 110 n.5
Hashimoto, O. K., 99, 101–2, 107, 109, 110 n.7

Haspelmath, M., 245, 246, 258
Hattori, S., 137, 154 n.5, 199, 211 n.12, 212 n.16
Heath, J., 30, 31, 32 n.6, 224, 256
Heine, B., 240, 260, 266–67
Hercus, L., 241
Herzog, M. I., 14, 268
Hetzron, R., 219
Hjelmslev, L., 212 n.27
Hock, H. H., 114, 117, 119, 128, 132 n.16, 218, 219, 222, 265
Hockett, C., 84, 154 n.19
Hoenigswald, H. M., 85, 220
Hooper, J. B., 228
Hopper, P. J., 5, 240, 244, 247
Hovdhaugen, E., 27
Hsu, R., 166
Huang, P. P.-F., 110 n.7
Hudson, J., 248

Illič-Svityč, V. M., 39, 58
Iris, M., 279–80

Jackson, F. H., 211 n.9
Jagić, I. V., 42, 45
Jakobson, R., 21–22, 54, 268
Jankowsky, K. R., 153 nn.1,2
Jeffers, R. J., 239, 240, 267, 268
Jespersen, O., 26
Johnson, S., 30, 83
Jones, Sir W., 45–47, 59, 64, 84
Joseph, B. D., 208

Kaiser, M., 40, 52, 53
Kantor, M., 42
Karlgren, B., 93, 110 n.3
Kaufman, T., 40, 76, 86 n.2, 138, 182, 208, 209–10, 213 n.39
Kay, P., 121, 266
Keller, R. E., 14–15, 20, 33 n.14, 234
Kim, C.-W., 149, 154 n.10
King, R., 78, 79
Kiparsky, P., 34 n.28, 79
Klausenberger, J., 228
Koch, H., 4, 7, 11, 12–13, 18, 28, 237
König, E., 266
Křepinský, M., 210
Kruszewski, M., 228
Kuhn, H., 132 n.12

Labov, W., 14, 22, 24–25, 26, 27, 91, 113, 131, 170–71, 268
Langacker, R., 203
Lass, R., 12, 14
Laughlin, R. M., 74
Laycock, D., 181
Leer, J., 30
Lehiste, I., 239, 240, 267, 268
Lehmann, W. P., 3, 114, 135, 219, 239, 240, 243
Lehrer, A., 266, 301 n.16
Leibniz, G. 42
Leskien, A., 135, 136, 153 nn.1,2
Le Page, R. B., 14, 21
Lewis, G., 271
Lichtenberk, F., 211 n.8
Lien, C., 23, 26
Lincoln, P., 24, 34 n.26, 213 n.35
Lisker, L., 149, 150
Litowitz, B., 279–80
Lloyd, A. L., 114
Lomonosov, M., 43–44
Lyell, C., 136
Lynch, J., 144, 185, 192

MacLaury, R. E., 266
Maddieson, I., 154 n.19
Maiden, M., 226, 229
Malkiel, Y., 20, 226
Manaster Ramer, A., 9
Mańczak, W., 232
Marchand, J. W., 114, 132 n.16
Martinet, A., 18, 20
Matisoff, J., 40, 57, 62, 267, 268, 272, 274, 282, 285, 296–97, 300 nn.5,7
Matthews, P. H., 228, 240
Maxwell, J. C., 136
Mayerthaler, W., 235, 251, 259
McDaniel, C. K., 121
McElhanon, K. A., 185, 211 n.11
McSwain, R., 188
Meillet, A., 7–8, 14, 47–50, 52, 56–58, 82, 114, 116, 128, 131 nn.4,5, 132 n.8, 209, 230, 240, 299–300
Meiser, G., 241
Mel'čuk, I., 267
Menner, R., 77
Menning, K., 282, 283, 301 n.11
Milke, W., 211 n.8
Miller, J., 273

Milroy, J., 14, 15, 16–17, 21, 22, 170–71
Milroy, L., 14, 15, 16–17, 21, 22, 170–71
Mitzka, W., 90
Moravcsik, E., 209
Mühlhäusler, P., 83, 209
Muntzel, M., 81
Muysken, P., 209

Nash, D., 282, 283, 301 n.11
Newman, J., 4, 11, 13, 91, 92, 105, 108
Newman, P., 40, 50, 61, 69 n.21
Newmeyer, F., 281
Newton, B., 213 n.41
Newton, I., 136
Nichols, J., 4, 6, 7–9, 10, 30, 32 n.7, 43, 51, 54, 60, 73, 181, 183, 208, 209
Nikiforidau, K., 266, 280
Norman, J., 92, 110 n.2
Norman, W. M., 76

O'Grady, J., 289, 293–94, 296
Ohala, J. J., 18, 19
Ohmann, E., 77, 78
Osthoff, H., 3, 85, 135–36, 153 nn.1,2, 209
Oswalt, R. L., 58
Ozanne-Rivierre, F., 213 n.39

Pagliuca, W., 266
Palmer, L. R., 226
Panagl, O., 241
Paul, H., 14, 33 n.12, 151–52, 155 nn.21,22
Pawley, A. K., 9, 185, 203, 211 nn.8,10
Peirce, C. S., 281
Penzl, H., 90, 110 n.1
Petruck, M., 280, 281
Phillips, B. S., 27
Prokosch, E., 115
Pulleyblank, E. G., 92

Rankin, R. L., 58
Ray, S. H., 185, 192, 199–202, 209, 212 n.24
Reh, M., 240
Reid, L. A., 211 n.8
Renfrew, C., 10
Ringe, D. A., 8
Ringen, J., 77, 79–80
Rivet, P., 82
Roques, M., 77

Ross, M. D., 4, 5, 9, 11, 13, 21–22, 24, 29–32, 34 n.26, 144, 182, 184, 185, 188, 192, 194, 197, 202, 211 nn.6,7,8,10,12,16,17,18, 213 n.37, 277
Ruhlen, M., 8

Sankoff, D., 120, 133 n.20
Sankoff, G., 211 n.6
Sapir, E., 81, 82, 83
Sasse, H. J., 205, 210
Saussure, F. de, 14
Schindler, J., 232–33
Schleicher, A., 14
Schooling, S., 16
Schuchardt, H., 16, 143, 153 n.3, 209
Shevelov, G. Y., 56
Sheveroshkin, V. V., 9, 40, 52, 53
Sievers, E., 85
Singer, S., 91
Smirnov, V. S., 43
Smith, A., 15
Smith, B. L., 150–51, 154 n.18, 155 n.20
Sommerfelt, A., 83
Stampe, D., 18
Starostin, S. A., 9
Stern, G., 265, 268
Stimson, H. M., 101
Stoneking, M., 39
Strauss, H., 271
Strehlow, T. G. H., 259
Strong, W. M., 192, 199–201, 212 nn.16,25
Svorou, S., 267
Swadesh, M., 32 n.6, 264, 282, 299
Sweet, H., 85
Sweetser, E., 266, 280
Syder, F. H., 203
Szemerényi, O., 4, 118, 127, 180

Tabouret-Keller, A., 14, 21
Thomason, S. G., 40, 182, 208, 209–10, 213 nn.39,41, 245

Thomsen, V., 153 n.2
Thurston, W. R., 21, 34 n.24, 183–84, 185, 202, 205, 209, 213 n.34
Tiersma, T. M., 232
Traugott, E. C., 5, 240, 260, 266–67, 281, 298, 299, 300 n.2
Tsiapera, M., 213 n.41
Turner, C. G., 39
Twadell, W. F., 114

Ullmann, S., 265, 268, 282
Ultan, R., 73
Unger, J. M., 13

Vaihinger, H., 136, 139
Vasmer, M., 56, 57–58
Vennemann, T., 228, 230
Verner, K., 135–36, 153 n.2
Voorhoeve, C. L., 185, 211 n.11

Wang, W. S.-Y., 17, 23, 26, 97, 104, 143
Watkins, C., 235
Weinreich, U., 14, 15, 17, 181, 205, 210, 213 n.33, 268
Wells, J. C., 34 n.27
Wilkins, D., 4, 10–11, 16, 18, 256–58, 261, 273, 278–80, 288, 296
Williams, J. M., 266
Wilson, R., 205, 210
Winter, W., 44
Witkowski, S. R., 278–79, 281, 300 n.2
Wolff, J., 148
Wurm, S. A., 137, 154 n.5, 199, 211 nn.12,16
Wurzel, W. U., 228–29, 233, 235, 236, 241, 253, 259

Yallop, C., 259

Zhang, H., 104
Zoëga, C. T., 117, 118, 131 n.13